CONVERGENT KNOWING

CONVERGENT KNOWING

CHRISTIANITY *and* SCIENCE
in CONVERSATION *with*
a SUFFERING CREATION

SIMON APPOLLONI

MCGILL–QUEEN'S UNIVERSITY PRESS
MONTREAL & KINGSTON · LONDON · CHICAGO

ISBN 978-0-7735-5443-6 (cloth)
ISBN 978-0-7735-5444-3 (paper)
ISBN 978-0-7735-5561-7 (ePDF)
ISBN 978-0-7735-5562-4 (ePUB)

Legal deposit third quarter 2018
Bibliothèque nationale du Québec

Printed in Canada on acid-free paper that is 100% ancient forest free (100% post-consumer recycled), processed chlorine free

This book has been published with the help of a grant from the Canadian Federation for the Humanities and Social Sciences, through the Awards to Scholarly Publications Program, using funds provided by the Social Sciences and Humanities Research Council of Canada.

We acknowledge the support of the Canada Council for the Arts, which last year invested $153 million to bring the arts to Canadians throughout the country.

Nous remercions le Conseil des arts du Canada de son soutien. L'an dernier, le Conseil a investi 153 millions de dollars pour mettre de l'art dans la vie des Canadiennes et des Canadiens de tout le pays.

LIBRARY AND ARCHIVES CANADA CATALOGUING IN PUBLICATION

Appolloni, Simon, 1962–, author

Convergent knowing : Christianity and science in conversation with a suffering creation /
    Simon Appolloni.
    (Advancing studies in religion ; 4)
    Includes bibliographical references and index.
    Issued in print and electronic formats.
    ISBN 978-0-7735-5443-6 (cloth). – ISBN 978-0-7735-5444-3 (paper).
    – ISBN 978-0-7735-5561-7 (ePDF). – ISBN 978-0-7735-5562-4 (ePUB)

    1. Religion and science. 2. Liberty – Religious aspects – Christianity. 3. Environmentalism – Religious aspects – Christianity. 4. Christian ethics. 5. Faith. I. Title. II. Series: Advancing studies in religion ; 4

BL240.3.A67 2018   215   C2018-904976-6
                                                           C2018-904977-4

This book was typeset by Sandra Friesen in 11/14 Minion.

Contents

Acknowledgments

To Stephen Scharper, for his abiding encouragement, warmhearted support, and generous wisdom, I am eternally grateful. To Hilary Cunningham and Ingrid Stefanovic, for their incisive comments and suggestions, and to Dennis O'Hara, Heather Eaton, Tim Leduc, and Christopher Hrynkow, who helped steer my thinking away from unnecessary crevasses along the road, I must express my sincerest thank you. Special mention goes to my family (Lucio, Luisa, Suzanne, Andrew, Janine, and Elena Appolloni), as well as to Katie Newton and Nancy Lunney for their vigilant editing eyes. I am also indebted to the insight and guidance of the two reviewers who helped me fine-tune the work so that it is more accessible, and to my editor, Kyla Madden, who guided my path through the publishing process with warmth and aplomb. Finally, to my daughter Elena who, while also having helped edit, offered me encouragement and patience, as her dad typed away all those nights and weekends, when he'd really have loved to watch that musical with her.

Preface

There is a saying one hears now and then – in various places – when travelling and seeking directions from the locals: "Oh, you can't get there from here!" While the weary traveller is not likely to enjoy hearing that she must turn around and begin the journey anew, and from a completely different starting point, there is solace in knowing that she will soon be on the right path. This book takes the religious tradition of Christianity as that weary traveller who beseeches the aid of a local citizen to help it arrive at a world that is both environmentally sustainable and just for all creation.

Imagine the scene: cognizant that the Christian tradition is currently on a path that is too focused on uncritical obedience to past wisdoms and literalist accounts of scripture, and noticing that Christianity seems uneasy with an Earthly route to begin with, you, the local, respond politely, and instruct Christianity that it, well, "can't get there from here." You suggest that it turn around and proceed in a far more Earthly direction, one guided, in large measure, by science. The tradition queries your instructions, declaring that it couldn't possibly be on the wrong path, because this is the route it has taken since it began its journey.

You point out to the tradition that the world has changed in many ways in the past half-century, and that as far as life on Earth for many Earthlings is concerned, the situation is dire. The oceans of the planet are becoming more hostile to life, with heat and acidity levels nearing or at dangerous levels. Already, you say, humans have brought on climate change, the sixth-largest rate of species extinction in Earth's history, changes to the global nitrogen cycle, the destruction of a good portion of Earth's fresh water, and the pollution of just about all parts of the planet's surface.[1] You remind Christianity that these problems are the product of a modern industrialized economic system and anthropocentric worldview that see the planet as merely an object to be used for human convenience. If it continues on the present course the tradition will perpetuate the "uncreating" of life that currently marks its complicity with this environmental crisis, something you know Christianity does not wish to do.[2] But it is not just the environment that Christianity must consider. Taking into account not only dollar per diem figures, but also the deprivation, social exclusion, and lack of participation of a good portion of the global human population, you point out that poverty rates are deplorable. The dignity of countless humans has been trampled by economic forces that are deaf to the cries of the poor. Moreover, you point out, the environmental problems that you outlined above will only exacerbate the social and economic problems facing the majority of humanity.

So, you set the tradition onto a surer path with a new starting point: the threatening anthropogenic global environmental destruction and the growing inequality and persistent poverty afflicting the majority of human beings on the planet. But first you impart four pieces of cautionary advice: first, along the journey, make sure the tradition maintains a close and prolonged association with science, and conserves a willingness to follow the evidence about the universe that science unveils, wherever it may lead; second, acknowledge a blurring of the epistemological boundaries between Christianity and science; third, remain focused on the liberation of not only the human, but the other-than-human, whereby subjects participate as agents in their own freedom from oppression; and, fourth, to the extent possible, include the voices and concerns of the entire Earth community, and multiple ways of apprehending reality, in its journey.

With all that information in hand, you send the tradition on its way. Will it take your advice seriously? Indeed, why did you stress such a starting point for the tradition? Are all your cautionary suggestions necessary? Surely, there must be a simpler route? To find out answers to these questions, read on.

CONVERGENT KNOWING

Getting Serious about the Liberation of All Creation

Since the last half of the twentieth century, Christian theologians, biblical scholars, philosophers, and ethicists have been struggling with the increasingly pressing issues that have arisen from a planetary environmental crisis and a growing inequality and persistent poverty afflicting the majority of human beings. Many have tried to reconcile these developments with discoveries from science about how our world functions, traditional ethical frameworks, and accepted affirmations of their faith. The struggle has been daunting, marked by a litany of concerned voices that argue that one or more of the issues or facets of the debate requires greater attention.

While today we are less likely to hear extreme claims from Christian thinkers that, for instance, "ecotheology" of any kind is "unbiblical or heretical in its view of God, humanity and nature"[1] – as had once been more common within Christian circles – debates are still encumbered by tensions, conflicts, fragmentation, and passionate arguments. They arise when one or more aspects of important spheres of concern – the environment, liberation, science, or faith – receives either too much attention or emphasis, not enough, or even none at all. Some give disproportionate attention to ecological values such as the integrity of ecosystems, sustainability issues, or evolutionary processes; others direct their attention mainly to liberation or social justice values such as liberty and equality, or issues like wealth distribution, sexism, or political oppression; still others focus their critical attention on Christian theology, history, and ethics, and how these issues relate to social and/or ecological issues.[2]

This struggle has been further intensified in recent decades, certainly within western society, by the greater authority society bestows on the natural sciences over religion as a means of describing and understanding the world. As Evangelical Lutheran theologian Philip Hefner puts it, "Today, the most fruitful and authoritative descriptions of the world are those of science."[3] Some Christian thinkers even acknowledge that it is the scientists who are playing the role of prophets today. Whether or not this is true, the fact that scientists are now referring to our era as the "Anthropocene" is telling. They employ this term to underscore the extent to which anthropogenic stresses on Earth systems have made sudden planetary environmental change a strong possibility.[4] While the term "Anthropocene" might make us feel uncomfortable about ourselves as a species, despite our achievements in science and technology, it is nevertheless appropriate because it describes our present geological period, when humans have reshaped the planet, to devastating results. We have already transgressed three environmental limits within which humanity can safely operate: climate change, the rate of species extinction, and changes to the global nitrogen cycle. According to scientists, crossing these limits means that we no longer have the assurance that life can continue relatively safely. Moreover, crossing these boundaries could exert further pressure on other biophysical system processes (e.g., atmospheric aerosol loading, global fresh water and land-system use, and chemical pollution), causing them to destabilize, thereby endangering potentially all life systems.

As some Christian thinkers have been pointing out loudly – and rightfully so – those marginalized by scarcity and lack of economic and political clout are far more susceptible to the ravages of climate change and the decline of other planetary systems. Considering that well over a billion people still live in extreme poverty, this vulnerability is significant. The outlook is not good. Despite some gains in raising incomes, if we exclude the developing economies of Brazil, the Russian Federation, India, and China, the absolute number of people living in extreme poverty, according to the United Nations Department of Economic and Social Affairs (DESA), actually increased from 1981 to 2005.[5]

What is implied and sometimes voiced within the testy tussle above is that in the process of building a just and environmentally sustainable world, each of the four spheres of concern – Christianity, science, the environment, and liberation – should be taken seriously. The works of four Christian thinkers – Rosemary Radford Ruether, Leonardo Boff, Diarmuid O'Murchu, and Thomas Berry– undergird this book precisely because, in large measure, they do just this. In the process, their works collectively pose three significant questions to their Christian faith:

1 How might we conceive the liberation of the human and the other-than-human when the future of life on the planet is at risk due to anthropogenic causes?
2 How and in what form might science and Christianity enter into a serious and sustained conversation to help effect the liberation of all creation?
3 What challenges and opportunities does the above conversation present for the Christian tradition?

A reasonable question to this claim might be, "Don't *all* Christian thinkers and academics approach their work seriously?" At a basic level, this is undoubtedly true. However, the context in which Christian thinkers today are being implored to do so is enormously complex. Humanity is being challenged with problems that seem to defy easy characterization, let alone any clear solution. What, for instance, does "common good," a prominent principle of Catholic social teaching, mean when the projected rates of biodiversity loss are anthropogenic, and so huge in proportion to the normal species loss that occurs every day that they constitute the sixth major extinction in our planet's history? These are problems that exceed our moral imagination; they are complex and defy ready answers. For this reason, they are sometimes referred to as "wicked problems." Within this context, one would expect a critical integration to allow the facts surrounding species extinction to permeate the character of the common good, as well as qualify it, that is, to modify or, in some way, limit it. Hence, the manner in which Christian thinkers today are being implored to approach their work seriously is redolent of a deep influence that weighs upon them. It requires an enormous degree of openness to allowing their religious tradition to be vulnerable to different perspectives, and to allowing the discourses and wisdoms of other traditions to deeply imbue, challenge, and even change their thinking.

This book describes how Ruether, Boff, O'Murchu, and Berry display this openness. These authors have challenged conventional approaches to the natural sciences, while also allowing the sciences to challenge previously held beliefs. The Earth, and indeed the cosmos, have become integral platforms from which these thinkers envision a new more biocentric ethic. Such an openness to other perspectives and concerns characterizes how they have taken the environment *and* liberation *and* science *and* their faith seriously, a feat many Christian theorists, theologians, biblical scholars, philosophers, and ethicists are still struggling to achieve.

It is not, however, just a particular hermeneutic of openness to other perspectives that enables Ruether, Boff, O'Murchu, and Berry to integrate these four spheres of concern. They use a particular epistemic framework that has greatly facilitated the conversation among these four spheres of concern. I label this framework "convergent knowing," which, as I will discuss presently, is characterized by a close and seemingly permanent relationship between religion and the natural sciences as two significant ways of knowing the world, where the epistemological lines are somewhat blurred. Moreover, convergent knowing includes the voices and concerns of the entire Earth community. As a result, it directs its focuses on liberating all Earth subjects.

I deliberately speak of "liberation" in this work and not "social justice." This is in large measure because it is the ethos motivating the work of the four interlocutors within this book. This does not mean that each of the four thinkers approach liberation in the manner I will be promoting here. Thomas Berry does not even employ the term in his writings. It is more the case that each presents one or more aspects of what I propose defines liberation, and a unique understanding of liberation at that. At one level, liberation, like social justice, implies a freedom from social, political, and/or economic domination or manipulation. Vital to the liberative process, however, is that the person, or subject, participates as an agent in her or his own freedom from oppression. A good way to understand this process is to consider the building of housing for homeless people. While both social justice and liberation principles demand that there be an ethical duty to build a house, liberation principles insist that the people who are to live in the houses participate in its design and construction.

There is more to liberation when one considers the global environmental destruction we are bringing about. Drawing from my chosen Christian thinkers, who have appropriated recent findings in cosmology, liberation takes on an even larger dimension. At the cosmic level, liberation entails following evolutionary impulses, leading to greater diversity, interiority, and communion, which means it therefore applies to all creation. Thus, for example, we find within ecosystems a complex and diverse community of producers, consumers, decomposers, and detritivores, celebrating a certain form of liberation, all interacting within the boundaries imposed by their physical surroundings. Through time, and by the processes of mutation, niche selection, and natural selection, each member of the community helps shape life: the detritivore (an earthworm, for instance) will ingest, then digest dead organic matter, from which a producer (a plant, for instance) receives nutrients. These evolutionary dynamics, however, can be and have been radically altered with the advent of the Anthropocene: even large consumers such as cheetahs, hippos, and gazelles are no longer evolving in the wild, but through interactions with human structures and actions; their location, size, and populations are in many ways determined by humans.

TRACING THE CONTOURS OF A SERIOUS CONVERSATION

In many ways, the phrase "take seriously" (quite often written, but sometimes merely implied) has become a popular trope for our time. The amount of literature in English-language scholarly journals with the theme of "taking something seriously" – usually pronounced within the title – is rather remarkable. Notwithstanding the sometimes pedestrian nature of this trope here, it merits attention for two main reasons. One is the ethos or, perhaps more pointedly, the pathos it evokes when it undergirds a conversation on the liberation of all of creation. When biologists refer to current and projected rates of biodiversity loss, they underline that this constitutes the sixth major extinction in our planet's history. In a similar manner, when Methodist Bishop Bernardino Mandlate of Mozambique addresses a United

Nations delegation about the millions of dollars in debt payment transferred yearly from poor African nations to foreign banks, governments, and international finance institutions of nations in the global North, he concludes, "African children die so that North American children may overeat."[6]

Another reason that this trope merits attention is the calibre of ethicists, theologians, and scientists employing the term. John Polkinghorne, for instance, a theoretical physicist, theologian, and Anglican priest, writes in *Quantum Physics and Theology* that one of the aims of his book is to encourage theologians to engage with scientists "a little more seriously than many of them have seemed inclined to do."[7] Polkinghorne does not only point his finger at his fellow theologians. He also enjoins his scientific colleagues "to take what theology has to say with a greater degree of seriousness than many of them display," noting that in the scientific community (of which he was a member), "the adjective 'theological' is sometimes used pejoratively to refer to a vague or ill-formulated belief."[8] Echoing Polkinghorne's views, theologian David Tracy points out that religion receives little consideration by scientists today, making it "the single subject about which many intellectuals can feel free to be ignorant." Tracy continues to paint the current scenario, where people believe they do not need to take religion seriously, debasing it "to something one likes 'if that is the sort of thing one likes.'"[9]

"Serious" is a curious term. It is charged with many different meanings: it could convey a matter of grave importance, often a situation that is critical, and gives cause for apprehension; it could connote a question that is not easily answered or resolved, and require deep concentration. Applying this term to someone could also tell us that person is being earnest, or that he or she is occupied in deep thought. Serious is also used to express the notion that much thought or work is required for a task, or that someone is deeply interested in a subject. While the meanings differ, all of them seem to have a common thrust: the need to engage a subject or issue with thoughtfulness, constructive resolve, and critical attention.

In this manner, Christian thinkers are taking a subject, issue, or concern seriously when they give critical attention to the complex and perhaps dangerous issues or perspectives. They also treat it with thoughtfulness by reflecting and questioning multiple perspectives, assumptions, concepts, methodologies, epistemologies, and theories, and weighing options judiciously, only after a thorough and honest examination. Those engaged in the process allow others' discourses to penetrate deeply, challenge, and even change their thinking. Finally, they take a subject or issue seriously by showing constructive resolve, that is, by being committed to addressing fruitfully the task at hand. In short, to determine whether Christian thinkers are taking each sphere of concern seriously, it is important to examine the degree to which they have applied critical attention, thoughtfulness, and constructive resolve to the spheres of concern.

A conversation that critically integrates these issues is arguably a more difficult endeavour. It requires a particular surrendering of sovereignty on the part of the participating disciplines, which requires a certain amount of trust among them. That is why it is perhaps more precise to look upon the conversation as being more transdisciplinary in nature, rather than interdisciplinary. This issue of trust is where both the Christian theorist and the natural scientist tend to struggle most.[10] A vital component within their conversation – if it is to be fruitful – will have to address the epistemological and methodological assumptions underlying their thinking. As philosopher Robert Frodeman insists, environmental issues resist simple division into separate categories of science and ethics. It will not do, then, he underlines, to employ within the conversation a scientific fundamentalism, one marked by an overemphasis on the scientific method and on rational analytic thought processes to the exclusion of other ways of knowing the world.[11] Both Christian theorists and scientists will have to learn new skills for thinking across categories.

David Tracy recognizes that a great turn must also occur in theology. He acknowledges that in the past, traditional Christian theologians, of whatever tradition, "preached and practiced a morality of belief in, and obedient to the tradition and a fundamental loyalty to the church-community's belief."[12] Obviously, Tracy is not eschewing the concept of obedience here, but an obsequious version of it that follows tradition uncritically and with a closed heart and mind. In contrast to this obedience, he maintains, the modern historian and scientist – whether in the natural or social sciences – must preach and practise a decidedly divergent morality, which cannot have a theologian investigate a cognitive claim with intellectual integrity while insisting simultaneously "that the claim is believable because the tradition has believed it."[13] Tracy notes that most Christians recognize today that much of the traditional Christian manner of understanding the cognitive claims made in the Christian scriptures ought to be abandoned in light of the findings of history and the natural and human sciences. But Tracy goes beyond mere rejection of a literalist account of scripture. The method he presents subjects the cognitive claims for its central symbols of revelation, God, and Christ, to an open-ended inquiry, critical reflection, autonomous judgment, and a skeptical hard-mindedness. Put another way, Tracy calls for a "willingness to follow the evidence wherever it may lead," even if such conclusions "may, in fact, negate a particular traditional belief."[14]

Building upon Tracy and Frodeman's suggestions above, I put forth the following criteria to assess whether the integration process is taken seriously: an openness to allowing each sphere of concern to affirm, clarify, inform, and qualify the others. The first two criteria are fairly straightforward. To be clear about the meaning of the last two, "inform" implies that the concerns, issues, or dynamics of one sphere are allowed to imbue and critically dialogue with the other(s). "Qualify" implies that the sphere is allowed to modify or in some way limit it. In other words, Christian thinkers must allow discourses of others to infuse deeply, challenge, and even change not only their thinking, but each of the other spheres of concerns.

For the liberationist thinker faced with the marginalized or excluded Other, be it the African children mentioned by Bishop Mandlate, or the myriad species becoming extinct, something more is required, which is also why a liberationist ethos undergirds this work: the liberationist thinker is compelled to subject him- or herself to a certain level of humility. This imperative involves a process of self-reflection that denounces any claim to seeing and understanding things from a universal or "God perspective." Rather, acknowledging his or her own situatedness geographically, socially, and economically, the liberationist thinker underlines that knowledge is particular. The thinker *must*, therefore, learn from the excluded, the poor, the Other. This self-critical reflection, then, becomes the overarching criterion in determining not only that Christian thinkers are taking liberation seriously, but that they are also taking seriously the integration of their faith and science in order to unite a liberationist agenda with an environmental ethic.

I am not suggesting that such a task is easy to fulfill. In fact, the opposite is true: it is very difficult to do, and throughout this work I will plumb the many reasons why. Yet, it is necessary. Tracy's own words are an apt summation of the import of my work: "There is no intellectual, cultural, political, or religious tradition or interpretation that does not ultimately live by the quality of its conversation."[15] Measuring the quality with which Ruether, Boff, O'Murchu, and Berry approach the four spheres of concern and integrating them into an ethical vision comprises a good portion of the first part of my work.

WHY THESE FOUR CHRISTIAN THINKERS?

In the process, Ruether, Boff, O'Murchu, and Berry have allowed their faith to become vulnerable to the open-ended inquiry with the natural sciences Tracy mentions above. In other words, they are allowing science and the liberation of all creation not only to affirm and inform their faith, but to clarify and qualify it.

There is more to my selection of these four theorists though. For one – and vital to the import of my book – in each of their writings, one finds a deep concern for the epistemological concerns underpinning assertions and assumptions about their faith, scientific findings, ethical systems, and the environmental crisis. These authors use convergent knowing as a particularly constructive epistemic framework. The blurring of the ways of knowing the world, which sets convergent knowing apart from many other epistemic frameworks, facilitates their conversation with the natural sciences, and allows them to approach not only science and their faith, but ethical issues as well, in a different light. Another reason I have chosen the works of these four is that each has assigned prominence to the liberation (as I present it here) of all creation. They take as the starting point of their thinking the anthropogenic global environmental destruction that threatens us, as well as the growing inequality and persistent poverty afflicting the majority of human beings on the planet. As will become evident, this makes a vital difference in the viability of their ethical vision.

It is not solely their epistemic framework that facilitates Ruether, Boff, O'Murchu, and Berry in integrating the four spheres of concern. Their willingness to follow evidence and to integrate their faith and science also arises out of a deep reverence they share for all of creation. The fact that they are all Catholic, I will show, is also significant, in that their Catholic imagination – which is not exclusive to Catholics – informs their relationship with creation as well as their employment of the natural sciences. Whether in the San Bernardino Mountains, the Amazon rainforest, the Irish countryside, or a North Carolinian meadow, Ruether, Boff, O'Murchu, and Berry each, at an early age, formed a loving, even reverential, relationship with nature as sacred and, initially at least, as a specific place. Such a sensitivity to the notion that revelation or God disclosing some truth or knowledge is not exclusively found in scripture facilitates not only their love for creation but their employment of science as the essential way to learn about creation. Berry describes this notion of revelation from science as being qualitatively different from the traditional scriptural "God sayeth" revelation, as understood intuitively by prophets. This novel revelation includes rational, analytic processes.

The priesthood of the three male interlocutors is not insignificant, since the religious communities to which they belonged (still belong, in the case of O'Murchu), formed much of their thinking. Boff was a priest of the Franciscan Order (later to resign), O'Murchu continues to be a priest of the Sacred Heart Missionary Order, and Thomas Berry had been a priest of the Passionist Order until his death in 2009. Ruether argued fervently for that entitlement to be granted to women in the Catholic tradition. This connection to Catholic priesthood is far removed from the clerical authoritarianism found in some Catholic circles today. It is best to understand the ordained statuses of Boff, O'Murchu, and Berry in relation to the liberationist ethos described above. For, each of them, at one point in his life, came to embrace the humility concomitant with the liberationist mindset that would eschew any obsequious obedience to traditional beliefs.

Finally, while the writings of Ruether, Boff, O'Murchu, and Berry are not homogeneous in content or approach, they are remarkably similar in many ways, most notably in their understanding of science, and, as just pointed out, in the liberationist intent I draw out of their respective works. Rosemary Radford Ruether was originally trained as a Christian historian; Leonardo Boff a liberation theologian; Diarmuid O'Murchu a social psychologist; and Thomas Berry a cultural historian. However, when approached all together into a communal conversation – as I do within this book – one can find each of their respective works affirming, clarifying, informing, and qualifying the others. Therein lies the ultimate fruit of choosing these four Christian thinkers.

To be sure, I do not present the four thinkers as an exclusive list. There are other Christian thinkers, such as Anne Primavesi, who attend, in one form or another, to the Christianity/science/environment/liberation nexus. Time and length preclude including more authors. The works of Heather Eaton are also promising, though, in my estimation, Eaton has moved too far away from the foundations of the Christian faith for her work to be considered here. Similarly, other Christian thinkers, such as ecotheologians Sallie McFague and Michael S. Northcott, have produced important works that engage with all four spheres of concern to various degrees. I exclude them from my work, however, because their interest in science is first and foremost to lend credibility to what they regard as important insights on ecology and justice into their Christian faith. Neither thinker permits science to inform (at least deeply) and qualify her or his faith.

Of course, there are some Christian thinkers who also engage with science without adequately applying the thoughtfulness or critical attention I described above. In the process though, they allow the science, perhaps too readily or without enough warrant, to inform and qualify their Christian faith, or ethics, such as self-professed New Ager David Toolan or evolutionary theologian and evidential evangelist Michael Dowd. Conversely, there are some Christian thinkers who are very thoughtful in their appropriation of science, such as John Haught, Ian Barbour, John Polkinghorne, and Philip Clayton, to name a few. What is missing from their discussions, however, is one or both of the other spheres of concern: environment and liberation.

THE DIFFERENCE AN EPISTEMIC FRAMEWORK CAN MAKE

As I alluded to earlier, convergent knowing is marked by a radical ethos of relationality, which according to Berry perceives the world as a communion of subjects, not objects. As a consequence, convergent knowing is inclusive of the voices and concerns of the entire Earth community, focused on liberating *all* Earth subjects. A salient feature of convergent knowing, then, and one that will become increasingly apparent in the course of reading this book, is that as a framework for knowing it seeks not first and foremost to arrive at an approximation of truth, but an assessment of it.

This last aspect is quite significant. In reading the works of these four interlocutors, one gets a sense that what they put forth is unique among the many ethical visions being proposed to address our planetary environmental and social crises: truth takes on what I call a "liberationally pragmatic" significance to it. Truth is measured more by the quality with which *all* subjects in creation can participate in their own (Earthly) liberation, than by merely being consistent with what we know of the world through science or indeed with the tenets of the Christian faith. By pragmatic, I am referring to a perspective that sees truth as an instrument used by human beings to solve their problems in a radically democratic fashion. In solidarity with marginalized subjects, it attempts to clarify the cause of suffering, with the goal of reconstructing (not just deconstructing) a just system within a democratic framework.[16] In this sense, I am not alone in asserting the merit of such an approach. Ethicist Willis Jenkins, working from a Christian perspective, also espouses a pragmatic strategy to ethics as the most effective means to ensure adherence to specific and concrete problems.[17] Hope is found in such an approach. Put simply, truth is bound up with the socially desired consequences, which, for my four interlocutors, is more definitively represented as liberation.

Given its liberationally pragmatic essence, convergent knowing sets out to reformulate the struggle above. Rather than inquiring how prevalent approaches to science, or traditional understandings of the Christian faith, or current ethical models can foster an ethical, liberationist vision for our time – the proverbial "trying to wedge a square peg into a round hole" – convergent knowing seeks out new paradigms for each of these spheres of concerns. It distinctly remains attentive to addressing interrelated questions not always manifest within the religion, ethics, and science debates: what kind of ethics, what kind of science, and what kind of Christianity do we need today and tomorrow when the liberation of countless subjects of creation is at stake? This liberationally pragmatic line of thinking even queries what kind of liberation is required when relationality undergirds our thinking: an eco-tethered liberation. This term I've coined applies what I have delineated above about liberation with regard to the human community and tethers it to all of creation. In this way, we include the concerns, realities, and the tendencies of all creation, from humans to nematodes to rivers, in all of our ethical deliberations. No one liberation can exist in isolation from the liberation of other subjects. It will become clear after reading chapter 5 that no vision can transpire from any "how-to" manual of ethics. Instead, as the works of Ruether, Boff, O'Murchu, and Berry attest, I am promoting what I describe as "messy ethics," one that is complicated, difficult to work with, far more humble in what we can presume to know about the world, and lacking in precision.

This book elucidates not only the kind of ethics of liberation that, on the whole, Ruether, Boff, O'Murchu, and Berry suggest we need, but the kind of Christianity, and science. In the process, it will become clear what they mean by professing a "mature" or "adult faith." Not unlike what we read from Tracy, such a faith eschews blind obedience to beliefs and encourages a dialogue that helps Christians unearth deeper truths. A mature faith is open to challenge, not necessarily as dissent (though that option is not excluded), but to serve as a corrective to ensure the faith unfolds and develops faithful to the guidance of the Holy Spirit, revelation, or divine disclosure about truth or knowledge, which is found throughout the universe and accessible to all. For Catholics in particular, a mature faith is far more in keeping with a post-Vatican II understanding of the tradition. It is thus a "pilgrim church,"[18] one that is ever-evolving, collegial, considerably less hierarchical, and deeply ecumenical and interreligious in that it does not pretend to stand as the exclusive expression of beliefs, structure, systems of thought, and practices that relate to God.

It will become clear that the science my chosen theorists describe stands in contrast to mechanistic, deterministic, reductionist, and dualistic classical Newtonian science. The science these theorists assert we need also stands in contrast to the neo-Darwinist, seemingly purposeless, and red-in-tooth-and-claw worldview. Instead, in what some label as "new science," we find contemporary concepts and understandings of reality from quantum physics and cosmology, incorporating transdisciplinary theories such as systems theory and the Gaia theory, with its inclusion of evolutionary biology and geology. To be sure, new science – along with its often cited sub-category of "new physics" – is not a precise term. Other writers on the subject apply a relatively new term: "post-normal science." This science, in contrast to abstract theory building, and atomized, and controlled-experimentation science – which has its place – is broader in scope. The term first appeared in the work of Silvio Funtowicz and Jerome Ravetz in response to "post-normal" environmental problems. They assert that especially in regard to the science of environmental sustainability, the issues of uncertainty and value loading need to be recognized along with a plurality of legitimate perspectives.[19] I find that the ethos underlying the term "post-normal" describes more fittingly how my chosen four Christian thinkers understand the science they appropriate. Working from a new paradigm of how scientists understand the universe, the term also eschews the reductionist and mechanistic assumptions associated with classical Newtonian science, and challenges assumptions that science produces final, precise estimates about reality that are free from uncertainty. Moreover – in keeping with the inclusive liberationist agenda of our four thinkers – it is also inclusive of normative social values and informed by inputs from community and stakeholders. Post-normal, as I am presenting it here, represents an apposite label for the science our four Christian thinkers appropriate, then, as it embraces multiple types of knowing, challenging the sharp dichotomy between expert and lay participants.

Because convergent knowing attends to inquiring what kind of science and Christianity we need today, it adds a new dimension to the religion–science debates, one that does not seem to be adequately represented by current leading typologies in the religion-science nexus. Many scholars working within the religion-science field have already identified various ways of understanding the closer relationship between religion and science. Depending on where an author places particular emphasis, whether on the epistemological presuppositions or concepts behind assertions, or on methods used, seldom do we find in religion–science literature emphasis on liberation or some sort of context of ecological justice. In fact, more often than not, we find an implicit or explicit goal of demonstrating either the plausibility of a deity, or the relevance of Christianity, or the authority of science, which – to continue the metaphor above – is changing the *hole* to match the peg. The question of what kind of science or Christianity we might need to address our pressing ethical problems entails reimagining both the *peg* and the *hole*, a practice that is not paramount in current religion–science debates.

When classifying the relationship my four principal interlocutors maintain exists between their faith and science, the intent behind their employment of these two powerful ways of knowing the world – addressing our pressing ethical issues – matters. Hence, while their appropriation of the natural sciences is designed to yield interdependent, collaborative, and reciprocal insights while still preserving the definitional integrity of each body, they undertake first and foremost to unite a liberationist agenda with an environmental ethic. For this reason, a clear distinction needs to be made between the religion-science debate in general and the liberationally pragmatic conversation being carried out by these interlocutors. I discuss this in chapter 8 of this book.

The import of this work is that as an epistemic framework, convergent knowing can assist Christian thinkers currently struggling to integrate science, environment, liberation, and their faith. To be sure, this work can assist scientists also concerned with the liberation of all creation. My focus here, however, rests on the theological endeavour, where Christian theorists can understand better, for instance, why a scientist can experience a new type of religious experience, distinct from but not unrelated to the religious-spiritual experience of shamans. Convergent knowing helps clarify why it is so difficult to demarcate an objective realm of "facts" distinct from subjective perspectives. As an epistemic framework, it allows the participant more readily see the connection among story, myth, dream, and cosmology, fostering intimacy with the universe.

Applying such an epistemic framework, Christian theorists are potentially better able to absorb their experiences with the natural world into their very being, thereby helping to counter powerful destructive myths, such as the illusion that human beings are souls captive within corporeal forms, or that our technology and science make us invulnerable to entropy. Applying convergent knowing, a Christian thinker is less likely to exclude rivers from the conversation on sustainability, expectantly ensuring that they do not run dry from damming before reaching open waters.

ASCRIBING A DEPTH-OF-BREADTH APPROACH

Readers will note that in my pursuit of a conversation, as described above, there is at times a lack of depth on some issues. Arriving at depth is not my aim. Instead, I have sought something novel yet imperative for our time: a fullness of breadth, a depth of breadth if you will, and the means to do it, which I believe underpins the import of this book. Through this depth-of-breadth approach, I present these four Christian theorists' work as a noteworthy and important example of how Christian theorists, theologians, biblical scholars, philosophers, and ethicists might reconceive their vocation in the Anthropocene.

In fact, one of the more intriguing aspects about this work is that there is little that speaks specifically and certainly fully to what the Christian interlocutors I explore are trying to do. The aim of their work is relatively new. What we are seeing, I want to stress, is not a synthesis of the disciplines of science and religion – as each maintains its definitional integrity. Nor is what we are seeing a mere merging of two "separate orientations" to our cosmos or "orderings of reality" that humans are capable of experiencing. It is, as will become clear through the course of the conversation that this work initiates, a convergence of sorts, much like what has occurred throughout millennia within the biological world, where hitherto distinct lifeforms have converged into permanent mutually enhancing or symbiotic relationships.

While the collective works of Ruether, Boff, O'Murchu, and Berry chart the process for a bold integration, it is chiefly when I bring all four interlocutors into a communal conversation, one in large measure realized by them and in part critically elaborated by me – allowing each of their visions not only to clarify and affirm but to qualify and inform the visions of the others – that we are presented with a more robust ethical vision. While attention is given to avoid conflating their visions, the communal conversation I weave among their various works uncovers a more robust ethical vision, one that addresses the challenges and/or weaknesses found within their individual ethical visions.

Part 1 of this book, "Delineating the Particular Contribution of Each Thinker," investigates each of the four Christian thinkers. Part 2, "Weaving a Communal Conversation," examines these theorists' larger epistemological dialogue with ethics and liberation, science, and their religion collectively, in light of the theme of "taking seriously" that underscores this work. I search for evidence that our theorists have allowed the dynamics and concerns surrounding the issues of environmental degradation and the marginalization of the majority of humankind, as well as those of science and their faith, to inform and qualify as well as clarify and affirm each other. It is here that I introduce and explain the new kinds of ethics, science, and Christianity needed for today, along with a number of new concepts, which I have introduced in this introduction. I have designed the work in such a way that ideas and concepts unfold progressively, becoming clearer as they are revisited from different perspectives. The work culminates in chapter 8 where I discuss more fully convergent knowing as a framework, and I describe its liberationally pragmatic ethos as a new typology in the religion-science debates. The book concludes by exposing a larger civilizational paradigm shift occurring that underlies a growing, albeit slow, convergence of Christianity and science.

The time to enact a viable vision for our time is running out. Old paradigms of knowing are proving inadequate to the task. We have arrived at a critical point in our planetary deliberations on ethical approaches to our environmental crisis and a growing inequality and persistent poverty afflicting the majority of human beings, where merely knowing from limited perspectives and conveying one or even a few things deeply is not enough. No one discipline or wisdom can address these crises alone. No one way of knowing the universe will suit the task at hand. Part of the struggle Christian theorists are experiencing today is an epistemological problem. Nothing short of a critical and, at times, bold integration process of a more Earth-based revelation will suffice for Christian theorists embarking upon the formation of a new ethical vision. There truly is a need for Christian theorists, theologians, biblical scholars, philosophers, and ethicists to reconceive their vocation in the Anthropocene, as stated above. To be clear, it is not just Christian thinkers or even natural scientists, but social scientists and all humanities scholars too who will need to reimagine their work in an era marked by "wicked" problems. Economists, for instance, can no longer ignore the effects of their monetary theories or conjectures on market systems on all of creation, and they will need to respect the "safe boundaries" within which biophysical systems operate. This is the Anthropocene, and bold Earth-based thinking is paramount for all disciplines.

The main concern of the serious conversation generated in this work, however, is to construct and elucidate for Christian theorists a process of serious integration, with convergent knowing serving as the means. That in the process, science, ethics, and Christianity are shown in a new light is an inescapable consequence of this bold process.

PART ONE

DELINEATING THE PARTICULAR CONTRIBUTION OF EACH THINKER

In each of the following four chapters that comprise part 1 of this book, I look separately at the works of each author, specifically her/his ethical vision and the science authoring it. Here, the reader will want to look for what is unique about the thinking of each author, and what is similar among all four.

To help in this regard, I have structured each chapter in the same way: each begins with an exploration of the author's starting points, since these are aspects of their personal biography that have influenced their thinking. I then examine the targets of their critiques, which will elucidate the rationale each puts forth for appropriating the wisdom of science. That rationale is invariably tied to how the author, in my assessment, conceives liberation, which ultimately underscores her/his ethical vision. This section is followed first by a section describing the science authoring the author's ethical vision, and then by a section analyzing that author's particular science-based ethical vision. Each chapter finishes with an examination of the epistemology and methodology backing that author's ethical vision. Highlighting their works first separately not only makes it easier to better understand each author's ethical vision, it sets the stage, so to speak, for the important analysis that follows in part 2: it will enable the reader to delineate and assess the particular contribution each thinker adds to the communal conversation I weave.

The order in which I investigate these authors is also purposeful, as it demonstrates, albeit roughly, the degree in which each author appropriates science, beginning with the least amount, with Ruether, then increasing in degree with Boff, then O'Murchu, and ending with Berry, whose appropriation of science in forming his ethical vision, I will demonstrate, is the most profound. Because many of the scientific theories or concepts are found in all of their works, I have chosen to discuss each scientific theory or concept (or an aspect of each) chiefly in one section and to build on that concept as warranted throughout the examination of all the ethical visions of all four thinkers. This process avoids repetition while also allowing me to emphasize which theory or concept receives a more prominent consideration by each author. This order of authors changes for chapter 7 where I mention Boff, Berry, O'Murchu, and Ruether. I do this to reflect, in ascending order, their degree of divergence from more orthodox teachings.

The order in which I investigate these authors also prepares the reader for the communal conversation I weave in part 2 of this work, specifically on liberation, discussed in chapter 5. When it comes to the liberation of all of creation, none of these four interlocutors "gets it fully right." I start specifically with Ruether and end with Berry, not only because of the extent to which each appropriates the sciences, but also because of the degree to which each positions the human as more central or peripheral to her/his respective ethical vision: with Ruether and Boff, the human, while certainly lowered from traditional (and prominent) Christian valuation, remains quite central; whereas with O'Murchu and Berry, as many commentators have noted with regard to the latter, the human appears far less important. I specifically do not begin with Berry (despite his adept appropriation of science, which informs that of the others) because he represents a non-traditional and novel voice within the communal conversation that is occurring within Christian circles; yet, it is also insufficient without the voices of people like Ruether and Boff. Put another way, while the first section does focus on science (because so many Christian thinkers still struggle with this sphere of concern), science, the reader will soon see, is but a *means*, while liberation is the overall *goal*. To this end, where one places the human within ethical-liberationist deliberations is considered key to future dialogues.

CHAPTER ONE

Rosemary Radford Ruether

INTRODUCTION TO RUETHER

Rosemary Radford Ruether was born in St Paul, Minnesota, in 1936, the daughter of a Catholic mother and an Episcopalian father. Her childhood was "generally pleasant," as she describes it, "climbing apple trees … [with] quiet moments of depth and mystery in the daily liturgy," and it was imbued with a love for art.[1] Notwithstanding these pleasant elements, Ruether speaks of the time her father died when she was only twelve. The family was living in Greece at the time, and her mother happened to be away when it happened, leaving Ruether alone to face the ordeal of death. Her recollection of this period of grief, waiting for her mother's return, is worth noting, as it is the chrysalis of her later thinking:

[I] remember feeling a strange detachment. I was haunted by a vivid image of my father in his grave, sinking down into the earth. Both then and in subsequent brushes with death, I have experienced a strong sense of human mortality, the finitude of the individual self … The doctrine of the personal immortality of the soul slipped away from me as an idea without real roots in my own better intuitions. Nature clearly cared only for the species, not the individual. If there is meaning in ongoing human life, it must be sought somehow in solidarity with the race, with the earth, with the matrix that binds us all together, not in the isolated self. This was the perception that took shape in my mind gradually.[2]

Ruether also speaks of her childhood as being religiously ecumenical, humanistic, and free-thinking, which, she believes, laid the foundation for a career as both a radically minded scholar and an activist. Taking a stark heteronomous stance to autonomous selfhood, she decided early in her life to believe only that which she found personally believable and not because the Church taught it. She embraces what she terms "an 'adult' stance toward institutional Catholicism."[3] Her sense of solidarity with all humans and the Earth, coupled with her search for a spiritual "environment of worship that would not insult [her] intellect,"[4] are the reasons why she can claim that her four years spent in a Benedictine monastery in the high desert area of San Bernardino (as a young adult writing her dissertation) remain a golden memory for her. Imbued with a sense of renewal that was coming out of the Second Vatican Council at that time, the monastery became a centre for people who were beginning to organize around civil rights and peace issues. She recalls in a somewhat poetic manner, "Rising just before dawn, I walk the small hills at the foot of the San Bernardino Mountains … as the sun slowly turns the desert to a rosy glow … The high desert spring boasts a carpet of exotic flowers … I hear the bell for morning prayers. A flock of ducks from the pond accompany me to the chapel, standing with heads tucked piously into their necks in front of the altar window. Swaying from side to side, in seeming imitation of the cowled monks swaying in chant inside."[5]

Ruether's involvement in the civil rights movement preceded her sojourn in the monastery. The experience would also shape her work in profound ways, leading her into the field of feminism. "I got involved in feminism through the Civil Rights critique of male dominance," she notes in an interview with the journal *Conscience*: "What you experienced in Mississippi was looking at the United States from the southern black side. You see the white dominance and the racism."[6] Since that time, Ruether has continued her activism in peace, liberation, and feminist movements, incorporating them into her academic work. Another important influence on Ruether's thinking has been her life as a wife and mother. Married to Herman J. Ruether – a scholar in political science – with three children (and now grandchildren), Ruether believes that these realities have influenced both her scholarship and her activism, emphasizing that "parenting essentially keeps you grounded in a lot of realities, not only in the whole work of bringing up little kids, but the questions that are important to young adults."[7]

Ruether received her PhD in classics and patristics from Claremont Graduate School in 1965. She has been described by scholars as a pioneer Christian feminist theologian, and as a feminist Christian historian, a social ethicist, and even a modern prophet. However, she has written in diverse fields such as the historical and theological roots of anti-Semitism, the Israeli-Palestinian conflict, the history of women in American religion, liberation theology, the mythology of the Near East, the historical and ideological patterns of how Americans view themselves, and, of course, ecology. The sheer breadth and depth of her writings (my last count was 49 books and close to 700 articles) seem to defy categorization. Still, it is undoubtedly the title of ecofeminist theologian that best characterizes her, as I investigate her engagement of science to unite a liberationist agenda with an environmental ethic. Not solely as a pioneer in Christian feminist theology, Ruether can also be considered a pioneer in ecotheology. When the environmental movement was in its infancy, Ruether was questioning environmental solutions and decision-making processes that excluded the majority of the human race.

Worthy of note is Ruether's involvement in different vehicles to express her dissatisfaction with the teachings and views of the hierarchy of the Catholic Church. She has been a board member of Catholics for a Free Choice: a contributing editor for *Conscience*, a journal for Catholics committed to free choice; a columnist for the *National Catholic Reporter*, an independent Catholic newspaper; and a firm supporter of movements in feminism and religion. In 1964, in her early days in teaching, she was working for the Immaculate Heart College in Los Angeles. In response to the Vatican's disapproval of contraception, Ruether wrote a piece for the *Washington Post* magazine entitled "Why a Catholic Believes in Birth Control." That article cost Ruether her position at the college but it also taught her an important lesson early in her career, which also explains why she has escaped sanctions from the Vatican: she says, "[the incident] gave me the basic message: don't work for a Catholic institution."[8] Indeed, Ruether has never worked for a Catholic institution since then. She worked for some time at Howard University School of Religion and then at Garrett-Evangelical Theological Seminary, became Carpenter Emerita Professor of Feminist Theology at Pacific School of Religion and the Graduate Theological Union, and presently is visiting professor at Claremont Graduate University.

THE TARGET OF RUETHER'S CRITIQUE

Ruether's *New Woman/New Earth: Sexist Ideologies and Human Liberation*, published in 1975, is one of the first ecofeminist texts to identify the key issue underpinning ecofeminist thinking: the interconnection between the domination of women and the domination of nature. In fact, Ruether was writing about ecofeminism before the term itself was coined by French feminist Françoise d'Eaubonne in 1974.[9] *New Woman/New Earth* critiques a hierarchical system of domination. In an oft quoted passage, Ruether lays out the extent to which social change must occur: "Women must see that there can be no liberation for them and no solutions to the ecological crisis within a society whose fundamental model of relationships continues to be one of domination. They must unite the demands of the women's movement with those of the ecological movement to envision a radical reshaping of the basic socio-economic relations and the underlying values of this society."[10] Within the same book and in numerous subsequent writings, Ruether explores the cultural and social roots that have promoted the domination of women and nature (at the same time extending this analysis to include not just women but class, race, and ethnic hierarchies). The system of domination, she maintains, is rooted in a larger patriarchal and hierarchical system. It is shaped and perpetuated ideologically and socially by creation myths, social and legal codes, and philosophies that have become embedded into institutional structures. On the ideological-cultural level, women are said to be "'closer to nature' than men, and more aligned with body, matter, emotions and the animal world."[11] This perception of the material world has been used to justify the claim that women lack the capacity for intellectual and leadership roles, and leaves them, on the socio-economic level, "relegated" to the sphere of reproduction, cleaning, food preparation, and the like.

This hierarchical system of domination was reinforced in the Greco-Roman era by the dualist thinking that pervaded classical Greek philosophy, such as mind/body, nature/non-nature, matter/spirit, and indeed male/female. By the end of late antiquity, the patriarchal-dualist social economic pattern of society was set. As Ruether puts it, "The chain of being, God-spirits-male-female-non-human nature-matter, is at the same time the chain of command."[12] By the modern era, such dualisms were deepened by the philosophical thoughts of Descartes, who viewed the body as mere dead matter mechanically impelled, not unlike a machine. In this way of thinking, the mind stands outside matter, independent of its influences, serving as a control system apart from the body. It is this western philosophical narrative, then, with its logic of domination and interrelated dualisms, that defines the root of the problem for Ruether. It is the source of a dysfunctional model of relationships that has structured western society for many centuries and continues to do so today. This patriarchal thinking explains, in part, why women, and countless people, because of their gender, class, race, and ethnic origin, are marginalized and dominated. It also explains why nature is also marginalized and dominated.

In contrast to this, as Ruether posits in *Gaia and God*, her goal is to bring about an Earth healing, "a healed relation to each other and to the earth" which, she stresses, "calls for a new consciousness, a new symbolic culture and spirituality."[13] This is what liberation is for Ruether: a restoration of the human to her or his true self, and a reintegration of creation with its true destiny as "God's kingdom." And as will become evident in this chapter, Ruether's employment of science plays a fairly considerable role in countering this logic of domination, thus ushering in a new consciousness and liberation.

THE SCIENCE AUTHORING RUETHER'S ETHICAL VISION

In fashioning an ecologically sensitive ethic, Ruether focuses on four areas of scientific exploration (though not all are given equal weight): the new story of evolution or cosmology (particularly as it pertains to Earth), the Gaia theory (as a subset of Earth's evolution), subatomic physics, and ecology (as a subset of biological science). Drawing upon the work of scientists Nigel Calder, Steven Weinberg, and Stephen

Hawking (through John Boslough), Ruether describes the scientific theory of the origin of the universe, beginning with what she believes has been unimaginatively termed "the big bang:" the rapid explosion of intensely charged, radiant light-waves that expanded "not into 'empty space,' but created space and time itself by its expansion."[14] She describes the continuous process throughout the first billions of years where various forms of force – from the gravitational to the electromagnetic, nuclear, and subnuclear – arranged the relation of everything in the universe, from atomic nuclei and atoms to the planets and galaxies. She demonstrates the connectedness of creation by emphasizing that apart from "the even older hydrogen and helium atoms, all of the atomic elements that make up earth, from rocks to the human body, are ultimately 'stardust.'"[15]

Ruether describes the same evolutionary process at work on our planet from its first 4 billion years, when it would have been inhospitable to life as we know it, stressing that notwithstanding the hostile molten seas, the atomic elements that would eventually combine to form life already existed. Relying a great deal upon the works of biologists Paul and Anne Ehrlich, she contemplates the history of biogenesis on Earth, a process that began some four billion years ago, noting how each stage of biotic development leads more rapidly to the next stage. Hence, while it "took about 3.9 billion years, some eight-ninths of earth's history, simply to generate photosynthesizing bacteria … the entire evolution of land plants and animals has taken place in the last one-ninth of earth's history."[16] One can see where Ruether is going with this: "Within that history of land animals, humans occupy a fraction of time, a mere 400,000 years, or less than one-tenth of 1 per cent of earth's history."[17] From the above, Ruether concludes that our anthropocentric claim of having dominion over Earth "appears absurd in light of the 4,599,600,000 years in which earth got along without humans at all!"[18]

Ruether continues her examination of the evolutionary process through the Gaia theory, de-emphasizing, as above, any human pretentions to be the universe's most important entity, as well as highlighting the finite nature of our planet. Her description of the theory, however, "that the entire planet is a living system, behaving as a unified organism"[19] appears too simple. Developed by atmospheric chemist

James Lovelock with the help of biologist Lynn Margulis, the theory is more accurately described by its author as "a view of the Earth that sees it as a self-regulating system made up from the totality of organisms, the surface rocks, the ocean and the atmosphere tightly coupled as an evolving system. The theory sees this system as having a goal – the regulation of surface conditions so as always to be favourable as possible for contemporary life."[20] Ruether incorporates little of the scientific details of the Gaia theory, as explained by Lovelock, into her work. She does not deal with the intricacies of how the atmosphere, biosphere, lithosphere, hydrosphere, and barysphere form a single self-regulating cybernetic system. Ruether relies instead on the biological science of Paul and Anne Ehrlich to demonstrate the laws by which nature, independent of human management, has generated and sustained life.

Ruether holds Gaia more as a metaphor for the sacramental nature of Christianity in a dialectic tension with the God of the covenant. The term Gaia certainly carries a religious-spiritual meaning – something understood by Lovelock himself when he chose it – as the name refers to the Greek earth goddess. However, Ruether does not suggest replacing the Christian male monotheistic God as a hostile concept with Gaia as an immanent female goddess. Gaia, for Ruether, serves as the other voice that calls us into communion, a voice that "has long been silenced by the masculine voice"[21] of power and law that – when authentic – speaks on behalf of the weak to protect the powerless and to restrain the power of the mighty. Still, while not exploring the intricacies of Gaian theory, Ruether uses it as a platform to present the work of paleontologist Pierre Teilhard de Chardin, which, she claims, not only meshes well with Gaia theory, but also represents an important step in incorporating new scientific developments in the Earth's evolution and quantum physics.

Teilhard de Chardin's explanation of Earth's evolution is important to Ruether's program, as it is to all the Christian thinkers I am studying, for it makes room for consciousness in the world in a way that eschews dualistic thinking, while simultaneously challenging any notion that thought implies a hierarchy of being. In addition to Earth's many interconnected self-regulating spheres as mentioned above, Teilhard de Chardin posits yet another sphere, the "noosphere," which Ruether describes as the thinking mind of the human "that is privileged to contemplate the cosmic process [which] beams outward from this one planet, and perhaps from this planet alone."[22] In Teilhard de Chardin's own words, with the advent of the human being, there was an instantaneous leap from instinct to thought, which he terms "hominization."[23] Earth, according to Teilhard de Chardin, "gets a new skin,"[24] the noosphere. His hypothesis ties the geogenesis to the biogenesis, ascending ultimately to a psychogenesis that terminates in what he calls the "Omega Point,"[25] the synthesizing cooperative and collective action of human minds – the noosphere – at the end of the world where a maximum level of complexity is reached. Teilhard de Chardin's thinking, then, offers Ruether a unique representation for the increasing organizational complexity found in evolution while simultaneously allowing for a raison d'être for the human that does not ascribe a managerial function to it.

Arguably most important to Ruether's ethical vision is Teilhard de Chardin's challenge to scientific dualistic thinking. Working from findings in quantum physics, Teilhard de Chardin posits that energy (which we will see can also be understood as spirit) and matter are not dichotomized but the inside and outside of the same thing. As Ruether explains, "When we proceed to the inward depths of consciousness or probe beneath the surface of visible things to the electromagnetic field that is the ground of atomic and molecular structure, the visible disappears. Matter itself dissolves into energy. Energy, organized in patterns and relationships, is the basis for what we experience as visible things."[26] To Teilhard de Chardin, all energy is psychic in nature, composed of *tangential energy* (as understood empirically by science) and *radial energy* (as hypothesized by Teilhard de Chardin, a cosmic energy that does not suffer entropy and constantly increases). Teilhard de Chardin states that to make room for thought in the world, he had to "interiorize" matter, which meant imagining how matter and energy are transformed with a view to an end, the Omega. Noogenesis, consciousness coming into being within the human, serves as the upstream rise against the current of entropy. It is this latter energy that is the spirit within. Our intelligence, according to Teilhard de Chardin, is an intense form of this radial energy. Mind is no longer the antithesis to body but the inside or interiority of matter. This thinking is important for Ruether, since mind or consciousness is no longer viewed as originating from outside nature or in some transcendent world. Mind has been present in some form from the beginning of time. The role of the human is underscored in this regard, for, as Ruether puts it, mind now represents "the place where nature itself becomes conscious."[27]

Applying the arguments above to nature and non-nature, and indeed male and female, Ruether can challenge the dualisms as well as the hierarchical thinking that undergird the logic of domination. Hence, in opposition to the chain of being described earlier, "The chain of being has been laid on its side, so to speak."[28] To be sure, to fully conclude this, Ruether needs to modify Teilhard de Chardin's thinking, which is unabashedly anthropocentric. She does this by looking for continuities between human consciousness and the radial energy of matter throughout the universe. In this way, for example, our intelligence, while special, is not without continuity with other forms. She states, "it is the self-conscious or 'thinking dimension' of the radial energy of matter."[29]

In summary, Ruether's studies of cosmogony, the evolution of Earth, and subatomic physics have allowed her to challenge notions that there exists a radical dichotomy between humans and other-than-humans, or between energy and matter. We are not only stardust but the elements of our bodies "have been circulated billions of times through other biotic and abiotic beings throughout the 4.5 billion years of earth's evolution."[30] Ruether suggests the story of Earth's "creation," as put forth by science, can serve as a myth in the classic sense whereby mandates for ethical relationships emerge. Through earth science and astrophysics we learn about a universe full of distant stars, galaxies, and life, one that is deeply interrelated and with which humans share a kinship.

This is not a romantic ontology that Ruether is painting, as she herself claims. Since spirit and matter are the inside and outside of the same thing, her framework represents an embodied or Earth-bound spirituality that is scientifically inspired. In this way, the spirit some Christians believe to exist in plants or animals should be considered not in anthropomorphic but in "biomorphic" terms.[31] Hence, from an ethical standpoint, echoing Martin Buber's framework, "We respond not just as 'I to it,' but as 'I to thou,' to the spirit, the life energy that lies in every being in its own form of existence. The 'brotherhood of man' needs to be widened to embrace not only women but also the whole community of life."[32]

The above investigation of astrophysics, Earth evolution, and sub-atomic physics lays a foundation for viewing the universe as deeply relational. It is the study of ecology as a branch of the biological sciences that receives the most attention from Ruether. She uses ecology to formulate a new ethical vision based on the radical interdependency of all Earth's systems. Here again, she relies much on the works of Paul and Anne Ehrlich. Ruether believes that ecology, unlike the modern physical and biological sciences, which are only descriptive, is "normative" or "ethically prescriptive."[33] In saying this, she suggests that we are restoring the classical role of science.

Ruether finds that ethical norms arise as one investigates the dynamics among the air, soil, water, plants, rock, and animals that sustain life. Conversely, our failure to take heed from what nature tells us is the cause for Earth's destruction. For example, she states, "The crisis of pollution that distresses modern civilization results, in large part, from its failure to imitate nature in [its] system of recycling."[34] Similarly, our oversimplification of ecosystems, as evidenced through monoculture farming, makes a crop prone to collapse by "cogenerating an excessive population of one type of insect that will feed on this one plant."[35] This process ignores the demand for diversity, a lesson learned by observing how Earth works. With the same line of reasoning, Ruether concludes that the escalating human population is equally unethical as one population, of humans, proliferates to the detriment of other-than-human populations, threatening the destruction of life on the entire planet. And since humans have no substantial predators, it is up to us to self-limit.

Equally unethical, if we are to treat ecology as normative, is the human-heightened regard western civilization has for competition. Here, Ruether is borrowing from Lynn Margulis's discussions about symbiosis, the merging of organisms into new collectives, and its importance within the evolutionary framework. Margulis's research demonstrates that life on Earth evolved in novel ways through symbiotic relationships. She finds evidence that suggests that parts comprising present microbes were once independent organisms. It was not a mere branching from one mutant cell to others that led cells to evolve, but the merging of cells, a fusion, so to speak that, through time, led to the development of organelles within cells, including the nucleus.[36] Life, Margulis shows, is symbiosis. Ruether concludes from this that, "Cooperation and interdependency are the primary principles of ecosystems, within which competition between populations stands as a subcategory that serves to maintain this interdependency in a way that sustains the balanced relation of each population in relation to the whole."[37] Consequently, Ruether maintains that our cultural concept of competition is mistaken, as it is mutually exclusive, always imagining the other side as an "enemy" that ought to be "annihilated."[38] The lessons from biology and ecology, however, demonstrate quite the opposite: that the "other" is a constitutive dimension of an interdependent relationship with the larger biotic community.

AN ANALYSIS OF RUETHER'S ETHICAL VISION

As a broad summation of Ruether's ethic, then, I cite her own words from *Gaia and God*: "Human ethics should be a more refined and conscious version of this natural interdependency, mandating humans to imagine and feel the suffering of others, and to find ways in which interrelation becomes cooperative and mutually life enhancing for both sides."[39] Ruether's employment of science upholds this natural interdependency – which is in keeping with her ecofeminist thinking – depicting an expanding universe that is relational, interconnected, interdependent, and finite. She thus presents a scientific basis for dismissing dualistic and hierarchical thinking that undergirds the logic of domination that prevails in western society. Science is providing a myth and guidelines, as well as models that can help us change how we see the world and ourselves in it. As early as 1983, in *Sexism and God-Talk*, Ruether summed up the process of obtaining a new ethical vision as the conversion of our minds to nature's logic, which means understanding – through science – what that relational logic of natural harmony entails. We learn to subsume our human anthropocentric ethic into the larger not-just-human "ecologic" that maximizes the welfare of the whole rather than undermining and subverting the life systems that support us.

Much along the lines of a bioregional model, then, we learn from nature how to cultivate the welfare of the whole ecological community. It is within such a model that humans can begin to develop the sustained relational logic of natural harmony with other humans and the entire Earth community. Ruether states, for instance, how western society as a whole has recently begun to look upon Indigenous communities of the Americas, Asia, Africa, and the Pacific Islands with a different lens, one of respect, as it becomes increasingly apparent how each of these peoples have formulated their own bioregional culture that has sustained the local human group as part of a larger integral community, comprising not only animals and plants, but the waters and air.[40] For Ruether, therefore, the ecologic of the bioregional model demands that the human and the concomitant need for justice be integral. She explains lucidly what she means: "Converting our minds to earth cannot happen without converting our minds to each other, since the distorted and ecologically dysfunctional relationships appear necessary, yet they actually support the profits of the few against the many. There can be no ecological ethic simply as a new relation of 'man' and 'nature.' Any ecological ethic must always take into account the structures of social domination and exploitation that mediate domination of nature and prevent concern for the welfare of the whole community in favour of the immediate advantage of the dominant class, race, and sex. An ecological ethic must always be an ethic of ecojustice that recognizes the interconnection of social domination and domination of nature."[41] There is in Ruether's writing, then, a dynamic, or dialectic, between ecological and social justice as two unique, yet inseparable, approaches.

Another dialectic worth discussing is the one between our vulnerability and dependency as embodied, finite beings on the one hand, and the necessities of responsibility and empowerment through community on the other. By converting our minds to nature's logic, or more simply to Earth, as Ruether also puts it, we are also accepting our vulnerability to the violent tragic force of nature, suffering, limits, and death. To be sure, such vulnerability does not imply the act of being wounded or in a situation of immediate danger; Ruether would say these should be avoided or reduced. Instead, vulnerability, viewed as a permanent anthropological condition, undergirds Ruether's ecofeminist thinking. Such vulnerability lies in contrast to patriarchal theology that seeks to escape the horrors of our Earthly, embodied existence in return for "immortal blessedness" or invulnerability that frees us from our finite limits.[42]

Vulnerability, for Ruether, implies an utter dependency on all the systems that support life. Hence, dependency is also a fundamental character of human existence for Ruether, a point noted by Lucy Tatman in her analysis of Ruether's ecofeminist theology.[43] Ruether posits that in recognizing that we are utterly dependent, we recognize ourselves as finite organisms that eventually "disintegrate back into the nexus of life and arise again in new forms."[44] Tatman, quoting from Ruether's *Women and Redemption*, underlines that Ruether sees redemption occurring when aspects of the mortal life, such as vulnerability, are accepted: "We can then recognize that the fragile fruit of the tree of life is indeed lovely and good for discernment, and eat the fruit with relish, making it a part of our bodies. This is the possible redemption of life on earth. But it is possible only when we put aside the impossible redemptions of final conquest of limits in a realm of immortal life untouched by sorrow, vulnerability, and finitude."[45] Borrowing upon the work of ecofeminist theologian Ivone Gebara, Ruether demonstrates that redemption on Earth comes only when we abandon notions of invulnerability. When we do this, death becomes an integral part of life, not something foreign to it, which, Ruether stresses, has been the claim of traditional Christian cosmology.[46]

Converting our minds to nature's logic facilitates our embrace of these fundamental characteristics of human existence, such as death. But since we cannot convert our minds to nature's logic without also converting our minds to each other, as indicated above, Ruether points to how vulnerability and dependence relate to responsibility and empowerment in a dynamic balance. To be precise, as Tatman points out, when Ruether is speaking of "other" she is referring to the entire community of being: past, present, and unknown future.[47] Such solidarity with the other in community – from the human community to the biotic community to the God/ess or the "empowering matrix"[48] in whom we live and move and have our being – is where the process of empowerment unfolds. According to Tatman, Ruether conceives of an empowering matrix marked by a "yearning or a desire for relational mutuality among and between all aspects of creation."[49] In this light, it is also not surprising that in many of her writings Ruether commends the work carried out by women religious communities and some of their ecologically oriented movements, such as Sisters of Earth in the United States. She states, "This movement recognizes that the private individual or even the nuclear family is too fragmented and isolated to be a base for ecological living. One must start with a community a little larger, living together with some roots in the land,"[50] as suggested in a bioregional model. Such a communal base, enjoined by an ecofeminist vision and its application in liturgical life and service, Ruether believes, has enabled women religious "to reclaim the best of past monastic life with the call to renewal."[51] Here, Ruether praises the work of various alternative agriculture movements that have organized collective and viable responses to corporate industrial (and unsustainable) farming. We can see this sense of empowerment through community in the organizations and movements she mentions, such as Sem Terra (a movement in Brazil of landless workers to gain land and economic and social justice) and *Via Campesina* (a global umbrella organization that defends small-scale sustainable agriculture as a way to promote social justice and dignity), including the fair trade movement. In this light, it is also not surprising that Ruether gives prominence in her later writings to the Earth Charter as a means to respond to our ethical challenges. This should not be surprising, since the Charter itself stresses global interdependence and universal responsibility.

Understanding the frameworks above, there is a sense of perhaps the most demanding aspect of Ruether's ethic: contending with different forms of life are valued: the human and other-than-human. As Steven Bouma-Prediger points out, value for Ruether serves as both a necessary and a sufficient condition for ethical obligation.[52] This being the case, because we depend on the collective life systems of Gaia, as well as on each other, Gaia and all humans should gain value. Does this imply an instrumental valuation of life forms? Not for Ruether, as each life form has its own purpose, its own right to exist. Nevertheless, consciousness, Ruether adds, allows humans an element of volitional power that seeks to rearrange patterns in nature to suit our demands. This last point is important for Ruether. With our self-conscious ability, she likens the human's role to that of a caretaker or gardener though not because nature *needs* us to manage its processes; quite the contrary. We inherit this role of caretaker because of our capacity to create dysfunctional relationships that destroy nature. This does not imply a freedom to do what we will, however, as we saw earlier: we are also constrained by nature's ecologic system.

The issue of valuation becomes more complex when trying to reconcile the preferential option for the marginalized human with that of the marginalized other-than-human. Ruether recognizes that there is violence and bloodshed in nature; however, with the exception of the human, she states, this takes place within its own built-in balances. Ruether notes how theologian Jay McDaniel once agonized about how the pelican, given two eggs so that at least one will survive, will peck the second to death once the first hatches and throw it out of the nest. So while sentimentality for the second pelican would be misplaced, as this is the logic of nature, sentimentality for an impoverished mother with two children whom she cannot afford to feed is not, as this is the logic of the human-within-nature. It is the human being alone that has no such built-in balances, through instinct or predation – other than through our ethics – which is telling us to self-limit. While this might sound problematic, Ruether explains, for example: "When I garden, I would be foolish to make a preferential option for the weak and the diseased. I need to root out the excess growth of many plants so that a few, the healthiest, can grow well."[53] Does this mean we ought to root out the excess growth of the overabundance of humans populating the Earth? The answer is a qualified yes. She does not suggest, however, that we root out the overabundance of humans through the same means she would weed or squish a slug eating her cabbage. Nor does she suggest culling the weak and diseased humans. Understanding the distinction here is crucial to understanding how Ruether envisions her ecological ethic.

Ruether posits that human consciousness includes impulses to loving care of others which allow us to self-limit, and in a way that is just. For example, we deal with the overabundance of humans populating the Earth not by force, but by limiting future births through education and by providing resources (such as contraception) to the mother of two children mentioned above; but it does not end there. We rectify the conditions (such as malnutrition and unclean water) that lead to an untimely death of her child. We could say – in keeping with our observation above – that within her bioregional framework, the ecological call to sustainability is held in an uneasy tension with the preferential option for the poor by correcting the destructive "option for the rich at the expense of the well-being of the whole community of life."[54] Ruether underlines, somewhat pragmatically, "To refuse to limit ourselves rationally means that these limits are imposed cruelly and violently."[55]

There are two logics at work in Ruether's ethic. While we recognize our vulnerability and utter dependence, we are also responsible and can become empowered through community. Hence, both the logic of nature and consciousness play decisive roles in Ruether's understanding of liberation. In this way, while "all life forms exist through an interdependency of consuming and being consumed,"[56] Ruether stresses that a different ethic must apply to the protection of human life because humans (because of our consciousness) live within a different context or "plane" of reality. She writes, "The ethical principles applicable to the protection of human life cannot be exactly identified with those appropriate for highly sentient mammals."[57] Does this imply a hierarchy? Not so, says Ruether. In ecological thinking, the hierarchical model of reality is misleading, as no part is intrinsically higher or lower. "Plants," she writes, "are not 'lower' than humans because they don't think or move. Rather, their photosynthesis is the vital process that underlies the very existence of the animal and human world. We could not exist without them, whereas they could exist very well without us. Who, then, is more important?"[58] With this same line of reasoning, Ruether finds the demand for animal rights to be morally unconvincing. She observes ambiguities and some arbitrariness from its proponents, such as Tom Regan, who readily extends rights to mammals. However, Regan is not clear about how those rights apply to fish and fowl, or even clams. This does not mean we are to condone cruelty to animals in laboratory experimentation, or in factory farming. But, in keeping with dynamic balance between different contexts or "planes" of reality, a blanket call to vegetarianism cannot be supported. Aptly, Ruether points out, "All humans do not dominate nature equally, view themselves as over nature or benefit from such domination."[59] Hence, she concludes: "we can hardly impose a vegetarian ethic on third-world peasants for whom the eating of the occasional chicken or pig that grows up in the barnyard is an indispensable part of an otherwise very limited diet."[60]

Again, as discussed earlier, Ruether is seeking a dynamic balance between justice and ecological sustainability, but, in doing so, appears to steer away from science. To understand this balance, we must see that it occurs within the larger philosophical-theological framework of process thought, which Ruether discusses in *Gaia and God* and incorporates into her other writings. Building upon the philosophy of Alfred North Whitehead, process theology postulates a dipolar God, which characterizes God, whose primordial nature contains the whole of potentiality of all entities that exist. This nature of God also provides the initial aim for these entities. Each entity, however, has its own subjectivity, the ability to adapt and actualize or even thwart this aim of God. But the fulfillment of this aim can only be partial. This thinking undergirds why, for Ruether, nature is never "perfect" or in a paradisiacal state. While Ruether believes nature can be cruel, it is not fallen; instead, nature is "marred and distorted by human misdevelopment."[61] In fact, Ruether eschews the Christian prelapsarian notion of a paradisiacal nature. Nature is not capable of completely fulfilling human hopes for the good. However, because our consciousness and aspirations also represent the evolutionary growing edge of what is "not yet" realized, humans take on a role of imperfect co-creators in an imperfect world. We pass on our ideals to the future by molding nature to reflect our ecologic ideals. This is a theology of becoming.

There is a certain reasonableness to Ruether's ethical vision. Within the frameworks she provides, an uneasy balance between the needs and desires of all life is supported. With this attention to the "not yet" "partial fulfillment" of creation, it should not be surprising that Ruether eschews ethical monism. Any application of a single set of principles that are all-encompassing has no place in her worldview. Instead, Ruether's is a moral pluralism where a plurality of values needs to be balanced in relation to each other. Her specific framework is crucial to understanding her ethic though, otherwise we unwisely spin our wheels, so to speak, on trying to make sense of the plight of the second pelican egg, ignore the plight of the woman and her child, or resist self-limitation, only to have limits cruelly imposed upon us down the road. But this does not mean her ethic is without difficulties.

Notwithstanding its logic, one has to question the extent to which Ruether's ethical vision has avoided a form of anthropocentrism. I contrast here what I term a strong anthropocentrism to a weak anthropocentrism. A strong anthropocentrism takes the view that value is to be accorded to the human, thereby placing humans above and apart from all other life forms. A weak anthropocentrism takes the view that reality can only be interpreted from a human point of view, thereby still according some centrality to the human. While it is true, as Ruether states above, that "the anthropocentric claims to have been given 'dominion' over the earth, and over all its plants and animals, appears absurd in light of the 4,599,600,000 years in which each got along without humans at all!," Ruether still seems to have us in the driver's seat of evolution and not simply because we are capable of destroying it. While humans take on a role of imperfect co-creators, or caretakers, in an imperfect world, Ruether stresses that humans are uniquely situated as mediators between the realities of the subatomic and the cosmic realms. This phenomenal position grants us a more engaged function beyond that of mere caretaker, since it is we who reshape nature to reflect our ideals. As it stands, we are the ones deciphering the logic we find in nature; and while this privilege carries with it a responsibility, it is nevertheless we, not the pelican, who decide what constitutes responsible action. While the anthropocentric character in her ethical vision appears to be more of the weak kind, it cannot be described as very weak either. Ruether does not make a distinction between these two understandings of the term, which is why I raise it here.

Related to the above, Stephen Bede Scharper takes issue with Ruether's insistence that humans are situated as mediators between realities while simultaneously rejecting any dualism between the male and female. He claims that in doing so, Ruether, despite her claims to the contrary, advocates a "managerial 'dualism'" between humans and other-than-humans, while eschewing any such hierarchical import between males and females. How can we account for this seeming inconsistency? Scharper states, "Since ecofeminists want 'humans' to act responsibly in regard to 'nature,' they seem to credit humans with the higher faculty of critical intelligence."[62] In fact, this is evident above with Ruether's reference to different planes of reality: the pelican does not receive the status of gardener. At the same time, as Scharper points out, for Ruether there is no higher or lower in this regard when it comes to men and women. Scharper suggests that Ruether is simply not recognizing the limits of dualistic discourse: she seems to be contending with different dualisms, one that is completely eschewed (the human–human) and the other, which is only partially eschewed (the human–nonhuman). Perhaps this discrepancy is a result of Ruether having two logics at work simultaneously. This is unclear, though.

Finally, readers might notice how Ruether appears to use redemption practically interchangeably with liberation, evidenced above, for example, when Ruether posits that redemption on Earth comes only when we abandon notions of invulnerability. Indeed, reading Ruether's various works, there is a noticeable blurring of the boundaries between redemption and liberation. The use of both terms, therefore, warrants some discussion. In *Women and Redemption,* she traces the notion of redemption back, in some ways, to its more original form as being Earthy, tied to a finite existence and the construction of the "kingdom" here and now. She does this by showing how it changes through time from its original Hebraic Earthy (social, historical) notion to its other-worldly reconciliation of the self with a God out there beyond Earthly existence. Certainly, with Ruether's strong emphasis on the person and community as a source of one's own redemption (not having to rely on an exterior saviour figure),[63] and with her severe downplaying of any afterlife that splits body and soul,[64] it becomes clear why she can speak of redemption as the transformation of the human into life-giving relationships – and not as any form of escape to the afterlife. Redemption, if it is to occur, happens here and now on Earth; it is a shift away from the modern western cultural other-worldly construct to a this-worldly hope. It is also not primarily about being reconciled with a God either, but more about reconciling ourselves to one another and Earth. She explains: "Redemption puts us back in touch with a full biophilic rationality of humans with their bodies and one another and rebuilds social relations that can incarnate love and justice. The redemption is about the transformation of self and society into good, life-giving relations, rather than an escape from the body and the world into eternal life."[65] She adds, seemingly as a theological caveat, "Other-worldly eschatology is usually not explicitly denied, but it is put aside."[66]

An inconsistency appears if I compare the above understanding of redemption with what Ruether writes about liberation in her book *Liberation Theology: Human Hope Confronts Christian History and American Power*.[67] Ruether argues that liberation is "a veritable resurrection of the self … a violent exorcism of the demons of self-hatred and self-destruction which have possessed [the oppressed] and the resurrection of autonomy and self-esteem, as well as the discovery of a new power and possibility of community with their brothers and sisters in suffering."[68] She further complicates the issue by suggesting an integral connection between the inner self-liberation as the conscientization process, and a redemptive rebirth;[69] conscientization here – which has always been used as a term to denote the process of liberation – is also redemptive. Indeed, when liberation is defined as a restoration of the human to her or his true self, and a reintegration of creation with its true destiny as "God's kingdom," how are we to distinguish it from redemption that has no other-worldly import? Even Mary Grey, in her foreword to *Introducing Redemption in Christian Feminism,* writes that redemption is more like a cluster of concepts that take in sin, salvation, grace, and the saviour figure. She concludes, "Redemption is clearly conceptualized on a global perspective as the path of liberation transforming both people and oppressive social systems."[70] Could it be that Ruether sees redemption as a means to liberation, which is the ultimate end? If so, why would she suggest we rid ourselves of redemption if it is the means? By way of another example, note how Ruether ends her book *Introducing Redemption in Christian Feminism*. In reciting the Beijing Women's Conference in 1995 as being all the redemption we need, she suggests, as well, that maybe the idea of redemption should come to an end, or at best be understood like this: "Bread. A clean sky. Active peace. A woman's voice singing somewhere. The army disbanded. The harvest abundant. The wound healed. The child wanted. The prisoner freed. The body's integrity honored, the lover returned … labor equal, fair and valued. No hand raised in any gesture but greeting. Secure interior – of heart, home and land – so firm as to make secure borders irrelevant at last."[71]

Of course, I could ascribe such blurring of the boundaries between redemption and liberation simply to lack of clarity from Ruether. I do not suggest here that Ruether willingly conflates the two terms – thus retaining a theological distinction between the terms for traditional theological purposes; rather, she wants to rethink our use of the notion of redemption, and play up its liberation elements while downplaying its salvific (other-worldly) elements. Reasons why notwithstanding, I think it reasonable, for the purposes of this chapter, to understand redemption and liberation, with regard to Ruether's ethical vision, as being virtually interchangeable terms.

THE EPISTEMOLOGY AND METHODOLOGY BACKING RUETHER'S ETHICAL VISION

When it comes to knowing, Ruether's feminist epistemological foundations become starkly evident. Ruether places her starting point on experience, though, in her case, it is unambiguously the experience of women where her investigation begins. As a result, Ruether is less focused on any discipline (be it cultural history, theology, or science) and more on context and relationality. Again, showing her ecofeminist credentials, Ruether eschews abstract hierarchical dualistic notions that emphasize the rational thinking processes over the intuitive, imaginative, and embodied ways of knowing. In *Sexism and God-Talk*, for instance, Ruether discusses the problem of using only left-brain thinking: this is linear thinking, she avers, which simplifies, dichotomizes, and focuses on parts and fails to see the larger rationality of interdependence. Not surprisingly, epistemologically, Ruether also seeks a balance of tensions, a point between linear thinking and spatial and relational thinking, which uses the whole brain, both its left and right hemispheres. And in keeping with her affinity to process thinking, like Leonardo Boff and Diarmuid O'Murchu – as discussed in later chapters – what we consider truth is an ongoing incomplete epistemological endeavour, which never ends, giving truth as she puts it, a "*status viatoris*."[72]

Ruether conforms to a feminist standpoint theory of understanding where knowledge about reality, while attainable, is nevertheless the product of a critical engagement within one's life as it is lived. This is readily apparent in Ruether's writing: "It became necessary to recognize that the world not only appears differently according to our standpoint toward it and methods of addressing it, but itself will be constituted differently by the stance assumed toward it. Rather than assuming a standpoint outside of and unrelated to reality, from which 'objective' knowledge is possible, the observer is an integral part of the reality observed."[73] Ruether is not espousing a purely subjectivist epistemology: while all standpoints differ, her way of knowing the world is also expressly communal. Lucy Tatman likens it to a shared "participatory discernment" that comprises self-critical reflection, "painstaking, roll-up-the-shirtsleeves, get-your-hands-dirty work … that requires that I acknowledge the other member of the epistemic communities of which I am a part."[74] It is for this reason that Ruether stresses, "But such a fuller integration of the sciences necessary for the fullest reflection on the question of human liberation today cannot be done by a single scholar. It waits upon a multi-disciplinary team work that can integrate the many sources of data and the types of reflection and symbolization around the core of theological reflection. Only with such a multi-disciplinary integration of human sciences can we begin to speak of the basis for a theology of liberation adequate to the present human situation."[75] Writing almost twenty years later, Ruether upholds this integrated way of knowing, saying, "Fuller exploration of ecofeminism goes beyond the expertise of any one person. It needs the cooperation of a team of historians of culture, natural scientists, and social economists who would all share a concern for the interconnection of domination of women and exploitation of nature."[76] These epistemic communities are not limited temporally, physically, or by any cultural or physical differences such as race, sex, or religion. And while less explicit than the other interlocutors I investigate here about where nature's voice comes into play, Ruether nevertheless maintains that nature's voice comes into the conversation through our empirical sciences and through our senses and our poetry. Addressing the role of our senses, in many of her writings she promotes Carolyn Merchant's "partnership ethic," which I discuss in more detail below.

Merchant speaks of hearing nature's voice, which comes to us through the senses: "through the semi-permeable membranes of our bodies," we are better able "to communicate with nature through sensuous experience ... Such consciousness can be reclaimed by listening to the voice of nature."[77]

The epistemic communities Ruether defines are, as Tatman suggests above, communities of "shared truths"[78] which, somewhat pragmatically, demand of their members a certain responsibility to ensure that the liberation of others is facilitated. What is constituted as the web of relationship, Tatman states, "will also be shaped by how we relate to it. The knower[s] must take responsibility for shaping the reality that is known in ways that are benign or destructive."[79] Truth comes about through a critical engagement with one's life. In this way, the features of Ruether's ethical vision discussed above, vulnerability and dependency and empowerment through community, serve as salient features for justifying truth. A truth is justified by whether or not it realizes just and authentic relationships within community (never descending from on high), where vulnerability and dependence are accepted and responsibility and empowerment are fostered.

The demarcation between ways of knowing blurs in Ruether's epistemology. Ruether points this out herself when speaking about the changing paradigm of scientific knowledge ushered in by Albert Einstein, Wolfgang Pauli, Niels Bohr, and others: "Just as science had broken down the Christian separation of spheres between earth and planetary matter and between humans and animals, so the new physics itself began to break down the distinction of spheres on which the separation of science from religion (and humanities) had been based. It no longer seemed possible to distinguish so clearly between matter and energy. Nor was it so clear that science could demarcate an objective realm of 'facts' distinct from subjective perspectives."[80] This breaking down of the distinction of epistemological spheres is supported, says Ruether, by the fact that all human language is symbolic. She says, "Scientists think the scientific language which is doing nothing but describing empirically proven reality is, of course, ludicrous ... they are oblivious to the other cultural ramifications of such language like big bang."[81] Ruether is referring here to the nomenclature we spoke of earlier, of "big bang," employed by scientists to speak of the origin of the universe, as opposed to something like the "cosmic egg," which Ruether believes is a far better metaphor. The point, however, is not so much whose language is more appropriate but that language and its symbolic nature matter. In other words, the scientist who does nothing but describe will fail to capture the full import of her or his experience. Speaking specifically to theology in her earlier writings, Ruether states, "Theologians today must be more willing to dissolve the traditional perimeters of their 'field,' its sources and content, in order to rise to the task of sketching the horizon of human liberation in its fully redemptive context."[82] This task of dissolving disciplinary walls is specifically vital with reference to liberationist-ethical issues, according to Ruether, for, "If theology is really to speak meaningfully about the mediating point between the 'is' and the 'ought' of human life, then it takes as its base the entire human project."[83]

To realize Ruether's relational program, it becomes clear that it "needs visionaries to imagine how to construct a new socio-economic system and a new cultural consciousness that would support relations of mutuality, rather than competitive power."[84] These are the poets, artists, and liturgists, as well as scientists and even revolutionary organizers, who work to incarnate more life-giving relationships in our cultural and social systems. This is why Ruether calls forth the "scientist-poet" as an ecological leader, one "who can retell the story … in a way that can call us to wonder, to reverence for life, and to the vision of humanity living in community with all its sister and brother beings."[85]

Ruether does not explicitly describe how her epistemological framework might function. Still, through some extrapolation we can get a picture of how it might unfold, in part, by how she describes the building of bioregional communities and, in part, through the model of Carolyn Merchant's partnership ethic, which Ruether promotes in many of her writings. Merchant's partnership ethic is explicitly a collaborative effort where negotiation and the seeking of consensus are key to engaging with others, replacing more contentious power over, legal, and litigation processes that are in vogue today. Ruether points out, for instance, that through the natural sciences, we can learn about chaos and complexity and learn that nature is not passive or mechanical, much less composed of dead matter. Consequently, we observe, "a meadow with many kinds of plants and insects balancing each other, each with their ecological niches, and then one learns to plant for human use in a way that imitates these same principles, in a more simplified and selective fashion."[86]

Ecofeminists, in turn, engage in the dialogue by asking who might profit from the intended method. For example, while the normative ecological requirement would have humans eat lower on the food chain, the ecofeminist would not deny a subsistence farmer the meat from a chicken or pig if that is the only source of protein for her family. How Ruether envisions the ensuing dialogue between the ecofeminist above and the scientist is less clear. I presume that a scientist-poet would be open to multiple epistemologies. Problems remain, however, since the welfare of the subsistence farmer above surely is not as guaranteed as Merchant's partnership ethic seems to presume: here, her/his welfare has to be negotiated within a larger communal debate. To be sure, Ruether's program rests more on the force of her principles and less on the intricacies of a system of dialogue.

There is, however, an embodied practice at play, be it meditation or just "tak[ing] time to sit under trees, look at water, and at the sky, observe small biotic communities of plants and animals with close attention, get back in touch with the living earth,"[87] which might allow us to engage more harmoniously with nature. This process, Ruether asserts, is meant "to assist releasing the stifled intuitive and creative powers of our organism, to draw and to write poetry, and to know that we stand on holy ground."[88] Similarly, according to Merchant's partnership ethic, humanity can learn to listen to nature's voice as revealed through ecological principles, ethics, poetry, and a reverence for our other-than-human partner. It is through such listening that we permit the river to flow freely. And while nature's language differs from our own, we can nevertheless listen through the membranes of our bodies. This action allows us to communicate with nature through the sensuous experience: "The rustling of leaves in an oak tree or an aspen grove is itself a kind of voice."[89] The intention of all this, Ruether seems to stress, is that we learn to respond – recalling the framework put forth by Buber – "as 'I to thou' to the spirit, the life energy that lies in every being in its own form of existence."[90]

CONCLUSION

I began this investigation of Ruether's ethical vision by discussing the starting points in her thinking, her life experiences that lead her to conclude that to find meaning in life we need to live in loving solidarity with *all* of creation. Early in her life she developed a mature stance to her faith and a readiness to fight injustices. It is not surprising, then, to see that the target of her critique is the logic of domination that marginalizes both the human, especially the woman, and the natural world. The two concerns are indelibly linked by the same corrupt values.

It is apparent from this investigation on Ruether that she is thoroughly concerned with meeting the needs and desires of the entire Earth community, while accessing abundantly the wisdoms of her faith and science. In all this, science, expressly ecology, regains a normative character. Yet, science is not exclusively authoring Ruether's ethical vision. As I have shown, her feminist intuition ranks prominently in her epistemological paradigm. Ruether, from her early life, intuited a finitude to existence long before she studied ecology, which teaches the same lesson. And long before cosmologists demonstrated our radical kinship among humans, trees, and ducks, Ruether experienced and valued an affinity among them all.

The result is an uneasy balance among disparate pressures that stem from her faith, what science is telling us, her feminist sensibilities, and her concern for the destruction of our planet. I say "uneasy" because some of the converging interests, as I will discuss in later chapters, appear to challenge understandings in science and important tenets of her faith, such as the view that humans alone are the cause of ecosystem imbalances or the downplaying of an afterlife. In fact, marking her ethical vision is a decided determination to arrive at a balance between a plurality of views, multiple ways of knowing, and between difficult-to-reconcile issues, such as the preferential option for the poor and environmental sustainability. The balance she speaks of, then, is not without tensions and contentions. This is not problematic for Ruether, though, but seemingly natural. What is important in all this is the participatory process in which this balance is achieved.

What is clear about Ruether's ethical vision, and something found in the ethical visions of the remaining three authors, is the importance she assigns to relationality here and now on Earth, our planetary home. Ruether's ethical vision is decidedly a grounded or Earth-bound spirituality that is rooted in the reality of our permanent anthropological condition of being vulnerable to finite limits of reality. It implies an utter dependency on all the systems that support life. Consequently, a relationality underpins the conversation between her faith and science. In fact, truths within this conversation are justified by whether or not they realize just and authentic relationships within community, which, for Ruether, describes liberation.

To be sure, some aspects of Ruether's ethical vision are not always clear, as I have shown. Yet, it should be kept in mind that her work spans some four decades, in which time some of her thinking has changed. While Ruether is adamant that converting our minds to Earth cannot occur without converting our minds to each other, she is not as clear on how such a process might occur, other than situating it within a bioregional context. Ruether also posits that there are two logics at work. If liberation is to be accorded to all creation, how is this biologic to work? It is not just Ruether, as will become evident in the ensuing chapters, who struggles with this issue.

CHAPTER TWO

Leonardo Boff

INTRODUCTION TO BOFF

Leonardo Boff was born in Brazil in 1938, and today he lives in Jardim Araras, an ecological wilderness area in the municipality of Petrópolis, Rio de Janeiro. Boff joined the Order of the Franciscan Friars Minor in 1959, where he underwent specialized studies of Franciscan spirituality. He was ordained to the priesthood in 1964. His fascination with St Francis and his mysticism are evident in much of his writings. St Francis, he states, "reclaimed of the rights of the heart, the centrality of feeling, and the importance of gentleness in human and cosmic relations."[1] According to Boff, the saint rehabilitated a worldview that Christianity had lost: "the encounter with God, with Christ and with the Spirit in nature, and accordingly the discovery of the vast cosmic kinship and the preservation of innocence – childlike clearsightedness at an adult age – that brings freshness, purity, and enchantment back to the afflictions of life on this Earth."[2]

A decisive experience that initially led Boff to embrace liberation theology was his work as a priest in the slum of Petrópolis, near Rio de Janeiro. There he came in contact with people who survived by rummaging through garbage dumps for food and yet found hope and maintained a sense of dignity through their connection to Christian base communities. The 1950s and 1960s were tumultuous times for the people of Brazil, as they were for most of the poor in Latin America. The populist government of Vargas in Brazil, for instance, inspired a nationalistic consciousness and much industrial development, which further marginalized an already struggling population, sending a large number of people into sprawling urban shantytowns. The process led to the rise of popular movements which, in turn, provoked the rise of military dictatorships – as was the case in Brazil – leading to further repression of those economically sidelined within society. The 1960s were also a time of renewal within the Catholic Church, which, in Boff's words, led many people to "take their social mission seriously."[3] The organizing of the poor into base communities of faith, where members had greater roles in liturgy and in the organizational decision-making processes, is an example of this. During this time, Boff would make frequent trips to the diocese of Acre-Purus which was in the heart of the Amazon jungle. There, he would eventually meet and befriend Chico Mendes, whom he supported for many years in his struggle for justice in the Amazon. Mendes was a Brazilian rubber trapper who saw the need to live and harvest within the rainforest sustainably. He helped form a union of rubber trappers and led resistance struggles against clear-cutting operations. In 1988, he was assassinated by a wealthy rancher. Mendes, and indeed the Amazon forest itself, would greatly influence Boff's understanding of ecology as well as his understanding of the role Indigenous peoples have on Earth. Mendes, Boff writes, "could hear the powerful call of the forest in his body and soul. He experienced himself as part and parcel of the land."[4] It is not surprising, in this light, to learn that Boff considers Mendes a secular and contemporary St Francis of Assisi.

Boff received his doctorate in philosophy and theology from the University of Munich, Germany, in 1970 and began his career as a professor of systematic and ecumenical theology at the Franciscan Theological Institute in Petrópolis. He is hailed as one of the founders of liberation theology along with Gustavo Gutiérrez. As he puts it, he "was present in the first reflections that sought to articulate indignance toward misery and marginalization with discourse, which later generated the Christian faith known as Liberation Theology."[5] Boff's reputation in Rome was of a different nature. In 1984, a doctrinal process was imposed upon him by the Vatican's Congregation for the Doctrine of Faith in Rome because of his book *Church: Charisma and Power.* By 1985, he was condemned to "obsequious silence" and was removed from his editorial functions and suspended from religious duties. While Boff was undoubtedly silenced, as he puts it, because of his trenchant views that society and the Church ought to be transformed so that the poor become protagonists,[6] it was specifically his "ecclesiological relativism," his teaching that the one true church can exist outside the Catholic Church, that landed him in trouble, as expressed by then cardinal Ratzinger, then prefect of the Congregation for the Doctrine of the Faith.[7] Ostensibly, Boff espouses a different model of church that lies in contrast to the current model where power rests with the hierarchy. Boff emphasized the Holy Spirit over current ecclesiological structures. While this first stricture was reversed to a large degree shortly after – due to international pressure on the Vatican – Boff renounced his activities as a priest under renewed threats of punishment from the Vatican in 1992, and, as he states, "promoted himself to the state of laity," underlining, "I changed trenches to continue the same fight."[8]

Boff currently serves as professor emeritus at the State University of Rio de Janeiro (UERJ). A prolific writer with some sixty book titles to his name, Boff is one of the most widely read South American writers within the religious field. He has also been involved in promoting many grassroots organizations in Brazil (among them, like Ruether, Sem Terra) and, notable for our purposes, was one of the authors of the Earth Charter. While it is not incorrect to speak of Boff as a Christian liberation theologian, that title does not fully capture the broad scope of his work, specifically his works since 1992, when the United Nations held a conference on environment and development in Rio de Janeiro. While Boff showed interest in ecological issues much earlier, it was at this time that he began to deal with ecological issues in a systematic way. Indeed, Boff was the first Latin American theologian to situate social and political liberation within an ecological framework. According to Andrew Dawson, since his renunciation of his holy orders, Boff has concentrated his writings less on understanding and developing the Christian theological paradigm and more on articulating the need for a globally relevant spiritual ethos that more aptly speaks to the worldwide situation.[9] In other words, Boff began focusing on the larger dimensions of liberation, not just for all humans but for the whole planet. As he put forth in his acceptance speech for winning the 2001 Right Livelihood Award, Boff considers himself an "integral theologian of liberation," which, as will become evident throughout this chapter, is perhaps a more fitting designation.

THE TARGET OF BOFF'S CRITIQUE

Boff targets what he labels a perverse logic of domination, based on self-aggrandizement and manipulation, which leads to the exploitation of both people and the natural world. Not surprisingly, given his experience in the slums and rainforests of Brazil, his early work targets global developmentalist models that lead to underdevelopment. An early critic of development theory, Boff notes how the ideal of development assumes an infinite supply of natural resources as well as possibilities. In such a scenario, both nature and humans become mere objects used for their resources and labour, respectively. Boff describes this vision as instrumentalist and mechanical: "people, animals, plants, minerals, in short, all living beings lose their autonomy and intrinsic value."[10] His analysis of development theory led him to conclude that capitalist industry flourishes by converting everything into accumulation mostly for the benefit of the few and only secondarily for the others. The foreign debts maintained by banks in wealthy countries to economically impoverished countries in the global South, for example, ensure that the rich control and dominate the poor, and indeed, the interest on the debt causes the system to perpetuate itself. The main critique from liberation theology is that such a model is incapable of creating wealth without also creating poverty and social exploitation.[11]

While neither the exploitation of the human nor of the natural world is new, Boff underlines that the ravages today are on a planetary scale and aided by the growth and application of science and technology. We first see his arguments on this develop in a systematic way (in their English translated versions) in *Ecology and Liberation: A New Paradigm*, published in 1995, and more thoroughly – especially in regard to its incorporation of new science – in *Cry of the Earth, Cry of the Poor*,[12] published in 1997. The cries that come from the Earth and the poor explain why liberation theology and ecology must discourse, for these cries "stem from two wounds that are bleeding. The first, the wound of poverty and wretchedness, tears the social fabric of millions and millions of poor people the world over. The second, systematic aggression against the earth, destroys the equilibrium of the planet, threatened by depredations made by a type of development undertaken by contemporary societies, now spread throughout the world."[13] In the context of woundedness, Boff underlines a grave imbalance not just between humans and the natural world, but among humans themselves. This is why he says that today's social system is anti-ecological: "The logic that exploits classes and subjects peoples to the interests of a few rich and powerful countries is the same as the logic that devastates the Earth and plunders its wealth, showing no solidarity with the rest of humankind and future generations."[14]

Underlying this anti-ecological logic of domination, which in later writings Boff refers to as a cosmology of domination, is a spiritual and cognitive malaise, representing a flawed consciousness that promotes a power over the other and eschews our universal connectedness to all that exists. Such a condition has fostered anthropocentric and utilitarian attitudes and the denial of the sacredness of the world, which have shaped how we conduct our economics and politics. Christianity, as far as it is complicit in inflicting both wounds, is also marred by its heightened anthropocentrism but also by its patriarchy, dogmatism, sense of election, its conviction that creation has fallen, and its heightened monotheism to the exclusion of other manifestations of God, as understood by Trinitarian theology. In more recent writings, Boff assigns materialist realism – the philosophical view that he states has prevailed over humanity for the last four centuries – as a cause for our crisis. Materialist realism marks a reality that is independent of the subject and exists in the form of independent objects, which he feels reduces the scope of reality, because it excludes any notion of subjectivity or spirituality. Like the cosmology of domination, this philosophical view further disconnects us from the whole, which is emptied of any sacredness or mystery.

To transform and heal our world, Boff calls for a new paradigm (a term he has used consistently since 1995), marked by a process whereby humans reinvent our understanding of ourselves as a species and our role. We are not living so much in an epoch of change as in a change of epochs, he states,[15] and the new era should be defined by a paradigm of care and connectedness brought about through a fundamental shift in consciousness. This is the process of "liberation," as he understands it. Certainly, it is understood in the traditional sense, as personal enlightenment, and in a more concrete collective sense, as the freedom from oppressive, political, economic, and social structures. But here liberation gains a wider ecological, even cosmological, dimension involving the conscious participation of humanity in the movement toward greater diversity, interiority, and communion with creation, inspired by science.

THE SCIENCE AUTHORING BOFF'S ETHICAL VISION

The scientists whose work Boff draws upon are numerous, and much of their work is ancillary to his more central arguments. Boff principally employs the works of chemist James Lovelock and biologist Lynn Margulis to discuss the Gaia theory; chemist Ilya Prigogine and physicists Erich Jantsch and Fritjof Capra to discuss systems theory; Capra again, physicists Nick Herbert, David Bohm, F. David Peat, and Menas Kafatos, mathematician John von Neumann, science historian Robert Nadeau, and – not a scientist, but with a strong background in science – Danah Zohar to discuss quantum physics; physicists Paul Davies, Stephen Hawking, and Steven Weinberg and cosmologist Brian Swimme to discuss cosmology.[16] The work of paleontologist Teilhard de Chardin is employed to emphasize the evolutionary aspect of the universe. Nevertheless, ecology – for which Boff relies much upon Lovelock's and Margulis's work to understand the historicity of nature, and, to a lesser degree, the works of E.O. Wilson and Paul Ehrlich – receives a pre-eminent position as the larger framework under which the many other sciences, as well as the many other ways of knowing the universe, coalesce. While Boff recognizes the scientific biological roots of ecology, as understood by biologist Ernst Haeckel (who coined the term in 1866), he also sees notions of connectedness and relationship underlining its fundamental nature and, hence, extends the term to cover *all* existing things (alive or not) and *all* their interactions. Specifically, it is a holistic, or integral ecology, that he refers to, a science that connects all things and "every type of knowledge," including all the branches of science. Boff thus defines ecology as "the science and art of relations and of related things."[17]

Boff argues, "If ecology is not holistic, it is not really ecology."[18] In opposition to modern science, which is "split up" and "disconnected," holistic ecology continually looks for relationships among all things and at all levels. This includes the social and mental processes that shape our environment. Thus, he speaks of a social ecology (the interaction of cultural systems and societies with their environment), and a mental ecology (the ideas, values, and prejudices that undergird our actions). These two ideally coalesce under the larger rubric of an integral ecology with a view to founding "a new alliance between societies and nature."[19] In this light, it is perhaps not surprising for Boff to say "more than any other science, ecology confronts nature as an organic, differentiated, and single whole," as ecology integrates other sciences.[20] Ecology, as his seminal 1995 book states in its title, *is* the new paradigm. Underlining this rather grand role Boff assigns to ecology is the dire social and environmental context in which it arises, where life and death of the whole planetary life-system is at stake. This new paradigm helps us to describe human beings "appropriately," a view of the human that stresses our connectedness to the Earth as well as our uniqueness. Thus, he concludes, "The human being is an animal of the mammal class, the order of primates, the family of hominids, the human genus, the species sapiens, with a body of thirty million cells, procreated and controlled by a genetic system produced in the course of a natural evolutionary process of four to five billion years, with a mind capable of forming global visions and constructing an indivisible unity, on the basis of some ten million of his or her ten billion neurons vibrating in unison, in order symbolically to create and recreate the universe and proffer an ultimate and all-inclusive meaning."[21]

According to Boff, the most basic insight of the holistic ecological approach is encapsulated in the Gaia theory with its deeply cooperative dynamics and interdependencies. As a scientific theory, it features rather prominently in many of his writings, which is not surprising, as Boff claims it serves to reprove our present mental ecology that places the human being at the centre of everything, or as an other-worldly being not of this planet. Boff sees Gaia as a "supra-organism" that functions as a single living entity under intelligent principles (given that it generated intelligent beings such as the human). For Boff the theory also serves as a transformative praxis carrying with it strong mythic qualities, which is why he employs it interchangeably with the Andean Indigenous term for Earth, "PachaMama" (akin to Mother Earth) in many of his writings, allowing for a maternal connection of human life to Gaia.[22] He further highlights this connection by comparing the human body's proportion of water (71 per cent) to that of the surface of the planet, and the proportion of salt in our blood (4.3 per cent) to that of the oceans.[23]

While Gaia is used to emphasize the human connection to nature, Boff also uses the theory to demonstrate that life and, as I will show, the human have an important planetary sense of purpose. In his collaborative work with Mark Hathaway, *The Tao of Liberation*, Boff, like Ruether, turns to the work of biologist Lynn Margulis, whose research on microbial life also reveals the great extent to which micro-organisms influence Earth dynamics. Margulis is quoted as saying this "bacterial web" which has "survived throughout the billions of years of life on the planet, play[s] a key role in the regulation of the conditions necessary for life."[24] Boff and Hathaway note, for instance, that the removal of CO_2 from the atmosphere has played a crucial role in allowing Gaia to maintain a relatively constant surface temperature over the past four billion years despite the fact that the sun's heat on Earth has increased 30 to 50 per cent in that time period.[25] Key to this happening, Lovelock and Margulis have discovered, myriad biological organisms that found ways to remove CO_2 from the atmosphere, mainly by burying the gas (in the form of oil or coal) or by locking it into rock (in the form of calcium carbonate that makes up limestone).

Boff makes an analogy between this key network of relationships among microbial life and the network of relationships among human beings. Building upon Teilhard de Chardin's notion of a noosphere – as I described with Ruether – Boff constructs a vision of evolution that moves toward some end that entails complexity, interrelationship, diversity, and self-awareness. Boff writes in *Cry of the Earth*, "The complexity of human brains, their growing number, the network of relationships being established between persons, continents, and cultures through all the means of communication, raise the possibility that we are laying the foundations for the emergence of a common consciousness around the Earth, which would function as the Earth's brain."[26] In this light, our presence, while demonic in its current logic of domination, is not inherently destructive to Earth. While anthropocentrism, for Boff, is "the worst sin of mental ecology,"[27] he nevertheless believes humans, with our consciousness, are an expression of Gaia itself, making us "co-pilots" of its evolution.[28] This *purpose* of the human is not assured though, as Boff notes it is possible that Gaia, with its own self-regulation in mind, could eliminate humans so as to allow the overall homeostasis to be maintained: "If Gaia has had to rid itself of myriad species over its life history, who can assure us that it will not be forced to rid itself of our own?"[29]

Notwithstanding this caveat, Boff is far more optimistic than pessimistic. In *Global Civilization: Challenges to Society and to Christianity*, he outlines how globalization – not what he refers to as the "dependent liberal-capitalist system"[30] but a globalization marked by a rise in social participative democracy and instantaneous communication (through Internet technology, for example) and more equitable market systems – represents a new phase in human evolution. It is evident where Boff is going with this: we are in the process of becoming the noosphere, as originally posited by Teilhard de Chardin, but reformulated to become the central nervous system or brain of Gaia. Indeed, Boff is taking his cue from Teilhard de Chardin when he says "the more evolution progresses, the more complex it becomes; the more complex, the more internalized; the more internalized, the more self-conscious it becomes; the more self-conscious, the more self-creating it becomes."[31] The above progression explains why Boff marks greater interiority as being an important part of the liberation process.

This Teilhardian notion – that the passage of time and evolution follow a pattern that increasingly creates complex, self-organized, and diverse entities – is shored up by Boff with the writings of Ilya Prigogine, whose science Boff greatly relies upon. Prigogine asked himself, How, if there is entropy – the process of increasing disorder or disorganization of a system through time, as explained by the second law of thermodynamics – can we explain evolution from lower to more complex forms? Prigogine reasons that entropy is not merely the downward slide toward disorganization but, under certain conditions, the progenitor of order. For this to happen, though, the system must be open, allowing it the possibility to import continuously free (useful) energy from the larger environment while exporting entropy (non-useful energy or waste); hence, the term "dissipative structures" is used, which is the title of Prigogine's theory. This continuous metabolizing nature of reality led Prigogine to conclude that reality, instead of being orderly, stable, and in a state of equilibrium, is seething and bubbling with this dynamic of change, disorder, or chaos.[32] Equilibrium, then, must be re-achieved continually through self-organization and an ever-higher level of internal organization. Physicist Erich Jantsch likens the process to someone who stumbles, loses her equilibrium, and can only avoid falling on her nose by continuing to stumble.[33]

While this way of seeing the world is non-mechanistic and non-reductionist, it is also non-deterministic, a point Boff stresses. He writes, "The system in some sense 'chooses' between several possible paths of transformation. Which choice it will make, however, is not predictable, although it depends on both the system's history and on the external stresses driving the transformation."[34] Causality, therefore, is not linear and, what is more, order and organization can actually arise spontaneously out of chaos. For the purpose of shedding new light on our global predicament, Boff underlines a salient feature of Prigogine's theory: that the more complex a system is, the more sensitive it becomes to external influences which could lead to change. Chaos is generative, which leads Boff to conclude, "Jumps in evolution can occur at any moment; it only requires enough accumulated energy to do so."[35]

Returning to Boff's take on globalization cited above, it is now clear how Prigogine, Lovelock, and Teilhard de Chardin's ideas coalesce in Boff's ethical vision. Boff writes, "The vast number of human brains currently at work along with the accumulation of knowledge and experiences, the increasing understanding of globalization, the perception that we are co-responsible for what may happen to nature, and to humankind enable us to put forward Teilhard's thesis of noosphere, that is, a collective consciousness or the unification of human minds."[36] Since, as Boff underlines, "even the action of a single individual can have an effect,"[37] I think it is fair to extrapolate – with regard to the noosphere – that this also means that one more brain can have an effect.

There is something decidedly positive in Boff's writing that favours – in contrast to Ruether – the idea of a growing world population. While Boff's assertion that one more individual could feasibly make all the difference might appear a fanciful appropriation of what the science says, Boff quotes Prigogine himself, who suggests, "We know that societies are immensely complex systems involving a potentially enormous number of bifurcations exemplified by the variety of cultures that have evolved in a relatively short span of human history. We know that such systems are highly sensitive to fluctuations. This leads to hope since even the small fluctuations may grow and change the overall structure. As a result, individual activity is not doomed to insignificance. On the other hand, this is also a threat, since in our universe the security of stable, permanent rules seems gone forever."[38] As with any system, be it the universe or a social institution, a continual flow of (new) energy and matter is possible when the system is open. Boff labels this avoidance of entropy in positive terms, as syntropy. He labels it as solidarity, in its social-ecological dimension. Boff uses syntropy (as he does solidarity) interchangeably with the term care; in any case, these aspects are the stronger force over entropy.[39]

Boff's employment of quantum physics serves to buttress what I have discussed so far: the importance of consciousness and relationality in the process of evolution, the more creative, non-linear processes of transformation, and the non-deterministic properties of these processes. All these notions are important to his ethical vision. I will concentrate here on how Boff approaches findings within the subatomic world to support these same notions as well as another: hope – that we are not without resources (help) in our present struggles for liberation.

When Boff refers to the particles of the subatomic world (called quanta), he is correct to point out that these particles cannot be described as "matter" commonly understood, because they are actually "energy at high level of concentration and stability."[40] Suitably, he asserts that one cannot even use the term "things" as this too is misleading. In fact, the vast majority of an atom's volume is empty space. Thus, within the atom there appears to be very little "hard stuff" to speak of. When one considers that the electrons within the nucleus are even smaller, it seems logical to conclude, as does Boff, that "particles are really not 'things' at all in the way we normally conceive them."[41]

What is curious about these particles is that they have no objective attributes of their own until they are observed. They appear as waves or as particles depending on the viewpoint of the observer. Their wave attributes and particle attributes cannot, however, be examined at the same time. Boff writes, "Either the exact position of the material particle is measured and one loses the velocity of the wave, or the wave is measured and the position of the particle is lost."[42] They exist, therefore, only as patterns of probabilities. Quoting physicist Nick Herbert, Boff writes: "By deciding what attribute you want to measure and deploying the appropriate instrument, you invite that attribute, but not its partner attribute, to manifest itself in the actual world."[43]

This strange feature of quantum physics led Werner Heisenberg to formulate what is called the uncertainty principle. While the principle outlines that it is impossible to know both the position and the momentum of a particle at any given moment, a further implication is that there can be no rigid distinction between the observer and the observed, since "the very act of observing causes the probability wave function 'to collapse' forcing a particular reality to become manifest either as a wave or a particle."[44] Boff notes that it is not the mechanical instruments "observing" the phenomenon that causes the wave function to collapse: an actual observer recording the measurement must be involved, which for Boff implies consciousness. This, Boff concludes, suggests a radically different epistemology, or way of knowing in science, one that is characterized by uncertainty and one that supports his understanding of the role of consciousness in the universe. Boff wants to understand how anything can exist if everything is based on this sense of uncertainty, adding, "who determined that we should cease to be probable and should come to reality, we mountains, sea, trees, human persons?"[45]

To answer this, Boff takes a cue from the writings of mathematician John von Neumann, who believed that the entire physical world remains in a state of pure possibility (for example, as waves), until a conscious mind "decides to promote a portion of the world from its usual state of indefiniteness into a condition of actual existence."[46] It should be noted that when Boff speaks of "observer," he does not limit this to the human alone. He uses "observer" as a tool for understanding a sense of interdependence at the most basic level of existence. An observer is any entity that dialogues and interacts with other entities. Hence, a proton interacts with another proton. In so doing, they mutually exchange energies and hold information together that neither can obtain separately. Adding a religious element to this, Boff holds that a dialogue between entities is always taking place forming, whether at the subatomic or macrocosmic level, a single system, "a connectedness, and a covenant of exchanges."[47] Yet, while not discounting the possibility that even plants might have some kind of consciousness, the emphasis here is clearly on human consciousness. Where Boff is going with this becomes clear: he suggests, given the findings in quantum physics, that mind in some sense "midwifes" reality.

While the mind can affect (he also states, "co-create") reality, Boff notes that causality – and not just with human actions – is not linear. He is referring to the notion of quantum entanglement. In the classical understanding of science, objects moved because some object or force acted upon them; however, with quantum entanglement, there is nothing pushing or pulling on anything else. The whole relationship of cause and effect is far more mysterious and complex, something Einstein famously referred to as "spooky action at a distance."[48] Quantum physicists have found that every particle is somehow linked to every other particle; in fact, no particle can be considered in isolation. This is a "non-local" connection or "entanglement" between particles that is independent of distance. Whenever two particles interact with each other, they somehow remain linked together from then on. In this way, what we do to one particle is experienced by the other instantaneously, even if it is separated over a long distance. This idea of quantum entanglement is important to Boff's vision. He quotes the work of science historian Robert Nadeau and physicist Menas Kafatos who put it thus: "[T]he universe on a very basic level could be a vast web of particles, which remain in contact with one another over any distance in 'no time' in the absence of the transfer of energy or information."[49] And given the deep time throughout which our universe has developed, Boff further suggests that is it safe to conclude that all quantum entities have already interacted with each other, becoming entangled. Redolent of the ethos put forth by St Francis, he adds, "As portions of the universe, we are all brothers and sisters: elementary particles, quarks, stones, snails, animals, humans, stars, galaxies."[50]

Given the ecological holistic sense that undergirds Boff's vision, cause becomes holistic itself, presented as a pattern of relationships. He cites a passage from Capra's writings, which is worth repeating: "In quantum theory individual events do not always have a well-defined cause … We can never predict when and how such a phenomenon is going to happen … This does not mean that atomic events occur in completely arbitrary fashion; it means only that they are brought about by non-local causes. The behavior of any part is determined by its non-local connections to the whole, and since we do not know those connections precisely, we have to replace the narrow classical notion of cause and effect by the wider concept of statistical causality."[51] Within Boff's larger project of a new globalized interconnected world mentioned above, the important role quantum physics plays for Boff becomes very clear: "We live in a cosmos whose foundations are built on deep rooted – or radical – relationality. On some subtle level, everything influences everything else."[52]

The question of where the energy behind all of this relationality might come from preoccupies Boff. In speculating about the quantum void, he finds a possible explanation and a source of hope. Boff notes how quantum physicists have found that at any moment a particle, along with its corresponding antiparticle, can spontaneously spring into existence from an apparent emptiness, and then the two can annihilate each other. The annihilation process is clear enough: for every type of matter particle scientists have found, there also exists a corresponding antimatter particle, or antiparticle. Antiparticles look and behave just like their corresponding matter particles, except they have opposite charges. For instance, a proton is electrically positive whereas an antiproton is electrically negative. Thus, when a matter particle and an antimatter particle meet, they annihilate each other, leaving behind the energy they were made of. But when particles spring into existence, from where do these particles come? No one knows.

This point causes Boff to raise the even larger question of the source of energy in the cosmos. According to quantum physics, and in keeping with the uncertainty principle, the vacuum state is not truly empty but instead contains fleeting electromagnetic waves and particles that pop into and out of existence. This is the quantum vacuum or what scientists refer to as zero point energy, which is the lowest energy state of a system. Boff likens it to a "pregnant void," for it appears more like a "vast sea of energy seething with possibilities."[53] Such a claim is not hyperbole. Physicists David Bohm and F. David Peat, Boff points out, contend that by some estimates, "there is as much energy in a single cubic centimeter of the void (or the space being manifest from the void) than would be generated if all the known matter in the universe were to disintegrate."[54] Reality, then, is "a kind of vibration arising from the pregnant void, waves on a vast ocean of energy."[55] From this, it becomes clear to Boff that while we are meant to "midwife" reality into being, we are not without the resources (energy) to support our venture.

While cosmology receives slightly less attention than do the other sciences in Boff's writings, it appears no less important in the creation of his ethical vision. Since his reading of cosmology resonates closely with Brian Swimme and Thomas Berry's *The Universe Story* – which I will discuss in more detail in chapter 4 – I will not go into much detail here. Certainly, the same themes I have discussed above are explored with cosmology. For instance, Boff highlights the creative nature of the universe. He describes the shift away from a static, eternal vision of the cosmos to one that is dynamic. He notes that at the initial moment of expansion of energy from the big bang, everything was entirely undetermined. Between the 10^{-11} and 10^{-5} second (of the initial moment of expansion) most of the particles (antimatter) disappeared into light. This left only a billionth of the initial mass of elementary particles. It was these particles that would eventually form the whole universe, including us. Once the particles were stabilized, there emerged the initial symmetries and structures in particle interactions, hence giving rise to the four original interconnections (gravity, the electromagnetic force, and the strong and weak nuclear forces). Boff concludes that these "inter(retro)connecting energies, which science has not yet been able to explain, should probably be understood as modes of primordial action through which the universe itself acts, interacts with its elements and is self-regulating."[56]

For Boff, the self-regulating nature of the universe is also creative, reasoning that throughout the process, choices are being made. The moment when the galaxies could form, for example, was decisive: "If the opportunity had not borne fruit, our cosmos would have remained an amorphous soup of energy and primitive matter with no real form or structure."[57] Boff concludes that creativity illuminates how things came into being despite the mathematical unlikelihood of our existence, given the calculations of physicist Stephen Hawking. Hawking states that if the rate of expansion one second after the big bang had been smaller by even one part in a hundred thousand million the universe would have re-collapsed before it reached its present size. Of course, the inverse is true too: had the expansion rate been infinitesimally greater, the universe would have expanded too rapidly and no stars would have formed; there would be no Earth, no humans.[58]

Boff's use of the anthropic principle merits some attention here as well. The anthropic principle has two versions: the weak version states that the universe is finely attuned to the existence of human life because humans are doing the observing. The strong version states that the universe must have those properties that allow life to develop within it. Boff appears partial to the stronger version because it suggests that the creation of humans was aimed at. Notwithstanding this strong assertion on the significance of the human, Boff underlines that the anthropic principle, even in its strong version, does not imply anthropocentrism, adding that it is not the amoebas or hummingbirds or horses that are engaging in reflexive discourse on the cosmos; only to the human does it have meaning. The difference with our self-reflective nature, he maintains, is not quantitative but qualitative. Boff, then, uses the anthropic principle to suggest further that human beings are a purposeful part of the original teleology behind the universe. Boff puts it quite succinctly, in a Teilhardian fashion: "In fact, looking back at the process of evolution that has now been unfolding for some 13.7 billion years, we cannot deny that there has been an ongoing progression: energy turns into matter, chaos organizes itself, the simple becomes more complex, from a complex entity life arises, and from life emerges consciousness. There is a purpose – a progression that suggests meaning – that cannot be denied."[59]

While he is cognizant that ideas of purpose or a directive principle are resisted within scientific circles, he responds by asking whether the more accepted idea of "struggle for survival" or the "selfish" nature of genes is any less purposeful. Purpose or intention for Boff does not necessarily imply the need for self-reflective consciousness either. Here he takes purpose as the principle of autopoiesis, the power of each thing to participate directly in its self-fulfillment and evolution. Not unlike the processes of dissipative structures outlined by Prigogine, and the self-regulating nature of Gaia, autopoiesis is that principle that explains how creativity, renewal, and self-regulation occur. This autopoietic character of the universe also underscores

Boff's understanding of liberation. He states, "Humans are made for participation and creation; we want not only to receive bread but to help produce it, so that we may emerge as agents of our own history."[60] Almost like a punctuation to his mantra, in *Cry of the Earth, Cry of the Poor*, Boff notes that physicist John Wheeler also saw, "very clearly," that the universe is participatory: "it is a most intricate web of relationships, enveloping everything, and human beings in particular."[61]

AN ANALYSIS OF BOFF'S ETHICAL VISION

For Boff, then, science offers a transformative and corrective vision of ourselves as the pinnacle of evolution, reproving mistaken ideas of separateness from, or power over others, and suggests we are conscious, spiritual, and corporeal beings that belong here. The message from science is made clear: we are all interconnected and there is a communication happening through consciousness. New science also empowers us to act in accordance with a holistic ecological approach with hope and determination. In this sense, it is also liberating, showing that social, political, economic, and personal transformation *are* possible. Recalling, for instance, that systems in a high state of chaos are sensitive to even the slightest fluctuation, might empower one individual to do his/her bit to change societal structures, no matter how small the contribution. Such a transformation also *ought not be so feared,* though the path is not assured nor easy. In short, the role of science is to "ensure" that this paradigm revolution succeeds.

In many ways, science serves to counter the spiritual and cognitive malaise Boff targets. As Fritjof Capra notes in the foreword to one of Boff's books, the scientific cosmology Boff puts forth "appears fully compatible with the spiritual dimensions of liberation."[62] Moreover, the sense of intimacy with all creation is borne out by the new conception of life found in new science. Perhaps this is why Boff feels it is appropriate to match this science-inspired transformative vision with that coming from a saint: humans, he states, need to follow less the example of Pietro Bernadone – the great and wealthy thirteenth-century textile merchant and father of St Francis of Assisi, who represents the culture of the satisfied, cynically ignoring the devastation he participates in – and more that of his son, whose burning "seraphic love for all creatures" we ought to emulate.[63] Such an emphasis on spirituality is also in keeping with Boff's claim that a new planetary consciousness is developing (the noosphere in the form of globalization), a mental and physical connectedness that serves as the foundation for a new paradigm of care, connectedness, and solidarity.

Given Boff's deep concern for the "other," it is not surprising that relationality is the most important lesson to emerge from science. Indeed, for Boff, all is relation and "nothing but relation exists."[64] To give an example, consider that while liberation is the primary aim for Boff, as it is for Ruether, it cannot be understood or realized in a vacuum outside the larger relationality. Closely related to relationality is the category of self-organization – autopoiesis. Life, we learn, is the interplay of self-organizing relationships and interactions allowing syntropy – or solidarity – to prevail over entropy. For this reason, the most important universal laws, for Boff, become synergy, syntropy, interrelationship, collaboration, cosmic solidarity, and communion in kinship.[65] The key to our survival, it would seem, lies in a gestalt of relationships interacting with each other which, in Boff's later writings, he would characterize simply as "love." Being ethical, then, begins by being in solidarity, which then demands that we learn to limit our human desires insofar as they lead to *our* advancement at the cost of class and planetary exploitation.

It is in the above sense that new science becomes normative. There are "oughts" implied from this interpretation of science. Further expressing how we ought to conduct our lives, like Ruether, Boff offers bioregionalism and the Earth Charter – respectively as model and mandate – as a way of informing our actions. We learn from the wisdom revealed in self-organizing mature ecosystems, for instance, that we must embrace limits, maximize diversity, and cooperate.[66] Everything possesses certain otherness. Everything has a right to continue to exist within the ecological balance, and this right produces a corresponding duty in humans to preserve this balance. For this reason, the common good, which Boff later reconfigures as an ethics of care, cannot exist solely for the human but must be for the whole terrestrial, biological world, with which humans share a destiny. This good is marked by our living in kinship with all that exists and assuming a responsibility for it.

For Boff, however, an ethics of care can never be understood as being for all time. Like Ruether, Boff's attention to the process of becoming, mentioned earlier in the form of noosphere, means we have to be attentive to change and adapt our ethics to what must be done at each moment. Boff's ethic, then, rests on a particular mindset that must be open to change. For this reason, Boff distinguishes between morality, which has more to do with customs – thus risking stagnation – and ethics, which is dynamic, "born out of a new definition of the human being and of its mission in the universe as understood by new science."[67] In this sense, liberation for Boff becomes a continual process of harmonizing of our conduct with the logic of the cosmos. And since liberation can never be realized outside the larger relationality, and is marked by the extent to which we participate with the logic of the cosmos, for Boff, like Ruether, it is something that can never be "reached."

However hopeful and holistic Boff's ethic may appear, it lacks clarity on some issues. Before the 1992 United Nations' Rio Summit, Boff's writing dealt specifically with a Christian theological paradigm that was decidedly from the viewpoint of the poor. We find, however, in his post-1992 writings, particularly in his more recent ones, a shift away from developing an ethic from the point of view of the poor to a more global view of the larger dimensions of liberation, not just for all humans but for the whole planet. In other words, his ethic has gained a view from everywhere. Andrew Dawson, writing on Boff's approach and use of new science recognizes this in his analysis, saying, "Having since exchanged his epistemological *locus standi* among the poor for the generalized experience of mystical connectedness, Boff's profession of ethical universals is no longer rooted in any particular context."[68] There is truth to this statement, and I am not discounting the possible benefits it can produce: for instance, we discern that it is not enough to cut down on greenhouse gas emissions in industrialized nations without a concomitant critical examination of the model of society, and paradigms of development and consumption that continue to champion economic growth. However, with the change of epistemological *locus standi,* is such an outcome still assured? One wonders if this will necessarily lead to fewer victims. If we are to view solidarity as a basic universal law, to whom, when conceivably all things appear equal, do we give the last or preferential say? Is compromise on preserving an ecosystem or local community always necessary?

The relation between humans and the natural world also remains ambiguous in Boff's ethic. It is true that animals, trees, and indeed the whole natural world gain intrinsic worth in Boff's paradigm. As discussed above, he asserts that everything that exists and lives deserves to exist. In what manner, however, can we really say that a cancer cell has a right to exist? It is doubtful Boff is referring to this; yet, clarification does not appear in his writings. In his analysis of Boff's ethical vision, Stephen Bede Scharper, arguing along the same lines, asks how the Earth has rights in the same way humans do.[69] How does the intrinsic worth of an animal compare with the intrinsic worth of the human? Can the former trump the latter? Such a distinction is not clear in Boff's analysis. Respectful dialogue on the plethora of choices to be made might not be adequate on a planetary level.

As with the case of Ruether's ethic, I question the extent to which Boff has avoided even some elements of a stronger anthropocentrism. Assigning the human as co-pilot (at times he also says guardian angel or even gardener, as Ruether does) is not precise in this regard, since a pilot is pretty much the most "significant" being on a plane, as far as survival of the whole goes. Despite the imperative of humility, love, or care that Boff assigns to the human, conferring to us the role of pilot carries a rather strong anthropocentric hue. A good pilot needs to know thoroughly how the entire plane functions and be able to control the plane in all circumstances. Even Boff's provisions with regard to the anthropic principle mentioned above seem uncertain. In pondering the unquestionable havoc we have wreaked upon the planet, taking countless wrong turns over the course of millennia, Scharper poses the amusing though fundamental question, "If we are co-pilots … what 'flight school' did we attend?"[70] In this vein, Boff's claim that a new planetary consciousness is developing – the noosphere in the form of globalization – presents itself somewhat like an apologetic to Gaia. It is almost as if Boff were saying to those in the camp of deep ecology, "Wait; it's true we have been demons to the Earth, but don't dismiss us just yet, we do have a valid and important role on Gaia."

Related to what I would designate the medium-to-strong anthropocentric nature of his ethical vision, I also question the assumption that underlies his thinking, which assumes that evolution and progress are two sides of the same coin of future development. Granted that Boff raises the possibility that humans could fail and that Gaia could be working to actually rid herself of our waywardness, the teleology in Boff's thinking is, nevertheless, unmistakable. Boff's ethical vision retains the evolutionary progression that places the human with our consciousness, seemingly as the end of a long process of evolution. Such a stance seems to imply that humans are quantitatively better than other-than-humans. While this is not what Boff would say, it is difficult not to arrive at this conclusion.

Finally, on the spiritual level, I have noted above that St Francis, the patron saint of ecology in Catholic circles, provides another ideal paradigm for helping us to live well, not better, in our world. To be sure, St Francis embraced a spirituality of radical poverty and abandonment to the will of God; he saw all creation as his brother or sister. Does Boff suggest that our entire world population will need to develop a St Francis-type spirituality? This would not be so much of a problem were it not for the importance of spirituality to Boff's program. There is no guarantee that all humans can or will spiritually interiorize the new experience before us which, Boff insists, is necessary for any ethic to take hold. To be fair, Boff does stress that since everything has its own interiority – something intuited by Teilhard de Chardin and supported by Prigogine – everything, then, is spiritual.[71] Still, does such a claim risk devaluing spirituality, the very goal Boff appears to be striving for? Moreover, Boff's promotion of a global consciousness, the noosphere, plays a large role in helping to raise the consciousness of our species (and we could surmise by that our spiritual awareness as well). But this premise is not as empirically verifiable as other concepts Boff has put forth. Undoubtedly, the key to understanding Boff's ethics, then, is its evolutionary and spiritual dimension. There is much hope placed on our ability to be creative and to continually evolve our ethics so that while questions persist now, they might be answered down the road as we gain more knowledge from new science.

It is fitting here, as well as significant to understanding Boff's ethical vision, to end this section, as I did with Ruether's, by underlining that Boff partly arrived at conclusions of our connectedness and solidarity before his appropriation of science. Unlike past notions of human liberation, though, a person's conscious participation in the unfolding of her or his life now becomes circumscribed by a gestalt of relationships, and therefore of "liberations" – and not solely of the human – each interacting with the other in syntropy. As with Ruether, then, there is an interplay between Boff's personal biography and what he learns from science. That Boff places relationality at the core of his ethical vision is certainly something that the new science affirms, but it is also something he understood long ago, following as a monk in the footsteps of St Francis of Assisi, and journeying with Chico Mendes. With a liberation critique of developmentalism, Boff came to the conclusion long before he penned *Ecology and Liberation* that we need to be in solidarity with the poor based on a knowledge that we are connected politically, socially, and economically. It was his introduction of an analysis of social ecology that led him to see that social and economic systems are structured so that resources are appropriated without restraints and that they are distributed unequally or, put another way, we can no longer address the cry of the poor without a concomitant embrace of the cry of the Earth. Like Ruether, ecological sustainability becomes pure nonsense for Boff if it does not take into account the story of the human person scavenging garbage dumps in Brazil for scraps of food: the forces that cause the creation of the dump are the same forces that leave this person little choice in her or his search for sustenance.

THE EPISTEMOLOGY AND METHODOLOGY BACKING BOFF'S ETHICAL VISION

Boff's epistemological stance lies in stark contrast to the classical scientific paradigm that isolates and controls. The latter can no longer be considered viable, as it denies the legitimacy of other kinds of dialogue with nature, such as common sense, magic, and alchemy. Ilya Prigogine, whose thinking on this matter heavily influences Boff's analysis, is quoted by Boff on this point: "We dialogue with the universe not only along experimental path of science and technology but other approaches to conversing with nature. All accounts that cultures have given of how they came into the world can help us better know and preserve ourselves and our habit. Thus it emerges that these are complementary approaches, and the monopoly of the modern way of deciphering the world around us is relinquished."[72] Boff maintains that only such an inclusive form of reasoning and communicating is appropriate to the complexities of our current reality. He puts forth a rich diversity of ways of knowing and understanding the world, each enriching the other: symbolic reason, reason of the heart, use of all bodily and spiritual senses, eros – understood here as passion and desire – pathos, sensitivity, what he calls daimon – nature's inner voice that speaks to us – and, of course, affect – feelings or sentiments such as fascination, wonder, and admiration at the diversity of cultures, the vitality of animals, or at the majesty of mountains, as well as awe at gazing at a star-filled sky.[73] In this way, "We learn from all human experiences and the way they handle nature, whether from those experiences mistakenly called primitive or magical, those using alchemy, shamans, those that are archaic and religious, or from contemporary experiences linked to empirical, analytic, and epistemological discourse. They all reveal the communication of human beings with our surroundings. They all attest to a truth."[74] With so much of Boff's ethic originating from the cries of the Earth and the cries of the poor, and with his concomitant earthy solidarity with their plights, it becomes clear why Boff says, "The world is one great message,"[75] whose divine revelation is knowable to us.

Relationality, then, while playing a key role in Boff's ethic, plays a similar role in his epistemology. For one, it means we cannot know an entity without knowing its own world of relationships or context. But interacting or entering into communion with the universe is also expressly democratic, since, "we are all in a process of dialogue and interaction with the universe; we all produce information and we can all learn from one another, from how viruses are transmitted, from how plankton adapt to changes in the oceans, and from how humans handle in different manners the challenges of extremely varied ecosystems."[76] To Boff, not only is "our own way of arriving at what is real […] not the only way,"[77] he is also stipulating that it *ought not be* the only way, for there are many ways of *getting to know* a being. Boff envisions a multi-directional dialogue happening that he defines as dialogical, an intra-universal way of communicating in communion with all that exists. He believes the logic of the universe itself is dialogical, as "everything interacts with everything at all points and under all circumstances."[78] This communal dialogue represents, for Boff, a vast process of universal interaction that began at the beginning with the big bang. And while we humans as a whole might have lost our understanding of this interaction, Boff contends, in light of the current ecological and social crises, that humans are developing a new sensitivity to the planet. This new sensitivity represents an "attitude of enchantment," not solely for science – though science appears the primary target – that refuses "to reduce Earth to an assortment of natural resources or to physical and chemical reservoir of raw materials."[79]

For Boff, arriving at what is real, what is truth, takes on an evolutionary dimension. Taking another page from Prigogine's writings, Boff states: "Order-disorder-order constitute the underlying force of reality as maintained by Ilya Prigogine. To get bogged down by the text and by the truth that is said and revealed in the same text is to fix oneself to a particular moment in the scenario of history and therefore to lose the open and evolving meaning of this truth."[80] Here, Boff is challenging the notion that traditional religious truths are static. He suggests that it continually unfolds and that no one subject can have more than a partial view of it. Boff is not saying that "everything goes" nor is he denying the possibility of the existence of an absolute truth. However, since everything, in one way or another, participates in the truth, the truth we should strive for, a more complete truth, is the one that more and more is relational and respectful of differences. Put another way, through humble dialogue one's own truth eventually disappears, replacing it with a truth accepted by all. Moreover, I mentioned above, having exchanged his *locus standi* among the poor for the larger ecological and mystical connectedness, a truth is no longer uniquely justified by whether it facilitates or hinders the poor being agents of their own destiny. Instead, truth, and by extension liberation for all creation, it would seem, is situated within a larger context by how well it supports or fractures the dynamic equilibrium, or common environmental good of overall ecosystems which, by definition, comprise the human community. As a criterion for truth, Boff presents the following: "The basic question in ecology is this: to what extent do this or that science, technology, institutional or personal activity, ideology, or religion help either to support or fracture the dynamic equilibrium that exists in the overall ecosystems?" [81]

To realize a liberating and sustainable society, therefore, humans have to engage in dialogue with all beings within their larger relational context. To do this, Boff proposes a perichoretic model as the best approach for realizing "the most inclusive stance possible," and "the one that is least inclined to produce victims," since everything interacts with everything at all points and under all circumstances. [82] His perichoretic model is an adaptation of the not very well-known (or used) Greek term, *perichoresis* which, in the Christian tradition, describes the mutual presence and interpenetration of the threefold nature and functioning of the Trinity (how God the Father, the Son, and the Holy Spirit relate to one another). He likens it to the ecological model that functions like a participative democracy whose members are spatially and temporarily unconfined, making his perichoretic model "transversal." [83] By transversal Boff implies a relation that extends simultaneously in multiple directions and in different manners: epistemologically and ontologically laterally among the ecological community; frontward, toward the future of that community; backward, into the community's past; and inward, into the complexities of that community with "all [its] experiences and all forms of comprehension as complementary and useful knowledge of the universe, our role within it, and in the cosmic solidarity that unites us to all." [84]

To be sure, such a vast process of universal interaction is difficult to envision within a bioregional model. How does Boff see the perichoretic model functioning at this level? The process appears to require a conversation among a large quantity of subjects, comprising the human, terrestrial, and other-than-human biological world, all interconnected amid complex sets of relationships. In *The Tao of Liberation,* Boff does stress that the process necessitates that humans can begin to relate only once they start to dwell in an area. "In the bioregional vision," Boff states, "we must fit ourselves into the ecosystem and natural economy of the particular place, rather than trying to mold the place to suit our personal taste (albeit, presumably, some mutuality of shaping does occur)." [85] Dwelling on the land implies that we listen to it, comprehending the kinds of soils, rock, and insects it has, as well as its carrying capacities; we do this through critical reflection, mutual engagement, and by what seems to be an interiorization of experiences. This inculcating of the natural world as part of one's inner nature allows us to identify with the land not by force but by letting the "land reclaim us like ivy growing over an old house."[86] This interiorization is facilitated through the "spiritual arts," which include practising meditation, spiritual dance, and movement.

This last matter on spiritual arts requires further explanation, since, as I have already discussed, they are vital to Boff's program. Recall that St Francis of Assisi is held as the quintessential role model of the type of person capable of fostering a new paradigm through the perichoretic model. This is not accidental. Boff avers that spirituality, one grounded in a mystical experience of the sacred, is key to his program. Spirituality complements our way of knowing by demonstrating the truth of the issues at hand. How is this? Boff theorizes that the human being is of two selves: the "conscious self" and the "deep self," also understood as the divine within us. In some of his untranslated Portuguese writings, Boff articulates this duality as being also head and heart. When the two meet through spiritual exercises, they form the "personal centre" of the being, which corresponds to the Jungian notion that human growth comes from a psychic source within.

In his work on Boff, Andrew Dawson suggests that for Boff, uniting the "conscious self" and the "deep self" corrects our misguided notions of being separate entities, and puts us in touch with universal values, thus serving to correct "any false consciousness by disposing the individual self to [in Boff's words] 'veracity.'"[87] While undoubtedly Boff does find that knowledge arises from this turn inward, as Dawson suggests, the degree it can claim "universality," again as Dawson aptly suggests, is questionable given Boff's democratic understanding of how we arrive at truth, as outlined above. While it is true that Boff states, "The more we know ourselves and know the sun that inhabits us … the more integrated we become, turned to that powerful center we call God,"[88] This notion is not in line with the pre-eminence he assigns to the wisdom of science. It would seem more accurate to conclude that Boff sees truth as being facilitated by the spiritual arts, allowing the person to gain more clarity to see things as they really are. What is "universal" about truths, partially accessible to the mystic, would come in the form of the principles of diversity, interiority, and communion which, to the scientist, would come in the forms of universal laws: differentiation, autopoiesis, and gravitation.

The assumption here is that we discern the common good or welfare of the biotic community not merely by accumulating knowledge and wisdom through dialogue, but through a multifaceted mutual reinvention of who we are, accompanied by a commensurate transformation in how we live. By way of an example already encountered, we can deepen our identity with the land through science, as Boff posits, by learning that the human body's proportion of water (71 per cent) is similar to that of the surface of the planet, and the proportion of salt in our blood (4.3 per cent) is similar to that of the oceans, as we discussed above. Boff seemingly rounds off his method of reorienting ourselves by having us also engage in the continuous cycle of meditation and experiential learning, rooted in place, where mind and body learn together – "not only by seeing and hearing but by tasting, feeling, and smelling" – we also find ourselves referring to the land as "PachaMama."[89] Our relationship to one another (culture) as well as to the land is further deepened through story, the transmitting of history, and the sharing of local knowledge. And since the bioregional culture is an open system, it interacts and enriches itself by listening to and mutually sharing with other bioregional cultures.

CONCLUSION

As in the section on Ruether, I began this investigation of Boff's work by discussing his starting points. Boff is concerned with meeting the needs and desires of the entire Earth community. His experience in the slums outside Rio de Janeiro and the jungles of the Amazon molded a vision within him whereby liberation for all of creation becomes paramount. Not just the human but the rivers, trees, and animals ought to be free to follow their own interiority without being dominated by political, economic, or social structures. Indeed, his ethical vision fosters a sensitivity for all creation.

Science also gains a normative role in forming Boff's ethical vision and, again like Ruether, we find that its role is not exclusive, as the Indigenous concepts of PachaMama and his mystical vision inspired by St Francis also feature prominently. The lines between the scientific and the more mystical ways of knowing become less distinct: on the one hand, science sets guidelines for our actions. On the other hand, science affirms a need to show solidarity with all creation, something that was clear to Boff long ago following in the footsteps of St Francis. Clearly, Boff assigns great importance to the concept of relationality here and now on Earth. His perichoretic model for how we know the world serves to affirm ostensibly what Ruether also posits, that the universe is widely participatory. Knowing then takes on a multidimensional character, one beyond its rationalistic dimension. In fact, this more inclusive way of thinking and communicating appears to Boff as the most appropriate approach to address the complexities of our current reality.

I account for the similarities between Boff's and Ruether's ethical visions, in part, by their starting points. Both were imbued early in their life by a concern for the poor or marginalized, whether through work in the civil rights movement or the slums outside Rio de Janeiro. Both were also infused with the excitement that surrounded the Church's renewal in the early years of Vatican II. And both found within science a powerful way to understand more deeply how grounded we are in Earth realities, therefore requiring our actions to become aligned with the logic of the cosmos. Liberation, each author is emphatic, is meant for all creation. On this last point, Boff's ethical vision, like Ruether's, is not without its difficulties. Boff's change of view, once decidedly from the view of the poor, now takes on a planetary lens. While this is an important step to foster liberation for all creation, the important question remains: how is this gestalt of relationships or liberations Boff refers to fostered for an entire planet where each subject is granted intrinsic worth? While Boff offers a more specific explanation of the bioregional model where the common good or welfare of the biotic community is of primary concern, the answer to this query is still not clear.

CHAPTER THREE

Diarmuid O'Murchu

INTRODUCTION TO O'MURCHU

Diarmuid O'Murchu is an Irish-born priest and has been a member of the Sacred Heart Missionary Order for over thirty-five years. He is also a social psychologist specializing in counselling for couples, the bereaved, and those with AIDS-HIV. O'Murchu has written many books and has contributed articles, essays, poems, and blogs for Catholic newspapers and websites – while also developing his own website. He facilitates many workshops that focus on adult faith development – in many cases addressing different Catholic religious orders – in Europe, USA, Canada, Australia, the Philippines, Thailand, India, Peru, and several African countries. And judging by his itinerary – openly accessible on his website – he is in much demand. The title "facilitator" seems to describe him well, given the energy he places on facilitating workshops, counselling adults, writing books, and maintaining a website directed toward adult spiritual growth. Still, as will become evident, O'Murchu might best be understood as an adult faith educator.

Deeply critical of religion as it is practised and configured today, O'Murchu – like Boff, though not to the same degree – has landed himself in trouble with the Congregation for the Doctrine of the Faith of the Vatican for his unorthodox views on the empowering of religious life, in some cases encouraging members of religious orders to leave the Catholic Church, thus placing religious life "far beyond" Catholic Church hierarchical control.[1] O'Murchu was not always as critical of the Church as an institution. He grew up and was educated in Ireland within a strict Catholic upbringing where "[a]uthority was absolute and the central doctrines of a ruling, controlling church, representing a harshly demanding God on high, dictated a very clear sense of right and wrong."[2] Having already developed a growing skepticism and growing mistrust of those who viewed the secular world as evil, O'Murchu states that reading the writings of Pierre Teilhard de Chardin in the 1970s "began to blow apart the inherited tenets of [his] narrow inherited tradition."[3] O'Murchu writes that when he read Teilhard de Chardin's *Hymn of the Universe* and *The Divine Milieu,* "Truly, my heart burned within me; everything I read resonated with a depth and conviction I had not known for many years."[4] He views his growing up on a farm within a milieu of Celtic spirituality as a main reason why Teilhard de Chardin's writings resonated so much within him, for in the Celtic mind the land was readily understood as sacred.

Indeed, it was throughout the entire era of the 1960s and 1970s, O'Murchu tells us, that he experienced a period of emotional turmoil, both religiously and culturally. This was a time when the growing Vatican II spirit of ecumenism was throwing the last vestiges of Catholic supremacy into disarray, and British soldiers were battling in Northern Ireland with "[*his*] fellow-countrymen."[5] O'Murchu cites a train journey in England, when he had a long conversation with two young British soldiers on their way to do service in Northern Ireland; he later found out that one was shot soon after by what he, at that time, understood as his own kinfolk. This experience placed him in personal confusion. As he puts it, "the insular religiosity that had fuelled [his] spiritual values for over twenty years" came into doubt.[6] Another incident that put his world into disarray was at an ecumenical service at a Taizé gathering in Southern France. His ecumenism, he confesses, was superficial, as he found himself feeling indignant when the group leader, an Anglican priest, invited him to concelebrate Eucharist with him. This episode was a deciding moment in his life, for even the ecumenism he had been embracing was elitist, a view that upheld the imperialist claims of the Catholic Church.

On closer examination, it seems like a blend of life experiences was instrumental in opening O'Murchu up to multiple worldviews. To this array of experiences, it is necessary to add his working so long as a psychologist, counselling believers and non-believers alike. His work as a counsellor is significant as O'Murchu claims he could no longer ignore the feeling that a spiritual hunger imbues the psyche of all humans and not just "church goers."[7] This feeling has guided him in his writings.

THE TARGET OF O'MURCHU'S CRITIQUE

Like Boff, Diarmuid O'Murchu is concerned with a spiritual malaise which, he maintains, is profoundly afflicting humanity at this point in history. In fact, this spiritual malaise is O'Murchu's chief concern. At humanity's deepest core, we desire wholeness, freedom, relationality, and creativity, which are features, as I will show, that O'Murchu maintains are inherent to the cosmos itself. However, these desires have been corrupted or frustrated by patriarchal, strong anthropocentric and dualist thinking, which seek to divide and control, leaving us alienated from ourselves, one another, and the world we live in. The result is that an adult or mature faith fails to develop, leaving us with a distorted picture of who we are and what our role ought to be as a species.

For O'Murchu, desire is the most fundamental trait that makes us human; it is a capacity humans have inherited from the universe and, therefore, there is something primordial about it. The denial of our primordial desires, such as the desire for relationship with other humans and other-than-humans, has led us to objectify people and nature, leading, ultimately, to social injustice, to speciesism, and to ecological degradation. O'Murchu points to reductionist science, which sees all elements in the universe as isolated and independent of each other, operating like a machine, contributing to this sense of separateness from other humans and the natural world, resulting too often in social and ecological catastrophe. O'Murchu likens this state of feeling separate from the other to living in exile from our planet and the larger, and now forgotten, evolutionary impulse. Much along the same lines of ecofeminist thinking, as I have discussed with Ruether, this sense of separation, even from our own bodies, is responsible for our refusal to accept death as a necessary good in evolution, instead of an evil as postulated by mainline Christian theology. Death, he contends, is not a punishment for our sins. This misconception about death only contributes to our spiritual malaise, as O'Murchu posits pointedly: "We cannot learn to live better for the future until we also learn to die better."[8] It might seem odd to advocate that we need to learn to die better, but O'Murchu seems to be restating what Ruether refers to as the denial of our anthropological vulnerability. O'Murchu captures here a truism of contemporary Western society: we employ our technology, build our cities, and gear our economic and social systems in ways that shun suffering (simply taking a pill to lose weight, for instance) and deny limits (building our homes on a flood plain). In this manner, learning "to die better" is really a way to learn "to live better."

It would be fair to say that the primary target of O'Murchu's critique is religion, and that it is mainly Christianity in its institutional form with its "insipid religiosity" that he critiques – though all forms of religion that seek to control or divide fall under his critique.[9] However, the science that excludes other ways of knowing and tries to dominate what can be considered as truth in the universe – which feeds a person's spirituality – comes equally under fire from O'Murchu. He writes, "Science tends to exclude God, while religion often brings in God prematurely. In both cases we are in danger of bypassing the challenge to the human imagination to engage more directly with the meaning of life."[10] In this regard, O'Murchu finds parallels between religion that dominates and science that controls: each treats inner human desire as a negative force. As the quote above suggests, science debases desire by explaining it in terms of genetic forces seeking survival for one's own genes, while religion seeks to eradicate it, because it is the cause of sin.[11] O'Murchu also maintains that both religion and science assume a generally pessimistic attitude toward human nature which, he suggests, contributes to many of our ecological and social problems. He points to the narrow scope of historical research on the human as a species, for instance, which concentrates exclusively on the past 8,000 years (as opposed to millions of years), as portraying our species solely as domineering, aggressive, and competitive.

What is needed to recover from patriarchal control, pessimism, and our sense of exile is knowledge of how our living systems, our world, and the cosmos operate and evolve. Ultimately, O'Murchu is advocating for a spiritual maturation as a species, or a mature faith that will allow humans to "embrace the grandeur, complexity, and paradox that characterize evolution at every stage."[12] Liberation, for O'Murchu, then, is tightly aligned with the extent to which humans and all living beings live out evolutionary impulses that desire wholeness, freedom, relationality, and creativity; for humans, it can be considered a process of maturation. And since "today science often outpaces religions in reawakening access to mystery and deeper meaning,"[13] he advocates turning to science to cultivate a true understanding of who we are really meant to be as humans on Earth and to provide us with guidelines to direct our behaviour so that we relate to the planet in a more harmonious way. In this sense, a new ethical vision, and indeed, liberation, can come about by listening and aligning ourselves with the larger cosmic story.

THE SCIENCE AUTHORING O'MURCHU'S ETHICAL VISION

O'Murchu's engagement with new science is arguably the most prolific among the Christian authors I am investigating. In his 1986 book, *The God Who Becomes Redundant*, O'Murchu deals with new physics and ecology, which includes the Gaia hypothesis. He expands on this initial exploration in subsequent writings, paying particular attention to quantum physics, chaos theory, Gaian theory, paleoanthropology, biology, and cosmology. Throughout his writings he has incorporated findings from a wide range of scientists: physicists David Bohm, David Peat, Lee Smolin, Stephen Hawking, Brian Greene, Fritjof Capra, Erich Jantsch, and Paul Davies; chemists Ilya Prigogine, James Lovelock, and Giuseppe Del Re; biologists Elisabet Sahtouris, Lynn Margulis, and Rupert Sheldrake; cosmologist Brian Swimme; primatologists Frans de Waal and Jane Goodall; and, certainly, paleontologist Pierre Teilhard de Chardin. More could be added to this list if we include the scientists whose work O'Murchu consults only once or twice and in one book, such as neuroscientist Karl Pribram, paleontologist Michael Brunet, biologists John Davidson, Humberto Maturana, and Evan Eisenberg, paleoanthropologist Richard Leaky, anthropologist and science writer Roger Lewin, physicist Mishio Kaku, and zoologist and ethologist Lyall Watson. Like Boff in his co-authored work with Hathaway, O'Murchu also tends to rely on scholars with backgrounds in science, such as Danah Zohar, and those heavily engaged in science, such as complexity theorist James Gardener; historian Theodore

Roszak; philosopher of science evolution and systems theory, Ervin Lazlo; and science writers such as Kitty Ferguson; and writer for the journal *Science*, Ann Gibbons. In a few writings, he also consults the works of author, inventor, and futurist Ray Kurzweil, who writes on the subject of science and technology in the future.

As the number and scope of scientist/scholars are extensive, it is difficult to pinpoint one field of science that receives more consideration. While O'Murchu's employment of quantum physics is arguably the field for which he is best known, he emphasizes other fields of science depending on the purpose or theme of a particular work. In *Quantum Theology*, for instance, while he looks primarily at quantum physics, he also explores the Gaia theory to understand the whole and dynamic reality of the universe so as to shed light on how theology should be done; in *Ancestral Grace* he relies a great deal on recent findings in paleoanthropology and biology to emphasize deep time to allow us to look differently at who we are as a species; in *Religion in Exile* and *Evolutionary Faith* he gives considerable attention to chaos theory within a cosmological framework to allow us to come to terms with natural processes with all their paradoxes and to reclaim our identity as a cosmic and planetary species on an evolving Earth; and in *The Transformation of Desire* he turns to his psychological roots; he examines desire in its planetary and cosmic essence and introduces bioregionalism as a means to help humans to align our desires with that of the whole planet. To be sure, these themes and scientific theories are not unique to each book and reappear in his other books. Still, I will divide my assessment of his use of science by these themes, all of which undergird his message of maturing as a species.

Much as we saw with Boff's analysis of quantum physics, O'Murchu sees quantum physics as evoking a new and profound way of understanding reality, one known to mystics for several thousand years. The discovery that subatomic particles are really vibrating wave packets invites us to see everyday objects as "living energy."[14] O'Murchu likes to use the example of a wooden desk, which to the naked eye seems to be a dead, inert material object. Yet, were there a powerful microscope available to observe what is happening, we would see a "sea-bed of minute 'moving' particles" which, "at very fine and sensitive levels, [are] affecting my psyche, just as I am affecting [them]."[15] He takes the metaphor of dance that Giuseppe Del Re, Brian Greene, and Brian Swimme each use to illustrate how everything interacts with everything else, a world of "rhythm, synchronized motion, and continual change."[16] Dance as a metaphor not only demonstrates the movement and dynamic nature of the universe, but, he underlines, it ties ancient wisdoms to what new science is telling, since dance, he maintains, "is the first, most ancient, and most enduring form of *religion.*"[17]

O'Murchu and Boff do share many common understandings of quantum physics. Where O'Murchu seems to part company with Boff's reading of this science is the degree to which humans determine reality. For example, O'Murchu acknowledges the historical significance of the Copenhagen interpretation of quantum physics. This interpretation (early 1920s), so named because its principal architect, Niels Bohr, was a Dane based in Copenhagen, is one of the earliest and most commonly taught interpretations of quantum physics. Comprising various contemporaneous understandings in quantum theory, such as Werner Heisenberg's uncertainty principle (as discussed in my chapter on Boff), the interpretation speaks to the wave function collapse as depending on which manifestation the observer is seeking; that is, there is no objective quantum reality beyond what is revealed by an act of measurement or observation. This phenomenon is significant for O'Murchu and Boff, because it demonstrates the role the observer ultimately plays in influencing the experiment. Further to this understanding of reality, O'Murchu also accepts much about the Teilhardian notion of noogenesis (as discussed in my chapter on Ruether), which he described as "that innate intelligence, not necessarily divine"[18] that governs life's unfolding. Recall that the noosphere is understood as the mind of the human in Teilhard de Chardin's framework, which can simply refer to Earth getting "a new skin," the human thinking mind.

However, O'Murchu accepts neither the Teilhardian nor the Copenhagen understanding of reality without a great deal of qualification. For example, O'Murchu steers clear of Teilhard de Chardin's understanding of noogenesis as the "crowning" domain surrounding Earth and its other spheres.[19] O'Murchu also decidedly restrains the anthropomorphic import of the Copenhagen interpretation of quantum physics. While Boff employs these ideas to support his claim that the human's role is akin to that of a co-pilot, O'Murchu downplays the role of the human, adding, "We humans do not and cannot determine the final outcome, except by quality of interference and control that is often deleterious than beneficial to progress and growth."[20] Placing us more as mere participators in a co-creative process than as co-pilots, O'Murchu eschews the strong anthropic conviction, "which claims that the highest possible levels of intelligence, information, and consciousness are those developed, or due to be developed, by human beings, *in their presently evolved state* [original italics]."[21] It is apparent where O'Murchu is going with this: we are not the final goal of evolution. Taking his cue here from Elisabet Sahtouris and James Lovelock, he makes a rather provocative statement from a Christian standpoint: "In Gaian terms, we are just another species, neither the owners nor the stewards of the planet. Our future depends much more on a right relationship with Gaia than on enforcing our self-righteous claim to be masters of creation."[22]

Indeed, the lessons from quantum physics lead O'Murchu to diverge even further away from Boff's understanding as illustrated in this passage: "That our only real hope for 'salvation' and new life is to humbly acknowledge how little we are in it all, let go of our masculine will-to-power, and allow ourselves to become the co-creative beneficiaries of an evolutionary process that far outstretches anything we ever dreamed of. In that sublime and poignant moment of letting go, and letting 'God,' we will rediscover who we really are."[23] There is more to this than a mere sentiment of humility. O'Murchu is being consistent in his thinking. He notes that the anthropic principle, by suggesting that we are the final outcome, "with nothing else of a higher nature to evolve," insinuates that we must therefore be "endowed with the wisdom and resources to resolve all of life's mysteries and riddles, especially the puzzle of meaningless suffering."[24] This, he declares, is not true; moreover, such thinking causes more suffering and angst, since by believing that we can solve all of life's riddles, we naively attempt to diminish suffering, a theme running throughout his works to which I will return later in this chapter.

While quantum physics prescribes a diminished role for us as humans, it underlines the relational character of the universe. For O'Murchu, it also serves to demonstrate that the whole is greater than the sum of the parts. Quoting Lee Smolin, he writes that radical atomism has failed: "Instead, if we want to give a complete description of an elementary particle we must include in the description every particle it may have interacted with in the past. This means that we can only give a complete description of any part of the universe to the extent that we describe the whole universe."[25] This concept of whole (also referred to as holism), he holds, is made nowhere more vivid or concrete than with an illustration of how the hologram works. The work of David Bohm, who proposed in 1971 that a hologram describes how the universe functions, is helpful in this regard. A hologram is a special type of optical storage system that uses laser beams. O'Murchu explains how it works: "If you take a holographic photo, say, of a dog, and cut out one section of it, e.g., the dog's leg, and then enlarge that section to the original size, you will get, not an enlarged leg, but a picture of the whole dog. We are dealing with a method of lensless photography in which the wave field of light scattered by an object is recorded on a plate as an interference pattern. If we look at it with our ordinary eyesight, we see a meaningless pattern of swirls, but when the photographic record – the hologram – is placed in a coherent light beam like a laser, the original wave pattern is regenerated; a three-dimensional image appears, and any piece of the hologram will reconstruct the entire image."[26] In this sense, the whole not only is greater than the sum of its parts, but is contained in each part as well. O'Murchu notes that Karl Pribram had suggested that the brain also functions like a hologram. But this detail seems secondary to O'Murchu's program, for, ultimately, he aims to show how the universe is relational: "Everything in the cosmos is made out of the seamless, holographic fabric of the implicate order."[27] From this, O'Murchu concludes that no whole is ever complete in itself.

Unpacking how this relational aspect of the universe might impact on our daily lives and our ethics, he quotes from Danah Zohar: "Quantum holism may be telling us, for example, that power relations are not the only, or perhaps even the most effective, way that people and events can be linked in society. The politician or the manager who tries to influence or control events may be less effective than one who can be sensitive to the spontaneous emergence of social or political trends. The individual who realizes that parts of his or her identity emerge through relationship with others may be less guarded and defensive."[28] In addition, contrary to an individualistic morality, one that assumes that the power to respond to ethical situations comes from the individual person alone, O'Murchu states that morality, in the quantum context, attends first to the whole and only secondarily to the parts composing the whole.[29] This might sound difficult to apply, especially when considering individuals. He states that "The values in themselves are not fundamentally different from those of traditional morality – honesty, truth, peace, justice, love, liberty etc." However, he adds, "How these values are *contextualized*, how they are incarnated in human social, and political structures, is what concerns quantum theologians."[30] The individual's response to moral situations occurs not as if the self were an isolated individual, but as part of a larger relational and interconnected reality. Further to the notion of relationality, he quotes business consultant Margaret Wheatley, who takes concrete lessons from quantum physics to guide her ethically in her daily actions. Her words are worth repeating here, at least in part: "My growing sensibility of a quantum universe has affected my organizational life in several ways. First, I try hard to discipline myself to remain aware of the whole and to resist my well-trained desire to analyze the parts to death. I now look for patterns of movement over time and focus on qualities like rhythm, flow, direction and shape … And last, I realize more and more that the universe will not cooperate with my desires for determinism."[31]

In short, morality in the quantum framework seeks to address the context, the system and the larger forces that affect individual and interpersonal behaviours: "The integrity, dignity, and rights of every 'part' (people included) can be promoted only within the relational context from which it emerges."[32] For O'Murchu, then, it is not our solipsistic individuality that matters; our independence and autonomy matter even less, for all of these are meaningless apart from the relationships that sustain us. For this reason, he prefers to speak of personhood, with relationality at its core. What does he mean by personhood? O'Murchu turns to Jungian psychology and the notion of the transpersonal, which means growing into a fuller sense of who one is by developing an awareness of his/her relationship with everything that constitutes the wider web of life. It is from that relational context that a person gets his/her deeper identity as a human being. O'Murchu puts it this way: "So, for example, in humanistic psychology … we use the phrase, 'I am at all times the sum of my relationships and that is what gives me identity'; and that is what I am challenging [in using personhood]. Ultimately our true identity as people is a relational identity even for us as individuals rather than an isolated separated identity." [33]

Relationality receives an added import from O'Murchu with the work of Rupert Sheldrake, whose hypothesis on morphic resonance highlights our capacity to relate through fields.[34] Much like gravitational or electromagnetic fields influence the world around us, Sheldrake posits that there are fields of influence, hidden to us and endowed with memory, that influence our behavior and thoughts. These fields are pooled memories, not unlike the collective memory-unconscious in the Jungian sense. Sheldrake himself likens morphic resonances to Carl Jung's theory of the collective unconscious.[35] Within the collective memory of humanity, people are more tuned in to members of their own family and race and social and cultural group, yet there is also the presence of a background resonance from all humanity. O'Murchu uses the oft-cited example of monkeys on Koshima Island in Southern Japan, who were observed in 1954 to have adopted a new mode of eating potatoes. By 1958, monkeys all over Japan had adopted this new behaviour even though there was no physical contact between the two groups. The hypothesis Sheldrake puts forth suggests that the monkeys communicated through the field of influence particular to their species. How could this occur? Sheldrake suggests that the form and behaviour of organisms do not arise merely from mechanistic interactions within their immediate environment. The morphic fields are like the signals from a TV set that are tuned to particular channels. Unlike TV signals, however, the communication is two-way: between the morphic field and organism and back. Sheldrake uses his hypothesis as a way of explaining why flocks of birds show such remarkable coordination and why termites building columns, which are adjacent yet separate, know how to build arches so that the two sides meet at precisely the right place in the middle.[36] From this – and in keeping with the holographic notion above – O'Murchu concludes that our communities, and societies, have a far greater influence on our lives than our individualistic culture acknowledges.[37]

For O'Murchu, the relational whole, which we are being asked to befriend, refers not just to the psychic-material dimension of the universe but to time as well. He takes insights from paleontology and ethology to demonstrate that our present model of being is more of an aberration of who we are as a species. To support this claim, he employs the work of Michael Brunet, who discovered in Central Africa the skull and jaw remains of a late Miocene hominid nicknamed Toumai: these remains are believed to predate the earliest previously known hominid remains, Lucy, by over 3 million years. O'Murchu concludes that the findings show us that human life began, not recently, but 7 million years ago.[38] The resultant "bigger picture" of human evolution determines that the relational model has prevailed throughout most of our "human" history, not the model whereby the human is seen as autonomous, atomistic, rational, and self-reliant. O'Murchu contends that such discoveries must lead us to different anthropological conclusions about ourselves: we become a far more convivial species than presumed.

Along the same line of reasoning, O'Murchu also looks at the work of Frans de Waal whose study of bonobo life and culture led de Waal to claim: "Had the bonobo been known to science first and the chimpanzee second [...] we might today have different ideas about the inevitability of violence in human society, about male dominance and male bonding in hunting and warfare."[39] Bonobos, de Waal asserts, are peace-loving and generally egalitarian apes, which distinguishes them from chimpanzees, who have received more scholarly attention and too often are used as prototypes of human behaviour. It is just such new exemplars that O'Murchu claims will help humans see themselves as more convivial beings: "The wisdom to realize that there are other prototypes we could use and adopt, some of which are far more congruent with our deeper story as human species."[40]

This more optimistic understanding of human nature is not the only lesson garnered here. Within this same deep-time outlook, our understanding of religion alters as well. Based on his study of paleoanthropology, O'Murchu posits that our spiritual journey must have begun some 600,000 years ago, not simply a few millennia ago; consequently, the major religions of our day, which came into being only between 3000 BCE and 1500 CE represent only a fraction of humanity's overall spiritual development. The implication he draws from this becomes clear: changing and even abandoning previously thought sacred eternal teachings and practices from religion becomes less problematic and, in fact, is a necessary step in our spiritual maturation.[41]

This openness to change that imbues much of O'Murchu's thinking is taken up again in his investigation of chaos theory through the writings of Prigogine, Sahtouris, and Lewin. Chaos theory is an attempt to explain the random components of systems. Popularly known as the butterfly effect, the theory posits that small differences in conditions of any system produce widely diverging outcomes. As a result, long-term predictions become impossible: "Chaos is a science of pattern, not predictability," he writes. "It reminds us that in nature an exact replication of behavior may lead to disaster rather than to progress."[42] Similar to his conclusion on sacred eternal teachings above, to O'Murchu chaos theory suggests that truths "will not be found within traditional religious institutions."[43] To find truth, we need to look to the peripheries of the fields of religion and science, and often well beyond them where currently ecological, New Age, and feminist movements, alternative medicines, and technologies are being created. In fact, O'Murchu suggests that chaos could be the precondition for launching a whole new way of being.

O'Murchu is not suggesting we abandon all past wisdoms, though: only those that are not congruent with the larger wisdom contained in the cosmos. He speculates that early hominids would have had the intimate awareness of cycles of birth-death-rebirth through intuition, adding, "Baffling and bewildering it may have been at times, but intuitively our ancestors recognized a fundamental paradox characterizing not merely human life but creation at every level."[44] In this sense, he is advocating for a re-embrace of a wisdom about the nature of the universe intuited long ago by our ancestors. *Homo ergaster*, he suggests, did not need a rational explanation for everything we do today. Suffering and death, along with birth and joy, would have been reflected in the human cycle and viewed not as a contradiction, which is how current patriarchal religion views it, but as a paradox accepted. He states, "Humans at that time would not have been happy about paradox, and like ourselves may have performed rituals (magic) to resolve it, but they would not have been caught up in the compulsive urge to control as evidenced in the anthropocentric world of our time."[45]

The ultimate lesson O'Murchu is suggesting here, one I touched upon earlier when referring to what he describes as our naive attempt to diminish suffering, is that instead of trying to control destruction, pain, and suffering at all costs, or trying to keep them at bay by defensive tactics of denial and scapegoating, we are to engage with them, listen to them, and learn from them. This is what he means when he says – as we saw above – we need to learn to live better by learning to die better: we come to terms with natural processes, as we once did.

AN ANALYSIS OF O'MURCHU'S ETHICAL VISION

O'Murchu suggests a metaphor of homecoming to denote our coming back from exile to our true selves, replete with the more optimistic understanding of our convivial nature, here on Earth as part of a wider community of beings. Homecoming as a way of being in the world not only embraces the relational nature of our universe but it incorporates the paradoxes, ambiguities, uncertainties, messiness, and struggles of life. And he suggests that bioregionalism – much like Ruether and Boff believe – can serve as a viable model for how a grounding or homecoming can take place.

Bioregionalism represents the bigger picture so important to O'Murchu's ethic whereby the human import is significantly limited. To this end, O'Murchu maintains, "The nation state has outlived its usefulness. Evolution is calling forth something quite different in our time."[46] In keeping with a holarchical (as opposed to hierarchical), collaborative, and empowering model, he suggests that at the local level bioregionalism can replace the nation state as a model for governance. It also represents a model that is small enough and yet still complex to honour the tenets of mutuality, participation, subsidiarity, cooperation, and diversity. The cycle of production and exchange will be determined by the quality and quantity of local resources, and power will be diffused and decentralized, with nothing being done at a higher level than necessary. The actual decision-making bodies will follow cellular principles, "in which families operate within neighborhoods, neighborhoods within communities, communities within cities."[47] O'Murchu concludes that with a bioregional grounding we are more likely to satisfy both our survival needs and our more enduring desires, as it will assist us in relating as the natural world relates, not in unrestricted competition but with intense co-operation.

In the end, this adult faith educator is suggesting that a more mature faith develops when we align our desires to those of the larger cosmic whole, most aptly modelled – at the planetary level – by bioregionalism.[48] Not unlike Ruether, who suggests we convert our minds to nature's logic, then, O'Murchu is suggesting that by learning through science how living systems operate within the process of evolution, we can ascertain who we are and how we should conduct ourselves. Within O'Murchu's framework, we are told to trust these cosmic processes or desires and to "attend first to the whole and only secondarily to the parts composing the whole," since, as he posits, new science shows us that "Creation has desires far more elegant and sophisticated than ours."[49] Thus, science, for O'Murchu, provides both guidelines and a vision of life and how we ought to approach it.

Trusting these "more sophisticated" cosmic processes or desires, and indeed looking first at the bigger picture, might seem contradictory to what one might expect from a liberationist ethic, especially if asking this, for example, of a poor and destitute Indigenous *campesina* from Guatemala, walking long and far for water. The term *campesina,* here in its feminine form, is a Spanish word that can be translated roughly as "peasant farmer." While I eschew the connotations of an uneducated person and the derogatory baggage that can come with this term – an Indigenous woman of few means living as a subsistence farmer with her community – this example serves as an apt way, here and throughout this book, of demonstrating how well O'Murchu, as well as Ruether, Boff, and Berry, attends to liberation of both the human *and* the other-than human.[50] On this issue of the whole, O'Murchu is not very clear how we might attend to the needs of our Guatemalan *campesina* if her needs conflict with those of the biotic whole. While I will return to this point, specifically the ambiguity surrounding O'Murchu's understanding of the whole, in chapter 5, suffice it now to say that O'Murchu – not unlike what Ruether does in distinguishing between the planes of reality of the human and the natural world – is at least clear about what he means by trusting cosmic processes. He makes a distinction here between cosmic and human processes, between meaningful and meaningless suffering. As we have little control over the paradoxes within the cosmic processes, we ought to learn to befriend them. Human processes, however, are often marred by wrong human intervention or human ignorance and, for this reason, any suffering that arises from it is meaningless and, according to O'Murchu, must be avoided or eased. The irony, O'Murchu avers, is that in befriending creation's cosmic paradoxes, we are less likely to go wrong in our interventions. Contrarily, our desire for a pain-free world, devoid of depletion and destruction, sets in motion our attempt to control life processes, which lies at the root of wrong intervention.

By way of example to help clarify this point, O'Murchu compares the January 2010 earthquake in Haiti, which registered 7.0 in magnitude, with Chile's most severe earthquake ever recorded, a month later, registering at 8.8 on the Richter scale. Though the earthquake in Haiti was nowhere near as strong as the one in Chile, far more people died in Haiti than in Chile as a result of the quake: the former resulting in some 230,000 deaths while in Chile – even though the quake struck during the early hours of the morning when the population was much more vulnerable – only 1,000 died. Comparing the two incidents, O'Murchu determines that the main factor explaining why Haitians suffered more from its earthquake was the quality of its buildings. Wishing away earthquakes will not help: were we somehow able to succeed in stopping earthquakes through advanced technology, it would be counterproductive, as earthquakes are essential to the flourishing of life on our planet. Yet, were technology used to construct earthquake-resistant buildings in Haiti – as was the case in Chile – that would be productive and just.[51]

With this distinction between meaningful and meaningless destruction in mind, we cannot always make sense of the apparent destruction and suffering, O'Murchu says. Nor should we always attempt to get rid of suffering, as there is a quality of suffering that is innate and essential to human evolution. As discussed earlier, if we try to avoid it, as he points out, "we get rid of life itself."[52] This is the paradox: something that does not make sense to our mind, a "surplus of meaning that cannot be contained within the structure of rational discourse." O'Murchu likens it to "a contradiction, with meaning written underneath it."[53] In this way, paradox should be approached much like one approaches Zen Buddhist koans: the person meditating accepts them without trying to "solve" them, and in doing so, gains insights.

In the course of distinguishing between the human and natural processes, humans learn where to place their energies. This discernment process – which will be discussed in more detail shortly – becomes crucial to understanding O'Murchu's ethical vision. He puts it this way: "Before we address these big questions, let's get our own house in order. Let's begin by resolving and dissolving all the meaningless suffering that we ourselves cause either directly or indirectly. Then the chances are that the other paradoxes that baffle us will not seem that irrational anymore ... then too, we are likely to be more at peace with the paradoxical enigmas of each day."[54] The task of the human, then, becomes not so much one of removal or avoidance of suffering but the discernment of which forms of suffering are needed for evolutionary development. Presumably with regard to the Indigenous Guatemalan woman walking long and far for water, trusting the more sophisticated cosmic processes should not deter us from giving immediate attention to her plight and addressing the social, political, and economic forces that created her situation in the first place. And similarly, in the earthquake example above, we realize that Chile has far more resources and money to ensure that its buildings are earthquake-resistant. This is not the case with Haiti. The difference is made more apparent by comparing Haiti with Japan, which experiences frequent earthquakes, yet suffers relatively few casualties. In Chile's case – and more so in earthquake-prone Japan – it has far more technology, money, and resources to implement legal directives for building codes and indeed to build such buildings. The central problem, O'Murchu concludes, "is that our world-system is fundamentally corrupt when it comes to justice and equality," adding that only indirectly did the planet kill 230,000 Haitians. Ultimately, "greedy human beings" who refuse to share justly and equally (and certainly not God) are the culprits.[55]

Notwithstanding the importance of discernment, actually distinguishing between meaningful and meaningless suffering remains somewhat uncertain. Is it always possible to distinguish between human and natural processes? While the occurrence of earthquakes is clearly non-anthropogenic, scientists are pointing to anthropogenic origins of climate change with its effects on ecosystems, flora and fauna, and the planetary hydrological cycle. Distinguishing between human and natural processes within the Anthropocene, therefore, becomes less clear. In this light, a good proportion of suffering on the planet – the suffering of amphibians who lose their habitat to sprawl or the demise of an insect species in the Amazon forest due to clear cutting, and arguably the reason why our *campesina* cannot readily find water nearby – runs the risk of becoming meaningless. O'Murchu responds to this difficulty by stressing, along the same reasoning of the French philosopher Paul Ricoeur, that *most* of the suffering in the world is actually created by humans directly or indirectly.[56] O'Murchu points to Hurricane Katrina in New Orleans in 2005. In reading the numerous commentaries on the disaster, he found a common thread of conclusions: that in all probability the problems that came about from the hurricane stemmed from wrong interventions that *contributed to* the destructive impact of the hurricane.

With this line of reasoning in mind, O'Murchu underlines that Leonardo Boff was justified when he posited that the issues of the poor can only be legitimately addressed when the ecological dimensions of people's lives are also embraced. O'Murchu concurs with Boff and Ruether, then, in saying that poverty arises when we mistreat the planet and other species. O'Murchu concludes from this that ethics can no longer be solely about the human being, but must encompass planetary life, and the rights of other species. He concludes, "Humans cannot hope for any kind of a meaningful liberation unless we are also seeking for some kind of liberation for a living Earth and the creatures that share the planet. In other words, liberation is not just a human project but an equal thing we desire."[57] He explains that liberation must apply beyond the human or the goal of homecoming – our coming back from exile to our true selves as being part of a wider community of beings – cannot occur, adding, "As long as we keep the word liberation at just the human level, I think we are in danger of staying at the anthropocentric level, and in danger of colluding more with our fierce cultural competition by where we compete all the time to dominate and control reality [which are the] complete opposite of befriending."[58]

By "some kind" of liberation, O'Murchu is not specific, other than to say that a big part of seeking liberation for Earth entails letting Earth systems do what they are meant to do: letting swamps be, for example. Liberation for an animal necessitates its being free to follow its evolutionary impulses. Recall earlier in my discussion on quantum physics that O'Murchu holds that "in letting go and letting God, we will rediscover who we really are." That same principle applies to how we are to deal with the natural world. O'Murchu likens this to a proverb he once heard: "A man is rich in proportion to the number of things he can leave alone." He clarifies this by framing the issue spiritually: "In other words, he doesn't interfere; to me that's the heart of mysticism in one sense. I don't understand this to mean we don't engage in any way with creation; I think we are meant to engage, but how to engage in a more benign eco-friendly way?"[59] O'Murchu points out, for example, that the lioness chasing a little gazelle in Africa is killing only for food. Liberation to both animals, while paradoxical to our reasoning, entails allowing them to carry out this prey-predator relationship. O'Murchu is less clear on how we reconcile conflicts that arise between the human and the other-than-human when, even in a "benign eco-friendly" approach to fostering liberation, the evolutionary impulses of one or both might have to be curtailed.

In the end, liberation does not imply the absence of suffering, whether for the human or other-than-human. In fact, full liberation, for the human at least, occurs when we transcend the delusion about suffering and "choose to honor the prerogative and creativity of the divine as seen from within the evolutionary story in its total context."[60] It becomes a long-term endeavour, and not an instantaneous release from suffering, and it begins by allowing ourselves to be vulnerable, which for O'Murchu ostensibly means being human.

This openness to vulnerability is important to O'Murchu's vision, but if not understood properly, it could understandably seem discomforting. As servants to a bigger process, he says, we cannot hope, let alone try, to control it. But has not our desire to control pain and suffering in the past led to major medical breakthroughs, which have saved countless lives? I do not think O'Murchu denies that such a benefit comes out of this desire. O'Murchu is more concerned with the current world order that cannot tolerate our anthropological vulnerability. He takes an example from his psychotherapeutic work, which often deals with cases of depression. The "flipside of depression," he states, "is frozen anger,"[61] hence, instead of prescribing people Prozac or some other medication, he explores with the patients some ways in which they can ventilate and articulate their anger. He finds that in this process of befriending their fragility or vulnerability, they find ways of releasing the pain. But this process could not have occurred if his clients tried to transcend their suffering, denying that it exists. O'Murchu also uses the example of our catching a cold or flu for which we end up in bed for three days. This is because our body needs to be in bed for three days. He suggests such rest is better for us than forcing antibiotics into our bodies. In this manner, the heavy weight of the illness becomes less of a burden, as it also opens up for us a viable way to better health. O'Murchu believes this process empowers humans to live in healthier ways. This is what O'Murchu means by saying, "Vulnerability is a graced gift."[62] by befriending our anthropological fragility, we are actually a healthier people; moreover, it keeps us close to the tenderness and fragility of all living things.

Ironically, O'Murchu's optimism for technology seems to challenge this process of befriending our fragility or vulnerability. Like Boff, O'Murchu's ethical vision is infused with the Teilhardian notion that we exist in a time of massive evolutionary change. While acknowledging the possibility that humans might be the cause of their own destruction, O'Murchu is also optimistic about the possible future of humanity. Again like Boff, he associates our own evolution with technological progress. He maintains that in billions of years of evolution to come, for instance, humans will be succeeded by other, more highly advanced, species.[63] O'Murchu, however, gives technology a greater significance in our own evolution. Prompted by the writings of Ray Kurzweil and James Gardener, he envisions – due to a human hybridity with technology – the development of the "transhuman" or "posthuman."[64] By way of example, he posits that the nano-technological shift (with its impact on human brain activity) will prove beneficial in the long term. While this could possibly be the case, it is certainly not assured. One has to wonder whether a posthuman being, highly advanced in biological functions – due to technological implants – will be able to share pain with lesser "naturally evolved" biological creatures. Put another way, will our hybridity with technology help us befriend vulnerability and "keep us close to the tenderness and fragility of all living things?" One need only consider a truism known to most teachers: that naturally talented students – whether in sport, art, or ratio-mathematical reasoning – sometimes have difficulty in understanding why others with less talent in that field cannot do what they do with relative ease. The same reasoning could apply to wealthy and healthy people who sometimes have difficulty understanding why a poor person suffering from a mental disease cannot "just get a job." Moreover, will a bigger gap arise between the rich humans who can afford the technology and the poor who never can? These questions remain unsatisfactorily addressed.

To be fair, O'Murchu responds to this query by underlining that the possible deleterious outcomes from technology largely depend on what kind of ethical safeguards we put in place. Suitably, he addressed my queries above by asking whether the industrial revolution of the seventeenth and eighteenth centuries, or the technological revolution of the nineteenth and twentieth centuries, diminished or altered the human capacity for empathy, concluding, "We cannot say they necessarily did." This is a valid point. Yet, as he concedes – thus giving my point credence – "Thus far movements in that direction are not very impressive." He adds, "We can only hope that the wisdom inherent in evolution will direct things in a benign direction rather than in a destructive one. Time alone will tell whether that optimism was wise or not."[65]

Similar to the shortcomings of his discussion of technology, O'Murchu's vision lacks a clear political economy approach which leaves some other elements underdeveloped: the case of the Indigenous woman seeking water, for instance. O'Murchu's ethical vision certainly incorporates her liberation and the injustices surrounding her predicament are denounced. However, the political, social, and economic forces underlying the perpetuation of such injustices are not dealt with in depth. To be fair, given O'Murchu's starting points and the target of his critique, this is understandable. He is a psychological counsellor concerned about the narrow and insular religiosity and institutional power structures that control our thinking.

Being a psychological counsellor might explain why O'Murchu is less concerned with our physical or cognitive evolution and more with our spiritual maturation. As much as science is employed to author its formation, Jungian psychology also plays an important role.

I have mentioned how Jung's notion of the collective unconscious resembles Sheldrake's morphic fields. But it is also Jung's notions on consciousness and unconsciousness that often come into play – the latter of which "represents the mysterious, suprarational within humanity and within creation."[66] Jung's psychology, mentioned in a number of O'Murchu's books, resonates deeply with the spiritual and mystical elements found within new science, and with post-normal science. It is sometimes difficult to distinguish where insights from psychology begin and where insights from the natural sciences end; the two are closely integrated. There is a marked similarity to the evolutionary processes O'Murchu speaks about and Jung's notion of individuation, which denotes a lifelong process, that, O'Murchu explains, "is the openness and receptivity to a larger reality: social, ecological, spiritual, cosmic [which] in its most highly developed stages, it merges with mysticism, and the boundaries of 'me' and 'not me' begin to melt away."[67]

Finally, and perhaps not surprisingly given his receptivity to a larger reality, it warrants mentioning that O'Murchu's ethical vision appears to be the least anthropocentric of the three interlocutors we have discussed thus far. While he accords a qualitative uniqueness to the human – not discounting his view that the human could evolve into something posthuman – O'Murchu nevertheless acknowledges that in our current state, "how little we are in it all."

THE EPISTEMOLOGY AND METHODOLOGY BACKING O'MURCHU'S ETHICAL VISION

Knowing, O'Murchu emphasizes, is rather elusive. Recall that for O'Murchu some things are forever obscure to our comprehension, such as the paradox of destruction and suffering. "Our universe is so vastly complex and mysterious," he writes, "that no one species (no matter how enlightened) and no one religious system (no matter how sophisticated) could comprehend and understand its totality."[68] In particular, for O'Murchu, it is illusory to think we can view (and understand) things in isolation. And while rational evaluation is incapable of capturing the inclusive whole that is always greater than the sum of its parts, there are still limits to how we know, what we can know, and when we can know something. O'Murchu suggests that even seemingly straightforward scientific notions like "autopoiesis" evade easy comprehension, citing its sophistication and complexity; hence, he maintains, "The process never can be comprehended purely on the level of rational thought or analysis."[69]

For O'Murchu, it is not merely science that is limited in fully knowing things. The lessons of quantum physics have O'Murchu assigning a certain vagueness to *all* reality: "The truth of the stories [of the evolving universe] rests not in whether or not we can verify the facts, because often we do not have the relevant information with which to do that; we access their truth more through intuition and imagination than through rational discourse and logical argument."[70] While O'Murchu assigns a slightly downgraded role to rational analysis (compared with other ways of knowing, such as intuition), it is not merely the quality of knowing that concerns him, but the quantity as well. He points to knowledge doubling at so rapid a pace that no one could be held accountable for it all, unlike one hundred or thousands of years ago.[71] This sentiment is supported by James Lovelock, who talks about there being too much information in the world today for anyone to comprehend: "While no one could understand the whole book [of knowledge], at least with the top-down holistic look, we can see the table of contents."[72]

With such limitations assigned to our knowing, what and how much does O'Murchu state we can know? Remarkably, O'Murchu maintains that there is nevertheless much we can know when we integrate rational thinking with intuition and imagination. Like Ruether and Boff, accompanying these cognitive approaches are more embodied ways of knowing such as dance, song, and drumming. Suggesting that the desire to dance is deep-seated in the human psyche, he states, "Dance emerged as a primary medium to make sense and meaning out of life … the medium used to establish archetypal communication with the heart of reality."[73] There are inner and outer dimensions to knowledge for O'Murchu. The desires of the cosmos, such as creativity, wholeness, and aliveness, O'Murchu seems to imply, can be found within us. Carl Jung's notion of a collective unconsciousness, for instance, suggests that human growth comes from a psychic source within. And while the collective unconsciousness plays a large role in O'Murchu's epistemology, so do Sheldrake's morphic fields. Remember that morphic fields link globally human imaginations and insights, which, O'Murchu concludes, grant "group thought" far more impact on us than contemporary culture recognizes. With this interiority of the collective consciousness and exteriority of the psychic fields – traditionally understood as Holy Spirit, according to O'Murchu – O'Murchu can speak about the mythic quality of the scientific endeavour, a mystical way of knowing that impels the work of scientists at the subconscious level. In fact, O'Murchu concludes, "what is driving the scientific imagination [...] is not rational logic, but a powerful subconscious mystical energy. The dreamer is outwitting the rationalist, the mystic outstripping the scientist."[74]

While O'Murchu does prescribe much weight to the dreamer in our search for answers, saying that we must at times continue down the road of scientific inquiry even "despite the paucity of facts,"[75] he is not really promoting competition between ways of thinking in lieu of integration, as O'Murchu speaks of the scientist him/herself integrating the dream into academic endeavours. He views science, for instance, as originally developing out of a spiritual hunger, offering British physicist Paul Davies (author of *God and the New Physics*) as an example of someone who sees science becoming spiritually more compelling than religion, since it uncovers an inescapable sense of mystery about the universe. Perhaps this coupling of science and mysticism explains why throughout his works O'Murchu is comfortable relying on theories of evolution from a wide assortment of thinkers: Henri Bergson with his élan vital, John Baptiste Lamarck with his notion of spontaneous generation, Teilhard de Chardin with his unceasing process of becoming and with greater complexity, and Sri Aurobindo who, like Teilhard de Chardin, speaks about a spiritual unfolding.

Like Boff and Ruether, then, O'Murchu promotes an integrated epistemology that begins with people's experience; only the human imagination plays a far greater role for O'Murchu in the creation of his ethical vision. He also places far more emphasis on participation from "non-specialists," which, for him, means the protean adult actor. He states, "In a sense, we are all intellectuals and ask intellectual questions," and underlines, "this interface between science and spirituality [for the past twenty years or so] is happening outside the academy and not within it."[76] O'Murchu insists, "People's wisdom is outpacing institutional knowing."[77] Accordingly, he maintains that our dialogue must include non-academics; though the academy is not always obliging. The essence of O'Murchu's epistemological program, it would seem, is captured by the image of breaking down barriers that currently fragment our ability to know the world, while empowering hitherto silenced voices. He seeks to bridge the rationalism associated with both science and religions with more imaginative and inclusive approaches to seeing and understanding our universe.

O'Murchu's understanding of truth follows a similar contour to how his integrated epistemology unfolds. We have already seen how truth receives a far greater evolutionary import for O'Murchu. Truth is always before us, rather than based on the certainties from behind us. But truth is also found in the whole, in all of creation, "rather than in human brains," he posits, thus suggesting a critical realist approach.[78] Critical realism is a philosophical view of knowledge that holds, on the one hand, that it is possible to acquire knowledge about the external world as it really is, independently of the human mind or subjectivity – hence, realism. On the other hand, it rejects the view of naive realism that posits that the external world is as it is perceived. Recognizing that perception is a function of, and thus fundamentally marked by, the human mind, critical realism holds that one can only acquire knowledge of the external world by critical reflection on perception and its world – hence, critical.

What concerns O'Murchu most about truth, however, is how it is arrived at and contextualized. Perhaps because of his training in psychology, O'Murchu sees truth arising from our unfolding stories: "We bring with us a deep inherited wisdom empowering us not merely to cope with the exigencies of daily life, but to grapple with the great mysteries that characterize our global embodied experience."[79] On the one level, then, the authenticity of what we know to be true is judged by how closely it conforms to the desires of the universe, a task for which the wisdom of science is crucial; hence, what matters is whether a truth liberates or empowers and fosters connectedness among individuals and communities, and "a convivial relationships with all sentient beings." Here, the provenance of truth matters too: does it come rehearsed from the past through the musings of a relative few, or is "coming from a deep intuitive place," inclined toward the whole, and assimilated without trying to shun paradoxes?

While not explicit on how he envisions a dialogue taking place among the various players and their ways of knowing, or how imagination and intuition can "unlock the deeper wisdom behind and within the scientific research,"[80] O'Murchu does put forth what he calls a "contemplative discernment process," which draws on a wide spectrum of experience, including insight, intuition, imagination, understanding, analysis, dialogue, and spiritual apprehension. Perhaps such a process is not surprising considering what I discussed about truth above. "Discernment" as a model, O'Murchu says, "provides a more reliable pathway to truth than rationality or the rigor of the scientific inquiry,"[81] since it incorporates a broader spectrum of ways of knowing. O'Murchu's model requires much listening and being receptive to universe about us, or more specifically, being open to the "logos,"[82] which is the creative divine energy or wisdom expressed in scripture. This task could be carried out through the simple everyday dimensions of our human engagement with life, be they contact with poor and suffering people, daily prayer, or sharing a sense of humour. Certainly, given the significance O'Murchu places on adult faith, it is safe to assume that the communal discernment among the human participants should be underscored by a sense of mutuality, transparency through open dialogue, and a concern for "sharing power with" instead of "enforcing power over" others, where adult learners can trust their intuition, take risks, and have their horizons of understanding continually stretched.[83] I also think it safe to assume that with an adult faith approach, life experiences and paradox are honoured, our anthropological vulnerability is accepted, questions are respected, and dogmatism gives way to trust.

Along with listening, dialogue, O'Murchu stresses, is key for a communal discernment process, where a critical vigilance is maintained in the face of excessive rationalism and dogmatic impositions. To be sure, the dialogue O'Murchu envisions is not just between humans. He asserts that like the mystics of every age, we need to converse also with creation itself, which he maintains is possible because "creation itself is a narrative experience, telling its own story across the aeons of evolutionary unfolding."[84] Specific to the bioregional context, he does assert that any dialogue among subjects must be more focused on values, explore commonalities (not differences), and be relational, holarchic, and inclusive and open to context. As a more concrete example of how this dialogue ensues, O'Murchu points to the process of networking as practised by NGOs throughout the globe. Here, the principle of subsidiarity, which seeks to foster decisions at the local level where possible, is meant to mimic biological processes. In this way, there is less a need for one "leader" such as the scientist-poet envisioned by Ruether, except to serve as a resource person who "facilitates" adult discernment.

To remain open and receptive to what is going on around and within us, O'Murchu recommends the practice of meditation, "a type of tuning-up process," he says, "facilitating communication between my being and the 'being' of life in the world around me (God if you wish)."[85] Meditation, he avers, helps us to focus our thoughts, clarify our observations, and deepen our intuitions. O'Murchu considers meditation to be a turn within, going from our conscious, through our unconscious, "into the experience of pure truth or God."[86] Likening the conscious and subconscious to the image of an iceberg, he states that the conscious mind represents only the tip of the iceberg, that one-eighth that appears above water, while the remaining unseen seven-eighths is the subconscious. Beyond the subconscious is the collective unconscious, the noosphere, universal consciousness, or the total Godhead. The ocean in which the iceberg floats is not only the means of communication between all the icebergs, but the collection of total truth to which we, as individual icebergs, have access.

While the above exploration of method is vague and lacks a precise framework, here is a slightly more tangible glimpse of how O'Murchu envisions such a communal dialogue or discernment process might work. The story below that O'Murchu narrates is about the Morgan fisher-folk, living on the southwest coast of Thailand. It reveals O'Murchu's concern for *how* truth is arrived at, ultimately allowing the Morgan fisher-folk to avoid meaningless suffering from occurring. On the morning of 26 December 2004, these people noticed that the familiar seawaters had receded far beyond their usual limits. O'Murchu goes on:

Things felt off kilter. Nature was not at ease … These primitive people – with no formal schooling or education – spend their entire time fishing and live in simple hovels along the coastline. Fish is their daily diet; fishing their life-long occupation. They looked intently upon those receding waters and upon the fishes leaping anxiously. They consulted their elders and in union with them quickly reached a collective decision: within hours they intuitively knew that massive waves would break upon their shoreline.

They gathered their meagre possessions and headed for the hills. On the way they met a group of Western tourists, some of whom ridiculed their story. But a few took them seriously and accompanied them to further heights. Thanks to those Westerners, we have inherited this amazing story. Those who dismissed and ridiculed their silly tale walked right into the eye of the storm and lost their lives. The fisher-folk and their accompanying visitors were totally safe![87]

In this narrative, O'Murchu sums up a process that is less about the facts before us, and more about trusting what we feel within. He concludes from this story, "By any set of standards this was a brilliant piece of discernment – and I use the term *discernment* in its full Ignatian meaning. What a different world it would be if more people would use this gift of the contemplative gaze!"[88]

CONCLUSION

Returning to O'Murchu's starting points, where I began this investigation, I find within him, as I did within Boff and Ruether, a deep reverence for all of creation. The writings of Pierre Teilhard de Chardin have played a pivotal role in changing how O'Murchu viewed his faith, the world, and indeed the universe. In fact, Teilhard de Chardin's writings play a pivotal role in how all three thinkers – and, as will be seen, with Berry as well – view both their faith and science. Like Ruether and Boff, O'Murchu also views the universe as deeply relational, and science, which gains a prescriptive role in forming his ethical vision, attests to this truth. Knowing, for O'Murchu, is vastly democratic and comes to us in many ways: at times embodied, at other times through reason or intuition, which is why epistemological lines between his faith and science are somewhat blurred. Again, like the other two, his is a mature faith, fashioned after the vision espoused by Vatican II.

Similarities found among Ruether, Boff, and O'Murchu can be explained by their common use of the works of at least five scientists: Hawking, Lovelock, Margulis, Swimme, and Teilhard de Chardin. But there appears something more profound at work here, as will become more evident in later chapters. A convergence of sorts between their faith and science is occurring, and the epistemological frameworks underpinning their ethical visions appear to facilitate this. With such a convergence, uncertainties and ambiguities are not dispensed with, but embraced.

Despite the many similarities among their ethical visions, divergences can be found in the degree to which importance is assigned to the whole and on the role assigned to the human. O'Murchu assigns less import to the human, eschewing any role to the human that carries with it even the remotest sense of importance, such as gardener or co-pilot. His ethical vision also lacks some of the deeper reflections on the roots of poverty and injustice found in Ruether's and Boff's works. Nevertheless, all three are in agreement that liberation cannot be found within a paradigm of domination and control. The importance O'Murchu assigns to liberation for all creation, as do Boff and Ruether, entails aligning ourselves with, and/or allowing the other-than-human to follow, the evolutionary impulses within creation. We are to engage less in understanding paradoxes and more in changing those situations in our world that we can change.

Finally, O'Murchu appears no more successful than Boff or Ruether in addressing how humans might foster liberation for the human in chorus with the liberation of all creation, other than recognizing that liberation can never be realized outside the larger relationality. However, the emphasis on accepting and even befriending our anthropological fragility, as I will show presently, is an important step in that direction. Thomas Berry, to whose work I now attend, is perhaps most emphatic in this regard, demonstrating that if we are fully to take the liberation of all creation seriously, we must first take our human anthropological condition, our vulnerability, seriously.

CHAPTER FOUR

Thomas Berry

INTRODUCTION TO BERRY

Thomas Berry was born in Greensboro, North Carolina, in 1914. He joined the Roman Catholic Passionist Order and was ordained a priest in 1942. It was actually upon his ordination that he took on the name "Thomas" (he was originally named William Nathan after his father), after Thomas Aquinas, whose thinking he admired. He obtained a PhD in western history at the Catholic University of America, and later studied Asian traditions, learning Chinese and Sanskrit, Indigenous traditions, and – eventually, in the last thirty or so years of his life – Earth history, its systems, science, and cosmology. Interestingly, Berry completed his most significant writings in the field of evolutionary cosmology after he retired from teaching at the age of sixty-three.

Berry's embrace of the study of Earth's history through science and cosmology was not due simply to interest or fascination but was a natural progression. From an early age he experienced a deep reverence for Earth. Berry speaks of the "magic" moments when he was eleven years old wandering through a meadow that, as he explains, "gave to my life something that seems to explain my thinking at a more profound level than almost any other experience I can remember."[1] Filled with white lilies, carved by a creek, and announced by the sounds of the crickets, this early experience, he believes, helped develop within him a sensitivity to nature, such that he could conclude, in an almost Leopoldian manner: "Whatever preserves and enhances this meadow in the natural cycles of its transformation is good; whatever opposes this meadow or negates it is not good."[2] Yet, through the course of his life, he witnessed the rise of a planetary civilization whose means for existing were destroying nature.

Berry's early background as a cultural historian at Fordham University in New York and his teaching career in the area of world religions, then, were valuable to his later writings that addressed Earth-human relations, as these permitted him to integrate skillfully the human story with the larger cosmic story. The writings of Teilhard de Chardin, however, were very influential to Berry's thinking in this regard, as they helped him in his formulation of a new cosmological story. From Teilhard de Chardin, Berry derived a deep understanding of developmental time and an appreciation for his law of complexity-consciousness. As Mary Evelyn Tucker points out, Giambattista Vico's philosophy also influenced Berry's thinking in this regard, as "Vico wished to show that providence was at work not only in sacred history but also in 'profane' history. Consequently, pattern and order are operative and discernible in history." Moreover, she adds, "Vico emphasized the poetic wisdom and creative imagination needed for the future."[3]

Berry did not consider or label himself a theologian, preferring to call himself a geologian – a scholar of the Earth. This choice is arguably a reason why he did not receive formal approbation from Church hierarchy for his writings. This does not mean he escaped rebuke or disapproval from conservative Catholics or mainstream Christians who feared he was not "Christ focused and human focused."[4] In fact, despite his popularity among many people, Christian and non-Christian, some Christians concerned with the environment distanced themselves from Berry when he suggested that we shelve the Bible for twenty years or so. He proposed this to challenge the exaggerated attention granted to verbal sources by Christians – in this case biblical sources – as a way of encountering the divine, to the point that they seldom notice how extensively they have lost contact with the revelation of the divine in nature.

Of interest here are not solely the influences upon Berry's thinking but the extent to which Berry's thinking has imbued a generation. Described by *Newsweek* magazine[5] as "the most provocative figure among the new breed of eco-theologians," his ideas, whether through his writings, video dialogues, talks, or audio-recordings, have inspired many scientists, environmentalists, spiritualists, theologians and, notably, an extraordinary number of Catholic nuns concerned with the spiritual and material dimensions of the ecological crisis. Berry is indirectly responsible for the formation of environmental-spiritual periodicals, community-supported sustainable farms, ecological institutes, academic research, conferences, films, and even musical compositions.[6] Berry's thinking also heavily influenced Boff and O'Murchu in the formation of their ethical visions, and while arguably less so for Ruether, his cosmology nevertheless pervades her cosmological vision and she even attributes Berry as being "the guru of the Catholic ecological movement."[7]

His importance to the religion-science-environment-ethics nexus, therefore, cannot be overstated. When Berry died at age ninety-four in 2009, author Richard Louv, whose book *Last Child in the Woods* Berry greatly admired late in his life, wrote a fitting accolade to this geologian: "Thomas Berry was the earliest and most important voice to describe the profound importance of the disconnection between humans and the natural world, and what that could mean for the future of our species. He often said that his own experience in nature as a boy transformed him and shaped all of his work … To spend time with him was like getting a soul transfusion."[8]

THE TARGET OF BERRY'S CRITIQUE

As indicated by Louv in the passage above, Berry maintains that the human has become disconnected from the natural world. We have forgotten how to listen to it at a basic level. Still, more than losing the capacity to communicate with the material world, Berry says that we have transcended it in spirit and mind, relegating our corporeal existence to a mere stepping stone to an ultimate afterlife. It was the Black Death, the devastating plague in the fourteenth century, which prompted such escapist thinking according to Berry. With the plague killing off nearly one-third of Europe's population in a short span of time, the human aspired "toward greater control of the physical world to escape its pain and to increase its utility to human society."[9] Such a deep estrangement from the world leaves it desacralized, making it easier to assert dominance over it; the world becomes an object or resource to be exploited and no longer a place to encounter a divine or numinous being. By the Enlightenment period, the human became the exalted spiritual being set apart and above a mechanistic other-than-human world. Berry concludes that we have created a dysfunctional cosmology in which the purpose of life and our existence is meaningless.

One could say that Berry primarily targets the pathological aversion against the human condition that has developed in western culture. He states, "There seems to be in the western psyche a deep hidden rage against the human condition, an unwillingness to accept life under the conditions that life granted us, a feeling of oppression by the normal human condition, a feeling that the pains of life and ultimately death are something that should not be, something that must be defeated."[10] It is not surprising, then, as Berry points out, that in recent centuries we have embraced a powerful myth of "wonderland" that denies our vulnerability while employing technology and science to snub entropy and magnify our own desires. He concludes, "So completely are we at odds with the planet that brought us into being that we have become strange beings indeed,"[11] adding with more force elsewhere: "We are the affliction of the world, its demonic presence."[12]

This last point requires an explanation. Berry is not assigning a demonic essence to human nature, but to the present human intent, which is part of a larger cultural paradigm. He recognizes that this assault we have perpetrated on the natural world has been carried out by good people, often for the best of purposes, such as the improvement of life for current generations. Moreover, much of this work has been performed within the ethical perspectives of our cultural traditions. He writes that while we all share a genetic coding with the natural world, an organic bond we have with the larger universe, we are "genetically coded toward a further transgenetic cultural coding whereby we invent ourselves in the human expression of our being."[13] The problem, then, is that our cultural coding, which is handed down by educational processes at both the familial and societal level, is no longer integrally related to our genetic coding. Our genetic coding, for Berry, is more comprehensive than our cultural coding: "It is integral with the whole complex of species codings whereby the earth system remains coherent within itself and capable of continuing the evolutionary process."[14] Yet our cultural coding has led us to deny or trivialize our cosmic or biotic imperatives, even though, ultimately, we cannot evade them. This is why, Berry concludes, for our species to remain viable we must go back to the genetic imperative from which human cultures emerge, reinventing a human culture that lives sustainably by returning to our pre-rational, instinctive, resources.

Because Berry targets the problem at the cultural level, our institutions – religious, educational, political, and economic – are themselves inadequate and cannot deal with our abuse of the natural world. The same applies to our ethics. Traditional religions as well as humanist ethics, then, are not equipped to effectively critique the devastation taking place. They know how to deal with suicide, homicide, and genocide, but they cannot deal with biocide or geocide. The problem speaks not simply to our ethics but to something deeper: our relationship with the planet, indeed the universe. In this light, Berry maintains that the problem is a spiritual one. As we saw with Boff, who maintains we are living amid a change of eras, it was Berry who first coined the idea that we are moving from the Cenozoic era, the period of biological development that has taken place during these past 65 million years, into either a Technozoic era, one defined by its increased exploitation of Earth as a resource, or into the Ecozoic era, "when humans would be present to the planet in a mutually enhancing manner."[15]

If the above, which describes our dysfunctional cosmology, is the problem, then a functional cosmology is in order. This entails reinventing the human, as he says, at the species level, which itself entails restoring the relationship between our cultural and genetic coding, so that we regain an intimacy with the planet. Such a future, he stresses, will only come about when humans understand the universe to be "composed of subjects to be communed with, not primarily as objects to be exploited."[16] In fact, although Berry does not employ the term liberation, I argue here that its ethos, as I have described earlier, is implied in part through his stress on treating all creation as subjects, and all that that term entails. That understanding will be realized primarily through the wisdom of science, which comes to us primarily in the form of a "New Story" of the universe, a cosmological narrative that provides us with a context in which life and our role on Earth can have meaning.

THE SCIENCE AUTHORING BERRY'S ETHICAL VISION

The scientists whose work Berry employs to help create a new story with a functional cosmology can fall broadly into three categories. First, those who deal with cosmology directly: mathematical cosmologist Brian Swimme and physicists Nigel Calder, Freeman Dyson, Paul Davies, David Bohm, and David Peat. I include here the work of paleontologist Teilhard de Chardin, who approaches cosmology from an evolutionary geology and biology point of view. There are those who deal with transdisciplinary theories such as systems theory and the Gaia theory: physicist Erich Jantsch, chemists Ilya Prigogine and James Lovelock, and biologist Lynn Margulis. Finally, those who deal with ecology: geneticist Theodosius Dobzhansky, microbiologist René Dubos, and biologists Paul Ehrlich, Anne Ehrlich, and Ursula Goodenough. I am including the works of biologists E.O. Wilson and Rachel Carson and forester Aldo Leopold in this latter category, although these three fit better under a fourth category of writers Berry borrows from: nature writers. These people, such as Loren Eiseley, Henry David Thoreau, and Wendell Berry, are not all scientists and their contributions are often used to determine the state of our environmental crisis. While Berry does single out some authors' work, delineating the exact influence of any of these authors is not always straightforward, as he tends to synthesize the findings of various writers and traditions; moreover, in much of his work, Berry does not incorporate footnotes or citations, but prefers to leave annotated bibliographies at the end of his books.

Berry depends most notably on Brian Swimme, with whom he co-authored *The Universe Story*, to help describe a comprehensive picture of the universe. Basing their findings on the cosmological principle that assumes the universe appears the same from all directions, they adapt Teilhard de Chardin's evolutionary perspective for understanding the universe as a cosmogenesis – a changing developing universe. Berry and Swimme take the cosmological principle one step further and assume that the form-producing dynamics of evolution are also the same at every place in the universe. With this in mind, and from what scientists have experienced and studied, they suggest that three principles or intensions govern the universe, which Berry and Swimme identify as differentiation, communion, and subjectivity. Only when we understand these three governing principles, they maintain, can we begin to understand the story of the universe.

Differentiation, also known as increasing diversity, complexity, or in biological terms as mutation, refers to the extraordinary variety and distinctiveness of everything in the universe. When the universe burst out in every direction some 13 billion years ago – as discussed with the work of Ruether – there was an expansive and differentiating force at work. This force embodied the pervasive insistence to create anew, which means no two things are completely alike. "To be," say Swimme and Berry, "is to be different."[17] Diversity in all its forms becomes important, for, "Were there no differentiation, the universe would collapse into homogeneous smudge."[18] The principle of communion immediately came into play when the universe began, as gravitation pulled the primordial particles together. Communion, also referred to as interrelatedness, interdependence, or kinship, and biologically as natural selection, is the ability to relate to other realities. Because of its relational underpinnings, communion receives much significance from Berry, who maintains that the universe is bonded. This bonding enabled the first atomic beings of hydrogen and helium to form. Within these first billions of years, galaxies also began to form – over 100 billion galaxies in all. This process continued and, because of communion, as Berry likes to say, the music of Beethoven also eventually came into being. Gravity, then, plays an important physical, if not poetic and, as I will show, an almost normative role, for, "without the gravitational attraction experienced throughout the physical world, there would be no emotional attraction of humans to one another."[19]

Additionally, as discussed with Ruether, Boff, and O'Murchu, with the principle of communion in mind, the universe can no longer be understood as being "out there," but as a mode of being of everything: all within it are intimately related to all else.[20] In this way, Berry views anthropocentrism largely as a result of our failure to think of ourselves as a species among other species: without a sense of communion, we see ourselves as "an addendum or intrusion" and, eventually, as a superior intrusion.[21] Finally, since all living beings, including humans, emerge out of this single community, Berry maintains in the Teilhardian sense – as I discussed with Ruether – that there must have been a consciousness component of the universe even in primitive form from the beginning. Consciousness here refers to the interior numinous component that Berry posits is present in all reality, which is the basis of subjectivity, also known as autopoiesis, self-organization, self-articulation, biologically as niche creation, and also, as Teilhard de Chardin referred to it, as complexification. The universe is filled with structures that exhibit self-organizing dynamics, a power or spontaneity that each thing has to participate directly in cosmogenesis, much as I discussed when reviewing the works of Prigogine and Jantsch in the chapters on Boff and O'Murchu. While Prigogine and Jantsch employed autopoiesis more in terms of self-preservation, certainly Jantsch does not exclude the idea of a primitive consciousness at play even in the pre-living world. Jantsch writes, "An *autopoietic* system is characterized by a certain autonomy *vis-à-vis* the environment which may be understood as a primitive form of the consciousness corresponding to the level of existence of the system."[22]

With these three principles in mind, it becomes clear how the Gaia theory, as put forth by Lovelock and Margulis – approached both in its mythic and mathematical-scientific form – fits appositely into the story of the universe. Berry maintains that Gaia provides a larger pattern of interpretation for understanding the self-organizational processes or subjectivity of our planet as well as the primordial expression of communion. It helps us understand "the dynamics of the earth as self-emerging, self-sustaining, self-educating, self-governing, self-healing, and self-fulfilling community of all the living and nonliving beings of the planet."[23] To understand what Berry means by this, consider what he says: "Nothing bestows existence on itself. Nothing survives by itself. Nothing is fulfilled in itself. Nothing has existence or meaning or fulfillment except in union with the larger community of existence."[24] In this light, not even Gaia is truly self-emerging or self-sustaining, only the universe is. In fact, to be truly comprehensive, Gaia must be understood within the larger universal context, explaining that this allows us to see Earth as commanding a special role of revelation.

For Berry, it is not just a matter that these principles organize not only Earth but the entire ever-evolving universe, or cosmogenesis to be more precise. It is the manner in which they do this that matters too. Taking his cue from geneticist Theodosius Dobzhansky, Berry maintains that these three principles continue to work together in the evolutionary process in neither a random nor a determined manner. In fact, Berry prefers the word creative. Thus, just as the early single cells, prokaryotes, mutated, showing novel depths of differentiation by eating the wastes and decay of other single-celled organisms, thereby "side-stepp[ing] disaster,"[25] so too did a constant creative differentiation among the human species bring forth different languages and religions, each with its own inner articulations. These three principles, then – understood within the broader context of the story of the universe – serve as the foundation of human ethics for Berry. Writing on this subject, Mary Evelyn Tucker suggests they serve as the basis for a more comprehensive ecological and social ethics where the human is dependent and intertwined with the Earth community. In fact, Berry's whole Universe Story, as she maintains, helps us to nurture "reciprocity between humans" and foster "reverence between humans and earth."[26]

Nurturing reciprocity and fostering reverence appropriately capture much of what Berry's ethical vision aims to do, as the Universe Story is meant to become our sacred story. The wonders that science brings forth to us through this story, and indeed the sheer awe of watching a sunset, serve to help us value the natural world. The assumption is that when we change our worldview to see the beauty and understand how we are interrelated with everything in the universe, our ethics likewise will be transformed. Some specific imperatives come out of this view. For instance, given that we are part of a single evolutionary process embedded within a larger Earth community, an important ethical criterion for Berry is that our human ethics be derived from the ecological imperative. In this way, human technology must integrate within the technology and principles of the natural world: the human economy must subsume itself under the Earth economy, and our democracy must yield to biocracy. "To advance the human economy," we learn, "by subverting the earth economy is an obvious absurdity ... there exists a governance too subtle for us to understand."[27] When it comes to dealing with specific other-than-human beings in the world, then, their subjectivity bestows them rights. Thus, rivers, plants, and birds all have rights. These rights, which I will discuss later in this chapter, are inherent and must be respected by humans. In this manner, Berry would say a river has a right to flow, but because the value of the river is determined in relation to the larger biotic community (communion), its waters must also circulate throughout the planet so that they can benefit other life-forms on the planet.

Ascertaining specific human rights within the framework of the three principles of the universe is not well defined in Berry's writings. However, with the concept of reciprocity in mind, and taking the example of a river's right to flow, above, it is not difficult to ascertain how the human might use its waters, whether for farming or energy. A brief illustration of the evolution of two animals, as given by Berry and Swimme, will show how this process of reciprocity might operate. The bison created its niche by butting heads for self-protection whereas the horse, which shared the same environment, chose to gallop. Why? Berry and Swimme say it was their self-articulations or evolutionary choices that made them that way. But at the same time, these animals were made within the context of their broader community of beings, or bioregion. In a biological sense, these animals did not enter into a fixed rigid external environment. Berry and Swimme conclude that the animals evolved within their relationship with its larger environment. A self-organizing dynamics is at play, explained earlier with Boff as autopoiesis. In another sense, the community said to the horse that "you may be a galloping energy," and to the bison that "you may be a ramming energy, but only if you include all of us and all of our concerns and realities in your life project."[28] Such a view of subjectivity, rights, and self-articulations denote the type of liberation I outlined earlier. The subject is participating as an agent in its own freedom to follow evolutionary impulses, yet the subject negotiates that freedom among the larger community.

In this manner, just as O'Murchu states that the rights of every "part" can be promoted only within the relational context from which it emerges, Berry is saying that if any animal, human or other-than-human, enters into a community, it must "pay attention" to the community and remain attentive to the needs of each member of the community. Returning to my example of the river, then, one can surmise from this illustration that if we are seeking access to the water from the river, we must listen – in a quasi-Leopoldian fashion – as just plain members and citizens of a larger biotic community, to the negotiations taking place between the river and the whole biotic community. Evident in the bison and horse illustration above, then, is a theme that runs through Berry's writings: microphase concerns (the individual's existence) need to give way to macrophase concerns (the communal larger existence). Here, he places the most value on the total community and not on any single mode of being.

A prominent motif underscoring Berry's ethical vision – one evident in the ethical visions of all our Christian thinkers, most notably that of O'Murchu – is the inescapable and necessary interconnection between destruction and creativity, between the basic ordering process (such as gravitation – "the primary discipline in the large-scale structure of the universe")[29] and disorder (such as the flaring forth after the big bang – the "wild, senseless deed that wells up from some infinite abyss in the expansive differentiating process of those first moments when all the energy that would ever exist flared forth in a radiation").[30] For the universe to exist there cannot be one without the other, the wild without the discipline, creativity without destruction. There is an inescapable cost to creativity, and conversely, many of the adaptations within the natural world are the result of beings meeting the limitations of the universe with creative responses. In *The Universe Story*, the science behind this conclusion is supported by Wolfgang Pauli and his Exclusion Principle – which states that no two particles can occupy the same quantum state (that is, no two electrons in an atom can be in the same state or configuration at the same time) – and the second law of thermodynamics – which states that useful energy deteriorates into waste or entropy over time.[31] By including with this the notion of autopoiesis – the tendency of all things to fulfill their nature or potential – Berry and Swimme present an account of violence and destruction as being fundamental to reality. Moreover, they state that destruction and creativity exist in "creative disequilibrium."[32]

Recall in discussing systems theory in the chapter on Boff that any system closed off from new energy will eventually decline and suffer entropy. Whether an ecosystem, civilization, or a single pair of aphids, each requires an influx of energy to sustain itself. But that energy, which is constant in the universe (the first law of thermodynamics) must come from somewhere; hence, there is an energy payment (a cost) to maintaining creativity. Berry and Swimme give the example of a single pair of aphids. If their desires were fully satisfied, after only one year they would generate over half a trillion offspring. Yet, this does not happen because their desires are held in what Berry and Swimme label a "fecund balance of tensions."[33] Such a creative disequilibrium means that constraints on creativity are fundamental: "Potentially infinite desire finds itself within a woven fabric of finite energy. This condition holds at every level of reality. The mollusk in the sand of the ocean, the bacteria in the rotting redwood tree in the forest, the tornado in the wind currents of the summer drought, the black hole in the center of the galaxy – each exists with demands in a world tight with constraints on the very energies necessary to satisfy these demands."[34] In short, the universe functions with imposed limitations: a star could not come into being without ever meeting resistance. And destruction is an inescapable part of creativity: our entire solar system could not have come into existence without the destruction of a supernova. The corresponding message here is clear. Despite understanding this reality, we humans, with our reflexive mode of being, have denied inherent hardships by avoiding the intrinsic costs involved in creativity, while simultaneously magnifying the intensity of our desires. For example, consider how economists posit endless growth while simultaneously seemingly ignoring the consequent impoverishment of the planet and its biosystems.

The ethical dimensions of this are apparent. Berry is speaking of sacrifice. Such a notion is embedded within reciprocity itself: if there is taking, then there must be giving. This is not some pursuit of pain for its own sake, however, which Berry together with Swimme rightly dismisses as pathological. It is, rather, a type of surrender of one's well-being for the sake of others, akin to the effort of a shaman who might sacrifice his or her security to assist in the empowerment of others. Linking an intuitive understanding of this scientific-based lesson, Berry and Swimme write, "The primal human insistence upon sacrifice can be understood as an early intuitive grasp of the essential truth in the second law of thermodynamics."[35] To refuse our inherent vulnerability in what Berry assigns as legitimate suffering "is to opt for a reduced existence."[36] Of course, such thinking returns us to Berry's contention that we must deal with this hidden rage against the human condition that is finite and limited. This rage not only is self-defeating but thwarts creativity, since, as I discussed earlier with Prigogine's theory of dissipative structures, creativity emerges out of tension.

AN ANALYSIS OF BERRY'S ETHICAL VISION

Berry assigns a pre-eminent position to the wisdom of science in creating his ethical vision. Science, he maintains, provides the epic evolution story toward the future. In fact, he holds, "We cannot resolve the difficulties we face in this new situation by setting aside the scientific venture. … If interpreted properly, it could even be one of the most significant spiritual disciplines of these times."[37] While Berry's New Story is primarily descriptive, Anne Marie Dalton explains how he interconnects story with myth, dream, and cosmology to serve as a "meaning-giver and driver of action."[38] The discoveries of science, Dalton suggests, serve as the primary authoritative voice to support the integral relationship of the human to the natural world. Hence, the story is telling us of concrete events in time, while also expressing a numinous quality of the universe to which the psyche of humankind has been attuned for ages, manifesting itself in the traditional myths. To be sure, the new intimacy humans are to discover with the universe means we must embrace both its creative side and its darker side of destruction. While Berry does not say, as O'Murchu does, that we must befriend the dark, he nevertheless believes we should accept it. Thus, found within his ethical vision – much like with Ruether, Boff, and O'Murchu – is a hermeneutic on how we are to approach the world. Moreover, within the New Story, with its governing principles, there are indications of what our human role might be: with our self-reflective consciousness, we are the universe reflecting on itself, enjoying and celebrating its grandeur and its mysteries, both the dark and creative. Our role is to tell this story and to let its norms imbue our way of living.

As I have done with the other three Christian thinkers, I want to consider whether Berry has avoided even a weak anthropocentrism.

Berry, like Boff and O'Murchu, certainly steers away from using "levels" to distinguish intelligences between the human and the other-than-human animal. Berry prefers to speak of qualitative differences and not quantitative differences, whereby concepts of higher or lower intelligence are rejected in favour of modality of functioning. Thus, he can say: "So in the world of the honey bee, the peregrine falcon, the rainbow trout, the dolphin, and the human – in each case the intelligence is appropriate to its function; each is perfect in its own order."[39] This would seem to eschew even a weak notion of anthropocentrism. Yet, as Stephen Bede Scharper points out, Berry's notion that we are the "self-consciousness of the universe" nevertheless keeps the human at the centre of all thought, as it is we who are making sense out of reality.[40] Does this assign a weak anthropocentric character to Berry's ethical vision? Recall that I described weak anthropocentrism to be a view that reality can *only* be interpreted from a human point of view, thereby still according some centrality to the human. Berry, however, does not claim that such interpretation can come *only* from the human: self-consciousness is qualitatively, not quantitatively, different from other means of knowing. If there is any claim to anthropocentrism in Berry's ethical vision, then, as it is with O'Murchu, it would have to be of a very weak kind.

Again, as I have shown with Ruether, Boff, and O'Murchu, while much of Berry's ethical vision comes in the forms of norms and models and not as a precise system of actions or oughts, one can nevertheless gather from Berry's vision some specific imperatives; for example, the principle of differentiation tells us that our modern world's increasing employment of monocultures and standardized industry is misguided, and, as discussed above, the human economy must subsume itself under the Earth economy, and our democracy must yield to biocracy. Not surprisingly, in the same manner of our other interlocutors, bioregionalism is offered as a viable model for nurturing reciprocity and fostering reverence for all life. Berry, however, devotes far more energy to explaining its import and function within the broader planetary framework. A bioregion for Berry is an identifiable geographical area of interacting life systems that is, for the most part, self-sustaining. But he underlines that bioregions are the quintessential communities that, as seen earlier in regard to Gaia, are self-sustaining, self-educating, self-governing, self-healing, and self-fulfilling. Berry's vision, therefore, places the onus on changing the human and all our cultural institutions to suit Earth and its processes, not the other way around. For this reason, our cultural coding must integrate with its organic base. With this premise, is Berry suggesting a return to the romantic concept of some kind of primitive paradisiacal existence? This is unlikely; Berry emphasizes that we should not over-romanticize primitivism. He applauds technology, as long as it is appropriate and respects Earth.

Where Berry's ethical vision does lack clear guidelines is on human-to-human social interactions. Indeed, as Dalton aptly points out, Berry demonstrates an impatience with our preoccupations with human concerns about the social problems of the human community to the exclusion of problems in the natural world. Dalton is not alone in her observation. Scharper puts the human-to-human issue into perspective with the Catholic principle of the preferential option for the poor.[41] He asks, for example, how is it that the poor, the marginalized subjects in the universe, can receive no preference? As we saw above, the second law states that each development has a cost. Scharper asks, then, whether this means a multinational corporation is justified in cutting down forests to serve its development needs. Does the principle of creative disequilibrium, this knife's edge on which we live, mean that we should value the poor being caught between the wildness of free markets and the discipline of social economics? The above questions point out how, without a political economy approach or certainly a principle like the preferential option for the poor, someone could appropriate the story to his or her advantage. While seemingly adhering to the ethic of self-limiting as implied by Berry and Swimme, they could be simultaneously exploiting the vulnerable. In short, the New Story, as comprehensive as it may be, cannot stand alone.

In a similar vein, Heather Eaton speaks of the "ambiguous dialectic" that exists between the micro and the macro ethical perspectives implied in this New Story.[42] Using the example of a sinking ship – the *Titanic*, in fact – Berry suggests we have appreciation for the daily concerns of the ship – its micro concerns, which include the welfare of individuals – in conjunction with the immediate concerns of saving the ship, the macro dimension. In this way, "our concerns for the human community can only be fulfilled by a concern for the integrity of the natural world."[43] Unfortunately, the human community has never had to consider such ethical demands on this grand scale before. This is why Berry contends that we have developed ethical responses to homicide, suicide, and even genocide, but not for geocide or biocide. Eaton feels, however, that Berry places greater concern upon the macro rather than the micro ethical dimensions. Indeed, Berry says, "Our human ethics are derivative from the ecological imperative."[44] Much in keeping with Scharper's caution, then, Eaton looks at how this approach could be interpreted by others and points out, "One can experience great pleasure in rethinking the cosmological horizon, and avoid addressing the urgent, difficult and entangled problems as seen from the ground." Poignantly, Eaton – returning to the Indigenous woman walking far and long for water who I introduced in chapter 3 – underlines that, "Obviously it is not those who are walking for days for water who are researching cosmological questions."[45]

To look for such a promotion of a preferential option for the poor human in Berry's writings, I suggest, is misguided. From his early life, Berry, having developed a keen sensitivity to Earth and all its subjects, was focused on that which will preserve and enhance the "meadow." But does this mean Berry ignores the plight of those most vulnerable? No. Dalton points out that in certain sections of his writings, Berry nevertheless reflects "a sensitivity to the plight of poor nations" and "a pathology that leads the Western world to think it is helping the poor while it devastates their natural environments."[46] Certainly when Berry says we ought to pay attention to the community and remain attentive to the needs of each member of the community, as discussed earlier with the story of the horse and bison, he is underlining how individuals and a community ought to behave if they are to "stay" in a larger community. While this illustration primarily explains niche creation, mutation, and natural selection in *The Universe Story*, it is not difficult to see the illustration as an indictment of the human species. Mary Evelyn Tucker and John Grim affirm this argument. They attest that Berry held immense feelings for the suffering that occurs in life. In his earlier life, Berry would make visits to meet Dorothy Day and Peter Maurin at the *Catholic Worker* in New York. Tucker and Grim point out this to demonstrate his "firm support" of social justice issues.

They also note that in their discussions with Berry over the many years they worked with him, "he would often comment on the suffering the environmental crisis is inflicting on these most vulnerable," citing how the 1978 experience of the toxicity level of Love Canal near Buffalo, New York, raised his understanding of how disproportionately the poor bear the burden of environmental destruction.[47] In his essay entitled "Economics as a Religious Issue," Berry points out that a moral-religious critique of the capitalist market system demonstrates its limits with regard to social justice. He underlines that we must have a special concern for the well-being of the society shared by all, "especially that the basic life necessities be available to the less privileged."[48] It seems apposite, then, to assign a certain level of concern within Berry's larger macro vision for the plight of those most vulnerable.

To be sure, then, Berry does not employ a political economy approach to his work. His forte lies in demonstrating the macro imperative: "A degraded habitat will produce degraded humans. An enhanced habitat supports an elevated mode of the human."[49] Nevertheless, it is also apparent that he recognizes that in any deliberations on economics, justice to those marginalized must not be overlooked. As I will discuss presently in the following section, Berry's epistemology and methodology ensure that the wisdoms from liberationist thinking are an integral and integrated part of a larger ethical vision.

THE EPISTEMOLOGY AND METHODOLOGY BACKING BERRY'S ETHICAL VISION

At the core of his epistemology, Berry conceives a universe that is knowable. And in the process of knowing something, Berry contends, there is a communication occurring between subjects, between the person who wants to know a being and that being itself. In keeping with his emphasis on relationality, he states, "Everything tells the story of the universe. The winds tell the story, literally, not just imaginatively."[50] Hence, on one epistemological level, he affirms that the mathematically formulated designs of scientists do refer to something ultimately real, implying that there is a definite interaction between reality and the knower. Nevertheless, on another epistemological level, Berry maintains that we can never know parts of the universe separate from the whole any more than we can understand the theme of a musical piece by listening to a musical phrase without the earlier notes. It is not just the whole but the mysteries within the whole that concern Berry. With the rational-empirical approach alone, he contends, we are often unable to feel or understand the mysteries of the Earth. These mysteries, he says, overwhelm us and cannot be expressed in human words: "People generally experience an awesome, stupendous presence that cannot be expressed adequately in human words. Since it cannot be expressed in language, people often dance this experience, they express it in music, in art, in the pervasive of the beautiful throughout the whole of daily life, in the laughter of children, in the taste of bread, in the sweetness of an apple. At every moment we are experiencing the overwhelming mystery of existence. It is that simple but that ineffable."[51]

The communication occurring between subjects, then, occurs not only at the verbal level but at the intuitive, aesthetic, and affective level as well. We are moved in the depths of our being by both terrifying storms and serene evenings. Whether as an aesthetic or painful experience, "The entire range of our poetry, music, and art resonate with the deep mysteries of existence experienced in the world about us."[52] It is important to note what Berry is saying here. It is not just that we *cannot* know the world fully through science. Science, he maintains, is inadequate in certain aspects of understanding and, therefore, *ought* not be the only way of knowing the world. The main epistemological issue for Berry is that our scientific preoccupations have left us with a diminished sensitivity to the natural world. He is often quoted as saying, "We have forgotten our primordial capacity for language at the elementary level of song and dance, wherein we share our existence with the animals and with all natural phenomena."[53] So while the story that we receive from the universe is "awakening in the depth of human psychic awareness a sense of ultimate mystery and how ultimate mystery communicates itself,"[54] we are having difficulties in hearing and listening to it. Other wisdoms, however, have not forgotten the "languages" that Berry maintains we need to listen to and hear what is, ostensibly, for him, revelation. This is why Berry proposes that humans integrate a four-fold wisdom into their ways of knowing the world: the wisdoms of women, the Indigenous, and of the many ancient traditions, along with the wisdom of science.[55] While no single wisdom, given its limitations and distortions, is sufficient to address the needs of our times, each enriches the other. But it is primarily Indigenous wisdoms that Berry invokes to help us regain our primordial capacity for a different way of communicating, "language at the elementary level of song and dance," so as to hear and understand the rivers, trees, and birds.

It is also important to note that while these wisdoms all enrich one another, Berry is not saying that the intuitive, aesthetic, and affective ways of knowing – certainly endemic to the wisdoms of women, Indigenous, and ancient traditions – pertain to these wisdoms alone, restricting the wisdom of science to the rational-empirical method. For Berry these epistemologies work as an integrated whole and, therefore, apply to all wisdoms. This means, of course, he maintains, that the driving forces behind the scientific effort are nonscientific. He says, "The excessive analytical phase of science is over. A countermovement toward integration and interior subjective processes is taking place within a more comprehensive vision of the entire universe."[56] To help us understand this integration, Berry speaks of a visionary experience, not unlike that which a shaman would experience, one that imbues the scientific process: "It can hardly be repeated often enough that the driving force of the scientific effort is nonscientific ... a far-reaching transforming vision is sought that is not far from the spiritual vision sought by the ancient tribal cultures, as well as by the great traditional civilizations of the past."[57] This is why Berry can claim that science is ultimately mythic in nature. The scientific endeavour is both impelled by myths and – especially when recounted as the Universe Story – serves as the progenitor of a new mythic structure that can help redirect human attitudes and actions to more congenial ways of being. It is for this reason that Berry can conclude that it is *within* and not from outside the scientific tradition that humans can find a new intimacy with the universe, replete with poetic and metaphoric expressions.

This seemingly trans-rational–empirical epistemology that Berry assigns to the wisdom of science can also be looked upon as a belief component. He points, for instance, to physicist Wolfgang Pauli, who attributed his discoveries to "archetypal dream experiences," and to Isaac Newton, who explored the mysteries of things through alchemy.[58] The importance of dream – which he sees as the awakening in us of a sense of ultimate mystery and how that ultimate mystery communicates itself – becomes key to Berry's entire epistemological framework. The term "dream" is used by Berry as both the psychic processes that take place when we are physically asleep and the "way of indicating an intuitive, nonrational process that occurs when we awaken to the numinous powers ever present in the phenomenal world about us, powers that possess us in our high creative moments."[59] Dream is, of course, the same power that poets and artists invoke. Berry sees the dream inspiring our future actions.

This does not imply that science is all subjective for Berry, but he insists that it must be looked upon as both a cultural and spiritual activity. "Every scientific formula is as much myth and mystery as it is rational understanding," he states, asking, "What is it that unifies the formula? The formula is nothing without its interpretation, so the understanding is not in the formula. (No formula is self-interpreting.) Scientists think it is there because they can make the equation work. I am not exactly arguing that the rational scientific process is a dream process, but it functions in the context of an even deeper mystery that many scientists are beginning to recognize. Our science does not reduce the mystery, it enhances the mystery."[60] In this light, Berry is placing science as a new type of religious experience, not quite the same as the experience of the early shamanic period of human history, but not too far from it either.

In short, Berry is describing a more unified way of knowing and hence, a new way of entering into a conversation with the world and certainly between religion and science; while we need the story, we also need the dream, which drives our action. In fact, the unity of the entire complex of galactic systems is among the most basic experience of contemporary physics. Although this comprehensive unity of the universe was perceived by primitive peoples, affirmed by great civilizations, explained in creation myths the world over, outlined by Plato in his *Timaeus,* and given extensive presentation by Newton in his *Principia,* nowhere was the full genetic relatedness of the universe presented with such clarity as by the scientists of the twentieth century.[61] The outcome of this unification cannot be overlooked. While Berry can assign a pre-eminent position to the wisdom of science in moving from democracy to biocracy, underlining that we cannot resolve our problems without science, the epistemological boundaries between science and religion are no longer distinct. This is why we find Berry – not unlike Ruether – invoking the way of the poet or artist with reference to his appropriation of science, "a renewed presence to some numinous presence manifested in the wonderworld about us."[62]

With this multidimensional epistemology, keeping in mind its emphasis on a dream process, it might seem that Berry espouses some form of idealism as a way of understanding truth-claims in science, religion, and other wisdoms. But this is not the case. While he does draw from the romantics and transcendentalists, as Anne Marie Dalton points out, Berry also criticizes Teilhard de Chardin for over-stressing spirit at the expense of the concrete universe itself. Dalton suggests, fittingly, in my estimation, that Berry follows more of a critical realist approach, asserting that we comprehend the truth as a result of experiencing, understanding, and judging. We can see this clearly in his collaborative venture with mathematical cosmologist Brian Swimme, where a more nuanced approach to objectivity is put forward, one that seeks to avoid bias values, give even-handed representation of the situation, and is open to debate.

With this multidimensional critical realist epistemology in mind, how does Berry justify truths? In *The Great Work*, as I discussed above, he speaks of his meadow experience in his youth as being normative for him, an experience he returns to throughout much of his thinking. Returning to the passage discussed earlier, where "Whatever preserves and enhances this meadow in the natural cycles of its transformation is good; whatever opposes this meadow or negates it is not good," Berry's orientation to truth becomes clear about the criterion for truth. Implicitly, then, Berry employs the three principles or intensions governing the universe to serve as the means for arriving at truth, which, in the way I have framed Berry's work, is liberation. In referring to the meadow, Berry suggests that we can judge the veracity of these principles for the meadow when this land, as an evolving biosystem, receives the opportunity to be itself and to express its own inner qualities. In this regard, much as I have shown with our other theorists, there is a liberationist and pragmatic bent to Berry's criteria.

With Berry's epistemological framework in hand, it becomes possible to understand how he envisions the necessary and challenging dialogue between religion and science to occur through his concept of bioregionalism. Berry refers to the "voices" one hears in the winds over the Hudson River Valley – voices that tell us of the distorted relationship we have with the land and its inhabitants. In what manner do the voices of these winds converse with the voices of scientists who tell us that our chemicals might be forcing the soil to produce beyond its natural rhythms? To answer these questions, it will be helpful first to understand more clearly what Berry means when he says we ought to pursue the way of the poet or artist in our appropriation of science. He maintains that the task of bringing together the four-fold wisdoms, with their perspectives and epistemologies, into conversation goes to the "integral ecologist." He describes such a person as the new spiritual guide for our times, one who is ecologically sensitive, a spokesperson or normative guide for the planet, a St Francis to the Pietro Bernadones of our time, and a person "who would understand the numinous aspect of a universe emergent from the beginning."[63] The integral ecologist provides leadership beyond what we can get from the traditional prophet, priest, yogi, monk, philosopher of the past and present, and certainly beyond any leadership that comes from the corporate leaders, engineers, and scientists who are the new guides of our era.

While the manner in which the integral ecologist might pursue a dialogue is not specifically laid out by Berry, Stephen Bede Scharper provides an overall framework for understanding Berry's approach, which he describes aptly as "listening." The approach involves, as it declares, listening and paying attention to nature. The bison-horse-grasslands example Berry gives to demonstrate how his three principles work is a good illustration of subjects listening to one another. If any subject, be it plant, animal, or human, enters into a community, it must "pay attention" to the community and remain attentive to the needs – and here I would add liberation – of each member of the community. There can be no reciprocity, mutuality, or exchange without the subjects involved first and foremost in listening to one another. And given Berry's epistemology, our listening may come in many forms or languages: through dance, song, poetry, and intuition, by the use of our ears, eyes, with or without scientific equipment.

In this way, it becomes clear how a biologist might tell us about the life systems and carrying capacity of bioregions, and the effects of human development on the bison, the horses, the waters, the air, and indeed all species. Berry finds that increasingly scientists are embracing a larger epistemological paradigm and beginning to experience a personal rapport with the Earth in their work. This explains why we see biologists like Dian Fossey and Jane Goodall giving names to the gorillas and chimpanzees they study. This is happening not through some analytic process, but through absorbing their experiences with the natural world into their very being. In other words, our biologist is listening not solely to what her instruments are telling her, but to what she is being told through a deeper and more corporeal level. At the same time, much like Dian Fossey and Jane Goodall, a biologist also listens to the Indigenous peoples, who arguably have not altogether lost the capacity of the mythic, imaginative dream experience; they perceive a numinous presence within that same bioregion and thereby recognize that each aspect of creation has its own inner life or subjectivity. I do not wish to suggest a romantic view of Indigenous peoples, and I do not believe Berry does either. However, it is not overstating the truth to suggest that an Andean Indigenous *campesino* would more likely see the mountain that towers over his village as being an *apu*, a mountain spirit that protects his peoples, while a businessperson from the global North might look at that same mountain and see it as a resource for copper.

Expanding the conversation to include economists, this person might learn how a market system within a bioregion ought to operate. By listening, the economist learns how even in the natural world, there is a constant interchange of values. There is the accumulation of capital and a search for more economical ways of doing things. And while Berry does not explicitly address the plight of the woman walking long and far for water, as I have discussed previously, he does explicitly incorporate the wisdom of women into the conversation; such wisdom, he maintains, "join[s] the knowing of the body to that of mind, to join soul to spirit, intuition to reasoning, feeling consciousness to intellectual analysis, intimacy to detachment, subjective presence to objective distance."[64] In this light, it is fair to assume that there would be a strong call within the larger conversation for a preference to be assigned to this woman's voice. As mentioned with Ruether, in assigning such a preference, we would direct our energies toward correcting the "destructive option for the rich" within the parameters of maintaining the "well-being of the whole community of life."

Finally, given that Berry's framework has us listening to (and presumably understanding) what the river and trees are telling us, it is important to mention his method for reconciling the inevitable clash of the rights of a river to flow free and fresh, with the rights to water and housing for our Guatemalan Indigenous woman carrying water and indeed her whole human community. To do this, Berry suggests we think analogically. He contends, as I mentioned earlier, that each being has rights according to its mode of being in the world. When we normally speak of the "rights" of a human and the rights of the other-than-human, we have trouble assessing the two because of their apparent differences, and too often end with human rights trumping the rights of the other-than-human. However, if we employ the term "rights" as an analogous term, we see similarities and differences. In this way, we can say "a river has rights." The river, however, does not have human rights because human rights would be no good for a river; the river needs river rights, such as the right to flow. How we can actually know what rights a river ought to receive is a deeper issue, one to which I will return in the following chapter.

CONCLUSION

A simple meadow in North Carolina formed early within Thomas Berry a deep reverence for Earth, a love that would later embrace the entire cosmos. The universe is not solely a subject of reverence. The story of the universe, deeply informed by science, influences how Berry, and the other three interlocutors, understands liberation: it broadly entails following the larger evolutionary impulses, described by Berry as three principles: subjectivity, differentiation, and communion. These form the basis for Berry's ethical vision, as does the need to embrace our anthropological vulnerability.

As with our other theorists, relationality lies at the core of Berry's ethical vision. As Ruether states, relationality invites us to stand back and consider how all subjects interconnect and cooperate rather than simply compete with each other. Even the act of liberation itself defers to the larger context of relationality, as one's own liberation is inextricably tied to the liberation of all subjects. Berry's writing is helpful in this regard, as it introduces a process of negotiation to reconcile desires and needs. This tethered liberation – as I will discuss in more detail in chapter 5 – is in keeping with Berry's larger ethical vision, since, for him, as well as for O'Murchu, Boff, and Ruether, the larger context of relationality speaks to the "holarchy" of the community – one where relationship is the core dynamic whereby no subject is considered in isolation from the whole, and a mutuality of responsibility (among humans) is required if the liberation of all subjects is to be realized. All our thinkers, then, give pre-eminence not so much to rational argumentation, but to a vast and communal discussion and negotiation through a democratic conversation for arriving at truths. The conversation among subjects within a community includes a plurality of voices encompassing their past, present, and future, myriad points of view, and multiple ways of knowing the world. In fact, we see evidence of a blurring of the traditional epistemological boundaries between religion and science.

There is evidence within the writings of all four of the Christian thinkers that each has embarked upon a self-reflective process that denies any claim to seeing or understanding things from "God's perspective." There appears a certain humility within their approaches, which accounts for the concern they place on listening, forming a conversation, and learning from the other subjects in the cosmos. Ruether and Boff are the most emphatic that that "other" be our *campesina* who is excluded from participating in her own history. At the same time, Berry, and to an extent O'Murchu, are emphatic that we not overlook the ecological necessities that impinge upon the *campesina*'s anthropological condition. The conversation I weave among these four thinkers on these concerns begins in chapter 5.

PART TWO

WEAVING A COMMUNAL CONVERSATION

The investigation in part 1 makes it possible in the subsequent chapters to investigate the larger epistemological dialogue that these theorists are pursuing collectively, and to address one of the underlying concerns of this work: whether these authors have taken seriously the four spheres of concern, and whether they have integrated them into a coherent ethical vision. It should be clear to the reader by now that it is indeed possible to pursue the works of these four Christian thinkers as one communal conversation.

What accounts for the many similarities among these four thinkers that allows for a fruitful conversation? I have discussed some points: each author is aware of the others' writings and, in many instances – especially with regard to the work of Thomas Berry – each author borrows from the others' thinking. While Berry is presented last in this series of examinations, it is his work, in many ways, that imbues the thinking of the first three interlocutors. Moreover, in many instances, albeit to varying degrees, all four employ the works of the same scientists, including Teilhard de Chardin. There is much at play here, including the Catholic faith they share. Aspects of these commonalities will be discussed in more detail in the chapters to come.

Emphasizing the merits of pursuing such a communal conversation, however, does not mean that I ignore those differences among their collective ethical visions, or overlook points where their arguments come across as weak. In regard to their individual ethical visions, it is true, for instance, that Ruether and Boff have divergent views on the value of population growth. Ruether eschews the universal propensities of Boff's epistemology. Ruether, Boff, and O'Murchu all take a process view to our evolving ethics, while Berry, taking a more substantive and providential view, finds that the three basic principles governing the universe were present from the beginning. I have discussed Berry's underdeveloped socio-political framework and have raised flags on the cogency of some of O'Murchu's claims, such as his belief and seeming enthusiasm for "people's wisdom outpacing institutional knowledge," and the creation of the "transhuman." However, these differences, I contend, are either a matter of degree rather than essence, or the problems they raise with respect to their larger communal vision are minimal.

Chapter 5 begins the second part of my book where I evaluate their approach to, and how they integrate, two spheres of concern: the environment and liberation. In chapter 6, I investigate how seriously these authors take other spheres of concern, and in chapter 7, how seriously they take their faith and how they integrate it into the four-fold nexus. Reading these three chapters, the reader will notice how they correspondingly speak, in broad strokes, to the three questions I posed at the beginning of this book. These are questions that the four thinkers collectively pose to their Christian faith:

1 How might we conceive the liberation of the human and the other-than-human when the future of life on the planet is at risk due to anthropogenic causes?
2 How and in what form might science and Christianity enter into a serious and sustained conversation to help effect the liberation of all creation?
3 What challenges and opportunities does the above conversation present for the Christian tradition?

This examination culminates with chapter 8, where I elucidate and evaluate convergent knowing, the epistemological framework that undergirds this entire work. Given the struggle Christian thinkers have been experiencing in trying to reconcile the four-fold nexus, in what ways might convergent knowing foster hope for a much-needed and fruitful conversation between Christianity and science?

CHAPTER FIVE

Toward a Serious and Sustained Reflection on the Liberation of All Creation

How have the four authors examined in this book dealt with the environmental and liberation issues of our time? Recall that to determine whether Christian thinkers are taking these spheres of concern seriously, I determined that it is necessary to examine the degree to which they have applied critical attention, thoughtfulness, and constructive resolve to each sphere. This is one aspect examined in this chapter. Have they also taken the integration of the environmental and liberation issues of our time seriously? I decided that there ought to be some evidence that these four theorists have allowed the dynamics and concerns surrounding the issues of environmental degradation and the marginalization of the majority of humankind to inform and qualify as well as clarify and affirm each other. This is the other aspect this chapter examines.

While these criteria are certainly useful for overall guidance, since it is specifically the spheres of the environment and liberation I am evaluating in this chapter, they are nevertheless too general to arrive at effective conclusions. To make these criteria more germane to my query, I suggest the following adaptation: does their attention focus on the entire creation as well as the current logic of domination that marginalizes both the human and the other-than-human? Is there within their ethical visions evidence of a thorough and thoughtful examination of what is required to unite a liberationist agenda with an environmental ethic, as well as a commitment to see this occur? Apart from critically examining their approach to and integration of these two spheres, the ultimate test of whether these four Christian thinkers have taken the liberation of all of creation seriously, I suggest, will rest on the feasibility of their ethical vision. Put another way, I will have to ascertain whether their ethical vision can "fly," so to speak. While I do contend that in the course of approaching these two spheres and their integration, the four Christian thinkers do so with much thoughtfulness and care, I do not conclude this without a qualification. It is when I bring all four interlocutors into a communal conversation, one in large measure realized by them and in part critically elaborated by me – allowing each of their visions not only to clarify and affirm but to qualify and inform the visions of the others – that a more robust ethical vision ensues. Such a vision addresses the challenges and/or weaknesses found within their individual ethical visions, as I outlined in the preceding chapters.

There is much within their communal ethical vision that supports my claim: concerned about the inadequacies of conventional modes of ethical thought, the four interlocutors have focused on forming not simply a new ethical vision, but a new ethical paradigm for our planet; they place a loving relationship with all of creation as the starting point of their ethical vision; they do not trivialize what is needed to change our present economic, social, and political structures, by stressing that we must embrace our anthropological vulnerability; they are adamant that all subjects in creation participate in their own liberation, which, by definition, necessitates a vast communal conversation when ethical decisions are made; in acknowledging the authority that science has in describing the world, these four Christian thinkers grant even greater power to this sphere by allowing it to author their ethical visions; and finally, embracing the ecological necessity of granting vital significance to the whole, while not placing it morally above its constitutive parts, the four theorists espouse a dialogic between the whole and its parts, offering new insights into what liberation might mean in the Anthropocene.

To substantiate my claim, I am subjecting the above features of their ethical vision to critical analysis. The ethical vision put forth by the four Christian thinkers examined in this book is demanding and unconventional in certain ways. In fact, I confer onto this approach to ethics what I am calling a "messy" character. I do not apply this term in a derogatory sense to imply careless reasoning, though. Nor do I suggest that "messy" conveys a system that is chaotic, where "anything goes." Yet, if messy is understood with its other meanings to convey a process that is complicated and difficult to work with, and lacking in precision, in many ways this characterization is not entirely inaccurate. Moreover, "messy" is used not so much to *define the ethical problems* (where the term "wicked" is more than adequate for the task, as I discussed in the introduction), but to *describe the ethical responses* to the problems. It is such an approach to ethics that Ruether, Boff, O'Murchu, and Boff advocate we need today.

I will begin by inquiring whether indeed conventional modes of ethical thought are as inadequate for the purpose of arriving at a liberationist ethic as our four interlocutors claim. I will discuss claims raised by philosopher David E. Cooper that question the feasibility of an ethic that exhorts us to revere nature or the environment, arguing that we cannot revere what we are not engaged with. Indeed, is it naive for the four interlocutors to be placing such emphasis on a loving relationship with all of creation as the starting point of their ethical vision? I will then inquire about the feasibility of an ethical vision that has us embrace our anthropological vulnerability when that vision purports to serve the needs of the majority of humankind that is, in many ways, already socially and economically marginalized. The question of what a vast communal conversation with all creation that the four theorists propose must also be addressed: is such a conversation necessary or even feasible? And if the conversation is to include the natural world, how, for instance, can we know what rights a river ought to receive? Many authors have argued, and still do, that it is wrong to derive *oughts* from what is empirically observed. In granting such pre-eminence to science as normative, I will have to determine whether our four interlocutors have committed the naturalistic fallacy. And finally, I turn to philosopher Ingrid Stefanovic's critique of ethical visions, which accord the biotic whole greater reverence, thereby grouping complex phenomena within a "totalizing paradigm."[1] This, she avers, can lead to questionable ethics, which would have us sacrifice the individual for the good of the biotic whole. Is this the case with the model of liberation I have drawn from the four interlocutors' respective works?

It will become evident throughout this chapter that their ethical vision is indeed viable and not *in spite of* the "messy" character to it, but *because of* it. Current approaches to ethics are proving ineffective in addressing the deepening poverty of countless human beings, the extinction of countless species, the acidification of our oceans, and the warming of our atmosphere. What appears "messy" and, therefore, supposedly ill-advised, I suggest, is actually a virtue for an ethical vision in the Anthropocene era marked by a dominant economics of neoliberalism. A radically new ethics marked by a process that is complicated, difficult to work with, and lacking in precision is precisely what the four interlocutors are proposing is the type of ethical vision we need today. Further, borrowing upon the thinking of various theorists, I will demonstrate that the concerns raised above that cast doubts about the thoughtfulness, constructive resolution, and critical attention with which our four theorists have approached the spheres of the environment and liberation are either unsubstantiated or unconvincing when the entire corpus of our four Christian thinkers is taken into consideration and examined critically. I will begin this query by examining the current context in ethical thinking in western society.

INADEQUACIES OF CONVENTIONAL MODES OF ETHICAL THOUGHT

Ruether, Boff, O'Murchu, and Berry are challenging conventional modes of ethical thinking insofar as they comprise simplified formulas, rigid procedures, decontextualized abstract reasoning, or reductionist analyses in the face of a real world, full of complex interconnections. Current thinking within some philosophical circles would suggest that conventional ethical frameworks, and even epistemological approaches to the environmental and social problems our planet is facing, are indeed problematic.[2] Philosopher Martin Schönfeld, for instance, underlines: "Doing business as usual is a recipe for failure."[3] He speaks to the failure of conventional ways of thinking in our world today to help us to arrive at a global ethics on climate change. He is particularly critical of mainstream philosophy that relies on postmodern thinking that stresses culture over nature, and overly analytical approaches that stress the breakdown of information, the isolation of data, and the separation of events from context. Such an approach, he avers, fails to provide us with solutions to a global climate change disaster.

While not employing as stern an assessment of the current state of ethical thinking in philosophical circles, philosophers Jim Cheney and Anthony Weston suggest that environmental thinking, in particular, is challenging the current relationship between epistemology and ethics, thus forcing us to rethink basic assumptions concerning ethics itself.[4] The epistemologies of modernism, they contend, have led us to remain detached from the world, "treating the nonhuman world and even the world as objects of domination and control."[5] Not unlike what Keith Douglass Warner finds in his examination of Catholic environmental ethics, where Catholic bishops merely "graft" environmental concerns onto already formulated social teachings,[6] Cheney and Weston question whether ethical theories can be "stretched to retrofit all new ethical insights."[7] They identify features of mainstream theories in ethics (what they call "epistemology-based ethics") that presume the world is readily knowable, that ethical knowledge is a response to our knowledge of the world, and that ethics itself is incremental and extensionist (a sort of continual expanding of moral concern from the familial onto newer, less biologically connected, individuals or groups). In this view, the two authors argue, ethics remains in the "orbit of facts" and merely builds upon "the stable and well-understood familiar world."[8] Examples they provide with regard to animal studies help explain what they mean: we must first know what animals are capable of, and *then* decide on *that* basis whether and how we are to deal with them ethically. Hence, it is only after gathering facts and figures on whether or not an animal feels pain, or is self-conscious that we decide whether or not to attribute rights to it. The presumption here, of course, is that we *can* know, even with precision, exactly what animals do or do not feel. This method, they say, is characterized by a sense of "familiarity" and "settledness" that thwarts our discovery of the new or openness to surprise.[9]

From a liberationist perspective, philosopher of liberation Enrique Dussel also argues that a new ethical framework is necessary. Our context, he maintains, is unique: we are at the end of a 500-year-old hegemonic system that has reached "absolute limits": the ecological destruction of the planet, and the destruction of humanity itself.[10] As a result, he maintains, we find ourselves constantly searching for solutions to problems we have to think about for the first time. Ethics, he contends, can no longer overlook the voices from the periphery, nor can it participate in conciliating the irreconcilable (such as a just society within a free market system), or covering up ruptures (like colonial legacies), so as to avoid conflict. Moreover, this process cannot occur by reading textbooks in the comfort of one's domain; rather, it can only be carried out by living "in the daily and historical experiences of our lives."[11] Such a rooted perspective is vital, as Dussel underlines with the example given by Bartolomé de las Casas, a Dominican friar of the sixteenth century. De las Casas arrived to the Americas with the first Spanish colonizers. He witnessed, and eventually felt morally compelled to oppose, the atrocities to which the Spanish subjected the Indigenous populations. He became the first bishop of Chiapas (now a state in Mexico), and among Indigenous peoples there is considered fondly, as their protector. Dussel writes: "Bartolomé De Las Casas would not have been able to formulate and articulate his critique of the Spanish conquest of the Americas if he had not himself lived in the periphery and heard the cries and witnessed the tortures to which indigenous people were being submitted."[12]

The problem that most concerns Dussel, however, is the destruction of peoples and communities in the global South that is perpetuated by a global capitalist world order. This problem is the product of modernity, which Dussel conceives as a centre-periphery system that began in 1492 when the first Europeans conquered the new lands of America, treating the land and its human inhabitants as possessions only to be colonized and enslaved to serve the centre. These are people who "never appeared as other"[13] and to this day remain colonized, economically, socially and, to a degree, politically too. While the centre of this now global system has shifted throughout the last 500 years (from various countries in Europe to the United States, and arguably continuing onto China and/or India), the basic rationalization of the lifeworld into simplified and, therefore, manageable economic, political, and cultural subsystems remains intact as a necessary way of managing the centrality of a world system of domination. Coloniality is not merely the underside of modernity, Dussel avers, but a constitutive dimension of it.

Affirming what, certainly, Ruether and Boff have been saying, Dussel contends that, for the most part, western ethics – or more broadly, European philosophy – is detrimental to fostering human liberation, as it perpetuates modernity's systems of domination and, by extension, the suffering and oppression that results. This happens because it accepts modernity (as he defines it above), as its point of departure – thereby rendering it capable, at best, of managing its deficiencies, or by degrading material needs with its disembodied, or abstract, thinking that universalizes what can only be particular, or contextual. It is not the universal per se that Dussel eschews, but a universal criterion that lacks empirical foundations and simply advances judgments of value. The present and dominant discourse on ethics works from abstract principles and ideas and procedures, and not from human life in its concrete, creaturely, "material" experience, with real needs and potentials. This disregard for the creaturely experience has produced a world where both humans and the Earth can be viewed as "exploitable."[14] True to his liberationist thinking, then, Dussel looks at ethics not from the perspective of the (European) centre, but from the countless people living on the periphery of this domain.

How do we even begin to comprehend the periphery and our ethical obligations? Ethicist Willis Jenkins provides a concrete example of the incompetency of our ethical traditions not only to take responsibility, but to interpret our "wicked" problems today.[15] Taking climate change as an example, he notes its indelible nature as a global commons problem where shared resources, such as the carbon sink of the atmosphere or oceans, are overused by myriad players, none of whom possesses an immediate incentive to limit emissions. Moreover, ecological problems are often worse for nations that are least responsible for carbon emissions, while the most damaging effects of climate change will affect generations not yet born. Some nations, like the Democratic Republic of Congo, could play a large role in helping absorb emissions by not cutting down their forests; yet such poverty-stricken nations receive little to no incentive to protect their forests, leaving them little choice but to invest in mining for resources.

Responding particularly from a Christian perspective, Jenkins adeptly asks, "What does love of enemies mean when enmity is mediated by nonlinear ecological systems?"[16]

Philosopher Chris J. Cuomo, I think, captures the salient problem at hand. She posits that we exist at a moral distance geographically, affectively, and epistemically to the people, communities, nonhuman species, and ecosystems of the planet, while at the same time being in close ethical proximity to them. She asks, "What might it mean to promote the good of a community you cannot even hold in your imagination?"[17] Yet, our money, the clothes we wear, our desires, and our work are "mobilized in the service of the exploitation of people all over the place, from midtown Manhattan to Malalaling." Traditional ethical theory, she concludes, provides very little to help us deal with these difficult dimensions of contemporary life: "Most traditional philosophical views assume the relationship between knowledge and responsibility to be straightforward, when we know of a clear casual connection between our choices and harm to others, there is a direct self-evident duty to alleviate that harm ... Utilitarians, deontologists, and virtue theorists agree: rationality demands that, if we want to do the right thing, and there is not much of significance competing for our attention, the right action will be obvious, and attractive." What Cuomo is saying rings true to the experience of anyone who regularly buys the groceries: the consequences of our actions and behaviours are difficult and sometimes impossible to know let alone address in a globalized world. The problems involve entities such as ecosystems and "dying cultures" that are "not easily accommodated by ethics that value people, utility, sentient beings, or communities of people." Moreover, Cuomo adds, these problems involve past and future generations, which calls for our current generation to cultivate a sense of responsibility that is unprecedented. In a sense, she sums up what the above thinkers are saying when she concludes: "[T]he endlessly flawed twentieth-century moral imagination is woefully inadequate to address the intricate webs of relation created by global capitalism, postcolonial realities, and the fact that the environment has no borders. We [apparently referring to global North] are prosperous/preposterous moral beings with a litany of responsibilities that seem nearly impossible to know, let alone enact."

The ethicists discussed above corroborate what Ruether, Boff, O'Murchu, and Berry are saying themselves about the dramatic disconnect that exists among humans and between humans and the other-than-human world. This is why a new approach is required. Currently – to continue the line of thinking from our philosophers above – the majority of humans living in the global North stress culture over nature, and *one* culture (the dominant western culture and its thinking) above all others, perpetuating a global system that favours the few at the expense of the many. We in the West prefer to remain in the realm of abstract reasoning, separating events from their contexts, thus keeping ethics from getting muddled in the day-to-day corporeal realities of countless subjects who suffer. With this mode of thinking we search for facts so we can know a world we believe to be knowable, while failing to recognize and acknowledge ourselves as living within a larger animate universe, in communion with other subjects.

In contrast to conventional modes of ethical thought, the four Christian thinkers I investigate here present an ethical vision that is "messy" and relational. As Ruether says, it invites us to stand back and consider how *all* subjects interconnect and cooperate rather than compete. There is no real "how-to" manual to their ethical vision. As O'Murchu puts it, we are to change from the traditional ethics of royalty or loyalty to one where there is constant mutual engagement of humans "as servants to a bigger process."[18] The complex web of relationships underlying reality appears to preclude a deontological, or one-size-fits-all ethics, and a utilitarian ethic, one that calculates the greatest good for the greatest number. Instead, the four Christian thinkers appear to be fostering first and foremost a sensitivity to all Earth subjects, which forces us to see things differently and from the perspective of alterity *and* from the whole. We are being asked to make a loving relationship with all creation serve as our starting point, to embrace our anthropological vulnerability, to facilitate a vast communal conversation when ethical decisions are made, to allow science to author their ethical visions and to regard liberation in a new light, as a constant dialogic between the whole and its parts. I turn to discussing these now.

STARTING WITH A LOVING RELATIONSHIP WITH ALL CREATION

In each of the first four chapters of this book, I began with an investigation of the respective starting points of the four Christian thinkers being examined, that is, the aspects of their personal biography that have influenced their thinking. It became evident that each formed, at a relatively early age, a loving, even reverential relationship with nature and, initially at least, a specific place – whether for the San Bernardino Mountains, the Amazon rainforest, the Irish countryside, or a North Carolinian meadow. This loving relationship, I suggest, is more than mere sentimentality but something akin to Albert Schweitzer's philosophy of "reverence for life," which he presented as the foundation of all ethics. As a starting point for their ethical vision, this love instills within the four thinkers a deep sensitivity to what is happening to all subjects of creation, obliging our authors to eschew simple answers to complex issues. Love, as I shall demonstrate, also serves as a means for further knowing and engaging with the world.

For Schweitzer, reverence is not simply an ethic of love or purely a system of thought. Later in his life he concluded that as an ethic, reverence for life "is the ethic of love widened into universality."[19] But even this definition does not seem to capture its full meaning. In its original German (*ehrfurcht vor dem leben*), the term carries overtones beyond what reverence evokes in English. One has to include feelings of "awe before an overwhelming force" to capture its fuller meaning.[20] Reverence stems from a knowledge, or recognition "apprehended by the most learned and the most childlike alike," that all life holds a "will-to-live."[21] Of this knowledge, Schweitzer writes, "It is reverence for life, reverence for the impenetrable mystery that meets us in our universe, an existence different from ourselves in external appearance, yet inwardly of the same character with us, terribly similar, awesomely related. *The dissimilarity, the strangeness* [original italics], between us and other creatures is *here removed*."[22] Such a will-to-live, he reasons, demands that humans share and preserve life. The notion, Schweitzer holds, is neither simple nor naive. He recognizes the full consequence of acting with reverence for all life, outlining the complexities and difficulties involved in constantly having to make decisions about life at seemingly every encounter. Since all "creatures live at the expense of other creatures,"[23] Schweitzer observes, noting that humans are not exempted from this reality, from the standpoint of reverence for life, ethical living demands a constant discernment or weighing of the options. Simple common codes of behaviours will not suffice, since for Schweitzer reverence is an attitude toward life, not a set of rules. Much like the four Christian thinkers, Schweitzer suggests that, when reflecting on the good, "good" is not fixed, but is that which sustains and advances life.

This attitude toward life finds expression distinctly within the bioregional model put forth by Ruether, Boff, O'Murchu, and Berry. Whether the demand is to convert our minds to one another and to Earth or Gaia, as Boff and Ruether would stress, or to live well and not better and to nurture reciprocity by aligning our desires with the evolutionary impulses found in the cosmos, as O'Murchu and Berry would more likely stress, the "good" is not fixed. In fact, while bioregionalism is the most concrete facet of the ethical vision espoused by these four interlocutors, as a model it nevertheless provides little in the way of straightforward rules or codes. What specifically constitutes "living well" within a bioregion, for example, is not so evident, especially since responses would reasonably differ from bioregion to bioregion. By way of a more concrete example, the question of whether one ought to become a vegetarian, or vegan is never clear-cut. Ruether reminds us that a chicken could be the only source of protein for a malnourished farmer living in the global South. Like Schweitzer's reverence for life philosophy, then, my chosen Christian thinkers make love for all creation a firm point of departure, and the process for discerning the "good" is ongoing and demanding. The way Schweitzer puts it – a way that resonates with Dussel's ethics of life – seems to encapsulate what the four interlocutors themselves are saying: "It is not by receiving instruction about agreement between ethical and necessary, that a man makes progress in ethics, but only by coming to hear more and more plainly the voice of the ethical, by becoming ruled more and more by the longing to preserve and promote life, and by becoming more and more obstinate in resistance to the necessity for destroying or injuring life."[24] Perhaps such an attitude explains, at least in part, why the four authors readily accept paradoxes and welcome ambiguities, and each of the four authors seems content to live with uncertainties. For, to do the contrary, to simplify or demand neat formulaic answers, could lead to meaningless suffering for another subject. As O'Murchu aptly puts it, the opposite of love is not hate, but indifference. The task, then, is not merely to learn to "leave things alone," but to discern constantly through "a love that liberates" – when suffering is deemed to be meaningless – how and when to act.[25]

At this point, I would like to consider the concern presented by philosopher David E. Cooper about ethics that exhort us to revere nature or the environment. From a phenomenological approach, he fittingly points out that one cannot revere what one is not engaged with, citing the Ganges River as an example. "It is absurd," he writes, "to suppose that the kind of attitude held by the Hindus to their river could be held by everyone towards everything."[26] Cooper's argument is persuasive and suggestive of Cuomo's argument above, that it is difficult if not impossible to promote the good of a community we cannot even hold in our imagination. The sensitivity Boff holds for the Amazon, for instance, is undoubtedly unique.

Yet, while the sensitivity the Christian thinkers examined here hold for all of creation is remarkably similar to Schweitzer's "reverence for life," it is nevertheless also grounded within a bioregional framework. This distinction is important. Cooper suggests, "The concerns of people conscious of the ancient ideal [obligation to one's children, avoidance of suffering, for example] will begin 'at home,' with *their* environments, the networks of meaning with which *they* are engaged."[27] In this sense, the reverence and sensitivity my chosen four thinkers are suggesting would also "begin 'at home,'" in their bioregion. This is not unlike what Willis Jenkins suggests by "privileging proximity." Taking the Good Samaritan as a case in point, he writes that "what matters for neighbor-love is not shared membership but near need."[28] This does not mean, however, that a reverence and sensitivity cannot also be held for all of creation at a different level. I surmise this is not unlike a Mohawk woman who, in travelling to Peru, can still show reverence for the Amazon River, though she is most at home along the St Lawrence River. She extends her deeply engaged concern for her river toward another river. She need not hold the same kind of attitude toward the Amazon as she does the St Lawrence to esteem the other river as a subject. Engagement, at some level, and not simply proximity, seems key here. In other words, a "reverence" for life need not mean that it occur, as Cooper suggests, on the same deep level and for every entity on Earth.

Starting an ethic from such a loving *relationship* with all creation is not unlike what Aldo Leopold wrote over half a century ago: "We abuse land because we regard it as a commodity belonging to us. When we see land as a community to which we belong, we may begin to use it with love and respect."[29] Whether as love or reverence, such an engaged relationality seems to matter. Leopold says, "No important change in ethics was ever accomplished without an internal change in our intellectual emphasis, loyalties, affections, and convictions."[30] Similarly, the call to a loving relationality promoted by the four authors examined in this work encourages solidarity or a communion in kinship. This attitude toward life mandates humans to imagine and feel the suffering of others, including the other-than-human, and to find ways in which interrelation becomes cooperative and mutually life enhancing for both sides. Making a connection with the writings of Aldo Leopold and Thomas Berry, Stephen Bede Scharper affirms that it is love that allows us to see the world as a communion of subjects and not a collection of objects. Scharper supports the claim that rules or contracts are insufficient alone to change our ethics. In fact, he concludes, "We can make ourselves more knowledgeable, change all our laws, fashion new policies, and even design cutting-edge sustainable technologies, but none of these will take hold until we change our relationship with creation."[31]

Love as a starting point not only obliges us to eschew simple answers to complex issues, it also serves instrumentally as a means for knowing the world. This is the argument put forth by Cheney and Weston. In contrast to conventional ethics defined above, which remains in the "orbit of facts," Cheney and Weston identify an alternative foundational assumption for ethics that is not dissimilar to what is being suggested above by Ruether, Boff, O'Murchu, and Berry. Cheney and Weston propose that an "ethics-based epistemology" (as opposed to the "epistemology-based ethics" described above) is increasingly gaining ground because the dominant ethics fails to resolve our pressing environmental and social problems. An "ethics-based epistemology," they write, seeks first and foremost to explore and enrich the world, and is characterized by less certainty and even disruption. This alternative view begins with the attitude toward life discussed above: love. "Love," they contend, "is in fact a way of knowing, but its dynamics are the reverse of the usual models," adding, "Love comes first, and opens up possibilities."[32] They continue: "Love in this sense is already an ethical relationship. It thus stands at the beginning, at the core, of ethics itself: a venture as well as an adventure – a risk, an attitude that may (*may*, for we cannot say for sure at the beginning) lead in time to more knowledge of someone or something, wholly wild possibilities."[33] In this fashion, the tools of the ethicist are to "listen" to give "space" to the subject, only pursuing any inquiry when "invited." The temperament of the ethicist becomes one of "courtesy, openness to surprise."[34]

Cheney and Weston refer to this stance as an "etiquette." They suggest it is a genuine means of discovery, which is being applied by researchers and environmental writers in general. By way of example, the authors relate a story that took place in an animal training facility where academics and the handlers or caretakers of chimpanzees were observed in how they related with the animals. The academics, who were there to observe operations in sign language, were, "psychically intrusive and failed to radiate the intelligence of the handlers … [who in contrast] walked in with a soft, acute, 360-degree awareness: they were receptively establishing … acknowledgment of and in relationship with all of the several hundred pumas, wolves, chimps, spider monkeys and Galapagos tortoises. Their ways of moving fit into the spaces shaped by the animals' awareness."[35] There is no arrogant inquiry happening here. Limits and inadequacies of knowing are recognized and accepted, a stance that contrasts with the current ethical framework, where we must first know what animals are capable of, and then decide on that basis whether and how we are to deal with them ethically. In their alternative view, Cheney and Weston write, "We will have no idea of what other animals are actually capable – we will not readily understand them – until we *already* have approached them ethically – that is, until we have offered them the space and time, the occasion, and the acknowledgment necessary to enter into relationship. Ethics must come *first*."[36]

Cheney and Weston believe that in contrast to conventional ethics, which has us treat the other-than-human world "as objects of domination and control," the ramification of such an "ethics-based epistemology" is profound: "others" are granted "universal consideration" that considers them to be valuable *at the outset,* thus reversing the usual burden of proof, "even though we may not yet know how or why, until they are proved otherwise."[37] In this manner, ethics and the love that precedes it are primary, and rather than constricting the way to knowledge, they facilitate it.

This thinking underlines what my four Christian thinkers mean by insisting that we are a communion of subjects. It also further illuminates, as I discussed in chapter 4, why some biologists are giving names to the animals they study. These scientists are not approaching animals through a value-neutral analytic process, but by absorbing their experiences with the natural world into their very being. Not surprisingly, as Ruether, Boff, O'Murchu, and Berry have themselves discovered, by beginning with love so as to enrich a world that is not readily knowable, possibilities can open up. At the same time, also not surprisingly, as Cheney and Weston affirm, this makes ethics pluralistic, at times discontinuous and even dissonant.

What my four Christian thinkers are proposing is not merely an ethical vision, then, but an ethical process, one that springs from a loving relationship and, as Chris Cuomo suggests, has us "recommit ourselves to the project of Getting Closer."[38] However, a loving relationship, while a viable starting point, cannot rest alone, as love could blind us to reality. More is needed within an ethical vision, such as a clearer understanding of ourselves as corporeal, finite beings.

EMBRACING OUR ANTHROPOLOGICAL VULNERABILITY

In the development of a viable ethical vision, the four authors examined in this work maintain that we must also address, as Berry puts it, our "deep hidden rage against the human condition, an unwillingness to accept life under the conditions that life granted us,"[39] that is, our anthropological vulnerability. This does not imply, as I discussed in chapter 1, the act of being wounded or in a situation of immediate danger; these should be avoided or reduced. Nor does it imply that we do not work to change our realities to live healthier and happier lives. It is, instead, a recognition of what philosopher Enrique Dussel states is our creaturely "material" experience, with real needs and potentials. Dussel's most recent work, *Ethics of Liberation: In an Age of Globalization and Exclusion*, particularly resonates with the liberationist trajectory of my four Christian thinkers. It outlines why it is necessary to accept, and even found, an ethic on our anthropological vulnerability, and why this, as I will demonstrate in the next section, necessitates a vast communal dialogue. Dussel's work further resonates with that of the four authors, as it also engages the entire world as a complex whole, offering a planetary dimension to his ethic. This ethic can only come about, he stresses, by being grounded in materiality. Dussel's "material principle," as he calls it, is "the obligation to produce, reproduce, and develop the concrete human life of each ethical subject in community,"[40] which means just what it says: one's life in its entirety. He substantiates this claim through empirical studies of the biology of the brain. A brief investigation of his reasoning will explain his overall ethic and affirm why it is important in an ethical vision to acknowledge our anthropological vulnerability.

Grounding his reasoning on biologist Humberto Maturana's proposal that we are a moment of autopoietic life (autonomous entities), Dussel looks at the human brain from a neurological-scientific point of view, as described by Nobel Prize-winning biologist Gerald Edelman. Edelman characterizes the brain as a "selective recognition system."[41] Dussel focuses on the limbic system and the base of the brain (the oldest part, already present in insects and reptiles), where some of the organs are the hypothalamus, the ganglia, the hippocampus, and the thalamus. This complex system of nerves and networks controls instincts, moods, and drives. For all animals, it is an evaluative system that allows or opposes the continuation or growth of the life of the organism. If animals did not have these functioning evaluative capacities, they would die. While "higher mammals" have more complex neural systems that allow them to discriminate more effectively, Edelman points to "higher species" – ostensibly the human – that possess self-conscious and language capacities that give us a unique ability to regulatehow we not only survive but thrive.

For Dussel, the difference between other-than-human animals and human animals (who possess self-conscious and linguistic-social capabilities) is important. For the former, there is no distance (in time) between stimulus and response. The animal simply receives a stimulus and reacts. Yet, for the human, according to Dussel, there is an added dynamic that occurs between the stimulus and reaction: "a space opens up between (a) the conceptual categorization, the conscious valorization, the responsible and the self-conscious linguistic process, and (b) the possible response."[42] In other words, the brain works directly to ensure that the human subject continues to live by conceiving and evaluating options that entail the entire human as a corporeal being living among other corporeal beings. This "space" to which Dussel refers denotes the self-conscious and linguistic-social processes that allow a human to choose life – as suicide, he stresses, *is* an option – thereby implying a responsibility to do so. "Life is under its own responsibility," Dussel states, adding that this is "exclusive to the *mode of reality* of human life: *to have it under one's own responsibility* [italics original]."[43]

Dussel reasons that because of this process, only humans live ethically, which he describes as one's self-responsibility for preserving one's life. He puts it as a syllogism:[44]

1 John, who is a responsible *human* living subject, is eating.
2 To live, it is necessary to eat.
3 If John ceases to eat, he would die.
4 As he is responsible for his life, he ought not to stop eating, or he would be guilty of suicide. *Ergo,*
5 John ought to continue eating.

Dussel does not leave this responsibility at the individual level, though. The material basis he affirms carries a logic of intersubjectivity, that is, a recognition of the autonomy and freedom before all other humans as well. One can see where he is going with this: the responsibility to produce, reproduce, and develop one's life becomes a responsibility to ensure others too can meet these ends.

Notwithstanding Schweitzer's framework above, Dussel's delineation between the *human* self-"responsibility" to produce, reproduce, and develop, and the "responsibility" *of all life* to do the same is not very convincing. As I stated above, Dussel extends the obligation to promote liberation to humans based on our self-reflective mode of reality. But can such an ontological delineation be cast between that which engenders the "will-to-live" in all life (as Schweitzer describes it) and the "material" experience for preserving life that Dussel assigns solely to humans? Dussel assigns this self-responsibility uniquely to humans, suggesting, without, I might add, sufficient evidence, that no animals have "feelings" in the way humans have feelings. Despite his unconvincing demarcation between the human and the other-than human subject, I think his ethics is helpful in explaining the larger issue of *why* liberation (here described as having one's life under one's own responsibility) is important in the first place. Dussel demonstrates that by being grounded in factual, empirical, and descriptive judgments, liberation becomes more than an abstract sentiment; it is an irrefutable obligation. His ethics is not dependent on a notion of class or intellectual reasoning. The desire for liberation stems from the "unconscious force field of drives"[45] grounded in our corporeal nature. In other words, Dussel's framework forces us to acknowledge, first and foremost, the daily anthropological vulnerability of the human.

It is not difficult to appreciate the significance of grounding ethics in our corporeal nature (and not on abstract or uncritical metaphysical reasoning) when one considers what has occurred (and continues to occur) throughout much of the colonial history of Latin America, where human suffering has been perpetuated under the pretense of "love." Such thinking motivates Dussel's critique of the Latin American bishops in Puebla who, in 1979 (in preparation to meet then Pope John Paul II), drafted a document that claimed to open "new directions." The document argued that the poor, "although deprived of everything, can still live with strength because of 'faith, as a word which nourishes.'"[46] Dussel fittingly counters, "Since when is it affirmed, and on what basis, that the word of God can replace material nourishment, proteins, and calories."[47] Dussel considers such thinking from Christian leaders to be one of the reasons for Latin American peoples' passive, tragic, and ahistorical resignation. For Dussel, the ethics the bishops are espousing can only be an ethics for angels or God for whom death is not possible. Fittingly, he says, "Without death, human life loses its vulnerability, its finitude; it stops being the criterion of truth; the logic of life no longer reigns in it; ethics becomes impossible: the angels or God are not governed by the ethics we are speaking about (which is an ethics of the living, within the horizon of death, always immediately possible), and even less by an ethics of liberation, which would be unnecessary under Cartesianism and, more than that, impossible."[48] Demonstrably, then, Dussel's philosophy of liberation bolsters the requirement set by my four Christian thinkers that we recognize and accept our anthropological vulnerability to the violent tragic force of nature, suffering, limits, and death. Not grounding ethics in the concrete daily life of all peoples – and the four interlocutors would add all life – permits the rationalization of the lifeworld of billions of excluded people into simplified and, therefore, manageable economic, political, and cultural subsystems.

Not unlike Ruether, Boff, O'Murchu, and Berry, who stress that we must respond to the needs of our Guatemalan Indigenous woman, Dussel insists that we must respond to what Rigoberta Menchú,[49] the Indigenous leader in Guatemala, is trying to articulate to those espousing a Eurocentric ethic. Menchú, if we listen to her – and to the millions of Indigenous peoples excluded from the conversation – tells us that her own anthropological condition must be recognized and nurtured within a liberationist perspective. Attending to our anthropological vulnerability in isolation to the larger liberationist import is imprudent, as it abandons the task of reconstructing an ethic of life. It must be remembered that for Dussel, for my four thinkers, the goal of reconstructing an ethics of life is to arrive at an intersubjective agreement whose validity rests on consensus, autonomy, and legitimacy. The construction of consensus must be plural and diverse and it must incorporate the participation of all affected members in the rational decision-making of such a community. How that conversation might unfold is where I now turn our attention.

SAFEGUARDING A COMMUNAL CONVERSATION

The communal conversation Ruether, Boff, O'Murchu, and Berry are suggesting might seem unwieldy at first glance – partly due to the fact that none of these interlocutors really spells out in any detail how the conversation might occur. Taking Boff's perichoretic model, for instance, he suggests it is the best approach for realizing "the most inclusive stance possible." He is not as clear about how it is also "the one that is least inclined to produce victims."[50] Yet, as I discussed above with regard to how a loving relationship serves as our starting point, a communal conversation would likely occur at the bioregional level and, if need be, among bioregions, in which case the framework need not be so unmanageable. Moreover, it would be absurd to suggest that the vast communal conversation include those subjects who are not involved in any way in the ethical situation that undergirds the conversation. Certainly none of the four authors I am examining suggest this. Already, then, delimitations on the vastness of the communal conversation become apparent.

Dussel's framework is also helpful in this regard. It substantiates the claim put forth by my four authors that a vast and communal discussion and negotiation through a "democratic" conversation occur and that it be integral to the process. Taking his cue from discourse ethics (an ethical system primarily concerned with the process employed to help people – especially those living within a pluralistic milieu – to arrive at ethical norms through reasoned debate), Dussel affirms the need for what he terms the "symmetric participation" of all those affected. This implies that those most affected participate more in the conversation. Nevertheless, he realizes the impossibility of identifying all those affected and *"all the 'possibly' affected."*[51] His point of departure, however, which delineates a major difference between the philosophy of liberation and discourse ethics, is the procedural "first question" that must always, and seemingly constantly, be asked: "Who may we have left 'outside' – without re-cognition?"[52] The primary consideration, then, is not so much how many are participating, but who is participating (i.e., the victim of an injustice). More precisely, though, Dussel underlines what must occur within that conversation: "The criteria of liberation would be that the unfulfilled demands of the victims, reflected in the alternatives suggested by the critical discourse, should be met. From then on, all future ethical decisions will be taken from the perspective of the victims. This means that life – and the choices it implies – would not be the privilege of a few but something common to every human being."[53] Perfection within the process is not attainable, and Dussel realizes this. What we can attain is a hermeneutic that consistently inquires who is missing from the conversation. Integrated into this vast communal discussion, Dussel adds, are "advisers," the experts, scientists, technicians, and those with experience.

Two main questions regarding Boff's perichoretic model and indeed those of the others still need to be clarified: how can the inclusive communal conversation proceed among humans, one that is especially accommodating of our Guatemalan woman and her community? And how are the subjectivity of the river and the discernment of its rights realized within the conversation? Fortunately, in their collective wisdom, the interlocutors examined in this work do provide some guidance on these points. And with the inclusion of the work of theologian David Tracy on the analogical imagination, I can describe the process well enough: all four of my authors stress the need for humans – and hence the development of our capacity – to listen, not only to the Guatemalan *campesina*, but to the river as well. Not surprisingly, the listening process begins by forming a relationship.

To listen well and understand the *campesina*, we need to enter into, and become involved with, her world. The process begins by forming a relationship and ends in solidarity. The strong liberationist methodologies of Boff and Ruether and the broader conception of liberation as understood by O'Murchu and Berry have them dwell with the poor and the suffering, being in regular contact with them. When it comes to including the natural world into the conversation, the process is somewhat similar in how it unfolds. We begin by dwelling on the land. Dwelling on the land, as Boff puts it, implies we listen to it, comprehend the kind of soils, rocks, and insects it has, as well as its carrying capacities. Dwelling, then, marks the first step in fostering a communal conversation. Taking his cue from father of liberation theology Gustavo Gutiérrez, Stephen Bede Scharper finds that this similarity in approach to listening to our *campesina* and the land makes perfect sense. He quotes Gutiérrez, who says, "Unless you know the names of poor persons, you are not in solidarity with them."[54] In this way, we are meant to actually know them as "Rigoberta" or "John." Scharper then suggests that Gutiérrez's statement has relevance for including nature in the conversation, for, "unless you know the names of certain species, learn how to communicate with them, spend time with eco-systems, with rivers, discern the patterns of animals that move across your life course, your ravines, you are not in solidarity."[55]

The actual engagement with the land that Ruether, Boff, O'Murchu, and Berry are suggesting occurs through critical reflection and what seems to be an interiorization process. Recall from the first four chapters of this book, that this process cannot be forced; instead we allow the "land to reclaim us like ivy growing over an old house."[56] Such an interiorization process is facilitated through meditation, spiritual dance, song, poetry, and intuition, by the use of our ears and eyes, with or without scientific equipment. Berry explains this process most adeptly when, as I have discussed with regard to scientists above, humans absorb their experiences with the natural world into their very being. This allows the biologist to listen not solely to what her instruments are telling her, but also to what she is being told through the very structure of her being.

How, in the process of decision-making, are we to understand what rights a river ought to have? Recall that Berry suggests we think analogically. He contends that each being has rights particular to its mode of being. When we normally speak of the rights of a human and the rights of the other-than-human, we have trouble assessing the two because of their apparent differences, and too often end with human rights trumping the rights of the other-than-human. However, if we employ the term "rights" as an analogous term, we see similarities and differences. In this way, to continue the thinking initiated in the previous chapter, "a river has rights," but it does not have human rights, because human rights would be no good for a river. A river needs river rights, which we can discern through the process of dwelling and interiorizing explained above. Analogy, as Berry uses it, is a way of ordering relationships and articulating similarities amid differences.

While Berry employs analogy to understand the needs of nature, theologian David Tracy contends that thinking analogically can also be employed to enable a viable conversation among humans, which is especially important given the plurality of voices that characterize such conversations. Conversations among humans can become frustrated by misunderstandings, leading to conflict or suspicions, notes Tracy. He advances the method of analogical imagination as a means for moving through such a morass, that is, as a way to enable a conversation. Tracy argues that the analogical imagination helps us to order relationships and articulate what he terms similarity-in-difference. He believes, "We understand one another, if at all, only through analogies."[57] A brief review of his argument will demonstrate its potential in this regard.

The goal in using the analogical imagination is to fashion some order out of disparate realities by recognizing congruities while maintaining real differences. Differences cannot be washed away under the banner of commonality or shared humanity, Tracy insists. In other words, in applying the analogical imagination, we are required to resist easy incorporation of another person's focus, thoughts, or claims into our own common ways of knowing, while simultaneously finding that similarity-in-difference that allows us to draw some kind of rough coherence, eventually steering us toward some form of harmony or order. This harmony, Tracy insists, can never be forced or it will simply turn into a form of domination. This runs the risk of debasing all information to all-too-common denominators, making no one at home in the conversation.[58]

In order to ensure analogy does not become some deadening single expression of truth for all places, and for all time, Tracy insists that it be accompanied by the dialectic – as portrayed most aptly through the methodology employed in liberation theology – as a necessary corrective. This dialectic comprises a logic of contradiction that negates illusions, pretensions, and wishful thinking, and challenges the status quo, saying no to ethical deliberations that would exclude the Guatemalan *campesina* from participating in her future. Tracy states, "Without the ever-renewing power of the negative, all analogical concepts eventually collapse into a false harmony, the brittle sterility, the cheap grace of an all-too-canny univocity or an unreal compromise pleasing no one who understands the real issues."[59] At the same time, he argues, the dialectical language must move into analogy if it is to avoid any false harmony that remains when the negation ends. The dialectic and the analogy, then, complement each other, and conflict becomes a reality that is welcomed. Where truth is being systematically distorted, Tracy states the conversation must yield to the dialectic.

Tracy's formulation of the analogical imagination, then, serves as a means for bridging the difficult path to understanding among humans. Moreover, it coalesces well with, and indeed requires, the liberationist paradigm put forth by my four Christian thinkers, one that challenges illusions, deceptions, or distortions of the truth. In other words, the analogical imagination, which necessitates the liberationist model, not only assists us in comprehending what the Indigenous Guatemalan woman is telling us, but ensures that neither her voice nor the voices of the other-than-human is excluded from the conversation. What begins as a dwelling that forms a relationship incorporating the analogical and the dialectic facilitates the communal conversation that includes our Guatemalan woman and the river. Their voices are vital to the ethical vision put forth by our four Christian thinkers.

HAVING SCIENCE AUTHOR AN ETHICAL VISION

The four Christian thinkers examined in this work have formulated guidelines and models from the natural world, which they suggest can help us change how we see the world and ourselves in it. The knowledge comes, in large measure, through findings in science. In other words, science, as a wisdom, also becomes vital to the ethical vision put forth by these thinkers. Boff, for instance, puts forth a dynamic ethics that is "born out of a new definition of the human being and of its mission in the universe as understood by new science."[60] In fact, while our conversation with a river can be facilitated through meditation, spiritual dance, song, poetry, and intuition, these four theorists nevertheless assign pre-eminence to science as a way of knowing.

With her understanding of ecology, Ruether concludes that the increasing human population is unethical, because it represents an extreme case of the proliferation of one population that threatens to strip the planet of its life. Ecology especially becomes normative or ethically prescriptive for these theorists, but quantum physics, systems theory, cosmology, as well as the chaos and Gaian theories, play a normative role as well. Through cosmology, the principles of communion, differentiation, and subjectivity that describe how the universe functions explain how all creation and not just the human are to live in harmony within biotic communities. At a fundamental level, then, science is used by all four to understand how the complex relationships within our environment are sustained and how we contribute to them, positively and negatively. In this manner, the four Christian thinkers employ science not solely to authorize (to sanction, lend credibility, legitimacy, or authority) but to author (to be the source of) an ethic: as Ruether suggests, we convert our minds to nature's logic through science; through the Gaian theory, Boff and Ruether maintain, we find principles for living well, not better; from quantum holism, as O'Murchu suggests, we eschew power relations, as they are not the only, or perhaps even the most effective, way of linking people and events in society; from the whole narrative, the universe conveys that we subsume our democracy under the governance of the larger biocracy.

This employment of science as prescriptive, that is, going from what *is* in the natural world, to what *ought* to be, is viewed within philosophical circles as committing a logical fallacy. Based on the Humean dictum that we cannot deduce an *ought* from an *is* in nature, many philosophers prefer to maintain a logical distinction between questions of fact and questions of value.[61] Hume, taking a subjectivist stance to ethics, was adamant that moral values are merely the product of natural human desires, not objective fact. Along somewhat similar subjectivist lines, the philosopher G.E. Moore argued that the *good* is an "object of thought"[62] and not an objective feature of the world. Moore believed that the notion of *good* cannot be defined, only intuited and, thus, cannot be defined in naturalistic terms; to do so would be committing the naturalistic fallacy. In both instances, the authors argue that it is wrong to derive *oughts* from what is empirically observed.[63]

It is important to keep in mind that the concerns surrounding the naturalistic fallacy involve more than the committing of mere "logical" errors, as potentially stakes can be high when fallacious conclusions are reached. A glance at how some authors approach the issue reveals that legitimate fears and concerns prevail over the potential misuse of science by scientists and non-scientists alike. Some scientists, such as biologist Frans de Waal, appalled at the vigour with which some Christians can embrace the harsh ideology of social Darwinism, call for a more cautious approach when reflecting upon animal behaviour, so as to avoid committing the naturalistic fallacy. "The problem is," de Waal writes, "that one can't derive the goals of society from the goals of nature."[64] Others, such as scientist Stephen Jay Gould, renowned for his argument that we preserve a sharp delineation between religion and science, is adamant that the former preoccupy itself with questions of morality, while the latter – at the most – only describe the conditions under which certain morals or values might have arisen. Christopher DiCarlo, lecturer on bioethics and philosophy of science, and John Teehan, professor of religion, suggest that underlining Moore's elaboration of the naturalistic fallacy was a special concern that evolutionary ethics might be allowed to define "good," since "those that are most knowledgeable about what things are more evolved (i.e., biologists) would become our authorities."[65] DiCarlo and Teehan also cite the case when philosopher Michael Levin argued that homosexuality, based on "science," is abnormal: the seemingly natural manner in which the penis fits the vagina and not the anus, following seemingly "mechanical" laws, according to Levin, obliges us to pursue only heterosexual relationships. The better fit leads to happiness, and to act contrary to what facilitates our happiness is abnormal. DiCarlo and Teehan sum up the issue at hand here: "It is, we believe, arguments like Levin's which cause the most anxiety over evolutionary ethics. The concern seems to be that if we allow evolutionary thinking into our ethics we are going to end up with a reactionary moral system which supports an oppressive patriarchal value system in which women are consigned to the kitchen, homosexuals to the closets, the poor and disadvantaged to the fringes of society, all in the name of the natural moral order."[66] While DiCarlo and Teehan relate their concerns to evolutionary biology, it is safe to assume that these concerns over oppressive ethics stemming from a prescriptive science are valid in other areas. This will be arguably an even greater concern in the future, as science continues to reign as the most powerful alternative explanation of the world. After all, as Holmes Rolston III points out, in the twentieth century alone, "science flourished as never before, but left us with deep misgivings about the human relation to the world."[67] This process does not seem to be subsiding.

While the above certainly supports the need for caution to avoid committing logical fallacies, it also illuminates why deliberating whether my four Christian thinkers have themselves committed such fallacies is important. It is a critical issue that requires critical attention. Have Ruether, Boff, O'Murchu, and Berry, then, derived *oughts* from what is, that is, failed to distinguish between questions of fact and questions of value? The answer is not straightforward. It is true that they have derived *oughts* from what is empirically observed in nature through science, but it is less certain that they have committed the naturalistic fallacy. When Ruether rejects the radical dichotomy between humans and other-than-humans or between matter and energy, she is not basing this purely on findings from subatomic physics. Similarly, her embrace of Carolyn Merchant's Partnership Model, while in keeping with the claims from scientists Paul and Anne Ehrlich, is also informed by her feminist epistemological perspectives founded on the experience of women and her feminist understandings of relationality. Note that when Boff views the Gaian theory prescriptively, he uses Gaia interchangeably with PachaMama. When Boff challenges the presumed static nature of religious truths by relying on what scientist Ilya Prigogine tells us about order-disorder-order, his conclusions equally rely on the messages from mystics, such as St Francis. Similarly, O'Murchu relies equally on the mystic – arguably more so – than on the scientist when he makes conclusions about the relational character of our universe derived from quantum physics. And while Berry, perhaps more so than our other three thinkers, gives pre-eminence to science in helping us understand the three principles that guide evolution, he includes the wisdoms of women, ancient traditions, and Indigenous traditions into his larger framework, as "Each [wisdom] has its own distinctive achievements, limitations, distortions, its own special contribution toward an integral wisdom that seems to be taking shape in the emerging twenty-first century."[68] Moreover, even if science alone were used to author an ethical conclusion, Berry and indeed all four Christian thinkers, view science as mythic in nature.[69] In light of the above, I think it logical to conclude that science is not so much *authoring* an ethic, but *co-authoring* it. On the one level, then, it would be difficult to claim that the four interlocutors have committed the naturalistic fallacy. If they have not, which I maintain is the case, then what is it they have done in their appropriation of science?

Philosopher Mary Midgley sheds light on what we are seeing here and, in doing so, arguably positions the whole naturalistic fallacy argument into a new perspective. Midgley is of the mind that the naturalistic fallacy is a "stuffed dragon and philosophers must finally stop marching around with its head balanced on their spears."[70] While I believe that the fears surrounding the possible misappropriation of science, as discussed above, might warrant the conversation not quite ceasing, as Midgley suggests, she does raise a valid point. She contends that while some thinkers do deductively reach conclusions from observing the natural world, their conclusions always stem from "a whole system of thought which they explain and defend in all its parts."[71] Midgley is not certain that facts and values can be so drastically isolated from one another, since the manner in which we make sense of the world always rests on a larger conceptual scheme. Our conceptual scheme frames how we interpret facts, she insists, concluding that "Moral judgments, if they are to be understood, can no more be arbitrary and isolated than judgments about causality."[72] In this light, it becomes apparent that when the four Christian thinkers examined here have science authoring an ethical vision, it always occurs within a larger conceptual framework in which they arrive at their conclusions.

But there is more going on, suggests philosopher Holmes Rolston III, when science is employed prescriptively, specifically within the framework of evolutionary biology or ecological science. If Midgley is not certain that facts and values can be so drastically isolated from one another generally, Rolston is not certain that the *is* can ever be isolated from the *ought* when we speak of ecosystem health or harmony. He explains: "Our account initially suggests that ecological description is logically (if not chronologically) prior to the ecosystemic evaluation, the former generating the latter. But the connection of description with evaluation is more complex, for the description and evaluation to some extent arise together, and it is often difficult to say which is prior and which is subordinate. Ecological description finds unity, harmony, interdependence, stability, etc., and these are valuationally endorsed, yet, they are found to some extent, because we search with a disposition to value, order, harmony, stability, unity. Still, the ecological description does not merely confirm these values, it informs them; and we find that the character, the empirical content, of order, harmony, stability, is drawn from, no less than brought to, nature."[73] The key point Rolston identifies is that value, or what we consider as *good*, is frequently – if not, perhaps, inevitably – encountered whenever we deal with evolutionary biology and ecosystem science. In this sense, it follows that Berry's sense of what is *good* is inevitably that which preserves and enhances this meadow, or that Schweitzer's sense of what is *good* is inevitably that which sustains and advances life. Rolston realizes that when we celebrate things such as biodiversity, order, and interdependence, for instance, biology, theology, and ethics become natural allies, and that "managing a landscape that has reared up such a spectacle of life becomes a matter of ethics and religions as well as of science."[74] Strictly speaking, he notes, these are only descriptive terms; yet, they also carry "quasi-evaluative" terms.[75] This connection of description and evaluation is complex in how it forms, for the description and evaluation "arise together" and determining a sequence of reasoning is impossible. Rolston's conclusion is not so much that an *ought* is "derived" from an *is* within the framework of evolutionary biology or ecological science, but that an *ought* is "discovered simultaneously" with an *is,* adding, "It is difficult to say where the natural facts leave off and where the natural values appear."[76]

If both Rolston and Midgley's analyses are sound, and I maintain that they are, it is easier to understand why Ruether's employment of science leads her to conclude that a natural interdependency exists, one that depicts an expanding universe that is relational, interconnected, interdependent, and finite, or why Boff concludes that new science provides a conceptual foundation for a holistic paradigm fostering relatedness. When it is life that is in question the human appears as a value-maker. When it is nature we are dealing with, and especially one we love – and here I include the human – value is synchronously present when we ponder ethical questions.

My four Christian thinkers read the science that describes the world, as Rolston suggests, "with a disposition to value." And given the larger conceptual scheme that frames the manner in which these Christian thinkers make sense of the world, the problem of the naturalistic fallacy is reframed less as an epistemological problem (deriving an *ought* from an *is*) to an ontological one: for what really is the *is* we are encountering? Is it a subject or an object? In this sense, Ruether, Boff, O'Murchu, and Berry become necessarily, as Stephen Bede Scharper suggests, "not the consciousness but the conscience of the universe,"[77] ensuring liberation for all subjects.

MAXIMIZING THE WELFARE OF THE WHOLE

In the effort to provide liberation for all creation, the four Christian thinkers examined here have journeyed between the Scylla of conferring moral consideration first to the human (individual and community), and the Charybdis of conferring moral concern above all to the biotic whole. This is not an easy journey to navigate, so it is necessary to see if they have done so with thoughtfulness, and allowed the demands and dynamics of one to inform and qualify the other. Philosopher Ingrid Stefanovic aptly expresses concern when ethicists accord the biotic whole greater reverence, thereby grouping complex phenomena within a "totalizing paradigm,"[78] that leads to questionable ethics, which would have us sacrifice the individual for the good of the biotic whole. Is this the case with the model of liberation that I contend grows out of the works of my four thinkers? I propose that while their ethical vision does accord much value to the biotic whole, it avoids the problem outlined above by comprising what I am calling an "eco-tethered liberation," which I will describe in this section.

While affirming the need to understand environmental issues *holistically,* Stefanovic is critical of various ways in which the term "whole" is understood and employed in environmental dialogue. The term is, at times, either vaguely described or naively applied to ethical reasoning, leaving us with questionable moral claims. Stefanovic cites, for example, Tom Regan's objection to "ecoholism" in that it amounts to what he calls "environmental fascism" by shifting moral considerability from the individual to the biotic wholes, potentially leaving an individual to be "sacrificed – with a clear conscience – for the good of the larger whole."[79] Fittingly, Stefanovic proposes, "[A]ny philosophy that tells us that we should sacrifice ourselves and our children for the good of the larger whole is itself morally degenerate from the start."[80] Stefanovic suggests that the problem occurs when "wholes achieve a substantial, metaphysical reality unto themselves beyond the existence of their individual parts."[81] In other words, the environment becomes so large an entity in breadth and scope that it becomes difficult, if not impossible, to speak about it and certainly any of its parts meaningfully. It becomes an abstraction and, ultimately, "an object separate from human beings instead of the very foundation of our experience."[82] Employing Cooper's argument above, she notes that this leads us to revere wholes, placing them morally above their constitutive parts. Such a totalizing and abstract view of holism, Stefanovic stresses, fails "to account adequately for implicit or hidden contexts, or for the significance of complex, synergistic relations that exceed the parameters of totalizing explanations."[83]

Stefanovic's argument serves as a valid warning to theorists who place wholes morally above their constitutive parts. It raises an important question for the four Christian thinkers of this work for whom fostering diversity, interiority, and communion for each subject is a vital part of their liberationist framework, for such a view of holism "may easily slip into a denial of difference, a denial of the value of the individual, component parts in favour of some abstract, totalitarian vision of the whole as superorganism," as Stefanovic suggests.[84] Can the principle of interiority, for instance, take hold when the subject is sacrificed for the good of the larger whole? The answer is, of course, no. However, is this what is occurring within their framework? Stefanovic would be justified in criticizing O'Murchu for seemingly doing just this. Recall that he claims, "Morality, in the quantum context, attends first to the whole and only secondarily to the parts composing the whole."[85] Still, as I discussed in chapter 3, O'Murchu seems to contradict himself on this matter when he also offers the hologram as an apt model of holism, which sees the whole not only greater than the sum of its parts, but contained in each part as well.

Notwithstanding this ambiguity, in my view the other interlocutors certainly do not present a totalizing and abstract view of holism. Certainly, as Berry maintains, we can never know parts of the universe *separate* from the whole any more than we can understand the theme of a musical piece by listening to a musical phrase without the earlier notes. It is not just the whole, but the mysteries within the whole that concern Berry. Rather than taking a totalizing view of the whole, Boff emphasizes the common good, which recognizes that humans share a destiny with the whole terrestrial, biological world. And Ruether, while subsuming our human anthropocentric ethic into the larger not-just-human "ecologic," which maximizes the welfare of the whole, simultaneously stresses that we cannot convert our minds to Earth without simultaneously converting our minds to each other. Evident here is the balance of tensions so apparent within Ruether's ethical vision. The tension also describes the manner in which Boff and Berry represent holism (and O'Murchu too, once we resolve the ambiguity surrounding his understanding: Stefanovic, for instance, considers the holographic model to be a more salubrious way of understanding the relation of whole to parts).[86]

It is a pragmatic response grounded in Earthly realities that realizes the ecological necessity of granting vital significance to the whole, while not placing it morally above its constitutive parts, for the parts are subjects, not objects. Rather than a totalizing view of holism, what these four theorists are espousing is more like a dialogical relation between the whole and its parts, one, as Stefanovic puts it, "where neither is ontologically primary."[87] In this sense, a subject is never "sacrificed" for the sake of the whole; rather, the four interlocutors simply affirm the paradoxical necessity of destroying other life. The key is to minimize this occurrence when/if possible and certainly, as O'Murchu states, to avoid meaningless suffering (such as factory animal farms) altogether.

The issue on maximizing the welfare of the whole and the challenges it presents, as Stefanovic demonstrates, brings us back to the question I have been investigating in the first four chapters of this book, a question not adequately answered by any of the four interlocutors individually: how do we actually take the liberation of all creation seriously? How are we to reconcile advocating for liberation for both the human and the other-than-human when conflicts of desires, needs, and interests arise? I will address this question in this final section.

EXPLORING AN "ECO-TETHERED" LIBERATION

While an acceptable answer to the questions above eluded my four Christian thinkers individually, in bringing their ethical visions into conversation, by way of some connecting-of-the-dots by me, I propose that they have led the way to a novel conception of liberation, which addresses the perplexing questions above. Below, I construct a conversation – which never did happen as far as I know, but is neither fanciful nor contrived – which demonstrates my point. It builds upon and adapts Gustavo Gutiérrez's threefold notion of liberation.[88]

While Gutiérrez applies his three dimensions to the human alone, I am applying them toward the larger other-than-human Earth community. The first level lies at the social level, which relates to liberation from unjust structures within society that exploit subjects. The second level lies at the personal level, which relates to an inner freedom so that subjects are in control of their own destiny or free to follow their evolutionary impulses. To ensure that one subject's liberation does not impinge on the liberation of another, however, Gutiérrez proposes a third and important dimension at a communal level. He refers to this theologically as liberation from sin. Gutiérrez's framework on liberation is comprehensive, though in a narrow way. It remains at the human level where Gutiérrez sees sin as the severing of a relationship (or friendship, as he also calls it) with God and other human beings, that is, only in loving relationship or communion with the other is each subject truly free from domination. This last point is key, for it stresses that both social and inner freedoms from oppressive structures are dependent upon the larger communal relationship one experiences with all subjects in creation.

All four of the Christian thinkers examined in this book also affirm that any authentic liberation must be a comprehensive liberation, though the web of relationships comprises the whole Earth community. Ecotheologian Charles Birch frames their reasoning well when he says, "It is a cock-eyed view that regards ecological liberation as a distraction from the task of liberation of the poor. One cannot be done without the other. It is time to recognize that the liberation movement is finally one movement. It includes women's liberation, men's liberation, the liberation of science and technology, animal liberation, plant liberation, and the liberation of the air and the oceans, the forests, deserts, mountains and valleys."[89] The difficulty here, and one not completely worked out by any one of my four thinkers, though evident when I bring their works into a communal conversation, is substantiating the claim above proportionately within an ecological *and* liberationist framework. What might this mean with regard to our *campesina*?

Given that liberation for the human does not represent a flight from the world, but is grounded and sought for in Earthly realities, a few matters are clear: authentic liberation can only come about if humans cease trying to escape the horrors of our Earthly, embodied existence in return for what Ruether calls "immortal blessedness" or invulnerability that frees us from our finite limits. In this light, liberation necessitates that we also accept our vulnerability to the violent tragic force of nature, suffering, limits, and death. In light of the third dimension of liberation put forth by Gutiérrez, this means that we accept that, as humans, we have emerged from, and exist as part of the living Earth community. There is, as Heather Eaton expresses, a deep continuity between Earth processes and ourselves, adding, "To persistently speak of humans and 'the environment' is ridiculous in the face of planetary dynamics, evolutionary processes, and emergent complexities."[90] Dennis Patrick O'Hara and Alan Abelsohn echo this sentiment, underlining what Berry himself made apparent, that "it is not possible to have healthy humans on a sick planet."[91] Continuing this line of reasoning and extending this conversation among all four Christian thinkers, discerned within their mutual conversation, is a novel truth about liberation: it can only ever be authentic – that is not exclusive to humans – if tethered to the larger bioregional context. A brief explanation will help explain what I mean.

On the one hand, Berry is arguably most adamant that we quell our "rage against the human condition," that "unwillingness of humans to accept life under the conditions that life granted us." Berry calls for nothing less than the ultimate subsuming of the human to the ecological imperative – which entails, among other things, preserving and enhancing the "meadow" – and accepting our anthropological vulnerability to the pains of life and ultimately death. On the other hand, Ruether and Boff, and to a certain extent O'Murchu, are equally adamant about the imperative to give preference to fulfilling the needs of our Guatemalan *campesina* walking long and far for water.

I suggest that Berry's sophisticated understanding of the darker side of creativity, and his insistence that we confer to the Earth primordial concern, ultimately induces Ruether and Boff to expose the preferential option for the poor itself to a certain vulnerability. One can almost picture Berry figuratively taking our liberation thinkers by the hand toward the dangerous, yet necessary, precipice of our anthropological condition, and ecological necessities with a clear understanding that only in this manner can humans *and* all Earth subjects find authentic and lasting liberation and, ultimately, the harmony they seek to live sustainably on Earth. At the same time, however, Ruether and Boff – for whom the liberation of the human in all its forms (corporeal, social, economic, and spiritual) must also be taken seriously – remind Berry, and to some extent O'Murchu as well, that while they certainly accept our radical dependence on Earth and recognize destruction as being an inescapable part of creativity, they maintain that the burdens that arise from these must never be disproportionately placed on an already vulnerable majority that is dominated socially, economically, and by gender or race, and is arguably the least responsible for our problems. In other words, the liberation of the Guatemalan woman and her community must also be taken seriously; burdens, then, ought to be portioned justly.

As I stated above, this conversation is neither fanciful nor contrived. Ruether, Boff, and O'Murchu already recognize a dynamic between ecological and social justice as two unique, yet inseparable, entities and Berry never suggests that the *campesina* ought to bear the burdens of giving preference first and foremost to Earth – and would find it abhorrent if she were to do so. I have merely connected the dots already drawn, which are undergirded by our relationality. The fruit of such a communal negotiation and the willingness to accept the vulnerable status of any liberation is, I think, a novel and important understanding of how one's own liberation is inextricably tied to the liberation of all subjects. Put another way, if a shared liberation within the larger Earth community can only occur within the constraints of a larger bioregional model, then any authentic liberation can only ever be a tethered liberation, or perhaps better labelled eco-tethered liberation. To understand an eco-tethered liberation more succinctly, consider the river, on whose banks humans need to settle and grow. It must be treated as a subject, never an object, and must, therefore, be accorded a say in how it is approached. The imperative to give preference to fulfilling the needs of our Guatemalan woman or her community can no longer – in light of what new science is telling us – be considered outside the larger ecological imperative.

Where conflicts between the two arise, the key is *not* to circumvent the liberation of the larger biotic community – as humans have been doing for some time now – but to address the larger and global preferential option for the rich, so that it is not the *campesina* who disproportionately bears the burden, or the river from which she draws water, but the entire human species that proportionately limits its actions. For, just as destruction is an inescapable part of creativity, so too is constraint an inescapable part of liberation. Their liberationist framework necessitates, therefore, negotiating communally with the wider bioregional community we discussed above, whereby the concerns, realities, and the tendencies of all subjects – here I would say their autopoietic nature – are included in the human life project. This is an ecological adaptation of Gutiérrez's third dimension of liberation: only in loving relationship or communion with *all of creation* is each subject truly free from domination. The significance of this insight can hardly be understated. Just as Berry has us reinvent the human at the cultural level, then, so too liberation of the human is reimagined in a new light: one unshackled from the anthropocentric foundation so common in Christian thinking and shared among all Earth subjects and, thus, inextricably consigned to an "eco-tethered" status.

To test the viability of an eco-tethered liberation, it might be helpful to conceive a scenario concerning the *campesina* and her Guatemalan community. Could an understanding of an eco-tethered liberation be used by wealthier communities to give ontological primacy to the land, thus denying the liberation of our *campesina* and her community? There is certainly a risk involved when the moral consideration of our Guatemalan community – arguably without much political and economic clout – is pitted against the moral consideration of the natural world represented by environmentalists with more political and economic clout. In this scenario, is there not a risk to *any* delimiting of the liberationist ideal? An example will suffice to explain what I mean.

It is not mere speculation envisioning the possibility of the *campesina* and her community – people already vulnerable – having their liberation tethered, unilaterally and in the name of the liberation of other Earth subjects, perhaps by ardent environmentalists who deem that a river's right to flow is more important than the community's right to use the rocks that lie along its border to build a school. Ramachandra Guha has made comparisons between the environmentalisms of the global North and South, for instance, and provides evidence that this has indeed been the case.[92] The environmentalism of the global North, he states, strives to save a natural setting *just for itself*, acknowledging an ethical responsibility toward "other species" while also enriching the "spiritual side" of human existence by preserving pristine wildernesses.[93] When such thinking surfaces in countries like India, Guha notes, the needs of entire human communities can be lost in the passion to save the land. Vast areas, as national parks and sanctuaries, can be protected from all "human interference" in the name of protecting nature, thus ignoring our own species, sometimes abruptly displacing entire communities deprived of political clout and without compensation from a territory on which they might have lived, and depended on, for generations.

While this is undeniably always a possibility, and one presumably more likely to occur as human populations continue to grow (especially in the global South) thereby increasingly encroaching on increasingly degraded natural lands, one cannot accuse my four interlocutors of ignoring this possibility, or in failing to provide a way to address it. When Ruether underlines the idea that converting our minds to Earth cannot happen without converting our minds to each other, she is also stressing that the option of the poor (for humans) cannot come about without also addressing the destructive "option for the rich," an option that currently prevails throughout the globe. The larger questions of production and distribution (which favour wealthier human communities) cannot be ignored when addressing the needs of the Guatemalan community. In this light, the four interlocutors are consistent in their thinking. Within the framework of relationship, any conflict between a river's right to flow and the right for our Guatemalan *campesina* to retrieve water from it is a false dichotomy.

CONCLUSION

Two main questions have guided my assessment in this chapter of whether the four interlocutors take and integrate environmental and social issues seriously: was the focus of their attention placed on the entire creation and the current logic of domination that marginalizes both the human and the other-than-human? And do we find within their ethical visions evidence of a thorough and thoughtful examination of what is required to unite a liberationist agenda with an environmental ethic, as well as a commitment to see this occur? I contend that to both questions the answer is "yes." The four thinkers have approached the liberation of all creation with much thoughtfulness and critical attention. Further, in their integration of the social and environmental problems facing our planet, there is evidence that they did not merely graft environmental concerns onto a social ethical framework. There was evidence of a critical conversation – in part elaborated by me – that had the two issues inform and qualify each other.

In the preface of this book, I brought up the saying one sometimes hears when seeking directions from local people: "Oh, you can't get there from here!" While it holds an air of lightness, I cannot think of a better metaphor than this to express the essence of the type of ethics my four Christian thinkers promote. For, on the one hand, it denotes that liberation for the entire planet can be reached only by a circuitous, complex, and messy route. These four theorists comprehend this. Conventional modes of ethical thinking are either bankrupt or deficient in one way or another. The moral imagination of the western tradition appears distressingly unable either to address the realities of the Anthropocene or to change the social, economic, and political structures that – as the Bishop of Mozambique points out in my introduction – seemingly allow African children to die so that North American children may overeat. In light of this reality, Ruether, Boff, O'Murchu, and Berry turned the tables and asked, What kind of ethics do we need today and tomorrow when the liberation of countless subjects of creation is at stake? Addressing this question paved the way to conceiving the liberation of all creation.

Indeed, a new ethical approach will have to represent a radically new relational paradigm for the twenty-first century that places the liberation of all creation above social, economic, and political structures. Any attempt to lessen the complexity of the path toward liberation – whether by taking a detour around the negotiation phase or by excluding those on the periphery – will only thwart us from reaching the harmony we seek among ourselves or between us and the natural world. Perhaps the main reason contemporary conventional ethics is proving inadequate for the task is that it takes detours around the complexities of ethical decision-making, as Dussel notes, by permitting the rationalization of the lifeworld of billions of excluded people into simplified, manageable economic, political, and cultural subsystems. It avoids the concrete everyday slow and complex – messy – process that my four Christian thinkers are telling us is the truer path toward liberation for all creation.

One might think that making a loving relationship with creation our starting point in ethics is too simple or unattainable, but this need not be the case within a bioregional context. Moreover, as I have shown, love as a starting point not only obliges us to eschew simple answers to complex issues, it also serves instrumentally as a viable means for knowing the world. One might wince at the level to which their ethical vision has us embrace our anthropological vulnerability, but this is our biological reality: ignoring it, these theorists point out, has proved and will continue to prove folly. Taking detours around this reality explains why our waters are warming, countless species are becoming extinct, and the majority of the human species live on the margins of life fed only too often by platitudes, such as "nourishment will come from faith."

One might think the four interlocutors are not being very serious when they propose a vast communal conversation among all of creation; yet, while daunting and arguably never fully realized, viewed from a liberationist point of view, the primary task here is to seek, first and foremost, to include the victims. Moreover, the task occurs at the bioregional level. And through use of analogy, discerning the rights of a river is not as impracticable as it might seem. One also might believe that the four interlocutors are committing a logical fallacy when they employ science prescriptively. But, is science even authoring their ethical vision independent of a whole system of thought? Besides, when the subject matter is all of creation, one we love, value is synchronously present when ethical questions are pondered. Finally, we might question the wisdom of granting such high value to the whole, noting the risk we take that could lead to a denial of difference or a denial of the value of the individual. Yet, when the relationship of the whole and the parts is perceived as dialogical, the focus put forth by the four Christian thinkers seems less precarious.

Yes, it is a messy ethical vision these four Christian thinkers put forth, but, as this chapter has demonstrated, it also appears feasible, and arguably more in line with the social and environmental needs of our day. What is more, it is unlikely that these thinkers could have articulated such a vision had they not approached both the liberation of the human and the natural world in the manner they did. By sheer force of purpose, they needed to allow the dynamics and concerns surrounding the issues of environmental degradation and the marginalization of the majority of humankind to inform and qualify, as well as clarify and affirm, each other. When brought together into a communal conversation, it became evident that their ethical vision is a product of this dynamic. The fruit of this integration is, I suggest, the notion of an eco-tethered liberation.

As will be shown more clearly in the ensuing chapters, Ruether, Boff, O'Murchu, and Berry appear much less concerned with arriving at an *approximation* of truth, and far more concerned with arriving at an *assessment* of truth. In fact, one gets a sense that truth takes on what I can only call a liberationally pragmatic significance to it, something I will attend to in more detail in chapter 8. A liberationally pragmatic truth is measured more by the quality with which *all* subjects in creation can participate in their own (Earthly) liberation, than by merely being consistent with what we know of the world through science or indeed with tenets of the Christian faith. By pragmatic, I am referring, in part, to the Deweyan perspective insofar as it sees truth as an instrument used by human beings to solve their problems in a radically democratic fashion.[94] Indeed, in the Deweyan tradition, as in the liberationist tradition, philosophical ethics ought to arise out of the everyday experiences of ordinary peoples, working in solidarity to attempt to clarify the cause of suffering, with the goal of reconstructing (not just deconstructing) a just system within a democratic framework. Like my four Christian thinkers, then, Dewey sees truth as being bound up with socially desired consequences, which, for our interlocutors, is more definitively represented as liberation.

The next chapter takes a deeper look at the quality with which these four Christian thinkers have appropriated the science. This is crucial, given the pre-eminence science receives in forming their ethical vision. The inquiry goes far beyond the possibility of committing logical fallacies though. For surely the quality of the conclusions attained from science will reflect upon the quality of their ethical vision. Have my chosen authors taken science seriously?

CHAPTER SIX

Toward a Serious and Sustained Reflection on Science

Having concluded that Ruether, Boff, O'Murchu, and Berry have taken the liberation of the entire planet seriously, adeptly integrating the related dynamics and concerns into a viable ethic, my examination turns to science. As I discussed in the introduction, it is the natural sciences, and more specifically, a particular understanding of the natural sciences, one I am broadly calling "post-normal," which is the kind of science these interlocutors advocate we need today. Why is this distinction important?

Post-normal science is a relatively new term, and I do not present it definitively here. Yet it is helpful for my purposes because it embraces the main tenets of what some label new science, and it appears far more open to an inclusive and more expansive epistemic framework. Thus, the science the four thinkers appropriate rejects a vision of the universe that is mechanistic, reductionist, seemingly purposeless, and competitive, and challenges suppositions that science produce final, precise estimates about reality that are free from uncertainty. In its stead, the science they appropriate works from a new paradigm, one that views the universe as being deeply relational, self-regulating, and self-determining and, therefore, open to uncertain outcomes. Understood as being mythic in nature, this science is open to the Gaia theory not only for its descriptive value of how the planet might operate, but also for its transformative praxis. Moreover, post-normal science is inclusive of normative social values and informed by inputs from community and stakeholders. In so doing, it embraces multiple types of knowing, challenging the sharp dichotomy between expert-lay participants. Importantly, in their appropriation of this science, all four authors depend on the writings of Pierre Teilhard de Chardin, which challenge scientific dualistic thinking, suggesting a fundamentally distinctive epistemology or way of knowing in science, an issue I will return to in chapter 8.

Investigating the thoughtfulness, constructive resolution, and critical attention with which the science is appropriated is particularly important, as the four interlocutors have assigned pre-eminence to contemporary findings in science to derive normative guidelines from nature. It is reasonable to conclude that the quality with which the science is understood and used by them will affect the quality of their ethical visions. It is worth mentioning that some of the scientists whose work they employ have pushed the boundaries of orthodoxy within their own disciplines. The main focus of this chapter, then, is not on their integration of science – for this was examined in the first four chapters of this book – but on the quality with which these interlocutors have entered into a conversation with science.

Much as I did in chapter 5, to undertake this examination, I will first need to be more precise as to what I mean by the criteria of thoughtfulness, constructive resolution, and critical attention, this time from a scientific point of view. Taking cues from various authors who have addressed this subject,[1] I suggest that to assess the quality of their appropriation of science, the following particular criteria should mark the works of my chosen four thinkers: a coherent and sophisticated understanding of the current scientific theories; a resolve to avoid conclusions not supported by current scientific evidence; a readiness to accept the challenges to previously held beliefs brought forth by scientific inquiry; and – related to the previous criterion – attention to potential incompatibilities between empirically based assertions and metaphysical claims. The point is not to determine whether their appropriation of science is faultless. Such a determination is not possible since, as I will show, science is not itself a homogeneous discipline with uniform methodologies or compatible theories. Instead, the aim is to determine whether or not any incompatibilities that might exist detract from the overall quality with which they appropriate the science.

Second, to undertake this examination, it will be useful to examine the current critiques of ecotheologians appropriating the natural sciences. To this end, I lean on the work of environment and religion scholar Lisa H. Sideris. Her work is significant because, like mine, it draws critical attention to a crucial epistemological question underlining the more fundamental claims of Christians appropriating science: what does it mean to take nature – and by extension, the science that describes it – seriously? Moreover, Sideris also investigates a number of ecotheologians who have appropriated science to develop a new ethic that speaks to the escalating environmental crisis.

Sideris is very critical of how many Christian thinkers, including my four interlocutors, misrepresent nature by neglecting and/or misappropriating basic scientific data. She contends that we ought to understand nature "as science understands it,"[2] adding "if details of the model are wrong, the ethics that emerges will, accordingly, be inappropriate."[3] But here lies the crux of the matter: Sideris is suggesting that none of my chosen authors have understood the nature of things in the world according to science. But *how does* science "understand" nature? While Sideris is not entirely clear on this crucial point, as will become evident, it is clear that Ruether, Boff, O'Murchu, and Berry differ with Sideris not only on what type of science we need when the liberation of all of creation is at stake, but on how science functions.

Sideris's work, then, will serve as a fruitful way of articulating some of the conceivable critiques of these four Christians authors' appropriation of science. I will begin this investigation by describing her argument in more detail, enumerating its strengths and weaknesses. Sideris's work is also helpful as it opens up debate on two larger and important issues surrounding my investigation of whether Ruether, Boff, O'Murchu, and Berry have taken science seriously. The first is that in appraising one's appropriation of science, how one understands the structures and processes in science matters. Assuredly, the authors of my investigation work from a decidedly different view of science than some of the mainstream approaches to science. Is theirs a viable view of science? Accordingly, part of this chapter will explore – in broad strokes, for this is too large a topic to portray comprehensively here – *how* science is structured, and some of its processes for knowing reality and communicating its findings. I will also discuss the nature of myth and metaphor in science and the powerful ways in which these shape how scientists understand and communicate their findings.

From this, it will become clear that the attention Ruether, Boff, O'Murchu, and Berry give to myth and metaphor is not unjustified.

I explore further this notion of what type of science we need when it is the liberation for the entire planet we are seeking, by examining the issues surrounding the Gaia theory. Sideris is not alone when she downplays the value of the theory. My chosen four interlocutors embrace the theory. It is in keeping with their approach to science, which is wide in scope and breadth, inclusive of multiple scientific branches, and one that takes into account the myths and imaginations that surround the broader issue. I contend that the Gaia theory addresses the above aspects of their approach, not exclusively, but certainly uniquely and adeptly, because it serves not only as a viable interdisciplinary platform to better understand the intricate and complex processes of our planet, but also encompasses an important transformative praxis for arriving at a viable ethical vision. The chapter closes with an appraisal of each of our four authors' appropriation of science.

HOW SOME CHRISTIANS ARE MISAPPROPRIATING SCIENCE

Lisa Sideris's concern is not whether Christian ethicists derive normative guidelines from nature; this she does herself. She is more concerned with the actual *oughts* or normative claims that these ecological theologians arrive at: in other words, how their normative claims are produced. She argues that too often the oughts "represent only a part of nature's *is,* as science understands it."[4] As a result, she holds that the misappropriation of science by ecological theologians has led to the formation of inappropriate environmental ethics. Specifically, Sideris's view is that many ecological theologians have not taken into account and, therefore, have not fully realized, the implications of scientific evidence on evolution when generating their ethics, namely, that "many ecological theologians have not dealt adequately with the implications of natural selection,"[5] as presented by Darwin. These thinkers, she states, downplay or gloss over the dark and negative Darwinian processes of the natural world, such as predation, competition, and disease by relying too heavily on rosy appropriations of lessons from ecology that characterize an interdependent, cooperative, and harmonious world. She concedes that "Darwin's darker vision of nature has never completely triumphed over a pleasant, harmonious interpretation. In popular imagination, as well as in the science of ecology, there has been an ongoing tug-of-war between ecological models of harmony and evolutionary accounts of struggle and disorder."[6] However, Sideris maintains that the lessons of evolution – the "darker vision of Darwinism" – cannot be brushed aside, which she claims these thinkers do to favour more "panglossian" Christian visions or sentiments. These visions or sentiments could be yearnings for a loving God that does not wish there to be suffering, or for Christian hopes for some ultimate redemption, or for an ultimate peaceful world where "the lion and the lamb, the child and the snake, lie down together; where there is food for all; where neither people nor animals are destroying one another,"[7] something that ecological theologian Sallie McFague apparently suggests.

In her appraisal of Ruether's ethic, Sideris contends that neither Ruether's romanticized understanding of science, nor the heightened role Ruether assigns to the human is consistent with the findings of science. With regard to the latter, Sideris concludes – and it is not unwarranted – that Ruether needs to establish greater congruence between the ethical implications she derives from nature and the biblical themes she develops in support of human responsibilities toward life. Taking her own description of interdependence more seriously would imply a more modest role for humans than that of arbiters of justice and purveyors of peace and health in nature.[8] In particular, Sideris is critical of Ruether's quote from Isaiah, who promises that "even the carnivorous conflict between animals will be overcome in the Peaceable kingdom,"[9] and of Ruether's claim that the science of ecology provides us with a "vision of humanity living in community with all its sister and brother beings."[10] Sideris also takes exception to Ruether's understanding of cooperation and interdependency as being primary principles of ecosystems. She quotes Ruether as saying, "Cooperation and interdependency are the primary principles of ecosystems, within which competition between populations stands as a subcategory that serves to maintain this interdependency in a way that sustains the balanced relation of each population in relation to the whole."[11] From this, Sideris concludes that Ruether is either ignoring the normative implications of evolutionary processes that posit struggle, predation, and competition in her conclusions, or believes those scientific findings "have no such normative import."[12] Sideris adds, "Because she wishes to uphold an ecological ethic of interdependency and coevolution, Ruether must dispel any 'survival of the fittest' reading that might creep into a nature-informed ethic. She invokes this phrase and expresses concern that such a reading of nature could distort an ecological ethic by mistakenly implying that 'the strong have a right to prevail over the weak and that, in the competitive struggle for existence, might makes right.'"[13] Sideris's main issue with Ruether's appropriation of science, then, is that there is nothing of nature within her vision that comes out of science, which is ultimately disturbing; moreover, if nature's processes are in disarray, it is because of "humans alone, in disobeying nature's limits and engaging in competition."[14]

It should be noted, however, that Sideris's reading of Ruether's appropriation of science is slanted, because she does not consult the multitude of Ruether's writings, just *Gaia and God*, and she fails to mention explanations Ruether provides that nuance her employment of Isaiah's quote, above. Accordingly, as I will discuss more thoroughly later in this chapter, Sideris overlooks some of the more cooperative and harmonious aspects of the Gaia theory that underscore Ruether's arguments. Where Sideris is justified is in pointing out that more recent findings in ecosystem science are not found within Ruether's – and admittedly the other three interlocutors'– writings. Sideris discusses the popular misconceptions of nature being in "balance" and "self-regulating." She presents a brief survey of the history of thinking on ecology, pointing out how ecologists and historians of ecology are, on the whole, moving away from the understanding of ecosystems as cooperative, co-evolving, and harmonious units that maintain some form of balance. The advent of chaos theory has led many ecologists to view the processes of nature as random, rather than as natural self-regulating communities.

Such a claim also potentially challenges the writings of all four of my chosen interlocutors. Because of the importance of ecology to all four of these thinkers, more attention is warranted here. Sideris's claim above, for instance, receives support from ecologist Peter F. Sale. While not using the term chaos himself, he affirms much of what Sideris is saying here: the idea that nature has some inherent self-regulating equilibrium-creating ability, while popular in our society, he says, is more a myth than reality. Nature is not in "balance," but in a continuous state of non-equilibrium and change.[15] Thus, in ecological studies there has been a shift from whole, finely tuned communities to natural systems that comprise what Sale calls "a mosaic of ephemeral patches [of communities] within which the component species exist as populations of individuals variously struggling to survive and reproduce."[16] These individuals struggle against a wide-ranging assortment of difficulties that might influence them suddenly and negatively: predators, a harsh climate or season, and unanticipated turbulences, such as famines. Sale concludes from this that natural systems are open dynamic "patches" of communities fraught with constant disturbances that place them in imbalance or a non-equilibrium state. Moreover, while disturbances are common within the natural world, many, such as mudslides, falling trees, or storms, occur "naturally." He adds, "Life is tough, but it is tough in varying ways from place to place and time to time."[17] In short, if nature's processes are in disarray, it is not solely due to humans disobeying nature's limits and engaging in competition.

Models emphasizing balance, Sale points out, rely on the concept of niche development where "no two species can occupy the same niche."[18] Where biologists were finding many similar species co-occurring, the thinking was that the species would continuously interact in density-dependent ways to homeostatically regulate the others' abundances, eventually leading to some form of balance. Rather than such a checks-and-balances model, however, biologists in the last half of the twentieth century were observing a patchwork of communities, some with a high diversity of species co-existing. This perplexed scientists, for, according to niche theory, one species regulates another, and if – as Darwinism maintains – only the fittest survive, then how, for example, is it possible that there can exist so many similar species of trees in a rainforest or species of fish on a reef? One obvious answer – especially since such occurrences were often found in tropical regions – is that there are sufficient resources for a diversity of similar species to exist alongside each other. However, ecologists were also finding that extinctions of species, as well as exponential population growth, were common occurrences within patchwork communities. In other words, any equilibrium that might be found was not due to, or had little to do with, the interactions among species. This being the case, Sale suggests that the niche concept carries no meaning and must be discarded. The absence of competition here means that there is no self-regulating mechanism that generates balance. Along the same line of reasoning, ecologists can find no mechanism that causes destroyed ecosystems to return to their previous state.

To be sure, Sale concedes there may still be interactions among individual local groups of species, and in predictable ways. Indeed, he points out that long-term equilibrium has occurred at various places and times, "but these patterns of interaction," he maintains, "are not universal, and they do not persist indefinitely, even within single local patches."[19] Sale concludes that we must take a less homeostatic view of nature that focuses *not on the group* but on the *individual organism's* struggle for existence. Here, chaos, as Sideris states, appears more the norm. The organism that can best tolerate harsh disturbances tends to win in the struggle for existence. These conclusions, as I will discuss later in this chapter, do not entirely correspond with the more group-focused dynamic of ecosystems presented by my chosen Christian thinkers, and seems to run contrary to a Gaian understanding of a self-regulating, self-renewing planet.

Finally, I turn to Sideris's critique of the appropriation of science "in mythopoetic form, as an enchanted 'epic of evolution,' a creation story common to all believers and atheists alike."[20] Sideris is, unquestionably, referring to the Universe Story, thereby extending her critique to all four of my chosen Christian thinkers.[21] Sideris is wary of the religious nature that these scientific narratives take on, since they narrow our understanding of the universe and our roles to one particular mode and vision. Sideris is also upfront in her criticism of using physics to arrive at an environmental ethics. Specifically, she does not believe physics should be used as a means of understanding interdependence at the ecological level.[22] When she mentions physics, in the context of its appropriation by Christian thinkers, she often speaks of it disapprovingly by coupling it with the adjective "postmodern."[23] While she does not explicitly say what she means by the term "postmodern physics," we do get clues on what it might mean from her reference to the infamous "Sokal hoax," whose architect (or perpetrator, depending on how one views the affair), theoretical physicist Alan Sokal, Sideris lauds.[24] She quotes Sokal as making "the reasonable observation that 'anyone who insists on speaking about the natural sciences – and nobody is forced to do so – needs to be well-informed and to avoid making arbitrary statements about the sciences or their epistemology.'"[25]

When Sideris criticizes "postmodern science" for its "abstruse theories and concepts"[26] that jettison subject-object dualisms, treat all creation as "subjects,"[27] and for its alignment of ecological perspectives with those from quantum science,[28] her thinking about science as a way of knowing the world appears to be very much in line with that of Sokal, who dismisses postmodernist thinking as "nonsense and sloppy." Sokal maintains that it is "subjectivist thinking" that "denies the objective realities."[29] Like Sokal, it would seem reasonable to assume, Sideris believes that ecotheologians, comparable to the leftist academics whom Sokal was targeting (mostly those in the humanities, but specifically those in cultural studies and studies of science), are "betraying their cause by challenging standards of logic, truth, and intellectual inquiry, in general, and the role of these concepts in the natural sciences in particular."[30] While Sideris concedes that there are forms of postmodernism that are not incongruent with scientific methodology, she holds that many ecotheologians have helped foster an overall suspicion of the cultural authority of science.

This point on the authority of science warrants attention, for, in granting authority to science – which is something all my chosen interlocutors do, as does Sideris – it stands to reason that we should understand how much, and in what manner, science ought to have authority. At the beginning of this chapter, I pointed out Sideris's contention that too often the *oughts* that ecotheologians arrive at "represent only a part of nature's *is,* as science understands it." But how *does* science understand nature's *is*? Sideris is not precise in how she outlines her epistemological understandings of science. To suggest that we should understand *oughts* conveyed by nature "as science understands it" without first knowing *how* science understands it would be unwise. What is it about the nature of science that should or should not warrant such doubt, ambivalence, or animosity in us? Are ecotheologians mistaken in being suspicious, or at the very least, cautious, of the cultural authority of science? Or is the argument surrounding the nature of science a matter of simply respecting, as Sokal suggests above, the standards of logic, truth, and intellectual inquiry within science? Can a viable conversation between religion and science ensue if suspicions one side has about the cultural authority of the other are left unexamined? If some suspicion is warranted, then in what manner can science be said to grasp and convey objective realities?

To address these questions, I will need to discuss how science arrives at its conclusions. Even if only in broad outline, it is important to have a better understanding of its processes for knowing reality and communicating its findings. Not only will such an exploration help in understanding the challenges in assigning excessive authority to science, but it will clarify why the four Christian thinkers within this book seek to understand our world in a non-reductionist and mytho-poetic scientific manner. Indeed, it would seem also that Sideris's critique of Ruether and our other interlocutors rests, in some ways, on a divergent understanding of the nature of science.

A CAVEAT TO GRANTING EXCESSIVE AUTHORITY TO SCIENCE

It bears mentioning that addressing comprehensively how science is structured and what processes it incorporates to know reality and communicate its findings far exceeds the parameters of this chapter, let alone this section. But I do not think such an expansive analysis of the structure and process of science is essential here. It is sufficient only to assess how well all four interlocutors have appropriated science (and why, by analogy, Sideris's critique of them is at times mistaken). Therefore, it will be necessary only to obtain insight into some of the key challenges and limitations inherent in how science as a discipline is structured, how it arrives at truths, and how it communicates them. I will examine these issues largely through the writings of Thomas Kuhn, along with incorporating the insights from other philosophers. In addressing science as an overall discipline, I do not suggest that it is monolithic. Far from it; methodologies, and theories, differ among the branches of science. However, all branches of science do share fundamental commonalities. Given that my chosen interlocutors are primarily working with "new" or "post-normal" science, Kuhn's work is especially pertinent, because it speaks to paradigm changes in science. Following this, I will look at the nature and significance of myths and metaphors in the formulation and explanation of scientific concepts, borrowing upon insights from Brendon Larson and Mary Midgley.

Thomas Kuhn's 1962 *The Structure of Scientific Revolutions* has been extremely influential in how we view the scientific knowledge-making process; it ushered in a new momentum in the philosophy of science, so it is fitting that I begin my examination with it.[31] Two outcomes arise from his larger thesis merit study, because they challenge popular conceptions on how, and to what extent, we can know the world through science. The first is that we cannot speak of scientific knowledge as progressively ascending toward an approximation of a fixed truth, but rather as a process that is continuously defined by a consensus of a scientific community by increased specialization. This process of increased specialization accounts, in large measure, for why it is increasingly difficult for the lay non-scientist to appropriate the knowledge gained by science. The second and more important outcome – which is tied to the first – is that we can no longer view the scientific method as an entirely rational process in which some logical processes filter our social and cultural influences in the process of discovery.

Kuhn characterizes science as a continuous puzzle-solving enterprise operating in two ways: as normal science and as revolutionary science. Normal science, the more common of the two, is highly regimented research, which is guided by paradigms (the laws, theories, applications, instrumentations, methods, and traditions that undergird and guide the scientific endeavour), replete with exemplars, or model solutions to puzzles, in the form of tried and tested methods and assumptions affirmed by the broader scientific community. While anomalies are certainly encountered, often, Kuhn states, these do not challenge the validity of the rules, or the paradigms used. This is because scientists test the phenomena, but do not examine the models of testing themselves (much like a chess player who follows the rules of chess to win the game but does not challenge the rules he or she uses to win the game). In this way, for instance, a scientist applies the rules for calculating certain properties of an atomic nucleus in quantum physics, but does not test the rules themselves. In defending paradigms, then, contending groups of scientists use their own paradigm to argue in defence of that paradigm, making the debate somewhat circular, for, in a sense, one is using the scientific method to judge the scientific method. Another way to look at it is by envisioning a scientist wearing glasses of a particular colour. If the glasses are orange, then the wearer sees reality accordingly.

Good science cannot, therefore, be defined by rules such as Popper's criterion of falsifiability (where, by design, hypotheses are considered testable by empirical experiment), and certainly not by positivist postulates (where logical and mathematical treatments of data are considered the exclusive source of all authentic knowledge). Instead, good science, Kuhn claims, is defined by how scientists perceive and apply these exemplars. Guided by the paradigm, however, science can be extremely productive. Kuhn states: "By focusing attention upon a small range of relatively esoteric problems, the paradigm forces scientists to investigate some part of nature in detail and depth [and] the profession will have solved problems that its members could scarcely have imagined and would never have undertaken without commitment to the paradigm."[32] When situations occur whereby normal problem-solving activities fail (that is, the exemplars themselves are put in question), normal science falls into a period of crisis. It is at this point, Kuhn maintains, that the nature of scientific inquiry within a particular field is abruptly transformed by the formulation of a novel theory, at which point controversies among competing schools of thought ensue. If the new theory is accepted by the scientific community, thus replacing the old theory, a scientific revolution has occurred and scientists work within a new paradigm. Kuhn likens this change to perceptual Gestalt switches, even religious conversions. The new theories, such as those ushered in by Copernicus, Newton, Darwin, or Einstein, Kuhn maintains, transform the world within which scientific work is done and, as a result, transform the scientific imagination.

For my purpose here – given how the four thinkers I am examining rely heavily on new science – it is important to learn why new theories are initially chosen. Kuhn explains that an epistemological crisis alone is not the sole reason for changing paradigms: "Something must make at least a few scientists feel that the new proposal is on the right track, and sometimes it is only personal and inarticulate aesthetic considerations that can do that."[33] Rational arguments on why a scientist changes paradigms might be put forth, but "these arguments, rarely made entirely explicit, that appeal to the individual's sense of the appropriate or aesthetic – the new theory is said to be 'neater,' or 'more suitable,' or 'simpler' than the old."[34] In fact, Kuhn cites five criteria that scientists employ to evaluate the adequacy of a theory: accuracy, consistency, scope, simplicity, and fruitfulness. Because no two scientists fully committed to the same criteria for choice of theory understand or give weight to each criterion in the same way, and because, when deployed together, these criteria often conflict with one another, the choice between competing theories rests on multiple objective and subjective elements. How a scientist initially works within a new theory is also significant. In rejecting an old paradigm in favour of a new one, Kuhn maintains, scientists must have faith that the new paradigm will indeed succeed, as the evidence provided by problem solving is not – at least fully – there.

Kuhn is not alone on this point. Physicist and historian of science Stanley L. Jaki, for instance, speaks about Michael Faraday's reliance on faith. Despite his initial failures in proving the interconnectedness of electricity and magnetism, Faraday never showed the slightest trace of wavering in his belief that there was such a connection. Jaki quotes Faraday speaking about his failures: "[They] do not shake my strong feeling of the existence of a relation between gravity and electricity."[35] Philosopher Hilary Putnam discusses the role of value judgments in scientific deliberations. He argues that values like "coherence," "simplicity," and even "reasonable" are *presupposed* by physical science. In fact, Putnam challenges the overinflated dichotomies between fact and value cited in science, arguing – along much the same lines as Kuhn – that there have been no successful algorithmic methods for hypothesis selection. Putnam concludes that what scientists consider as objectively *reasonable* may seem so in a conventional sort of way, but this verdict carries a value judgment. Notwithstanding the above, the subjective character of acceptance of a theory does not, in Kuhn's mind, mean truth in science is all constructed. If a paradigm is to be accepted, he underlines, it must gain the support of a few scientists "who will develop it to the point where hardheaded arguments can be produced and multiplied."[36]

Subjective values do not only affect hypothesis selection. Philosopher Ingrid Stefanovic demonstrates how taken-for-granted assumptions and the context in which questions are asked within the scientific endeavour can drastically shape how scientists interpret facts and view the world, thus drastically influencing the policy-making process. By way of example, she cites a case whereby scientists interpreted an identical set of laboratory studies in different ways. A government ministry had cancelled the registration of the herbicide "alachor" by Monsanto (an agro-bio-chemical company), because its assumptions of risk and safety were markedly different from those considered by scientists within the company.[37] But the issue does not lie just with assumptions, as Stefanovic notes: biases are also problematic. In this light, the notion that science is guided, as Alan Sokal would suggest, solely by the scientific method, construed as a set of rules rigorously to be followed, seems too simplistic. Further, it becomes clear why circumscription is needed when granting cultural authority to science to describe nature, for, within the Kuhnian framework, science is not especially open-minded or critical.

Another aspect of the scientific method of which Kuhn speaks is the greater articulation and increasing specialization of knowledge that occurs during the period of normal science: as new specialties are formed, scientists develop instruments, practices, and concepts suited to a narrower range of phenomena. This point, one raised by all four of the Christian thinkers examined in this book, is of great significance. The result of increased specialization is an increase in predictive power, which is a good thing, but only within the context of normal science where scientists are working within a coherent paradigm. Moreover, this greater specialization leads to greater fragmentation within science as a whole, something physicists David Bohm and David Peat cite as the most pervasive and serious difficulty afflicting science today.[38] Another downside to this increasing specialization of knowledge, Kuhn points out, is the "unparalleled insulation of mature scientific communities from the demands of the laity and of everyday life."[39] In other words – in contrast to post-normal science – while the insulation has never been complete – since the scientist, arguably more so than any other professional (be it a poet or theologian), is working only for an audience of colleagues who take standards and the specific scientific language for granted – lay appropriation of the science is not a priority for the scientist. This issue, I suggest, will prove to be a decisive problem in the religion-science-environment-liberation debate in the decades to come since – as Kuhn effectively demonstrates – science invariably becomes increasingly specialized and complex as time passes.

This examination portrays a picture of the scientific process that is not a purely rational process, but one that includes the entire spectrum of human experience: it takes place within a fragmented social community, with social forces, habits, and biases; within a particular culture that influences what science is carried out; and within a certain paradigm that is rarely questioned. Not only are there key challenges and limitations inherent in how science arrives at truths, but also in how it communicates them. This becomes more evident when considering the use of myths and metaphors in science.

MYTHS AND METAPHORS IN SCIENCE AS AN IMAGINATIVE PROCESS

Myths and metaphors are important to the processes of science, and considering the weight Ruether, Boff, O'Murchu, and Berry give to them, they merit a separate discussion. That scientists are influenced by myths in formulating their theories should not be surprising. Writer and futurist Alvin Toffler reminds us that science is an open system embedded in society and linked to it by very dense feedback loops; it is, therefore, powerfully influenced by external environment. Its development is shaped by cultural receptivity to its dominant ideas. This explains why the acceptance of the mechanistic view coincided with the rise of a factory system and why the rise in technology (i.e., railroad, steel, textile, and auto) seemed to confirm the universe as an engineer's "Tinkertoy."[40]

On the matter of myth, Midgley writes, "We are accustomed to think of myths as the opposite of science. But in fact, they are a central part of it: the part that decides its significance in our lives. So we very much need to understand them."[41] Kuhn's thinking already opens the doors to understanding science as a not purely rational endeavour. And since science is a fully human experience, and not some natural or mechanical process, and because people are essentially purposive beings, Midgley concludes that myths naturally reflect what is important to us. Not all myths are good, however. Midgley believes Richard Dawkin's notion of a selfish gene, for instance, in which competitive interactions between organisms bespeak the survival of the fittest, is mistaken about our purpose, as it presents a world in which enlightened self-interest is a sufficient force to lead life along its evolutionary path to where we are today. But it is also inappropriate, a needless drama, she explains, that suggests self-interest and competition are deciding factors in life. Myths are not lies but "imaginative patterns, networks of powerful symbols that suggest particular ways of interpreting the world. They shape its meaning." She concludes, "The way we imagine the world determines what we think is important in it."[42] Midgley contends that the mythical quality that has many scientists reject the concept of Gaia – which I will discuss shortly – is no less present in Dawkin's selfish gene.[43] Myths are powerful, as Berry himself has shown us, and once they gain a footing in the consciousness of scientists and the larger society, they can be sustained for a long time.

Environmental scholar Brendon Larson tells us that a metaphor is no less important in scientific inquiry. There is a close relationship between metaphors and myths, notes Larson, not only on how they are both replete with values and how they each affect our view of reality, but in how one influences and even grows into the other. Metaphors over time may become myths, Larson states, and myths can inform metaphors. The use of metaphors by scientists is far more explicit, he adds.[44] Brian Greene, for instance, in trying to convey the science of string theory to his readers, "tried to stay close to the science while giving the reader an intuitive understanding – often through analogy and metaphor – of how scientists have reached the current conception of the cosmos."[45] Many more examples could be given. In the educational video series *Journey of the Universe: An Epic Story of Cosmic, Earth, and Human Transformation*,[46] Mary Evelyn Tucker, the host, has conversations with leading scientists on the subject of science and our human transformation on Earth. In explaining the science behind the origin of the universe, the scientists, it seemed, could not help but use metaphors to explain concepts. As one example, physicist Todd Duncan places our solar system in the "suburbs" of the Milky Way (our galaxy), observing the cosmic microwave background radiation is as if we were looking at "baby pictures of the universe."

Although many scientists have traditionally denounced metaphors as imprecise rhetorical embellishments, Larson tells us, metaphoric reasoning lies at the core of what scientists do when they design experiments, make discoveries, formulate theories, and describe their results to others. Put succinctly, metaphors enable us not only to understand one thing in terms of another, but also to think of an abstraction in terms of something more concrete and commonplace.[47] Author Nancy Abrams concludes that scientists have to use metaphors, which she considers a form of art that helps us figure out what is going on in reality. She says we need mathematics to come up with pictures of reality, but we need art, poetry, and language (by way of metaphor) to understand and "buy into it."[48] While scientific texts will always strive for accuracy and to narrow polysemy, Larson concludes, metaphors will continue to be an integral part of science.

The significance and seeming ubiquity of both myth and metaphor in science requires those appropriating scientific knowledge to be particularly discerning when they use imaginative patterns, symbols, figures of speech, and comparisons that might undergird and illuminate the concepts scientists are conveying. This is of particular concern in environmental inquiry, since metaphors often carry normative claims, as the implicit distinction between facts and values is not always clear. Not unlike what I discussed in the previous chapter on the naturalistic fallacy, therefore, trying to separate the *is* from the *ought* often proves very difficult. As an example, Larson uses the metaphor "earth is warming." Here "earth" and "warming" are "co-constituted" by factual and normative elements: "At a minimum, the former relies on all the scientific interest in documenting such change, and the latter relies on evidence that there is enough of a problem that we need to do something."[49] Metaphors can also be performative. When scientists say "the health of the Great Lakes has recently declined," for instance, "health," while imprecise as a term, nevertheless not only describes the reality, but changes (or at least sets out to change) reality. Despite the influence metaphors have, Larson points out that scientists are not always circumspect when they choose metaphors: some are effective, others not. This is why Midgley is critical of metaphors like "selfishness" and "clockwork" while approving of "Gaia": since the way we imagine the world determines what we think is important in it, metaphors like "selfishness" and "clockwork" are not useful. Larson agrees. Charged with symbolism, "Gaia," he says, "is a positive form of personification that focuses on our relationship with our home planet."[50] Such a metaphor, as I will discuss presently, could then allow us to begin to question other predominant paradigms, such as the mechanistic view of our world.

In light of the powerful influence metaphors and myth have upon both the formation of scientific knowledge and its dissemination and, indeed, what I have pointed out about the nature of science, its structure and ways of knowing, the challenges to any appropriation of science for the purposes of arriving at an ethic become significant. There is much a scholar should discern before he or she decides not simply how much authority science as a discipline should be granted, but how much weight or credence he or she must give to a particular idea, concept, or even theory. The discernment is ongoing and challenging, yet absolutely necessary. Helpful in this regard is the work of biologist and historian of science Jacob Bronowski.

Bronowski suggests that we think of science as an imaginative process, an infinitely human endeavour. In this light, he does not distinguish it from other imaginative activities such as art: both find order and meaning in our experience through discoveries of hidden symbols. "Science, like art," he says, "is not a copy of nature but a re-creation of her."[51] This, he explains, is why science (and art, for that matter) cannot be carried out by machines or insects. It is the creative process, the exploration of likenesses, that counts here. I think this view sums up well my exploration of the structure of science, how it arrives at truths and how it communicates them. This is also why I challenge the view, as put forth by Sideris, as well as Sokal, that we ought to understand nature "as science understands it." It seems too simple and, arguably, misguided – given what has been learned above – to grant science such decisive authority: any appropriation of science takes place under the influences of social forces, habits, and biases, within a particular culture that influences what science is done, within a certain paradigm, influenced by certain myths that are rarely questioned, and often disseminated by powerful and influential imaginative patterns, symbols, figures of speech, and comparisons that are not always accurate or appropriate.

Does this mean all scientific knowledge is constructed? No. For one, there is a definiteness to electromagnetic waves that allow me to write this book on my computer. Moreover, the critical realist approach to science taken by all four of my chosen interlocutors assumes that what one understands and judges the real to be is the result of experiencing, understanding, and judging what is observed or experienced. And, as a continuous puzzle-solving endeavour, when scientists find – or are shown – that their ideas no longer conform to what they and others observe in reality, the ideas are eventually discarded in favour of new ideas, concepts, and theories. Again, Jacob Bronowski puts it well: "Science is a very human form of knowledge. We are always at the brink of the known; we always feel forward for what is to be hoped. Every judgment in science stands on the edge of error and is personal. Science is a tribute to what we can know *although* [my emphasis] we are fallible."[52]

A POST-NORMAL GAIAN APPROACH TO SCIENCE

Equipped with a more accurate understanding of how science functions, and the processes it incorporates to know reality and communicate its findings, the question remains: How indeed are we to approach it? I am in accord with Mary Midgley on the matter of hermeneutics and standpoints when she contends that these affect how we see and approach the world, and ultimately the conclusions we draw. She quotes William James, who contends that the observer's spirituality and temper, as well as standpoint, "inevitably produce different responses and would do so even if what confronts them outside is actually the same for all."[53] Earlier I quoted Midgley saying, "The way we imagine the world determines what we think is important in it." In this light, a better question for my purpose here might be, How do we draw from the wisdom of science when it is expressly appropriated for the purpose of addressing our environmental and social crises? Context matters, as I have discussed in the previous chapter with the work of Rolston: our current context consists of vexing and sometimes incomprehensible problems, seemingly unsolvable interrelated issues, and extremely complex processes affecting the life and liberation of countless subjects. Before we even approach science, we have a goal in mind. But there is more occurring here. In light of the complex and vexing nature of our global situation, one that requires an understanding of how the entire complex planet functions, ought we to ignore the wider scientific context? Will one or two branches of science suffice to provide us with the worldview we seek? Sideris's challenge to Ruether's understanding of ecology and evolution, for instance, stems primarily from what the biological sciences are saying about the ecological and evolutionary (Darwinian) science, with some discussion on chaos and complexity theory especially in light of discussions on ecology. This understanding of our world rests mainly on the scientific interpretations from thinkers within these branches of science, with little of substance from other scientists from different specialties. Is such a limited perspective advisable? Can we afford to ignore the transformative powers that some scientific theories entail?

In this section of this chapter, then, I argue – as all four of my chosen Christian thinkers do – that the most viable approach to science, when it is the liberation for the entire planet we are seeking, is one that is wide in scope and breadth, inclusive of multiple scientific branches, and one that takes into account the myths and imaginations that surround the broader issue. Furthermore, I contend, it is the Gaia theory that addresses the above requirements, not exclusively but certainly uniquely and adeptly, as it serves not only as a viable interdisciplinary platform to understand better the intricate and complex processes of our planet, but encompasses an important transformative praxis for arriving at a viable ethical vision.

Mary Midgley affirms that the world we are trying to understand is often a great deal more complex than one scientific approach is ever likely to satisfactorily capture completely, and calls for a pluralism not only among the sciences but among all ways and branches of knowing our world. Paraphrasing the biologist J.B.S. Haldane, she says the "world is probably not just much queerer than we suppose but much queerer than we *can* suppose."[54] Midgley thinks the more profound physicists of our day have already understood this. Different questions are asked depending on the perspective; hence, different answers will ensue. She writes, "No one pattern of thought – not even in physics – is so 'fundamental' that all others will eventually be reduced to it. For most important questions in human life, a number of different conceptual toolboxes always have to be used together. And there is no single law showing us how we should combine them."[55] Along the same line of thinking, physicists David Bohm and F. David Peat call for greater creativity and communication in the sciences with a greater emphasis on the whole and not on fragments. Fragmentation, they argue, is not the same as simple specialization. The division of knowledge into various subdivisions in science is necessary to its developing precise knowledge about reality. It is when boundaries are rigid, however, that problems occur. For this reason Bohm and Peat conclude: "[I]n general, science today is becoming more and more specialized so that an individual scientist may spend a lifetime working in a particular narrow field and never come into contact with the wider context of his or her subject."[56] The two authors call for fluid boundaries between specializations and a greater awareness of the wider context by other scientists.

Each branch and subdivision of science asks different questions and sees the world from a unique perspective, and these alone cannot hope to capture fully the story of evolution. Elisabet Sahtouris, an evolutionary biologist herself, argues that we need to take a broader, more holistic cosmological look at evolution. In doing so, we find, on the whole, that life, represented in its earliest stages as ancient bacteria, while having "competed with each other for resources as they caused major planetwide problems such as starvation and global pollution [...] invented new technologies to solve them, but finally had to negotiate and learn to cooperate in communities and in the ultimate symbiotic bacterial community."[57] In other words, with this wider perspective, Sahtouris can conclude, with Ruether, about "cooperation and interdependency being the primary principles of ecosystems," and Midgley, about "fittest" as being the most "social," that "the best life insurance for any species in an ecosystem is to contribute usefully to sustaining the lives of other species, a lesson we are only beginning learn as humans."[58]

Taking a broader, more holistic cosmological look at evolution has enabled Berry to understand the universe as a communion of differentiated subjects. A cosmological approach revealed to the four Christian authors in this book that we are stardust, sisters and brothers with all creatures, connected not only to the first living cell, but to the supernova whose implosion led to the creation of solar system. The four thinkers affirm this broader, more holistic approach ardently in their writings. Diarmuid O'Murchu, for example, makes a point of charting the three principles (differentiation, autopoiesis, and communion) with *all* their dimensions: cosmological, biological, and philosophical, explaining that in this manner: "[T]he dynamics involved in the process of cosmogenesis, with key concepts of Darwinian theory reconceptualized to provide a fresh synthesis. The résumé suggests that instead of modeling the grand sweep of evolution on a biological (animal pattern), the biological pattern itself reflects the creative unfolding of the greater reality."[59]

This wider approach, one with fluid boundaries, specifically within the Gaian perspective, has Lovelock conclude, "Our interpretation of Darwin's great vision is altered … It is no longer sufficient to say that 'organisms better adapted than others are more likely to leave offspring.' It is necessary to add that the growth of an organism affects its physical and chemical environment; the evolution of the species and the evolution of the rocks, therefore, are tightly coupled as a single, indivisible process."[60] The Gaia theory, referred to by physicist John Ziman as "The Challenging, Inspiring, Irreducible Pluralism of Gaia,"[61] undergirds a good portion of the four interlocutors' ethical vision. It has reframed how we understand evolution. Gaia is the natural domain for discussion among the sciences, a place where the world of life, the world of consciousness, and the world of the social come together and engage. Ziman sees this pluralism of the sciences as not so much a weakness of the human intellect, but as the "product of the physic-bio-psychic history of our Gaian abode."[62] Gaia, then, is emblematic not only of the broader scientific approach to life and evolution; it is an affirmation of the commingling of the mysterious spiritual thinking with the scientific empirical thinking so needed today.

While the Gaia theory has gained the acceptance of a good portion of the scientific community, thus elevating it from its previous status as hypothesis, the theory is still not without controversy among scientists: its very name evokes hostility for some, because it implies Earth is a living entity; others note that reference to Earth as a goddess creature has sanctioned some "flaky" interpretations from a diverse population of writers.[63] Some, like Peter Sale, who still refers to it as a hypothesis, reject the theory, as he is critical of notions of balance in nature and group selection. Yet, he does not reject all self-regulating mechanisms. By placing emphasis on the individual mechanism and not the group mechanisms,[64] he accepts the "far simpler mechanisms in play that continue the survival of particular genomes,"[65] but rejects, for instance, there being any mechanism working to force the forest back to its previous state after a fire. Along similar lines, Richard Dawkins criticizes the theory because the group mutualisms that lead to optimal conditions for life pose a problem for evolutionary theory, that is, they are susceptible to "cheats" (organisms *not* contributing to optimal conditions for life, but participating in the benefits). Such cheats "would outreproduce [their] more public-spirited colleagues and genes for public-spiritedness would soon disappear."[66] Dawkins cannot see how Gaia itself can be a product of natural selection.

Given the above contentions as well as the prominence Gaia theory plays in the ethical vision of our four Christian thinkers, it seems judicious to inquire about the manner in which my chosen four authors have approached the theory specifically. Have they demonstrated a coherent and sophisticated understanding of the evolutionary theory and Gaian theory? Have they given critical attention to potential incompatibilities between empirically based assertions and metaphysical claims? This last question is significant as each of the thinkers finds within the Gaia theory not only an acceptable scientific way of understanding planet-wide homeostasis, but a spiritual paradigm that serves as a transformative praxis for helping humans to live more harmoniously within creation.

One of the problems in discussing the scientific issues behind Gaia is that the discussions are ongoing and new insights and definitions frequently arise.[67] A further challenge surrounding discussions of the theory is the inherent interdisciplinary nature of the topic. Until a few decades ago, the editors of a volume of discussion that came out of the Second Chapman Conference on Gaia in Valencia, Spain, tell us that the Earth sciences, for the most part, approached their research through disciplinary lenses: biology, chemistry, geology, atmospheric, and ocean studies. Ziman ponders why scientists might find Gaia disconcerting. He suggests that scientists find that it "can't be squeezed into any of their established pigeonholes: it mixes together concepts from the chemical, biological and physical sciences," which makes it difficult to combine these into a coherent, unified representation or vision. He suggests that "this intrinsic pluralism is one of its glories and fascination."[68] Yet, as biologist Lynn Margulis points out, the theory itself cannot be understood without collaboration from biologists, especially microbiologists, geologists, geochemists, atmospheric chemists, and even meteorologists "to understand science outside their own fields."[69] Margulis appears to imply the same reasoning when she quotes geneticist Theododius Dobzhansky, saying, "nothing in biology makes sense except in the light of evolution";[70] yet Margulis goes on to qualify, "Evolution is simply *all* of history"[71] (original italics), adding "The study of evolution is vast enough to include the cosmos and its stars as well as life, including human life, and our bodies and our technologies."[72] On the positive side, the editors of the volume mentioned above note, "Happily, the evolution of interdisciplinary science into the mainstream and the ongoing development of Earth system science have promoted scientific inquiry seeking and elucidating Gaian – and nonGaian – mechanisms within the Earth system."[73] In fact, they suggest, in the Kuhnian framework, that Gaia is "exiting its 'revolutionary' phase – of vociferous controversy and ostracism from the scientific establishment – and is entering its phase of 'normal' puzzle-solving science."[74]

While conclusive statements regarding Gaia continue to elude the scientific community, it is interesting to note that the objections raised above have been considered by other scientists. David Wilkinson, for instance, posits that, contrary to criticism of Gaia by evolutionary biologists, such as Dawkins (who cannot see Gaia being a product of natural selection), biosphere regulation is theoretically possible. If we shift our attention from "investment mutualisms" (where both organisms provide some service to their partner at some cost to themselves) to "byproduct mutualism" (where a waste product of one organism is used by its partner), he reasons, "regulation can emerge in a system without active selection for regulation."[75] Rather than looking at this process within Gaia as a process of natural selection, Wilkinson suggests that we see it as an emergent property of a complex system, thus challenging notions that Gaia is necessarily teleological in character. In other words, he maintains that criticisms from scientists like Dawkins do not hold, because Gaian systems do not have to be a product of natural selection.[76]

Scott Turner takes a physiological view of the emergent process for arriving at homeostasis and, using insights gained from studying termite-fungus symbiotic relationships, he suggests that metabolic complementarity (as seen with the termite-fungus relationship, where together they produce more efficient enzymes to break down woody material), could play a large role in emergent homeostasis. He suggests that there could be a co-opting of the physical environment, modifying, for instance, fluid densities, wind speeds, and concentration of particular substances through emergent processes to arrive at homeostatic conditions. Such co-opting, evident within the termite-fungus association, can be transferred onto a Gaian physiology, thus potentially accounting for the homeostatic condition of the planet. Turner also suggests that there is within the biotic systems an ecological inheritance whereby "Gaia may require a sort of extracorporeal genetic memory, shaping the selective milieu in which the biosphere's many extended organisms operate."[77] Certainly with regard to the termite-fungus association, "the modifications of the soil environment associated with the colony outlast any individuals within the colony, and the success of future generations of workers and fungi depends in part upon the structural legacy left to them by previous generations."[78] Such hypotheses suggested by Turner could address Sale's concern raised above, as they offer possible explanations why forests can revert back to their previous states after devastating fires.

Finally, scientists Francesco Santini and Lodovico Galleni tell us that the assumption that Gaia theory and evolutionary theory are incompatible has proven false. They and other evolutionary theorists are increasingly finding compatibilities between the Gaian and Darwinian theories.[79] There is now widespread consensus among scientists that life can drastically affect or "regulate" the biosphere. Few today would argue against Margulis when she says, "If the earth's surface were not covered with oxygen-emitting bacteria, algae, and plants, as well as methane- and hydrogen-producing bacteria and countless other organisms, its atmosphere would long ago have degenerated to the same carbon dioxide-rich steady state that today can be found on Mars and Venus."[80]

Controversy persists however, and probably will for some time, on how and why a system regulates. So while scientists can agree with the Gaian science – as I discussed in earlier chapters – that the Earth has maintained a relatively constant surface temperature over the past 4 billion years, despite the fact that the sun's heat on Earth has increased 30 to 50 per cent in that time period, they are not yet in agreement on *why* and *how* all this happens. Nevertheless, theoretical arguments that regulation is fully a product of chance, Wilkinson notes, are becoming increasingly difficult to maintain. He himself rules this out, as recent modelling studies "hint at the possibility" that it is more than "luck" that life has survived so long on Earth.[81]

What is certain about the Gaia theory, given the planetary context of environmental degradation in which it arises, its inherently interdisciplinary nature, and the significance of its name, is that any discussion of this theory can never be fully or even satisfactorily addressed by one scientific discipline. The theory has taken on a multidimensional character that necessarily comprises the natural sciences, philosophy, religion, and environmental ethics. Mary Midgley argues that this broader union between the empirical and the mystical or spiritual is exactly what we need to address our environmental crisis. The theory in both its scientific, metaphoric, or mythic form "suddenly open[s] the window which, for a century, had been firmly closed between modern scientific thinking and the spiritual world that our ancestors, and most other human cultures, had always assumed was there around them."[82] Midgley, who understands the powerful relationship between myth and science, reminds us that not all myths are good. Gaia can serve as an excellent myth and therefore a bridge not only among the various branches of natural sciences, but between the natural sciences and philosophy, and we can include religion here. She sums up the matter well, saying, "The idea of Gaia – of life on earth as a self-sustaining natural system – is a powerful tool that could generate solutions to many of our current problems. It does not just lead to new applications of science and technology. It can also counteract the corrosive forms of social atomism and individualism which infuse much current scientific thought. Its approach, once fully grasped, makes a profound difference, not just to how we see the earth but to how we understand life and ourselves."[83] Such a metaphor evokes a positive relationship with the planet. It could allow us to begin to question other predominant paradigms, such as our mechanistic view of our world.

Ostensibly, as Midgley puts it, the notion of evolution can seem like a game of chance, as biochemist Jacques Monod believes, or more mysterious and having some kind of order. This latter type of thinking, she insists, is how Darwin saw the universe. Such an approach to the world fits well with the approach of many physicists today "who are struck by the coincidences that are emerging in the cosmic order."[84] One can repudiate the Gaia theory, as Sale does, or refute its ability to provide normative guidelines, as Sideris does, but this is becoming increasingly harder to justify on scientific grounds and arguably on ethical grounds too. Science writer Fred Pearce, on discovering in 1994 that Lovelock was considering changing the name of the theory because of its mystical connotations, wrote the following in *New Scientist*: "Gaia as metaphor; Gaia as a catalyst for scientific enquiry; Gaia as literal truth; Gaia as Earth Goddess. Whoever she is, let's keep her. If science cannot find room for the grand vision, if Gaia dare not speak her name in Nature, then shame on science. To recant now would be a terrible thing, Jim. Don't do it."[85] Lovelock, in fact, chose to keep the name in the end, not wanting to lose the poetry and emotion it evokes, as these "keep us in good heart while the battle goes on."[86] Gaia holds promise as a scientific theory and wields transformative power as an ethos.

Deciding the exact role and manner the Gaia theory ought to play in the creation of an ethical vision is not straightforward. It requires us to keep in mind how science is structured and how it knows the world and communicates its findings. If, as Bronowski puts it, science is more like art in that we do not "copy" nature but re-create it, then, like any art, our spirituality and temper cannot be overlooked. We cannot afford to dismiss Gaia. Nor can we afford to approach it without scientific rigour. Have Ruether, Boff, O'Murchu, and Berry taken the Gaia theory seriously? I believe they have. Have they taken the whole of science they appropriated seriously? I will turn to this question in this final section.

IS SCIENCE BEING TAKEN SERIOUSLY?

With the exception of Diarmuid O'Murchu, my chosen interlocutors do not deal at any length with Darwinist thinking on evolution. This is unfortunate, as Midgley points out how Darwin's thinking can deepen our understanding of how connected we are to the natural world, especially animals. However, this is not problematic – certainly not as problematic as Sideris claims – since, as I will point out, all four of our authors maintain a balance between the hope that comes from reading science and the dark paradoxes that, they insist, we must accept.

There is, to be sure, some legitimacy to Sideris's contention that Ruether's writings do not seem to pay sufficient attention to the darker side of *natural* (at least nonhuman) processes, focusing instead on the darker side of *human* actions – a claim, to a degree, that I attribute to Boff as well. But does this mean they entirely ignore this darker side to nature? To answer this, it helps to look at Ruether's other writings. In fact, I suggest that Ruether's views on the darker side of nature appear to have evolved since having written *Gaia and God*, the sole source Sideris uses on Ruether. Recalling what I discussed in chapter 1, Ruether does mention that the logic of nature suggests that any sentimentality for the second pelican that is pecked to death by its parent would be misplaced.[87] A more contextual reading of Ruether's employment of the passage by Isaiah, cited by Sideris above, leads to somewhat different conclusions about Ruether's appropriation of science than those arrived at by Sideris. While it is true that Ruether quotes Isaiah, Sideris also notes (at the beginning of the chapter with which Sideris seems to have the most difficulty) that Ruether's intention was to "explore two lines of the biblical thought and Christian traditions that have reclaimable resources for an ecological spirituality."[88] Important to note, and something Sideris fails to mention, is Ruether's caveat preceding this point regarding the resources in both biblical thought and the Christian tradition: "I am *not* assuming that these are the only or the best religious traditions for ecological ethics and spirituality; and I am *not* assuming that these traditions can be reclaimed and made usable without change ... Both these traditions are marked by a legacy of patriarchalism and must be reinterpreted."[89] The italicized words above are found in the original version by Ruether. In fact, Ruether demonstrates her doubt that such a legacy can even be purged and, in reference to all past traditions, adds, "The radical nature of this new face of ecological devastation means that all past human traditions are inadequate in the face of it. Whatever useful elements ... must be reinterpreted to make them usable in the face of both new scientific knowledge and the destructive power of the technology it has made possible."[90]

In keeping with the larger motif in her writings of maintaining dynamic tensions, Ruether is not accepting any simple throwing-away-the-baby-with-the-bathwater mentality: her aim is for the Christian not to forsake the tradition entirely, because some wisdom for our time can still be found within it. With the above in mind, it does not seem entirely accurate to assign romantic tones to Ruether's ethical vision, because she does recognize the reality of cruelty in nature. Sideris, for instance, does not mention Ruether's criticism in *Gaia and God* of the deontological approach to animal rights advocated by ethicist Tom Regan: "To attempt to derive this mandate [an animal's inherent right to life] from 'nature' runs into the contradictory reality of predation as an unavoidable part of nature. Not only do carnivorous animals depend for their existence on eating other animals, but all life forms exist through an interdependency of consuming and being consumed. Nor is it sufficient to claim that one does not eat beings with whom one can have an interpersonal relation."[91]

If anything, it appears more like Sideris is misreading Ruether by focusing on her one book and, even then, not in its entirety or always accurately. Moreover, Sideris relies much on one writing of Lynn Margulis and Dorion Sagan to critique Ruether's interpretation of the Gaia theory (then hypothesis) as illustrating a world that is harmonious and life-sustaining. Margulis and Sagan's work, "God, Gaia, and Biophilia" – part of a larger volume looking at Edward O. Wilson's biophilia hypothesis – focuses on the mistaken ideas of the human role in causing destruction to Gaia, and not, as would be expected, on Gaian evolution.[92] Nevertheless, the topic of Gaian evolution is still discussed and Sideris is certainly correct in pointing out, as do

Margulis and Sagan, that "Gaia is Darwin's natural selector,"[93] yet Sideris does not mention that within the same article Margulis and Sagan also write, "Gaia is simply symbiosis seen from space."[94] Again in that same work, Sideris fails to mention a significant point made by Margulis and Sagan – which I discussed above – that were Earth's surface not covered with oxygen-emitting bacteria, its atmosphere would long ago have degenerated. Yet, this point seems to support Ruether's claim about cooperation.

Notwithstanding the omissions of these more cooperative and harmonious aspects of Gaia, the point I am raising here is that Sideris's critique does not incorporate the actual works Ruether employs in *Gaia and God* to discuss evolution and Gaia. Ruether, for instance, borrows heavily from the writings of Anne and Paul Ehrlich, such as their book *Earth*; in reading this work, she would have been well informed about the wisdom behind evolutionary nature. It was Margulis and Sagan's larger work, *Microcosmos: Four Billion Years of Evolution from Our Microbial Ancestors*, that Ruether accessed. Some investigation into its main points will help to understand that Ruether's putative "panglossian" view of the science – if just based on this particular work by Margulis and Sagan alone – is not so misguided and that Ruether does not appear to misrepresent the "science" as much as Sideris claims. Recall earlier where Sideris quotes Ruether as saying cooperation and interdependency are primary principles of ecosystems. Sideris claims this is a misrepresentation of the science, yet Margulis and Sagan tell us, "Although we would be foolish to propose that competitive power struggles for limited space and resources play no role in evolution, we show how it is equally foolish to overlook the crucial importance of physical association between organisms of different species, symbiosis, *as a major source of evolutionary novelty* [my emphasis]."[95] In fact, the authors add, "It is folly not to extend the lessons of evolution and ecology to the human and political realm. Life is not merely a murderous game in which cheating and killing insure the injection of rogue's genes into the next generation, but it is also a symbiotic, cooperative venture in which partners triumph."[96]

While the brief investigation above might demonstrate that Ruether has not necessarily misread her sources, a larger question remains: has Ruether misrepresented reality as understood by the science? We know that Sideris's darker understanding of evolution relies much upon her reading of Darwin. Borrowing upon the work of evolutionary theorist Peter Kropotkin, Midgley reveals a more nuanced understanding of what Darwin might have meant by "struggle for existence." Kropotkin became interested in the works of Charles Darwin in the late nineteenth century. He was in full agreement that the "struggle for existence" played a key role in evolution, but he rejected the ideas of Thomas Huxley, who placed great emphasis on competition and conflict in the evolutionary process.[97] From reading Kropotkin, Midgley finds evidence, not unlike what Ruether maintains in her writings, that "the fittest" members of an interdependent animal community "are not necessarily the strongest, nor indeed the cleverest, but the most sociable: those whose temperament most inclines them to friendly cooperation."[98] Indeed, Midgley finds that Darwin shows how "friendly order and cooperation – how much, indeed, of what we call humanity – there is already in the lives of other social animals,"[99] which emphasizes how much our animal nature is not alien to but part of who we are.

Consider as well the matter of self-regulation within ecosystems discussed above by both Sideris and Sale. While Sale and other ecologists might not be able to find evidence for self-regulation, what ecologists Paul and Anne Ehrlich say about the seeming self-regulating capacity of soil cannot be ignored. Soil fertility is maintained by a conversion process within complex ecosystems in which fragments of rock are mixed with waste products of organisms. Indeed, a gram of rich soil contains myriad tiny organisms, more than 80,000 single-celled protists (algae, protozoa), 400,000 fungi, and 2.5 billion bacteria. A square metre could contain 45,000 minute relatives of earthworms, 48,000 mites and insects, and 10 million round worms. The Ehrlichs point out that "some of these inconspicuous microbes often live in intimate association with the roots of plants in the legume family (peas and beans): in return for energy-rich products of the plants' photosynthesis, the bacteria enrich the soil with nitrogen."[100]

In the end, Sideris was not without some justification in challenging Ruether for her omissions of details on how ecosystems work or in finding remnants of anthropocentric thinking in her writing. In my analysis of Ruether's ethical vision, I already discussed the problems with having humans act as "gardeners" to the rest of creation. And Sideris's critique of Ruether for her "hopes for a final restoration of nature that will usher in right relations among all creatures, thus 'healing nature's enmity,'"[101] while arguably problematic, viewed within the whole of Ruether's writings, is less challenging. I also discussed in chapter 1 Ruether's simple explanations of some scientific aspects, such as the definition of the Gaia theory. She refers to Gaia as being "alive," a "living planet," which at the metaphoric level is fine; but left at that, ignores, as Lovelock himself has gone to great lengths to explicate, the importance of precision in scientific reasoning. And, as mentioned in chapter 1, Ruether incorporates little of the scientific details of the Gaia theory, as explained by Lovelock, in her work. She does not deal with the intricacies of how the atmosphere, biosphere, lithosphere, hydrosphere, and barysphere form a single self-regulating cybernetic system. Also, Ruether's incorporation of the science, while fairly broad in scope, is limited in quantity. Her understanding of ecology was solely from the Ehrlichs, and her treatment of cosmology was minimal. There was very little in the way of systems theory or quantum physics. Moreover, after *Gaia and God,* she does not seem to have continued her research, relying on the same research in subsequent writings.

While a larger Gaian and cosmological framework challenges Sideris's and Sale's arguments on ecosystems, like Ruether, Boff, as I have discussed, can be faulted for an un-nuanced account of nature being in "balance." Moreover, one wonders why Boff could logically even speak of a "balance of nature" while simultaneously supporting the Prigoginian systems view that finds disorder, instability, disequilibrium, and nonlinear relationships as being the norm in reality. Further, Sale's discussion of the ephemeral nature of communities within which the component species struggle amid an array of nonhuman disturbances, does make Boff's pointing to the human as the almost exclusive perpetrator of its disturbances less convincing. However, Boff's research, unlike Ruether's, is far more comprehensive (notably in his collaborative work with Mark Hathaway, who has a background in science) and, it would seem, somewhat ongoing, as his later writings examine newer research from biologist Humberto Maturana. The reflections from physicist Fritjof Capra on Boff's (and Hathaway's) *The Tao of Transformation* shed light on some mutual incompatibility of ideas, and some incompatibility of ideas with the framework Capra has developed.[102] On the mutual incompatibility of ideas, Capra is most critical of Boff's consideration of Sheldrake's ideas on morphic fields. He believes them to be too unscientific, "a sophisticated form of vitalism." He believes Boff misunderstands "attractors" (patterns that a system tends to settle into. Think of the motion of a pendulum that, over time, settles at the lowest and middle point of the swing).[103] Capra suggests Sheldrake's morphic fields are more easily understood within a systems theory framework where fields are "analogous to the idea of an attractor that creates a kind of boundary for forms and behaviors."[104] The point here is not whether Sheldrake's morphic fields hypothesis is a viable way of looking at the world, only that how it is presented within a framework of scientific credibility is important. To be fair to Boff and Hathaway, they do make this distinction. On another issue, in contrast to Capra's own conceptual framework, while Boff states that the mathematics of chaos theory does not exactly explain why creativity seems to be inherent in the very fabric of the cosmos, Capra believes to some extent it does "as it explains the process of emergence, i.e., the creation of novelty, which is a characteristic of all nonlinear systems." Capra stresses that these incompatibilities, while some are "esoteric and definitely outside the scientific mainstream,"[105] are not major. In fact, he concludes overall that "Nevertheless, they succeed admirably in demonstrating the emergence of a new coherent scientific understanding of reality." Capra adds that Boff (and Hathaway) argue correctly that "the emerging scientific cosmology is fully compatible with the spiritual dimensions of liberation." In short, the incompatibilities mentioned above, according to Capra "do not detract from the overall value of the book."[106]

Of our four interlocutors, O'Murchu appears to be the most avid in maintaining an ongoing research into what the latest science research is telling us.[107] However, at times, the inferences he draws from reading the latest science are not always empirically verifiable. For instance, as I demonstrated in chapter 3, O'Murchu takes Danah Zohar's conclusion from quantum holism as indicating that power relations are not the only, or perhaps even the most effective, way that people and events can be linked in society, and that the politician or the manager who tries to influence or control events may be less effective than one who can be "sensitive to the spontaneous emergence of social or political trends."[108] While admirable as a principle, the suggestion that this notion can be found through a study of quantum physics is stretching the science. And it also seems a stretch of the science to affirm, as business consultant Margaret Wheatley does, that we can take concrete lessons from quantum physics to guide us in our daily actions. O'Murchu tells how Wheatley's growing sensibility of a quantum universe affects her organizational life. Wheatley does this by disciplining herself to remain aware of the whole and to resist her "well-trained desire to analyze the parts to death."[109] To this list of more imaginative interpretations of the science, I also apply Capra's critique of the incorporation of Sheldrake's morphic fields, which is something O'Murchu does. In short, O'Murchu's insistence on applying imagination and intuition which, as I have discussed, is not incompatible with appropriating the science, is nevertheless at times too generous – especially in cases where there exists a "paucity of facts"[110] – to a point where the scientist might not recognize the science behind the conclusions. In other words, the care with which O'Murchu attends to potential incompatibilities between empirically based assertions and metaphysical claims is not always consistent. Finally, in light of Sideris's main contention, it is important to mention O'Murchu's keen understanding of paradoxes – that darker side of reality that comes from taking nature seriously that Sideris deems many thinkers gloss over – inherent in reality. He does not attempt to marry naive Christian eschatological hopes to make us feel better about death and destruction, as Sideris claims many Christian eco-theologians do. Rather, his ethical vision constructs a hermeneutic for embracing the dark, the paradox.

Last, given the above exploration of science, of our four interlocutors, Berry is undoubtedly the most precise in his appropriation of science. His assertion that science is ultimately mythic in nature, serving as a meaning-giver and driver of action, is not fanciful metaphysical thinking. Instead it is an accurate description of how science operates. Similarly, when Berry says there is a belief component to science, the writings of Kuhn, Jaki, and Putnam confirm this to be accurate. Where Berry also conforms to a method of scientific rigour is, like O'Murchu, the acceptance of the dark side to nature, underlining that there is a cost to creativity. As a matter of fact, O'Murchu stresses that he is much indebted to Berry and Swimme, whom he considers to be the best contemporary scholars to have understood the paradox of creation and destruction as being part of life. O'Murchu writes, "Contrary to other theorists, they do not seek to get rid of the violence, and neither do they accept it as a fait accompli, in the face of which we feel powerless and all seems helpless."[111] Berry received his greatest compliment from mathematical cosmologist and collaborator Brian Swimme, who writes, "Thomas Berry's achievement is to position himself within the knowledge that scientists and all the rest of us regard as obviously true. His starting point is natural selection and genetic mutation, the second law of thermodynamics, the initial singularity of spacetime, the innate releasing mechanism of neurophysiological response. His starting point is the universe as it has been discovered by contemporary scientific modes of understanding. By taking the universe as primary, he is able to work out a cosmology that is meaningful to anyone educated in modern ways of knowing."[112] Swimme maintains Berry avoids conclusions not supported by current scientific evidence, adding, "He is not interested in adjusting the world of the sacred to fit categories of thought."[113]

Might not Sale's argument also challenge Berry's discussion on niche creation, which he likens to subjectivity, autopoiesis, self-organization, and self-articulation? Berry's understanding of niche creation undergirds his own view of how the bison and horse live together in a biotic community. And recall Berry's discussion of a single pair of aphids, each requiring an influx of energy so as to sustain itself: if their desires were not held within a "fecund balance of tensions," problems would arise. Does Sale's view, which greatly downplays self-regulation within an ecosystem, along with his challenge to niche development, mean Berry is incorrect in his assumptions on the science? To begin – as far I can tell – Berry nowhere speaks simply of "balance." Actually, with regard to the aphids, as seen in chapter 4, he speaks of a "fecund balance *of tensions*" (my emphasis) that hold constraints on creativity under a larger state of "creative disequilibrium." In other words, with a careful reading of Berry's understanding of niche and "balance," a far more nuanced interpretation appears, one more in line with ecosystems existing primarily in a non-equilibrium state. In the end, I think it safe to conclude that Berry's appropriation of science, which finds its way into the thinking of the other three interlocutors, is certainly comprehensive and thoughtful.

CONCLUSION

I was not long into this chapter when it became apparent that to judiciously pass judgment on my four Christian theorists' appropriation of science, and to judge the reliability of Sideris's claims, it was important to have a better understanding of how science is structured, and some of its processes for knowing reality and communicating its findings. The scientific process is not purely rational. It entails the entire spectrum of human experience: it takes place within a fragmented social community, with social forces, habits, and biases; within a particular culture that influences what science is carried out; and within a certain paradigm that is rarely questioned.

It also became apparent, in discussing the role of myths and metaphors, that a viable approach to science, when it is the liberation for the entire planet we are seeking, is likely one that is wide in scope, inclusive of multiple scientific branches, and takes into account the myths and imaginations that surround the broader issue. The Gaia theory, which continues to meet many of the challenges presented to it by scientists, addresses the above requirements, not exclusively, or fully, but certainly uniquely and adeptly. That the four Christian thinkers of this book rely on it in forming their ethical vision, then, seems understandable and judicious.

In the end, I submit that what Fritjof Capra says of Boff's work applies to all four interlocutors: the incompatibilities and imprecisions found in their work do not detract from the overall value of their ethical visions. In fact, each of these Christian thinkers, while varying in degrees, demonstrates a remarkable level of seriousness when appropriating the wisdom of science. There is within their writings, on the whole, a coherent and sophisticated understanding of the current scientific theories. It is seldom that our interlocutors "misread" or (in the case of O'Murchu and his somewhat promiscuous inferring) "misrepresent" the work of scientists. But what happens when details are not quite accurate, as this does happen? Might the scientist her- or himself, in choosing the wrong metaphor be somewhat at fault, as Larson points out above? Historian and scholar of philosophy of science Mara Beller presents an intriguing argument that places some of the blame for the excesses of the postmodernist critique of science – with regard to the Sokal affair – on the philosophical pronouncements of scientists themselves, such as Bohr, Born, Heisenberg, and Pauli.[114] If scientists – and the venerated ones – are responsible for some of the excesses, the challenge to Christian ethicists in appropriating science becomes that much more demanding.

While this cannot excuse someone from misreading the science, it does point out how exacting and time consuming is the task of the non-scientist when accessing the works of even prominent scientists. It is evident that a fairly high level of scientific literacy is required to maintain a critical hermeneutic of suspicion when engaging with any scientific work. Engaging science, especially for the non-scientist, is a demanding task. It requires not only that the author demonstrate a coherent and sophisticated understanding of the current scientific theories but that the author remain abreast of new theories, or challenges to current theories. To avoid making conclusions not supported by current scientific evidence requires that one's engagement with science remain a never-ending research endeavour, or as Kuhn refers to it, a continuous puzzle-solving enterprise.

This might sound overly demanding, but I do not think there is any other way around it. None of my chosen interlocutors delve into string theory, for instance. Should this matter in future discussions of ethics? And how might the recent findings concerning the Higgs boson particle, often referred to as the "God particle," affect our understanding of how the universe works?[115] In regard to our relation as a species to nonhuman animals, only O'Murchu seems to continue research into the works of various ethologists such as Marc Bekoff, primatologists such as Frans de Waal, and the work of various paleontologists to discern our common ancestry with other species. Yet, the contributions of the works of ethologists and primatologists could prove significant when considering Christian understandings of meta-ethics, a point to which I will return to in the conclusion of this book. I mention this specifically because it is O'Murchu's ethical vision that is, of the four we have seen, the least anthropocentric. Might this worldview have something to do with which branches of science he employs? After all, just with regard to the voices from science alone, it seems, no one viewpoint, no one appropriation can do justice to our understanding of nature.

Perhaps the discrepancies I found over how science is understood among my chosen four Christian thinkers, Lisa Sideris, and the other interlocutors, such as Mary Midgley, speak, at least in part, to the paradigm each interlocutor choses to embrace: one where the universe is either mechanistic, reductionist, and dualistic with no discernible purpose, or one in which the universe is deeply relational, a communion of subjects such that parts of the universe cannot be known separate from the whole, and knowing occurs not only at the verbal level but at the intuitive, aesthetic, and affective level as well. The former paradigm tends toward fragmentation, leaving the work of science to the experts. The latter paradigm, to which I am referring here as post-normal science, tends toward an interdisciplinary approach, incorporating the larger population into the process.

Ruether, Boff, O'Murchu, and Berry are engaging with a post-normal science, a kind of science that is more democratic in how it chooses its metaphors, inviting the larger population to engage in the process. It is a science that understands that the way we imagine the world determines what we think is important in it. At this point in this work, it is easier to understand why Ruether is so adamant in her call for a scientist-poet, that ecological leader "who can retell the story … in a way that can call us to wonder, to reverence for life, and to the vision of humanity living in community with all its sister and brother beings," and why Berry invokes the way of the poet or artist with reference to his appropriation of science. Recall that he says, "We might think of a viable future for the planet less as the result of some scientific insight or as dependent on some socioeconomic arrangements, than as participation in a symphony or as renewed presence to some numinous presence manifested in the wonderworld about us."[116] This is a science that is concerned with the liberation of all creation. It is also a science that is open to taking Christianity seriously.

CHAPTER SEVEN

Toward a Serious and Sustained Reflection on the Christian Faith

It might seem odd that the aim of this chapter is to determine whether *Christian* theorists take their *own* faith seriously. Yet, a good number of Christian theologians, like Van A. Harvey and Michael Northcott, suggest that there is a limit to the degree to which Christian beliefs can be revised to accommodate modernity, postmodernity, or new findings from scientific research.[1] In fact, the four Christian authors I am examining in this work are very critical of many current Christian beliefs and practices. They argue that without profound change their tradition cannot address the environmental and social crises we face. On top of this, they engage their faith with a view to arriving at an ethical vision that seeks the liberation of *all* creation, while simultaneously profoundly appropriating insights from science. In light of the criteria for taking and integrating something seriously, then, such an engagement with liberation, environment, and science should involve current Christian beliefs and practices in some way. But as some theologians, such as the ones cited above, suggest, while some challenges are to be expected and are nourishing to a religion, there should be a limit to the degree a religion can change. Is this assumption correct? How might one discern whether, in critically approaching environment, liberation, and science, Boff, Berry, O'Murchu, and Ruether are also approaching their faith with thoughtfulness, constructive resolution, and critical attention?

It is important to understand first that consistently reflecting upon their faith in light of the realities they have seen, heard and, in one form or another, experienced, the four Christian thinkers I am investigating

– notwithstanding having or not having "official status" as theologians – are doing theology. Taking theology broadly to mean what the eleventh-century Archbishop of Canterbury Saint Anselm believed is "faith seeking understanding," one finds in their writings that there is a close, almost dialogical relationship between what they believe (faith) and a thirst to understand it in light of the times (theology). There is, in fact, a natural speculative nature to theology where human reason is applied to experience in the pursuit of better understanding one's faith. Since the four Christian thinkers I am examining approach Christianity with such a querying faith commitment, to assess the manner in which they have approached their tradition, it also seems necessary to assess the quality of their overall theological undertaking.

This query, however, is not as straightforward as it might seem. While theology does entail that never-ending search for understanding in light of one's faith, certain understandings or doctrines exist, certainly within the Roman Catholic tradition, while not infallible, nevertheless carry much authority because they have been taught by the Church bishops, or Magisterium. There are even a set of doctrines that are considered divinely revealed truths and, therefore, infallible: dogma. Many followers within this tradition adhere staunchly to such dogma. There are even others who adhere dogmatically to doctrines that are not considered divinely revealed. As will become abundantly clear in this chapter, Christian theology is pluralistic, employing a multiplicity of methods, cognitive models, and starting points. Even the Catholic tradition, as a subset – albeit the largest – of Christianity, a tradition to which these four interlocutors belong, is characterized by diverse and even conflicting interpretations of the Christian faith. Among the four interlocutors themselves there is a range of theological approaches: from ecofeminist theology, to eco-liberation theology, to radical liberal ecotheology, to historical and cultural and ecological interpretations of faith. Certainly for Boff, a liberation theologian, and Ruether, an ecofeminist liberationist thinker, theology is a second act. The lived experience of the poor, and solidarity with them, come first, not thoughts about God. For Berry, the universe represents primordial revelation. While O'Murchu would not doubt Berry's view, his emphasis lies within experience that is at once personal, interpersonal, planetary, and cosmic. In short, no one "orthodox" understanding of

Christian beliefs and practices exists, nor is there any one theological approach from which to measure, with any degree of satisfaction, the quality of the theological reflections of these four authors. Instead, as I propose here, there appears a more viable way of assessing their approach to Christianity: recognizing this multiplicity to Christian theology, and the various points of view and cognitive models that undergird it, and taking this understanding of doing theology in our current historical context as a starting point for theological reflection – as many theologians, especially those involved in ecumenism and interreligious dialogue, affirm we must do.

Borrowing from the writings of Gregory Baum, Leonard Swidler, and David Tracy, I will discuss the merits of using a relational model of assessing truth to discern the quality of their theological reflection. The model takes the plurality of viewpoints and cognitive models that characterize current Christian theology as its starting point and, thereafter, seeks only to arrive at a relative adequacy of conclusions. Moreover, a relational model views dialogue as being the most viable method for arriving at communal understandings. In this light, I adapt the criteria for assessing whether something is taken seriously to the relational model of doing theology, and ask the following: do their reflections serve as thoughtful corrections to current thinking and practices? Do their reflections pay critical attention to hidden or silenced perspectives, different points of view and cognitive models? Is there a provisional character to their reflections? Within this framework, it will become clear that they approach their faith with thoughtfulness while *simultaneously* approaching the liberation of all creation and science with constructive resolve. There is evidence that Boff, Berry, O'Murchu, and Ruether not only engage their faith in a conversation with science and liberation to clarify, affirm, qualify, and inform both, but that they allow these spheres to clarify, affirm, qualify, and inform their faith. Notwithstanding this integration, I contend that they are not only thoughtful in their approach to Christianity, but actually drawing heavily from its wells, wanting to bring it into an intense conversation with science so as to arrive at an ethical vision that fosters liberation for all creation.

In searching for possible reasons to clarify what it is about their faith that so inspires them to seek liberation for *all* creation, and to engage profoundly with the empirical natural sciences, I suggest three probable explanations, although not without some qualification. All three underscore the *Catholic* nature of their faith: their predilection toward natural theology, which sees God as immanent in creation, and its closely related natural law tradition, which purports that normative claims about human nature can be found within nature through the use of reason; the influence from Catholic priest and scientist Pierre Teilhard de Chardin, whose writings present a world imbued with a sense of the divine, and lay an important foundation for the development of an epistemological model to engage science and Christianity in a deep conversation; and finally, their Catholic imagination, as conveyed by author and sociologist Andrew Greeley, which has cultivated within them a deep "ease" with the natural world.

The works of Leonardo Boff, Thomas Berry, Diarmuid O'Murchu, and Rosemary Radford Ruether definitely lie on the margins of their own denominational church thinking. Here, as you have probably noticed, I have changed the order of their names to reflect, in ascending order, their degree of divergence from more orthodox teachings. I will begin this investigation, then, by identifying more clearly what exactly it is they declare that so challenges the orthodoxy of their faith, followed by a discussion of why this does not necessarily signify that they do not approach their faith seriously.

CHALLENGES TO CHRISTIAN ORTHODOXY

While the works of these thinkers do lie on the margins of their own denominational church thinking, one could say that this is, arguably, because the powers-that-be within the Church, in large measure, wish to keep them there. This is certainly the case for Boff and to a lesser extent for O'Murchu too. And while neither Ruether nor Berry has suffered official censorship or rebuke, they achieved this by being strategic: Ruether by refusing to teach at a Catholic institution, and Berry by maintaining that his thoughts are based on his work as a geologian and not a theologian. Such censure should not surprise us: the four interlocutors do not mince their words when they declare that their own Christian tradition cannot address the environmental and social crises we face alone, or without profound changes, which entails extending much more authority to the wisdom of science. Moreover, as discussed in previous chapters, it is not the wisdom of science alone that these four interlocutors embrace. Whether the Tao, ecopsychology, ecofeminism, deep ecology, or the wisdoms found in Indigenous traditions, all play a role in fostering a planetary transformation, as well as what O'Murchu calls the development of a more "adult" faith, one that recognizes the individual as a feeling, embodied, thinking subject, living and negotiating life in communion with a diversity of other subjects. A brief overview of how each has challenged traditional beliefs and practices will serve to clarify why the powers-that-be within the Church might wish their writings to remain on the margins of their own denominational Church thinking.

Leonardo Boff's earlier works on liberation theology had caused many theologians, including then Archbishop Ratzinger, head of the Sacred Congregation of the Doctrine of Faith, to accuse him of reducing human life to the political realm. Boff has remained firm that the attention to the political and corporeal elements of the human is necessary to address the grave situation in Latin America, where a majority of its peoples are non-persons. Liberation is a political as well as a social and economic issue, and not something theology alone can deal with. The incorporation of Marxist theory into liberation theology, which had caused – and still causes – some to question the authenticity of the theology, has always served as a mere tool for analysis.[2] But it was Boff's ecclesiology – notably in *Church Charism and Power*, comprising essays in "militant ecclesiology"[3] – which placed stronger emphasis on the Holy Spirit in granting validity to ecclesial structures than to ecclesial authority that raised more concern from the Vatican. In more recent works, building upon evolutionary theories from Ilya Prigogine and Pierre Teilhard de Chardin, Boff – and here I include to various degrees the other three interlocutors – envisions a new global civilization or paradigm coming to fruition, one in which the traditional Christian Church that centralizes power in the hands of clergy, excludes women from roles of leadership, and relegates community-based Christianity to a passive role plays no role. Boff continues to be very critical of the hierarchical Church in his blogs, citing, "The present Catholic Church is submerged in a rigorous winter."[4]

As discussed in chapter 4, Thomas Berry maintains that the current geocide perpetrated on this planet cannot be critiqued or addressed effectively from within the Christian traditions: our cultural coding, out of which our religious traditions were built, needs to conform to our genetic coding. In *Befriending the Earth,* Berry questions the "excessive concern with the individual, historical Jesus,"[5] adding his dislike for the idea that "any one religion has the fullness of revelation."[6] Berry also suggests that Christians "shelve" the Bible for a couple of decades so as to reorient themselves to the universe as primordial revelation. For these reasons, he has received rebuke or disapproval from the conservative Catholics or mainstream Christians who feared he was not "Christ focused and human focused."[7] A former director of the Environmental Justice Program for the US Catholic Conference of Bishops, Walter Grazer, for instance, believes Berry is "far too left" to effectively influence American Catholics. And despite Berry referring to himself not as a theologian but as a geologian, people like Grazer believe his "impropriety" in suggesting that we shelve the Bible only adds fuel to those who consider environmentalism as pagan and therefore idolatrous.[8] Berry does not see paganism as idolatrous, though. In fact, he states, "the salvation of Christians lies in the unassimilated elements of paganism."[9] He suggests, for instance, that we extend the ritual of Christian baptism, which traditionally brings humans into a relationship with the divine as well as within the religious (human) sacred community, to the Earth. Berry puts forth the Omaha Indian ceremony as a good example of this: the ceremony presents the infant to all regions of the universe, imploring the spirits of the Earthly world and the subsoil – the trees, animals, and insects, along with humans – as well as the spirits of the heavens, to make the path of the child smooth.

Diarmuid O'Murchu, reflecting upon the deep time characterizing human evolution, advocates abandoning many teachings and practices from religion previously thought sacred and eternal as a necessary step in our spiritual maturation. Recall that O'Murchu stresses – and arguably more so than our other three thinkers – that if theology wants to retain a degree of relevance and meaning, "it must now adopt the great paradoxical pathways it has so often advocated for its adherents," and, "die to its own supremacy." While it is true that all four thinkers believe Christianity, as O'Murchu puts it, "must become the servant of a higher and more embracing wisdom," and that it must learn to mediate new truths that are dawning upon our world, allowing itself – in conjunction with all the other sciences – "to be born anew!,"[10] O'Murchu is most vociferous in the call for Christians to outgrow what he terms "adolescent" attitudes toward religion. The tradition, as it stands for him and presumably for his many followers (recall that he is a much sought after facilitator, especially for women religious orders), no longer nourishes him; it is "not big enough" for him.[11] "We need to let go of the monotheistic, patriarchal dogmas of our recent past," he states, adding, "No matter how well they may have served us, they are no longer appropriate or adequate for the emerging world [from what new science is showing us] of our time."[12] How we do theology, O'Murchu concludes, is changing rapidly and dramatically. It is far more participatory and, as is evidenced in his study of quantum theory, for instance, far more open to the findings from the natural sciences.

No less outspoken on Christian patriarchal teachings, Rosemary Radford Ruether maintains that the radical nature of this new face of ecological devastation means all past human traditions, not only Christianity, are simply inadequate in the face of it. She is candid about her disagreement with Church hierarchy on women's ordination and contraception, and – like O'Murchu, Berry, and Boff – she is very critical of a religion that does not treat its followers as adults. Early in her academic career, Ruether published *The Church against Itself: An Inquiry into the Conditions of Historical Existence for the Eschatological Community,* where she refers to a "crisis theology" or modern dialectical theology that is needed to create a viable theology of radical change – something, she points out, the hierarchy cannot do as long as it clings to outdated doctrines from the past.[13] And as discussed in chapter 1, Ruether suggests, as Berry does with the Bible, a sort of shelving of any other-worldly understanding of eschatology so as to foster greater emphasis on a this-worldly liberation.

Reading the above challenges, it is not unreasonable to ask whether these four thinkers have taken their Christian ethics, beliefs, and structures – in short, its theology – seriously. While my study remains focused on the ethical Christian visions of these four thinkers, none of their individual visions escapes touching upon at least some of the central Christian theological matters: the role of scripture, ecclesiology, Christology, soteriology, or eschatology. In all four cases, all four thinkers believe Christianity, in one form or another, as O'Murchu puts it above, "must become the servant of a higher and more embracing wisdom … to be born anew!" Is there indeed, as some theologians suggest, a limit to the degree Christian beliefs and practices can be "born anew"?

As will become evident in the following section, however, this question and the criticisms that have come from theologians such as Harvey and Northcott appear misguided. For one, notwithstanding the above challenges these four chosen thinkers present to Christianity, it should be noted that all of them remain firmly planted in its soils, not merely Christian soils but the loams of the Catholic tradition. In fact, despite being silenced by Church authorities and renouncing his priesthood, Boff remains a Catholic, professing his love for the Church. Ruether and O'Murchu also remain steadfastly within the Church, as did Berry until his death. Moreover, Boff's theology, notwithstanding his ecclesiology – in my opinion – remains, in many ways, fairly orthodox: he does not put into question the divinity of Christ as the son of God, the resurrection of the body, and the afterlife, though he interprets them from a liberationist viewpoint; and the Trinitarian framework plays a vital role in his theological enterprise. Berry – somewhat ironically – refers to himself as a "conservative Christian."[14] In fact, while their works remain on the margins of denominational Church thinking, within various Christian circles their works are very well received. As a result, a simple evaluation of whether our four interlocutors take Christianity seriously, then, will prove to be more difficult than merely assessing their status within their faith tradition. Not unlike my discussion on science, it will be necessary first to understand what is meant when speaking about the Christian theology. What indeed, is the nature of theology? And can one speak of Christian theology in such monolithic terms?

UNDERSTANDING THE NATURE OF CHRISTIAN THEOLOGY

Theology can be described simply as faith seeking understanding, as described above, or more precisely as the study or systematic reflection of God and the relationship of everything else to God. Yet such unassuming descriptions do not seem to relay the full weight of its meaning. Peter C. Hodgson writes, "There is something intrinsically radical about theology. After all, it purports to make assertions about *God*, about the ultimate meaning and purpose of things, and it offers strong judgments about human behavior from a prophetic perspective."[15] Even with this more far-reaching description, the problem remains that there is no one standard or "orthodox" systematic theology from which to assess the quality in which they approach their faith. Currently in Christianity – and, many would argue, since its inception – there co-exists a multiplicity of doctrinal utterances, practices, and beliefs, each understandably claiming to have approached their faith, and even the world, with thoughtfulness, resolution, and critical attention. What is more, theologians today employ a pluralism of cognitive models. Thus, it is not solely the controversies over the ultimate meaning and purpose of just about everything within the universe that abound, but how these meanings and purposes are derived. It is this pluralistic nature of theology that merits discussion first to appropriately decide whether Boff, Berry, O'Murchu, and Ruether have taken their faith seriously.

As David Tracy states, "Any observer of contemporary Christian theology cannot avoid noticing how pluralistic, how diverse, even how conflicting are the theological interpretations of Christianity in our period."[16] This is neither an understatement nor a new phenomenon. Theologian David F. Ford portrays an image of theology that is so fragmented that even the definition of theology itself is open to debate. "Christian theology since 1918 has been immensely varied," he writes, adding, "This has not just been a matter of diverse approaches and conclusions, but also of fundamental differences about what theology is, what modernity is, and what Christianity is, and which questions within these areas are to be given priority."[17] Ford accounts for such diversity in our times by listing the multitude of historical events with which Christianity has had to grapple throughout the past centuries: the Reformation, the colonization of the Americas, the Enlightenment, the American and French Revolutions, the Industrial Revolution, the rise of nationalism, and the rise of the natural sciences, technologies, and medical and human sciences. In this list Ford includes the combined impact of the rise of constitutional democracies, new means of warfare and communication, mass education and public health programs, and movement in the arts and philosophy. Aptly, he concludes that by the beginning of the last century, the context for doing theology had permanently changed.

To capture this diversity, Ford broadly categorizes theologies into five main types. Imagining a continuum, at one end we find an "extreme" type of theology that attempts to repeat a traditional version of Christianity with little to no recognition of the realities of the time, or the varied perspectives that have arisen. At the other end, we find another "extreme" theology giving the modern reality priority (perhaps in the form of a secular philosophy or worldview) with Christianity becoming valid insofar as it conforms to that reality. Between these two radical types we find theologies that differ in the degrees to which they give primacy either to Christianity or to fostering a dialogue between modernity and the Christian tradition.[18]

Tracy also suggests models employed in contemporary theology, five of them, each employing its own style or type of reasoning. The models range from the orthodox – which does not come to terms with the cognitive, ethical, and existential counter-claims of modernity – to the liberal, which attempts to reconcile modernity's values and reinterpretations of Christianity's historic claims.[19] Newer models have continued to come into existence since Tracy has written, suggesting that a typology that describes only five models of theology might be imprecise. The recent growth of Radical Orthodoxy, constructive theology, along with contemporary calls for a new Radical Liberalism is a case in point.[20] Notwithstanding the magnitude of models or types or even schools of thought that characterize Christian systematic reflection upon God, within recognized categories themselves there are further varieties of theologies and even some inconsistencies. In some cases, one can find among theologians different understandings of terms such as Liberal Theology or Revisionist Theology. In others, terms such as Liberal and Progressive are employed interchangeably.[21]

The point of this brief exposé is not to sort my chosen Christian thinkers into any one category – for this issue will be addressed more appropriately in the next chapter – but to make it clear that when speaking about theology, there is no clear "orthodox" account to which one can measure the "correctness" of others whether in content or method. This, however, does not mean one cannot therefore speak of Christian theology. Despite its diversity, one can still speak of Christianity with at least a rough semblance of agreement or coherence. As Tracy illustrates, while pronunciations differ widely for reading and writing, there is nevertheless a "syntax" and a "grammar" that have remained relatively stable that allow one to speak of the Christian reflection on religious experience as a single expression with rough coherence.[22] Indeed, as Rosemary Radford Ruether and Marion Grau clarify, "a 'persistent multiplicity' of doctrinal utterances, practices, and beliefs coexisted with the assertions for orthodoxy throughout the centuries and millennia."[23] To this end, they cite the words of historian Rebecca Lyman, who says, "'Christianity' defined as 'orthodoxy' rests uncomfortably on a history of inner conflict and persistent multiplicity. This intractable problem of diversity together with the ideological claim of unity only reinforces the cultural uniqueness or ideological paradox of Christian exclusivity in late antiquity."[24] Ruether and Grau appropriately posit that such a conclusion raises the question whether there has *ever* existed an orthodox Christian theology. The task of judging the quality of their theological reflection, therefore – at least by deciding how well it measures up to any one norm – becomes difficult, if not impractical.

One might argue that since all four of my chosen interlocutors are Catholic, a ready "orthodoxy" from which to measure their systematic reflections upon God, and the relationship of everything else to God already exists. But this is a simplification of how the Catholic Church understands revelation and misrepresents the state of current Catholic theology, which is widely understood as being pluralistic itself, as David Tracy declares. Moreover, the notion of *sensus fidelium* ("the sense of the faithful"),[25] along with the primacy given to a Catholic individual's conscience in matters of faith, which resurfaced at the Second Vatican Council, makes it clear that the 1 per cent of clerics and bishops who lead the now 1.2 billion Catholics of the world can never realistically represent *the* standard orthodoxy. Most disturbing to many theologians today is that the majority of lay theologians – who are entrusted with faithfully interpreting the *sensus fidei* (sense of the faith) – are not consulted by the Magisterium when deciding upon theological questions.[26] Writing on Roman Catholic theology after Vatican II, Paul D. Murray notes how there has been a concerted effort from the post-conciliar popes to reverse the central thrust of the theology put forth at the Second Vatican Council. Murray comes to the conclusion that the Catholic Church finds itself in "a dysfunctional situation": on moral issues alone (initiated in large measure by the issuing of *Humanitae Vitae*), he believes the Church is in crisis.[27]

It is clear, then, that "orthodoxy" (or whatever systematic or constructive reflection on God one believes represents it) cannot facilitate my assessment of how the four thinkers have approached their faith. Might accepting this multiplicity of theologies, then, be a fundamental starting point for our analysis? First, it might be helpful to understand better *why* such diversity exists – apart from Ford's analysis above. For a case can be made that the current situation in Christian theology is not simply a matter of recognizing a multiplicity of points of views brought on in part by a world in flux, but a diversity of cognitive models that underscore how theology is approached. Few theologians would espouse the neo-scholastic intellectualism so prominent in the medieval era (though not absent today), which viewed revelation as a store of mysterious supernatural teachings that were pondered through reason. Currently, though, it is not solely reason but, increasingly, the totality of the human that most theologians today employ when reflecting upon God.

In their edited volume *Rethinking Theology and Science: Six Models for the Current Dialogue,* editors Niels Henrik Gregersen and J. Wentzel van Huyssteen argue convincingly that there exists a diversity of *cognitive* models at work within Christian theology today that, in turn, have helped to foster the theological pluralism I have discussed above. This phenomenon is not unlike what I have described in the previous chapter with regard to how science is carried out: various methodologies and styles of reasoning fashion how each branch of science develops. Gregersen and van Huyssteen reason that this cognitive pluralism is especially problematic when religion and science are in conversation: "With the inescapability of theological pluralism, it has rendered it almost impossible to talk about the 'theology' side of 'theology and science' as if the existence of one true theology could still be posited in such a generic uncomplicated way."[28] The authors submit that a number of factors have led to this situation: the postmodern jettisoning of the grand narratives of modernity, the role that discrete experiences increasingly play in theological reflection (compare the experiences of our *campesina*, discussed in chapter 5, to your own experiences, for example), and the increase of specific, local theologies (liberation, feminist, womanist, and various ecotheologies) have all rendered any simple evaluation of different theologies unfeasible.

This phenomenon is no less evident when looking at Christian ethics. In *Reviewing Christian Ethics: The Catholic Tradition*, Michael E. Allsopp concludes that the state of ethics in the Christian community is "bedeviled by a lack of any clear understanding of how Christians ought to approach moral problems."[29] Allsopp notes that Christian ethics has undergone tremendous change in the last hundred years: it is less rationalistic, far more attuned to the social wellbeing of individuals, and mindful of context. For this reason it has necessarily become more modest and tentative in its claims than it used to be. How Christians do theology, as O'Murchu suggests, does indeed appear to be changing.

A RELATIONAL MODEL AS A WAY OF DOING THEOLOGY

Not surprisingly, the cognitive pluralism, along with the multiplicity of viewpoints that characterize much of theological discussion today, have contributed to the re-evaluation – and perhaps the end – of absolutism. The ecumenical movement that began in the 1960s helped to generate this reality. Gregory Baum writes that when he studied Thomistic theology in the early fifties, he was "firmly convinced that [he] was acquiring the concepts and the method [he] would use in theological research and reflection for the rest of [his] life."[30] It was the rise of the ecumenical movement that "profoundly affected" his theological thinking and understanding of truth. It introduced him to the understanding of dialogue as a way of truth: "Dialogue opens ourselves to perspectives hidden from us before."[31] Baum concludes that dialogue "gives theological reflection a certain provisional character."[32]

Taking this understanding of how truth is arrived at further, Leonard Swidler points out the dramatic shift in the understanding of truth that has taken place through the nineteenth and twentieth centuries, first in western civilization, and subsequently beyond it.[33] Swidler outlines the limitations surrounding the discernment of truth that many Christian thinkers have come to understand: truth and the meaning of something have to be understood in relationship to the historical context, the intention of the speaker, the speaker's standpoint, and the paradigm in which she or he works. Indeed, the very limitations of language, he adds (as Wittgenstein and others have shown us), contribute to the "de-absolutization"[34] of truth, for, although reality can be viewed from many perspectives, language is limited in what it can express. Further, much like science is carried out, as discussed in my previous chapter, he notes that we do not simply receive reality passively but frame it and give it specific categories.

Swidler concludes from this that Christianity can only work within a new relational model of truth. He, like Baum, maintains that the model for arriving at truth is dialogic in character and, therefore, necessitates dialogue. Paul Knitter, also renowned for his work on religious pluralism, writes about a new model developing in how theology is carried out where "truth will no longer be identified by its ability to exclude or absorb others. Rather, what is true will reveal itself mainly by its ability to *relate* to other expressions of truth and to *grow* through these relationships: truth defined not by exclusion but by relation. The new model reflects what our pluralistic world is discovering: no truth can stand alone; no truth can be totally unchangeable. Truth, by its very nature, needs other truth. If it cannot relate, its quality of truth must be open to question."[35]

Renowned for his work on religious pluralism, David Tracy seems to affirm the views above. As Baum himself attests, Tracy finds different perspectives and cognitive models not as dissents, but as healthy "correctives" or warnings to the larger community that it has dangerously narrowed its perception of the whole and, in so doing, has not quite "got it right;" such an embrace, he insists, can serve as a positive role.[36] In doing so, we accept only the "relative adequacy" of any one point of view, system, concepts or understandings, and never give them any claim to "final adequacy." With such a view in theology,

Tracy recognizes, as I discussed in the introduction to this book, that a great turn must also occur in how theology is done. Tracy acknowledges that in the past, traditional Christian theologians, of whatever tradition, "preached and practiced a morality of belief in, and obedient to the tradition and a fundamental loyalty to the church-community's belief."[37] In contrast to this obedience, he maintains, the modern historian and scientist – whether in the natural or social sciences – must preach and practise a decidedly divergent morality: it cannot have a theologian investigate a cognitive claim with intellectual integrity while insisting simultaneously "that the claim is believable because the tradition has believed it."[38] Tracy claims that most Christians recognize today that much of the traditional Christian manner of understanding the cognitive claims made in the Christian scriptures "should be rejected by the findings of history and the natural and human sciences."[39]

But Tracy goes beyond merely rejecting a literalist account of scripture. The method he presents, which perhaps stretches the boundaries of the relational model of theology described above, subjects the cognitive claims for its central symbols of revelation, God, and Christ, to an open-ended inquiry, autonomous judgment, critical reflection, a skeptical hard-mindedness, and a "willingness to follow the evidence wherever it may lead," even if such conclusions "may, in fact, negate a particular traditional belief."[40] Tracy concludes from all this: "There is no intellectual, cultural, political, or religious tradition or interpretation that does not ultimately live by the quality of its conversation."[41] It is for these reasons above that Tracy maintains, "Conversation is our hope."[42] Thus, the ability to listen becomes key.

It is the relational model for doing theology, one that understands dialogue as a way of arriving at truth and one, borrowing from Tracy, which must therefore accept the "relative adequacy" of any one understanding, avoiding claims to "final adequacy," that I employ to evaluate the quality with which Boff, Berry, O'Murchu, and Ruether have approached their faith. I say this not solely for the force of logic behind it, or because it happens to resonate with the ethical framework of these four Christian thinkers, which is itself relational in character, but because this model appears to be the way in which Christian theology, in large measure, *is being* done. This is certainly the case with the World Council of Churches.[43] In fact, given the existence of a plurality of points of view that underscore theological reflection, the plurality of cognitive models for engaging with reality, and the absence of any one "centre" from which to come to theological truth, I contend that a relational-type model is the most feasible vantage point from which to evaluate any Christian reflection at this point in time.

IS THEIR FAITH BEING TAKEN SERIOUSLY?

In light of the relational model, then, the following question arises: do we find evidence within the work of my four chosen Christian thinkers that their reflections serve as thoughtful corrections to current thinking and practices? Do their reflections pay critical attention to hidden or silenced perspectives and different points of view and cognitive models? Is there a provisional character to their reflections? And since I also want to assess the quality of integrating issues, dynamics, and concerns from the other spheres, some of which are divergent, I have to also ask: do we see evidence that these interlocutors have allowed each sphere not only to affirm and clarify but also to inform and qualify the others?

Boff's emphasis, much as I have shown with the other interlocutors, is on finding a way of experiencing Church in a world where the poor and the natural world are crying from oppression. When he criticizes the present authority structure of the Church, which does not assign enough significance to the role of the Holy Spirit in revelation, it should be remembered that he makes a distinction between Christianity and his faith, much like O'Murchu distinguishes religion from spirituality. Official Christianity, Boff believes, has committed the mistake of identifying itself with faith, when, in reality, faith is larger than any one religion can embrace. When Boff criticizes ecclesial structures, he is not against the notion of a hierarchy per se; he sees it as essential, but only if "it does not subsist in and for itself."[44] In other words, Boff is pointing out that the Church hierarchy is not paying critical attention to different perspectives and silenced points of view that are themselves listening and discerning the messages of the Holy Spirit.

Boff has also clearly demonstrated an openness to allowing liberation concerns to inform and qualify aspects of his faith. I have shown the fallout from this – when he was condemned by the Vatican for espousing a more participatory and liberationist ecclesiology. And while Boff also readily employs the Gaia theory and cosmology to clarify and affirm why St Francis could call all beings brothers and sisters, his emphasis on Franciscan spirituality, one grounded in a mystical experience of the sacred, is key to dispelling false consciousness when anyone – including a scientist – engages with science. Indeed, Boff looks at the complementarity of spirituality and science, stating that great scientists themselves gain a spirituality when they come face to face with the complexity of reality.

If Berry says the salvation of Christianity lies in the unassimilated elements of paganism, he is suggesting that such wisdom could serve as a corrective to the excessive other-worldly attitude prevalent within Christianity that ignores the divine presence on Earth. Moreover, he points out – correctly – that assimilation has been part of the Christian heritage: Christians have assimilated Greek wisdom and even Oriental wisdom in the form of meditation techniques. Similarly, when Berry suggests "shelving" the Bible for a while, he does not suggest that it be abandoned for good. This is a provisional measure, however, as our disproportionate concern with salvation and the saviour personality, Jesus Christ, has led us to ignore the immediate crisis on Earth and the divine revelation that is found within the natural world. Berry has also stated that we should put Webster's dictionary on the shelf because we need a new language to guide us into an ecological future. In this sense he is consistent when he warns us that "we cannot deductively get our guidance from the past";[45] a new revelatory experience that comes to us in large measure through science is giving us a new sense of life and what it means to be Christian. He likens the situation to a sinking boat: when it gets a hole, we place our attention on fixing that first and foremost. Berry adds, "Excessive concern with the historical Christ is presently just not that helpful."[46] Berry puts forth an understanding of Jesus as a "cosmic person," which, if allowed to be differentiated, could serve as a religious shared phenomenon.[47]

Certainly more than Boff, Berry demonstrates much openness and readiness to allowing the lessons from science to inform and qualify

Christian tenets of faith. But he is also very clear why this is the case: our cultural coding, out of which our religious traditions were built, needs to conform to our genetic coding. And it is science that is providing us with knowledge of the latter. Berry is equally adamant that the primordial capacity for language at the elementary level of song and dance is needed by humans to listen to and hear what is – ostensibly for him – revelation. It is not so much Christianity, but the larger religious phenomenon or dream, that is informing, qualifying, and enriching the scientific endeavour. It is the dream that awakens in us a sense of ultimate mystery and the numinous powers ever present in the phenomenal world about us, powers that possess us in our high creative moments.

When O'Murchu speaks to the spiritual malaise that is afflicting humanity, he does not see Christianity itself being the problem, but a Christian religion that is not open to context. Human desires have been corrupted or frustrated by patriarchal, anthropocentric, and dualist thinking. A turn to science, he insists, can aid us in cultivating a truer understanding of who we are really meant to be as humans on Earth, and to provide us with guidelines to direct our behaviour so that we relate to the planet in a more harmonious way. For instance, O'Murchu does not eschew the teachings of Jesus, but reveres them. The difference is that he pays critical attention to the "rebellious subversive" Jesus who he finds manifest aptly through the medium of poetry.[48] O'Murchu is trying to correct the excessive concern for a religion that dominates and excludes other ways of knowing (recall that he is equally harsh with a science that does the same). In its place, he points to spirituality in all its expressions as being the path of enlightenment and liberation. This is O'Murchu's message to scientists and religionists: we cannot explain the deep search we seek in mere rational terms; it demands a contemplative mystical gaze that relies on other ways of knowing, including intuition.

When Ruether is critical of the logic of domination that permeates the Christian tradition and states that Christianity must be reinterpreted to "make [it] usable in the face of new scientific knowledge,"[49] she is bringing our attention to the deep wells within the tradition whose waters have become "toxic or at least complicit in Earth destruction."[50] These toxic elements that surface in the form of distorted creation myths, hierarchical social and legal codes, dualistic philosophies, and dysfunctional cosmologies, have become embedded into institutional structures. Science serves as a considerable corrective in countering the logic of domination that distorts the tradition.

The science also affirms that we are "stardust," therefore, Earthlings. Ruether, while not explicitly eschewing salvation in the afterlife, puts the matter aside for the present so that we place our focus on being Earthlings and place our energies on facilitating the liberation of women and all subjects that are dominated in the here and now. This last point attests to the degree to which Ruether, like Boff, readily allows liberationist concerns to inform and qualify her faith. The ecological concerns that stress a finite planet, in contrast to what is implied within current Catholic teachings on birth control, also inform her view on population control. But it is also her faith in a world imbued with the presence of God that informs and qualifies her view of how science is done. The scientist who does nothing but describe will fail to capture the full import of her experience, she notes. This is why Ruether calls for an embodied practice, be it meditation or just taking time to sit under trees and look at water. These bring the scientist-poet – indeed all of us – back to wonder, to reverence for life, and to know that we stand on holy ground.

In the end, I conclude with reasonable assurance that the reflections of these four interlocutors are serving as thoughtful correctives to Christian beliefs that give excessive concern to the human at the expense of the other-than-human. Their reflections – each approached through the lens of her or his specialty – pay critical attention to hidden or silenced perspectives and cognitive models of the majority of humans as well as to the voices of the natural world, thus forcing the Christian tradition to re-examine how it does theology. In fact, the challenges to Christianity and theology from these four, and the firmness with which each engages his or her own faith, appear not as a trivialization of Christianity, but more like the fruit of an intense conversation with it to *equally* engage with the social and ecological realities facing our planet, pre-eminently with findings from "new science," with the ultimate purpose of uniting a liberationist agenda with an environmental ethic. There is evidence that while the concerns for liberation for all creation can inform the four interlocutors' Christian doctrines and beliefs, so does their Christian faith inform a love for Earth and all its inhabitants. Just as science informs and qualifies their religion, so does their religion show science the power of the dream.

INSPIRATIONS BEHIND THEIR THEOLOGICAL PROJECT

It may seem at this point that all four Christian thinkers are less concerned with demonstrating the viability of the Christian religion and far more preoccupied with discerning the viability of the human and the role science plays in authoring an ethical vision, one that fosters liberation for all of creation. This view is not entirely incorrect, as liberation figures most prominently within their visions. However, it would be a mistake to make a clear distinction between their faith and their attitude toward science, and their love and concern for the environment and for human beings, especially those most sidelined in local and global societal decision-making processes. In fact, I contend that their loving relationship with creation, their call for the liberation of all Earth subjects, and their embrace of science as a co-author of an ethical vision arise, in large measure, because of their faith.

In this final section of this chapter, I will discuss three inspirations, which are more specifically Catholic in orientation, to make my case: the approach to understanding their faith and moral guidelines through natural theology and the natural law tradition; the writings of Pierre Teilhard de Chardin; and the Catholic imagination, as described by Andrew Greeley. I do not suggest that these are exclusive markers of their particular orientation to their Christian faith, the employment of science, and the love and concern for all of creation. Still, there is a reason why these particular four Christian thinkers take the environment *and* liberation *and* science *and* their faith seriously, while other Christian thinkers, notably some Protestant theologians, do not. The catholicity that marks these four Christian thinkers plays a significant role in this. A short discussion of each of the inspirations identified above should suffice to make my point.

It is difficult to slot theorists into neat categories, as will become clear in my discussions in chapter 8. However, as a way of trying to broadly portray the thinking of these four Christian thinkers in how they approach the world and their faith, a turn to the natural theology method seems appropriate. When trying to arrive at moral norms, in broad terms, they do employ aspects of the natural law tradition. While neither is exclusive to the Catholic tradition, both, mainly natural law, are used by Catholic thinkers who are sensitive to the notion that revelation from God is not exclusively found in scripture.

Natural theology, in its widest sense, refers to the study of God and God's nature with the understanding that these can be interpreted through God's work, or creation. Many thinkers employing this theology begin their study from nature – and correspondingly through scientific data – and reflect upon these observations in light of their faith. Natural theology emerges out of the medieval view that distinguished between insights about God from nature and supernatural revelation (which included that which was revealed in scripture). While I do not wholly place the four Christian thinkers studied here within this theological category, it is fair to argue that all four view creation as a means for arriving at understandings about God. As a case in point, as I discussed in chapter 4, Berry surmises that we have such a wonderful idea of God because we live in such a gorgeous world. Were we to live on the moon, our ideas would change, as "our sensitivities would be dull because our inner world would reflect the outer world."[51]

The natural law tradition, at least in Catholic thought where it is most employed, maintains this nature-revelation distinction found in natural theology. While there is no monolithic understanding of natural law among Christian thinkers, making a definitive definition difficult, by and large it holds that moral obligations, norms, and values should, as James A. Nash puts it, "reflect the reality of the human condition."[52] These truths are discovered, and then subjected to evaluation through natural human reasoning capacities without the aid of supernatural revelation. The implication here is that facts are not morally neutral. It is easy to see how such thinking challenges the naturalistic fallacy I discussed in chapter 5, because the natural law tradition does hold that an *ought* can be derived from and defended in terms of an *is*.

While it is clear from my examination of the ethical visions of the four Christian thinkers studied here that they do indeed believe that moral norms can be derived from nature, or even that nature is somehow an extension of the mind of God, the natural law tradition, as it is currently and popularly understood, does not adequately describe what these four interlocutors do. For one, natural law, commonly understood, is less about following nature and more about assuming the norms of our human nature. Such an approach has traditionally raised the human being above and beyond the natural world, and stressed the use of reason over other ways of knowing the world, thus giving it a strong anthropocentric character. The process of ethical discernment, however, is always more than reason and intellect. Some proponents of natural law propose that it can be revised in such a way that the human is viewed as being part of nature and that our approach to the world could could include a broad epistemology. Still, even within this more ecological-friendly skin placed on natural law, other scholars have their doubts about its efficacy, as it can be too static or hierarchical.[53] After all, it has been used in the past to promote slavery, racism, and gender inequality. Disagreement about natural law's relevance also arises from what scientists are saying about the strangeness and counterintuitive character of the natural world. Notwithstanding these inconsistencies between natural law and the approach to ethics by Boff, Berry, O'Murchu, and Ruether, I think it is fair to say that there is nevertheless a continuity between their visions and this primarily Catholic concept – with its underlying theories, shared with the vision of natural theology that finds God in creation.

It is precisely a world viewed as enchanted, imbued with a sense of the divine, that underlies the writings of Pierre Teilhard de Chardin. Teilhard de Chardin sought a scientific understanding of the world that did not separate the sacred and the profane. Teilhard de Chardin was a Catholic Jesuit priest, a very competent paleontologist, and an inspired thinker whose writings tremendously influenced not only my chosen four Christian thinkers, but an entire generation (and continue to do so). Recall from chapter 3 how O'Murchu felt after first having read the writings of Pierre Teilhard de Chardin: "Truly, my heart burned within me; everything I read resonated with a depth and conviction I had not known for many years."[54] In fact, in *Divine Milieu,* which has so inspired O'Murchu, Teilhard de Chardin writes, "To repeat: by virtue of the Creation and, still more, of the Incarnation, *nothing* here below *is profane* for those who know how to see. On the contrary, everything is sacred to the men who can distinguish that portion of chosen being which is subject to Christ's drawing power in the process of consummation."[55] John Grim and Mary Evelyn Tucker write that as a Catholic and a scientist, Teilhard de Chardin "sought to unite his scientific affirmation of the world of matter with his formative Catholic faith in the divine."[56] As Teilhard de Chardin himself puts it, "There is a communion with God through the earth."[57]

Teilhard de Chardin was the first person, Grim and Tucker point out, to describe the universe as having, from its beginning, a psychic-spiritual and physical-material dimension. As Boff, Berry, O'Murchu, and Ruether insist, this allows the human story to be identified with the Universe Story. Human beings can now see themselves as being fully Earthlings within a cosmogenesis. Hence, one of Teilhard de Chardin's remarkable legacies is that he presents an intellectual and affective synthesis of evolution that draws in the spheres of religion and science. As he stated himself, Teilhard de Chardin had originally set out to dramatically shift the science of his day, which was analytical.[58] Interestingly, in the course of trying to give a scientific description of the whole (phenomenon of the human being), he viewed religion, with its sense of the mystical, as completing the act of knowledge. In fact, Teilhard de Chardin regarded the convergence of science and religion as inevitable, as one needs the other to develop "normally." He writes, "Neither in its impetus nor its achievements can science go to its limits without becoming tinged with mysticism and changed with faith … religion and science are the two conjugated forces or phases of one and the same complete act of knowledge."[59] He writes more on the notion of this convergence in his preface to *Phenomenon of Man*: "Like meridians as they approached the poles, science, philosophy and religion are bound to converge as they draw nearer to the whole. I say 'converge' advisedly, but without merging, and without ceasing, to the very end, to assail the real from different angles and on different planes."[60] Teilhard de Chardin thus helped lay an important foundation for an epistemological model to engage science and Christianity in a deep conversation. This and his view of an enchanted world, one imbued with a sense of the divine, are two important inspirations for the four interlocutors of this book.

While I place the Catholic imagination as an inspiration in its own category, a reasonable case could be made that would place it as the larger vision under which we could suitably place natural theology, natural law, and the work of Teilhard de Chardin. Since the concept of the Catholic imagination is very useful in helping us understand the distinction between it and the Protestant heritage, it merits a more exclusive discussion. The Catholic imagination, as posited by Catholic writer and priest Andrew Greeley, is a view of the material world that is enchanted and sacramental, infused with the creative and providential work of God.[61] Such a view nourishes not only a loving relationship with the physical Earth and indeed the universe, but moderates the distinction between the sacred and the profane. With his concept of the Catholic imagination, Greeley offers an insight into what underscores the works of Boff, Berry, O'Murchu, and Ruther, and what facilitates for them a more profound rapport with the natural sciences as a means of engaging with the material world.

Greeley writes that Catholics tend to see the world as enchanted, "a world of statues and holy water, stained glass and votive candles, saints and religious medals, rosary beads and holy pictures." Whether a practising or lapsed Catholic, to such a Christian, he avers, these "paraphernalia are mere hints of a more persuasive religious sensibility which inclines Catholics to see the holy lurking in creation."[62] Fittingly, he notes that this view could also be called sacramental, as "it sees reality as a 'sacrament,' that is, a revelation of the presence of God."[63] Yet, by using "imagination," he seems to convey the understanding that Catholics actively participate in an enchanted milieu. Greeley does not limit this enchantment to our planet, though, as "black holes, dark space, the non-locality of particles, big bang inflation and the great attractor suggest that science may have an enchantment of its own."[64] In fact, according to Greeley, "Everything in creation, from the exploding cosmos to the whirling, dancing, and utterly mysterious quantum particles, discloses something about God and, in so doing, brings God among us."[65]

In distinguishing between the Catholic imagination and the Protestant heritage (or Protestant imagination), Greeley is not stating that belief necessarily separates the two. Rather, the former invests these common Christian beliefs with their distinctive sensibility, "developing Easter lilies and Santa Claus, and the Feast of Corpus Christi."[66] Such sensibilities arise as the Catholic imagination emphasizes the metaphorical nature of creation where the material world "hints" at the nature of God to us and "makes God in some fashion present to us."[67] So while the Catholic imagination stresses what is similar through metaphor, or analogy, the Protestant imagination emphasizes what is not similar. Greeley takes the work of Protestant theologian Paul Tillich as an example. Dissatisfied with anthropomorphic language to define God, Tillich tries to avoid this by talking about a "God beyond God, about whom nothing at all could be said or known except negatively."[68] In fact, taking his cues from the writings of David Tracy, Greeley cites the negative or dialectical, which describes the Protestant imagination in contrast to the analogical, which describes the Catholic imagination. Greeley proposes that probably the most significant difference between Catholics and Protestants – apart from most of the latter dismissing votive candles, stained glass, and religious medals as "superstition and perhaps idolatrous"[69] – is that the former tends to accentuate the immanence of God while the latter accentuates the transcendence of God. By placing God in creation, Protestants emphasize that we risk superstition and idolatry. Contrarily, by placing God outside creation or as only marginally present, Catholics move into a dangerous world where God is remote.

There is evidence to support Greeley's claim that the Catholic imagination plays a role in how Boff, Berry, O'Murchu, and Ruether approach the material world. Recall in chapter 5, when discussing the living relationship with all creation, how each of these Christian thinkers had formed, at a relatively early age, a loving, even reverential relationship with nature and, initially at least, a specific place – the Amazon rainforest, a North Carolinian meadow, the Irish countryside, and the San Bernardino Mountains. The universe for them is enchanted and sacramental, and this continually forms their love for it, which, in turn, fosters an urgency to seek liberation for all creation. By way of example, the Catholic imagination infuses Berry's writings – and this could be said to varying degrees of the other three thinkers – most notably through the Universe Story, which sees the universe as the primary religious reality, and with his concern for assimilating elements of paganism, which sees within creatures and trees "revelations of the divine and inspirations to our spiritual life."[70] To be sure, Berry is less concerned with statues and holy water, stained glass and votive candles, and more concerned with falcons and rivers. Yet the main point holds: the primordial revelation is the universe, not scriptures. Boff, likewise, sees reality as a sacrament and, therefore, a revelation of the presence of God. He writes, "The sacred texts and traditions that attest to revelations are only possible because the sacred and the revelations are first in the world,"[71] adding, "It is because things speak and are charged with sacramentality that enthusiasm, poetry, painting, invention, and all the inspiration present in each type of knowledge up to the most formal knowledge of modern physics are all possible."[72] His panentheistic views of creation (which posit God as both immanent and transcendent), as well as his cosmic Christology, attest to this.

An interesting example of why her catholicity has influenced her ethical vision comes from Ruether. She tells of the time when she was teaching at Berkeley and at the Sophia Center for Culture and Spirituality in 2006. The Center was, at one point, not sure if it could continue where it was based (at Holy Names University), so members from the Center were casting around for an alternative venue. The Sophia Center, for Ruether, was a place she felt comfortable speaking about the Universe Story, ecology, and ecofeminist thought. Since the Graduate Theological Union (GTU) at Berkeley had taken in a lot of programs in the past, she thought she would inquire as to whether the Sophia program might locate itself there. The story she recounts is interesting, and it lends anecdotal support to Greeley's hypothesis, because resistance to the idea came from one Protestant denomination:

The Pacific School of Religion [which is a participating member of the GTU] has the United Church of Christ as one of its affiliations and, basically, the answer from the college was "no" and rather hostilely. And it was not clear whether they saw Sophia as using a kind of language that was unacceptable to them. I was totally surprised because we were talking about nature in sacramental terms which was something that they, as Protestants, couldn't accept. I was really kind of surprised, because it was almost like they were harking back to [the] old history of their tradition that really had not recognized this kind of dimension. I was actually surprised [as] what was kind of sacramental language of nature [which we used at the Sophia Center] was taken for granted at Holy Names, which was really hard for them. There were several people that spoke forcibly [against the application, but] they didn't know how to counteract it. That was the end of the Sophia Center's application there.[73]

While a far more thorough account of the Catholic imagination would be needed to discern the exact influence it has upon the ethical visions of the four interlocutors, I submit that their views of a world that is enchanted and infused with sacredness and their proclivity to finding analogies between creation and God have greatly inspired their visions. Their Catholic imagination has served not only to help foster a love for all creation, but to find readily within the material world a platform from which to learn about creation, God, humans, and our role on Earth. And since science is the quintessential means of learning about the world, it receives a pre-eminent role in fostering an ethical vision.

Might not this same worldview stem from a Protestant imagination as well? It certainly can, and Greeley himself does not discount this, and certainly the works of Sallie McFague and Michael S. Northcott attest to the deep concern and love they share for creation. Furthermore, not all Catholics equally share this form of imagination. Catholic bishops in the United States, as late as 1999, were still "uneasy" with the use of the term "sacramental" within pastoral letters on the environment.[74] Greeley, however, suggests that Catholicism is unique as a religion since it possesses a very high comfort level with creation: "Of all the world religions which emerged in the last half of the millennium before the Common Era and the first half of the first millennium of the Common Era, Catholicism is the most at ease with creation. It has never been afraid (at least not in principle) of 'contaminating' the purity of spirit with sensible and often sensual imagery."[75]

To this notion, according to their critical survey on Christian thinkers and the environment, Bakken, Engel, and Engel note that a comprehensive review of the response to environmental issues in

American Protestantism from 1970 to 1990 found on the whole that "a major shift toward environment concern within Protestantism to be internally divided, unclear about its 'community' model of the ethical life, lacking in philosophical and scientific rigor, and politically naïve and uninformed."[76] I also point out that the criticisms Lisa Sideris raises with ecotheologians misappropriating science are directed at (with the exception of Ruether) Protestant ecotheologians: for instance, Michael Northcott, Sallie McFague, John Cobb, Jürgen Moltmann, and Charles Birch.[77] Sideris recognizes this and suggests one reason for this "may be that Protestantism has been more closely wedded to scripture and its significance for orthodoxy than has Catholicism. Protestants have thus also been an easier target for critics who trace environmental destruction to certain key scriptural passages that seem to encapsulate and perpetuate the 'Christian' anthropocentric, instrumental attitude toward nonhuman life."[78]

While the anecdotal evidence seems to bolster Greeley's conclusion that Catholicism is the religion *most* at ease with creation, I am not prepared to accept such a sweeping claim. I think it better to say that this is one way of viewing the world, one predominantly embraced by Catholics, though not by all Catholics, nor exclusively by Catholics. This worldview is very conducive to cultivating within individuals an "ease with creation." After all, as Greeley astutely notes, a metaphor is a two-way street: when we use metaphors as tools to understanding God, these in turn affect how we view the world. Romeo, who compares Juliet to the sun in Shakespeare's play, Greeley aptly notes, is thereafter going to look at the sun in a different way.[79] Similarly, the clover St Patrick uses to describe the Trinity, once accepted, is more likely thereafter to be viewed in a fresh light and arguably with more reverence. The metaphors of PachaMama or Gaia for Earth, as I discussed in chapter 6, imprint within us a different way of approaching the planet. Carolyn Merchant has described this phenomenon in her historical analysis of human views of nature in *The Death of Nature*: "The image of the earth as a living organism and nurturing mother has served as a cultural constraint restricting the action of human beings."[80] She explains how miners, before seeking metals within "the uterus of the Earth," "offered propitiation to the deities of the soil and the subterranean world, performed ceremonial sacrifices ... observed fasting before violating the sacredness of the living earth by sinking a mine."[81] Considering my earlier discussion on metaphors, and what Merchant acknowledges, when the mother image of Earth turns into that of a "wicked stepmother," as happened in Saxony, the metaphor can be used to serve commercial interests.[82]

CONCLUSION

Asking whether my chosen four theorists have taken Christianity seriously is not entirely an odd question. Given the great degree to which they are asking their religion to change to meet the needs of a wounded planet, a healthy dose of suspicion is warranted. Nor is the answer entirely straightforward.

It became clear that there is no one "orthodox" view of Christianity or methodological and cognitive model for doing theology – and more important, could not be – in which I could assess the question at hand. The plurality of approaches and viewpoints, as well as cognitive models used in theological deliberations that characterize the current state of theology, precludes this simple approach. Instead, a relational model for discerning truth serves as a viable way of discerning the quality in which the four thinkers have approached Christianity. The model takes the plurality of viewpoints and cognitive models as its starting point, and thereafter seeks only to arrive at a relative adequacy of conclusions. Dialogue becomes the most viable method for arriving at mutual understandings. I therefore inquired whether their reflections serve as thoughtful corrections to current thinking and practices. I asked whether their reflections pay critical attention to hidden or silenced perspectives, different points of view and cognitive models, and I questioned whether there is a provisional character to their reflections.

While it became clear that these four interlocutors have taken Christianity seriously within the framework provided above, I found that they have also treated the integration of environment, liberation, science, and their faith with care, allowing each of these four spheres to affirm, clarify and, more important, to qualify and inform the others. In fact, these four interlocutors' challenges to Christian theology, and the firmness with which each engages his or her own faith, appear not to trivialize Christianity, but, more like the fruit of an intense conversation with it, to *equally* engage with the social and ecological realities facing our planet, pre-eminently with findings from science, with the ultimate purpose of uniting a liberationist agenda with an environmental ethic. Evidence suggests that while the concerns for liberation for all creation can inform their Christian doctrines and beliefs, so too does their Christian faith inform their love for Earth and all its inhabitants. Just as science informs and qualifies their religion, so too does their religion show science the power of the dream and the importance of embracing a certain mysticism when exploring the universe. There appears to be no simple grafting occurring here.

Finally, I queried why these particular four Christian thinkers are taking the environment *and* liberation *and* science *and* their faith seriously, while other Christian thinkers, notably Protestant thinkers, seem to struggle with the task. I suggested that their gravitation toward a form of natural theology, and natural law, might play a role in this. Through reason, both these methods purport to find evidence of God and the values humans are to follow within creation. Neither, however, fully explains the force with which the four Christians engage with science, nor the ease with which they relate to all of creation. The writings of Teilhard de Chardin that have inspired the ethical visions of all our thinkers, I suggested, have further inspired their understanding of an immanent God and have laid a groundwork for an epistemological model for engaging science and Christianity in a deep conversation.

However, I found that it is, notably, the Catholic imagination that seems to capture the overall inspiration behind the ethical visions of our four Catholic thinkers. The Catholic imagination, as Greely conveys it, conceives a world that is enchanted and infused with sacredness. It seeks analogies between what is found in creation and what one believes about God. The Catholic imagination that inspires these four Christian thinkers has served not only to help foster within them a love for all creation, but to see the material world as a platform from which to learn about creation, God, humans, and our role on Earth. And since science is the quintessential way to learn about the natural world, it receives a pre-eminent role in fostering an ethical vision. Does the Catholic imagination sufficiently account for why the

Christian thinkers who take liberation, environment, and science as well as their faith seriously happen to be Catholic? Not necessarily, but it could explain why Boff, Berry, O'Murchu, and Ruether seem to be so at ease with all creation and the employment of science and why their ethical visions are so grounded in the realities here on Earth.

The question posed at the beginning of this chapter remains: is there a limit to the degree to which Christian beliefs and practices can be revised to accommodate the pressing realities of our time and, more important, new findings from scientific research? This is a question to which I will return in the conclusion to this book. As suggested in chapter 5, my four chosen theorists appear much less concerned with arriving at an approximation of truth, and far more concerned with arriving at an assessment of truth. Whether it is the concept of redemption in the afterlife, ecclesiology, Church dogmas, or the employment of the Bible in our daily lives, any "truth" must be assessed in light of whether or not it fosters liberation for all of creation. Just as the concept of liberation needed to become open to change so that it could be more inclusive of all creation, the positive science, with its discursive mathematico-logical reason, needed to become open to other ways of knowing the world, including the mystical, so that it could more adequately describe the world. So too is Christianity being asked to be open to accepting the relative adequacy of its promulgations. This requires of Christians an open-ended inquiry, autonomous judgment, critical reflection, a skeptical tough-mindedness, and a "willingness to follow the evidence wherever it may lead."

For now, a more pressing examination of the communal conversation that these four Christian thinkers generate between their religion and science needs to take place. Apart from the Catholic imagination that fosters a sense of ease with the material world, and therefore concern for its welfare, and an openness in employing science that explores it, there is more at play here that has allowed these four Christian thinkers to integrate their faith with science. There is a deep convergence occurring characterized by a vast communal conversation. It is no longer clear in this conversation when the sphere of Christianity starts speaking and when the sphere of science stops. Describing this conversation and its characteristics is the aim of my last chapter.

CHAPTER EIGHT

Between Hope and a Hard Place

In this last chapter of my examination, I am taking a step back to assess what has come to light in the previous chapters. The four theorists appear to be fostering a close and seemingly permanent connection between their religion and science as two significant ways of knowing the world. The conversation they envision is widely inclusive of a multitude of ways of apprehending reality, and encompasses the concerns and needs of a vast number of subjects, both human and other-than-human. The goal of all this is to arrive at an ethical vision that fosters liberation for all creation. In regard to Christianity and science, there is something distinctive about the manner in which knowing occurs, as the epistemological boundaries between these two spheres of concern appear blurred. In fact, I suggest that the image we discussed in the previous chapter in which Teilhard de Chardin depicts religion, philosophy, and science seemingly converging "like meridians as they approached the poles" adeptly captures in broad strokes the epistemic dynamics we are observing here between religion and science.

This notion of a convergence between religion and science, and more specifically between Christianity and science, is an idea shared by many. Alfred North Whitehead speaks of Christianity and science converging to address pressing issues.[1] In more recent times, scholars attending a forum at the 1999 Parliament of the World's Religions, concerned about the current environmental crisis and the religious implications of science, produced a book with the title *When Worlds Converge: What Science and Religion Tell Us about the Story of the*

Universe and Our Place in It. And while "convergence" is "clearly in the wind," writes Jim Kenney, who concludes the book with his chapter, "On Convergence,"[2] the manner and form in which a convergence between religion and science will occur is anything but settled. Kenney employs the analogy of spokes in a wheel, following the Hindu story of the sacred wheel, "a symbol of the richly variegated human quest."[3] The rim represents knowledge at the most superficial level. The hub represents the common source and deepest level of each and every way of understanding. Kenney explains that, "as one moves 'along a spoke' and 'toward the center,' one begins to apprehend the necessity and the power of encounter and dialogue with the other. As the distance between spokes diminishes, as their convergence becomes more apparent, it becomes increasingly urgent to reach out and engage the other way of knowing."[4]

While Kenney's spokes of a wheel are a helpful metaphor of a convergence, it is not clear what exactly about religion and science is converging. Interestingly, Teilhard de Chardin uses the word convergence "advisedly" in his analogy of meridians because there is no merging into one homogenous entity. Given his credentials as a scientist, as well as a Christian thinker, we can take this to mean that the definitional integrity of both religion and science body are somehow preserved. In Teilhard de Chardin's parlance, differentiation is maintained, but in unity. This analogy appears to be more in tune with what Ruether, Boff, O'Murchu, and Berry are suggesting when they discuss what type of Christianity and what type of science we need today. If there is a type of convergence, then, but no merging, what is it that is occurring? How can we understand it? What are its implications for Christians who are engaging with the natural sciences and the broader Earth community to arrive at a viable ethical vision for our time?

I set out here to answer these questions. In so doing, one of the main conclusions of this work surfaces: that the communal conversation that these four Christian thinkers have generated between their religion and science reveals a new epistemological framework for Christianity and science, one I am calling convergent knowing. It is a framework formed by an *epistemic* convergence between Christianity and science, marked by a close and seemingly permanent connection between their faith and science. This framework serves as the epistemological means that facilitates the thoughtful and, at times, bold integration process whereby each sphere of the four-fold nexus – Christianity–science–environment–liberation – is allowed not only to affirm and clarify, but to inform and qualify the others.

To demonstrate this, it will help to recount the epistemological framework the four chosen theorists employ, as investigated in previous chapters. Given the great similarity among their frameworks, referring to them as a whole is not problematic. What is problematic is trying to categorize what we understand of their framework in light of current typologies that theorists are employing to describe how religion and science relate to one another. What the four interlocutors are promoting does not fit readily into any one established classification of the religion-science relationship. One reason for this is that the relationship being promoted between Christianity and science is specifically an *epistemic* convergence. Another reason is that current typologies are not chiefly concerned with the environmental and social contexts of our time, or the question of what kind of science or Christianity we need to address our pressing problems. Both are paramount for Ruether, Boff, O'Murchu, and Berry.

A SHARED COMMUNAL "SYMPHONY" OF TRUTHS

Reality for all four interlocutors, recall from my discussion in previous chapters, is relational. This means we cannot fully know any subject without entering into some form of relationship with that subject and perceiving the subject from her, his, or its own perspective. Indeed, each subject has her, his, or its own relational paradigm (temporally and spatially) with the rest of the universe, which must be taken into account to help us know the subject. Since such a feat is ultimately impossible to achieve, we accept that there are limits to our knowing. Employing a variation of critical realism that acknowledges the contextual nature surrounding truth, which forever escapes our grasp, the four Christian theorists within this book accept that the universe multidimensional. Everything might tell a story, but a multidimensional nature to reality implies that there are many layers to the story, each layer manifesting itself differently and simultaneously: as myth, fact, or feeling, for instance. "To know" means to embrace an integral relationship among the past and present of a subject along with her, his, or its dreams and desires of a future. As this directionality of reality also extends spatially, we are to embrace the participation from the voices of subjects from the entire globe, which includes the entire natural world. The immensity of this embrace is delimited by the importance given to bioregionalism, wherein the greater part of the conversation occurs. Finally, given the simultaneous multi-strata to the story, knowing must occur in chorus with commensurate ways of apprehending reality: through sensory observation, at one level, for example or, in some cases, at an intuitive and even visceral level; the process of knowing uses dance, song, and poetry alongside rational discourse.

What is key to note here about this vast epistemological paradigm that Ruether, Boff, O'Murchu, and Berry propose is that there is no distinct separation among these facets of knowing. Nor does there appear any defined hierarchy to ways of knowing: while the scientist obviously makes use primarily of a discursive scientific rationality in reaching her conclusions, there is no sharp delineation as to how she arrives at conclusions, where, for instance, mathematico-logical reasoning ends and the intuitive begins. Knowing is ultimately an integrated enterprise of engaging a multidimensional epistemological dialogue. It is indeed, as Berry says, a shared communal "symphony" of truths that requires of us, first and foremost, a healthy competence to listen. In short, in their use of science, the four Christian thinkers present a framework whereby the epistemological boundaries between religion and science are less distinct than popularly thought. This is not to be confused with E.O. Wilson's notion of consilience, where he espouses the synthesis of knowledge from different specialized fields of human endeavour. What we are seeing, I hold, is not a unified knowledge, or even a synthesis of the disciplines of science and religion – because each maintains its definitional integrity. Nor is what we are seeing a mere merging of two "separate orientations" to our cosmos or "orderings of reality" that humans are capable of experiencing. It is, as Teilhard de Chardin and Kenney describe, more a convergence of sorts. Allow me to explain, as the distinction here is important.

Anthropologist Stanley Jeyaraja Tambiah, for instance, proclaims that there are at least two modes of understanding our world. Tambiah was greatly influenced by the work of Lucien Lévy-Bruhl, a philosopher whose thoughts on the human mind challenged contemporaneous assumptions on the "primitive"[5] and modern mentality. Tambiah labels these two modes "participation" and "causality." The former represents the more relational and affective dimensions of reality, and the latter refers to the rules and methodological processes of positive science with its discursive mathematico-logical reasoning. Causality represents the cognitive aspects of distancing and neutrality whereas participation identifies a relationship of closeness in space or time occurring among persons, groups, animals, and natural phenomena. This relation of contiguious relationship can manifest itself in many ways: through people's identification with the land of their ancestors, communion with nature, protection of land from pollution, memorials, and even amulets: "an ensemble of relationships," as he puts it.[6] While accepting two complementary orientations to our universe acknowledges that there are other viable ways of knowing the world, Lévy-Bruhl's and Tambiah's two viewpoints remain distinct.

I suggest that holding such a rigid distinction between ways of knowing the world might explicate some if not many of the reasons why Christian thinkers are struggling to arrive at viable ethical visions for our planet. Even in cases where scholars define a very strong dialogue between religion and science, too often a strong epistemological divide is maintained between these two spheres, leaving science to "describe" the world and religion to "prescribe" how we ought to be and act in it.[7] Such a rigid distinction between ways of knowing the world, especially on matters pertaining to "logical reasoning," is more likely to exclude ways of knowing other than logical reasoning. Moreover, as discussed in chapter 5, this demarcation is somewhat artificial, because we arrive at an understanding of our world by means of a whole system of thought, where science co-authors an ethical vision. Might recognizing the integral and inclusive nature of knowing make a difference in how theologians approach science, the environment, and liberation?

I suggest it might indeed. Returning to my discussion that opened this book – where Christian theorists are struggling to reconcile the environmental and social crises with discoveries from science about how our world functions, traditional ethical frameworks, and accepted affirmations of their faith – I put forth that maintaining this demarcation between ways of knowing the world could be a main reason why these theorists are failing to construct and elucidate a process of serious integration. As long as these orientations to our world remain distinct, we are more likely to continue hearing that *eco*theology is "unbiblical" and therefore heretical in its view of God, humanity, and nature. Without such an understanding of the integral nature of knowledge, it seems more likely that we will continue to hear some scientists use the adjective "theological" in pejorative terms, to designate a vague or ill-formulated belief. They might walk away from the communal conversation with theologians if the latter refer to "life" principally as a metaphysical comportment such as "I am the way of life," while eschewing any discussion of biological "life."[8]

But the struggle refers to scientists as well. Because they hold rigidly distinct orientations to our world, the likelihood that scientists will recognize the power of the dream and the importance of embracing a certain mysticism when exploring the universe remains distant. Such scientists, unlike Jane Goodall, whose methodology I discussed in chapter 5, are more likely to assign numbers to the animals they observe, rather than names. It is also more likely that these scientists will continue to employ metaphors uncritically, such as the "selfish gene," ignoring the normative aspects that are built into the term. I suggest, as well, that with such a demarcation between ways of knowing, theologians are more likely to continue to be challenged by scientists upholding physicalist accounts of reality, ones that view life as the product of a blind process of replication and selection, thus relegating humans and animals to being mere robots or machines. Equally as important, without an inclusive way of knowing, policy makers are apt to continue their inaction on debt cancellation for the millions of people of Mozambique and/or mitigating climate change for the sake of countless species – including the human – throughout the planet, ostensibly sanctioning their suffering and even their death. If the rivers of the world remain excluded from conversations on sustainability – as is likely the case in an epistemological framework that excludes their "voices" from the decision-making processes – the rivers are more likely to continue to be dammed and to run dry before reaching open waterways.

Such a rigid distinction between ways of knowing the world is the antithesis to the thinking of my four interlocutors. Instead, they understand there to be no thought-tight compartmentalization between how religion and science are arriving at truths; the epistemological distinction between the two spheres or orientations to our world becomes less distinct; the exchange of understanding the world between them is more fluid than supposed. What is more, when focused on the liberation of all creation, the conversation encompasses the larger Earth community. Knowing then becomes an integral and inclusive process, realized relationally.

I suggested earlier that the kind of science our four Christian thinkers believe we need today and for our future is akin to a post-normal science, as described in chapter 6. This is a science that eschews reductionist and mechanistic assumptions, and challenges assumptions that science produces final, precise estimates about reality that are free from uncertainty. It is a science that is broader in scope: it also encompasses normative social values and is informed by inputs from community and stakeholders. At the same time, the kind of Christianity our interlocutors believe we need today and for our future is one that maintains an open-ended inquiry with science and with all of creation, and one that upholds the liberation of all of creation. It is a mature faith that encourages its adherents to be part of the dialogical process that helps them unearth deeper truths. The approach to integrating the insights from both their faith and natural science requires a messier ethics than those to which our world is accustomed. This is an ethics that is complicated, difficult to work with, far more humble about what we can presume to know about the world, and lacking in precision. It is relational and concrete, never ignoring the material experience of subjects, with their real needs and potentials. It is evident, through all this, that the chosen Christian thinkers are espousing a specific relationship between their faith and science. What is not evident, though, is where within the current religion-science nexus we can locate this relationship.

CLASSIFYING THE FRAMEWORK

Classifications are difficult, especially as not all scholars define categories similarly. Many authors recognize this. Writing on the theme of naturalism, for instance, neurobiologist Owen Flanagan presents an argument that there are far too many meanings of naturalism (religious or secular) in use today to make any strong demarcation of who could be classified under that category.[9] A generally well-accepted classification of the many perspectives on the religion-science nexus comes from Ian Barbour, who posited in 1990 four models for understanding the relationship between religion and science: conflict, independence, dialogue, and integration. The epistemological approach of the four Christian thinkers within this book appears to fall within his last classification, which Barbour sees as a more systematic partnership between science and religion.[10] Authors falling into this category call for extensive and systematic reformulations of traditional theological ideas, which is certainly true of our thinkers.

Barbour further divides his integration category into three subsets: natural theology, theology of nature, and a systematic synthesis. This is where difficulty arises in trying to characterize the epistemological dialogue my four Christian thinkers are pursuing. While Berry's program appears similar to Barbour's understanding of natural theology,[11] and is consistent with the personal response of "awe and wonder" that Barbour affirms many scientists experience in their work, the way Barbour defines natural theology makes it consistent mainly with a God of deism, an intelligent designer that is far too remote from the world Berry understands. Moreover, the seeming uni-directional (as opposed to dialogical) epistemology understood in Barbour's natural theology suggests it is inappropriate to serve as a characterization of Berry's thinking: if one starts with science, for instance – which is what is implied – and then merges findings with less empirical ways of knowing, the world would have to be mediated first and foremost by science, which is not accurately depicting what Berry is saying. Conversely, Barbour defines theology of nature as starting not with science but from theology. Again, at first glance, while this classification might include Ruether (which is where Barbour himself places her), Barbour appears too strict about the uni-directional ways of knowing: he holds science and religion as being rather independent sources, which is not what Ruether posits. Moreover, Barbour is far too conservative about the extent to which only some traditional doctrines need to be "reformulated" in light of current science. In light of Ruether's ecofeminism, this demarcation whereby a primacy is given to historical revelation is too strict and is anathema to Ruether's program.

Finally, while Barbour's systematic synthesis has "both science and religion contributing to a coherent worldview elaborated in a comprehensive metaphysics"[12] – a point that does suggest it could serve as a category in which all our thinkers could fall – Barbour delimits the parameters of inclusion by assigning process thought as the most "promising" paradigm of such a systematic synthesis. Notwithstanding the veracity of his stance on process thought, it precludes Berry from the list. Moreover, depending on how process thought is understood, the other interlocutors might also have to be excluded. Stephen Scharper, for example, notes that in light of John Cobb and Jay B. McDaniel's process theology, the human is positioned too hierarchically over the rest of creation, which is not what any of our thinkers wish to do.[13] So while Barbour's systematic synthesis comes close to serving as a possible articulation of the epistemological dialogue that our Christian thinkers are pursuing, on one level it is too limiting with its inclusion of process thought, while on another level it is too broad to give meaning to the intricacies of our interlocutors' program.

William B. Drees raises a good point about Barbour's categories: they do not pay sufficient attention to which kind of religion is supposed to be in conflict with, or independent from, or integrated with, which kind of science. He suggests it is better to focus on debates and contexts to understand the particular relationship between science and religion.[14] In this light he presents a model that classifies the religion-science debate into nine relationships. While this breakdown certainly offers more precision on definitional matters, it also narrows the parameters of inclusion, which, as Drees defines them, exclude my four Christian thinkers from coming under any one classification. I suggest this is because Drees's ultimate aim is to present a radical naturalist position, which considers "metaphysical" epistemological claims as being separate from and not integral to the scientific endeavour.

Drees's denunciation of supernaturalism also increases the epistemological divide between science and religion. With Drees, then, we have the same problem as we have with Barbour.

Similarly, Ted Peters presents an eight-fold classification. His first six categories look carefully into the languages each domain uses, and the way each views reality. They certainly allow us to see the conflict, independence, and dialogue debates – as understood by Barbour – more clearly.[15] Peter's seventh category, "ethical overlap," places the pressing social and ecological ethical issues at the forefront of the debate. Were he to leave it at such a broad definition, while not very helpful in adequately explaining the epistemological paradigm of my Christian thinkers, I would certainly place them within this category; however, Peters also emphasizes a clear program of *how* theologians ought to approach the ethical problems within this category, advocating for an "eschatological redemption,"[16] which is problematic, certainly for Ruether and arguably for all four interlocutors. In his eighth category, "new age spirituality," Peters assigns Berry as a prime candidate, suggesting that a certain meta-religious naturalism undergirds its ethos. Clearly none of the above classifications by Peters will do.

Concentrating more on methodological issues, John Polkinghorne presents a framework that portrays a "cousinly relationship" between science and religion.[17] He describes a critical realism that is similar in understanding to that espoused by Ruether, Boff, O'Murchu, and Berry. Helpful in this regard is his promotion of critical realism as the most viable method for a religion-science relationship, as such a stance does not deny the existence of a reality independent of our thinking about it. While all my interlocutors do fall within that category to varying degrees, we are nevertheless left with a classification that is still far too broad. Moreover, Polkinghorne's overall framework is far too focused on methodological similarities and his delimiting of the use of imagination in the realm of science presents problems, certainly in regard to how O'Murchu sees its use.

Philip Hefner presents six interpretive models based on the assumption that all models describing the religion-science interface relate ultimately to our human search for meaning. The resultant convergence or controversies that arise from debate are products of this more fundamental search.[18] His model, entitled "postmodern/

New-Age option: constructing new science-based myths," incorporates many features of the epistemological paradigm employed by Ruether, Boff, O'Murchu, and Berry, such as the construction of a new science-based myth that gives meaning to humans. While this aspect certainly applies, labelling my interlocutors under a postmodern approach is problematic. While it is true, as Hefner asserts, that postmodernism "is impressed with the inadequacy of traditional religion to play its role as provider of a meaningful life-world,"[19] given postmodernism's tendency to reject meta-narratives, there is difficulty placing Ruether, Boff, and O'Murchu. Moreover, postmodernist claims (at least as Hefner sees them) to having "no specific ethic, racial, or gender grouping"[20] impel me to exclude Ruether. Finally, the New Age label also makes classification here difficult for all four thinkers. Hefner, like Peters, assumes Berry, specifically, is New Age. While neither Hefner nor Peters defines what exactly he means by New Age, the classification is definitely inappropriate for Berry, who himself refers to it as "ineffective."[21]

John F. Haught provides a brief typology of five different ways in which religion and science relate. His first three, conflation, conflict, and contrast, do not apply here.[22] Contact, his fourth typology, forbids any confusion between science and religion, while recognizing that some interaction between the two is necessary; thus, cosmology can have an effect on theology. Confirmation, Haught's fifth way of relating religion and science, seems to complement contact: it suggests that while keeping the two ways of understanding the world separate, theology can nonetheless "quietly confirm" the scientific enterprise.[23] Haught's typology here is too narrow, because his typology of contact follows a definite theology of nature paradigm, which for the same reasons outlined above with Barbour, precludes all our interlocutors.

A more promising typology from John Haught comes in a later book of his that speaks specifically to religion and science as they deal with evolution.[24] On this issue, Haught organizes the religion-science debate into three categories: opposition, separatism, and engagement. Obviously it is his third category that concerns us. Haught presents a framework for a new evolutionary theology based on a metaphysics of the future (in a Teilhardian sense) which embraces the full force of evolution but within a decidedly Christian-process-thought paradigm. Apart from the import given to process thought, which, as we have seen, causes problems, there is still much within his presentation that resonates with the program of my four interlocutors, especially his understanding of reality as a cosmogenesis (though he does not employ that term himself).

Nevertheless, Haught's promotion of what appears to be a revised Christian orthodoxy makes his classification difficult to use. While he states that an embrace of evolution implies a radical reinterpretation of Christian doctrine, for instance, many doctrines appear inviolable in his schema, and any reinterpretation he gives exhibits characteristics more of theological-tweaking than radical re-visioning. His emphasis on ecological eschatological promise is another example: while taken to mean more than just survival in the "next world," but a totality of reality shaped by God's presence, it does not capture the Earthy import of what all four Christian thinkers in my work are conveying. What is more, such eschatology precludes Ruether from this category. Also, Haught's enthusiastic embrace, albeit somewhat nuanced, of a hierarchy of beings within creation stands in contrast to what my interlocutors are trying to achieve in regard to the dangers of anthropocentrism. While, as discussed in earlier chapters, my interlocutors, to varying degrees, have not avoided anthropocentric claims altogether, nevertheless, they all do attempt to distance themselves from it, making Haught's nuanced *embrace* of it problematic. Finally, Haught's program clearly does not begin from either the ecological or social global crisis we are facing. His main aim appears more to prove the relevance of the Christian tradition within an evolutionary framework.[25]

Finally, Stephen Bede Scharper constructs a typology of Christian thinkers that comes very close to classifying the four Christian thinkers of this work, because it is expressly engaged with ecology. He separates Christian responses into three categories: apologetic, constructive, and listening.[26] In the listening category, authors are less concerned with defending the Christian tradition or reforming it by exhibiting its doctrine, images, and beliefs in a new light. Instead, relying far less on its tradition or scripture, these thinkers, as Scharper puts it, "[strive] to nurture a religious consciousness that 'listens' to nature and creation itself."[27] In this category, the human connection to nature, and indeed the cosmos, is highlighted and – not surprisingly

– so are the natural sciences (though not so much the social sciences) along with non-Christian and cultural resources.

Scharper's own contribution to this configuration is the inclusion of a political theology of the environment, which fully takes into account the economic, political, social, and cultural concerns, along with the pressing ecological issues. As a result, it encompasses the import of the ethical visions put forth by my interlocutors, as well as their overarching approaches, such as liberationist, ecofeminist, and Gaian systems. Nonetheless, the fit is not exact. For one, while Scharper places Berry squarely in this category, and we can add to it Boff and O'Murchu,[28] ecofeminists – and by extension, Ruether – fall under the constructive category, which he describes as adopting a "self-critical perspective in dealing with the accusations leveled at the Judeo-Christian tradition by Lynn White Jr."[29] This is understandable, as Ruether "expresses sensitivity to the wide variety of Christian practices, traditions, and expressions,"[30] and tries to incorporate the ecological enterprise within the theological enterprise. However, a case could be made that Ruether could also fall under the listening category, as her embrace of Merchant's Partnership Model stresses that humans must learn "to listen to nature's voice as revealed through ecological principles, ethics, poetry, and a reverence for our non-human partner." It should be recognized that Scharper made this analysis in 1998. I have already identified how Ruether's thinking has changed over the years. Arguably, it could very well be Ruether's more recent work at the Sophia Center that would have her fit more appositely in the listening category. Scharper's typology also does not explicitly include the sphere of science, which is problematic considering the pre-eminence Ruether, Boff, O'Murchu, and Berry assign to it. But more important, Scharper's typology does not explain the particular epistemological paradigm our four interlocutors are putting forth. While I find much that is valuable in Scharper's typology, the designation of listening as an approach, were I to place all our interlocutors there, while fitting in many ways, does not fully capture the multidimensional character of their epistemological dialogue. To be sure, Scharper grants much elasticity to his typology, recognizing that certain authors "write from several vantages."[31]

ARTICULATING A NEW TYPOLOGY

With this above survey, which is not meant to be exhaustive, but paradigmatic of the leading thrusts within the religion-science debate, the difficulties inherent in classifying the four Christian thinkers of my work under current options become clear. Depending on where an author places particular emphasis, whether on the epistemological presuppositions or concepts behind assertions, or on methods used, and seldom on liberation or some sort of ecological justice context, categories are either too narrow or too broad. Moreover, predominant within most of the writings we find an implicit or explicit goal of proving the plausibility of God (the strong anthropic principle, for instance) or more often, the relevance of Christianity. While Boff and Ruether might partake in this undertaking at times in their writings, this is not their main impetus, it is not at all Berry's concern, and it is something O'Murchu would consider an anathema. In fact, for all four interlocutors, what we find first and foremost is a deep concern for coming up with a new ethical vision and the means to make it work.

Where does all this leave us? In *Science, Religion, and the Human Experience,*[32] the debate is presented in a slightly different light. James Proctor, editor of that volume, challenges the two underlying models assumed by academics when speaking about the issues that are subsumed in Barbour's typology – and I would, by extension, include the typologies of the other theorists discussed here. In brief, Proctor suggests that those who prefer to keep religion and science as two discrete domains, the former concerning itself with values and the latter with facts, try to assuage tensions by merely granting each its own separate validity. This Proctor calls "conciliatory dualism." Proctor uses the example of paleontologist Stephen Jay Gould, who sees these two domains as "non-overlapping magisterial" or NOMA. Peace can only be maintained by clearly demarcating facts from values. Conversely, a "convergent monism," as Proctor calls it, is promoted by those who propose a belief in the unity of science and religion in their claims on reality. He cites physicist Paul Davies as an example of science speaking to the soul, so to speak, and religion speaking of deeper truths about reality. Proctor believes neither domain works. One falls into a naive taxonomy of false distinctions, as in the case of conciliatory dualism, or meaningless, oversimplified unity, as in the case of convergent monism. This notion is supported somewhat by Hilary Putnam who (chapter 6) believes that the fact/value dichotomy in religion and science is overinflated. Proctor suggests a third option: bringing human experience into the forefront of our discussions of science and religion, which has the benefit of emphasizing that both science and religion are fully human enterprises. Proctor is taking a page from Whitehead's philosophy when he places emphasis on process and experience. In Proctor's framework, the dualist or monist understandings of the relation between science and religion break down. In its place we find the third option: "By bringing the human experience into science and religion, we have not so much gone from two to three, or two to one, but rather have found a point somewhere between one and two, somewhere between the denial of difference (and hence the possibility of relation) that so bedevils monism and the metaphysical gap that defines dualism."[33]

While Proctor's emphasis on experience does not help position my thinkers within any specific typology, it is valuable in demonstrating how all discussions of typology can only be derivative of a particular experience that precedes any understanding of the religion-science nexus. Is this not what Jacob Bronowski means (chapter 6) when he describes science as being a very human form of knowledge? Is this not also what Hefner is attempting to do in describing the religion-science interface as relating ultimately to our human search for meaning? Or what Drees is attempting to do in redirecting our attention to which kind of religion is supposed to be in conflict with, or independent from, or integrated with, which kind of science?

If this is the case, and I sense it is, before adequately classifying the epistemological dialogue recreated in this work within the larger science-religion debate, it is necessary to ask consistently, "What issue is at hand? Is it methodological, conceptual, metaphysical presuppositions, or cognitive claims that preoccupy us?" It is also essential to ask, "What is the context?," "Which science is being addressed?," and "Which religion is being addressed?" In the cases above, Barbour, Drees, Polkinghorne, Peters, Hefner, Haught, and Scharper all present their typologies based firmly on their observations about reality, which, ultimately, fit their particular worldview and concerns. If left at that, there would be no problem, as these thinkers would merely be arguing from a particular point of view. Instead, with the exception of Scharper, each attempts to universalize his categories and, as I have shown, numerous exceptions and stipulations arise. I suggest that the reason it is so difficult to fit Ruether, Boff, O'Murchu, and Berry into their categories is because they presume that their categories are fully objective and can sufficiently address the gamut of the religion-science debate. Clearly, this is not the case and such a conclusion should not surprise us. In the discussions above, I have already considered the problems in assigning any universal objectivity to our knowing the world; why should a classification of categories be any different? In other words, to a large extent, the standpoint of the author circumscribes the typology.

I propose that there is a clear distinction to be made between the religion-science debate in general and the one being carried out by the four Christian thinkers in this work. Still, I think it is important to remind ourselves that the religion-science debate is not your ordinary academic endeavour: it relates to issues of life and death and – as is wont to be in regard to human nature – is always slanted in a particular direction. Philip Hefner puts it well when he says, "The interaction between science and religion is a field in which individuals, cultures, and an entire historical epoch wrestle with some of the most fundamental issues of human existence. This is so because the science-religion conversation is a medium for our search for meaning today."[34] This understanding of the religion-science debate leads me to wonder whether it would not be more fruitful to look at the debate squarely from the point of view of intent. It seems disingenuous to classify the science-religion debate by trying first to be objective and then superimposing more subjective interpretations as a way to "resolve" the issue. Points of view and standpoints matter, especially, as Hefner suggests above, in the religion-science debate. And since epistemic claims and methodological approaches underpin points of view, it appears to me that the best option is to create a new typology for the religion-science debate that rests more openly on the intentions and worldviews of our interlocutors: a typology, if you will, that is defined by what is most meaningful to those within it. Moreover, this, in fact, is what our four Christian authors *are* doing: meaningful to these Christian thinkers is their engagement with new science to unite a liberationist agenda with an environmental ethic. Specific to their intent, epistemological issues become paramount because they are not seeking so much to achieve an approximation of truth, as an assessment of truth. This understanding, then, must ground the typology that I am setting out to formulate: in this case, one that is liberationally pragmatic. How can we characterize this typology?

CONVERGENT KNOWING UNDERSTOOD THROUGH METAPHOR

It was in reading the work of microbiologist Lynn Margulis and her theory of "serial endosymbiosis" that I found an apposite metaphor for describing the particular epistemological dialogue that my four theorists are pursuing. I will first need to explain her theory here before presenting my adaptation of it. Margulis's research, which entailed gathering much evidence and synthesizing a large number of contributions from hundreds of scientists and thinkers, led her to conceive her serial endosymbiosis theory (also known as SET).[35] Etymologically, *endon* is the Greek term for "within," *sym* refers to "together," and *biosis* to "living," which together denote the coming together of cells of different histories and abilities. "Endo" is key here, as it denotes an embedded merging. Margulis's main thesis, and the reason why it was received with much difficulty from the scientific community, is that evolutionary novelty is explained in large measure by cooperation and not, as neo-Darwinian thinking proposes, by the gradual accumulation of small random mutations and chromosomal alterations. In lay terms, the theory goes like this: billions of years ago single cells were eating other cells (perhaps due to harsh conditions, to survive). Margulis surmises that the cell consumed, for some reason, could not be digested, or the cell served to help the consuming cell in some way; either way, the consumed cell remained intact but within the consuming cell, and continued a cooperative relationship with that cell. This process explains, for instance, how chloroplast is found in plant cells: billions of years ago, non-digested green photosynthetic bacterium, once a free-cell that was able to obtain its food from the sun, was incorporated into another cell and became the chloroplast to that cell. Mergers, Margulis concludes, continued and the inner parts that we find within cells today, such as chloroplast (the part that works to convert the light energy of the sun into sugars that can be used by cells as food), but also mitochondria (the powerhouse of the cell that creates and converts food particles into the energy), are really "organelles," that is, they were once free-living bacterium that became "symbionts."

Margulis notes that such partnerships always happen for a reason, likely from a hunger that unites predator with prey. She gives an example of endosymbiosis occurring with a strange sort of seaweed found along the beaches of the English Channel. While it looks like a plant, it is really flatworms grouped together. They are all green because their tissues are packed with *Platymonas* cells, which are photosynthesizing algae, and live in the worm. The theory goes that at one point in their evolution, the photosynthesizing algae were ingested but not digested and thereafter a relationship began. Margulis explains how this partnership works: "Sunlight reaches the algae inside their mobile greenhouses and allows them to grow and feed themselves as they leak photosynthetic products and feed their hosts from the inside. The symbiotic algae even do the worm a waste management favor: they recycle the worm's uric acid waste into nutrients for themselves. Algae and worm make a miniature ecosystem, swimming in the sun. Indeed these two beings are so intimate that it is difficult, without very high-power microscopy, to say where the animal ends and the algae begin."[36] It is important to note that in her theory, these cells that merge are only distantly related, and the merger is permanent; neither can ever live without the other.

Where am I going with this? I am suggesting that in an analogous way, my interlocutors are promoting an epistemological dialogue between religion and science as a partnership that functions in the manner Margulis mentions above. To be sure, the analogy requires qualification: unlike what is implied with endosymbiosis, where one living entity lives *within* the body of *another*, there is no such order (implied by Margulis's prefix *serial*). Here, both science and religion as two hitherto separate ways of knowing the world have epistemically converged (as "organelles"). These are unlike epistemologies brought into intimate and mutually benefiting relationship. It is not a new organism I am suggesting – that is, a merging of science and religion disciplines – but a new epistemological paradigm that, again, not unlike Margulis's theory, has different ways of knowing come into partnership, under the circumstances of harsh conditions, to survive. The relationship or partnership, they seem to suggest, is permanent. Thus, just as Margulis can say, "The origin of new species is hypothesized to correlate with the acquisition, integration and subsequent inheritance of such acquired microbial genomes,"[37] can it not be said of the epistemological paradigm put forth that the origin of truths is hypothesized to correlate with the acquisition, integration, and subsequent inheritance of such acquired ways of knowing? Can it not also be said that just as the integrity of the chloroplast is respected, and that it nevertheless shares a common denominator with the rest of the cell, so too the integrity of an empirical-rational epistemology is respected, yet it shares with other ways of knowing an underlying myth? I put forth that the partnership of the *Platymonas* cells, where there exists a back-and-forth mutual engagement, serves as a metaphor for the back-and-forth mutual engagement among ways of knowing that my Christian thinkers are promoting.

I do not wish to belabour the analogy here, only to characterize an apparent dynamic that helps elucidate what Berry means when he says," [S]cientific inquiry ... establishes a basis for a new type of religious experience differentiated from, but profoundly related to, the religious-spiritual experience of the earlier shamanic period";[38] or what O'Murchu means when he maintains we need to break down barriers that presently fragment our ability to know the world, while empowering hitherto silenced voices; or what Boff suggests with the process of indwelling in bioregions whereby we let the "land reclaim us like ivy growing over an old house"; or what Ruether means when she says, "Just as science had broken down the Christian separation of spheres between earth and planetary matter and between humans and animals, so the new physics itself began to break down the distinction of spheres on which the separation of science from religion (and humanities) had been based." Indeed, the correspondence is striking: just as Ruether goes on to say, "It no longer seemed possible to distinguish so clearly between matter and energy. Nor was it so clear that science could demarcate an objective realm of 'facts' distinct from subjective perspectives,"[39] is this not similar to what Margulis, speaking of the *Platymonas* cells above, means when she states: "These two beings are so intimate that it is difficult, without very high-power microscopy, to say where the animal ends and the algae begin"?

Many of the implications surrounding the process of convergent knowing as an epistemic framework became evident through our discussions in chapter 5. It is worth revisiting some of these here. Accepting a framework whereby the epistemological boundaries between religion and science are blurred allows both scientist and Christian theorist to see more readily the connection among story, myth, dream, and cosmology. Such a connection can serve, as Berry has shown, as a "meaning-giver and driver of action,"[40] to both the Christian theorist and the scientist so as to foster that "new intimacy" with the universe. Applying such an epistemological framework to forming an ethical vision, the scientist and Christian theorist are better able to absorb their experiences with the natural world into their very being, thus helping to counter the powerful myth of "wonderland" that denies our vulnerability, while employing technology and science to deny entropy and magnify our own desires.

To understand better what is meant by "absorbing" experiences with the natural world into our very being, Stephen Scharper offers a helpful account. He suggests that too often we overlook the "agency" of other-than-human nature, a concept that has always been understood by a number of Indigenous cultures. By "agency" Scharper is referring to the capacity that other-than-human nature has to "exert influence over us," not unlike what O'Murchu describes with the Morgan fisher-folk whose way of knowing about the pending flood is seemingly a mix of one-part facts before them, and one-part a trusting of what they feel within, as influenced by their surroundings. It is in this same way that, as Scharper puts it, "When Danny Beaton, a Mohawk activist, says, 'Brother fire is helping me,' he really means what he is saying. The fire is not just an element that has no connectivity to him, or just some physical relation that keeps him warm; it interacts with him."[41] Recognizing this intersubjectivity is what impels biologists like Jane Goodall to give names to the chimpanzees, whales, and gorillas they wish to learn more about. This is not a trite romanticizing of nature. My earlier discussion (chapter 5) explained how greater knowledge about Earth arises out of an approach that begins with reverence for the other-than-human. Knowledge, hitherto unavailable to us, can arise out of a sense of love and a willingness to listen. The opposite could be said of not accepting such a framework, which is often the case today in science: animals are numbers, caged in laboratories, serving as objects for our needs.

At a practical level, as Proctor suggests, with convergent knowing it no longer becomes tenable to keep religion and science as two discrete spheres of concern, the former concerning itself with values and the latter with facts when dealing with environmental and social questions. We gain clarity on why an *ought* seems to be discovered so often simultaneously with an *is*. The epistemic convergence means that a scientist can no more adequately or certainly fully know our world through analytical, mathematical-rational thought alone than the Christian theorist can, through intuitive mystical contemplation unaccompanied by an empirically arrived at knowledge of the world. As Teilhard de Chardin posited over half a century ago, "Religion and science are the two conjugated forces or phases of one and the same complete act of knowledge."[42] This is why, as I concluded in chapter 7, it is important to recognize the Gaia theory as a tremendous transformative power: it facilitates the commingling of the mysterious spiritual thinking with the scientific empirical thinking.

In the end, convergent knowing prompts the scientist and the Christian ethicist to reject assigning rigid epistemological boundaries between their two spheres of concern. By understanding knowing to be an integral enterprise of engaging a multidimensional epistemological dialogue, each learns to listen with a readiness to change her or his view and a resolve to accept the relative adequacy of truths. Moreover, such a model can prompt the scientist and the Christian thinker to recognize the value of an epistemic convergence of science and religion in effectively addressing the pressing issues of global poverty and environmental degradation. Both spheres of concern exist within the *same* world struggling with some of the most fundamental issues of human existence. This is so because, as Philip Hefner reminds us, the science-religion conversation is a medium for our search for meaning today.

This search for meaning is at a critical point today as we witness the sixth major extinction of life in Earth's history by the work of human hands. The relational model of knowing presented here reveals an inescapable interdependency and, subsequently, propels the concomitant need to surrender epistemic sovereignty among spheres of concerns. In this manner, the vulnerability I explored in chapter 5 *does* become a virtue. Just as a scientist must be open to rejecting sometimes treasured theories, so too should the theologian be content with accepting the relative adequacy of her or his truth claim. Just as a Christian thinker accepts the challenge that deep time presents to the belief that the world has been created ultimately for the human, so too the scientist accepts that myths are basic to the scientific venture. Also found within this model is a definite groundedness in our Earthly existence. We accept our anthropological vulnerability, and understand that our own liberation is inextricably tied to that of the larger biotic community. This is why we need to consign it to an eco-tethered status. Understanding occurs in the back-and-forth movement of the conversation, where knowing entails a vast communal and multidimensional conversation and negotiation. Since convergent knowing is inclusive of the voices and concerns of the entire Earth community, focused on liberating *all* Earth subjects, our Guatemalan *campesina*, her community, and the river they rely on are more lilkely to be assured of a place at the table where the communal conversation and conversation takes place.

The liberationally pragmatic essence behind convergent knowing clarifies why Ruether, Boff, O'Murchu, and Berry set out from the beginning to reformulate the struggle that opened this book. They are less interested in gauging truth by how consistent it might be with what we know of the world through science or indeed with tenets of their faith than by the extent to which *all* subjects in creation – the Guatemalan community and the river – can participate in their own (Earthly) liberation. This starting point changes everything: when one begins her query from the standpoint of liberation, it no longer becomes feasible to also begin with steadfast beliefs, rigid scientific methodologies, or off-the-shelf ethical models. Convergent knowing ultimately leads one to query: what kind of ethics, what kind of science, and what kind of Christianity do we need today and tomorrow when the liberation of countless subjects of creation is at stake?

CONCLUSION

Ruether, Boff, O'Murchu, and Berry have fostered a new epistemological framework in their appropriation of science. It is a framework described as an epistemic convergence between Christianity and science, marked by a close and seemingly permanent connection between their religion and science as two significant ways of knowing the world. The conversation they envision includes a multitude of ways of apprehending reality, and comprehensive of the concerns and needs of a vast number of subjects, both human and other-than-human, for the sake of arriving at an ethical vision that fosters liberation for all creation.

The appropriation of science to co-author an ethic is not to be understood as an intrusion of the rational-empirical methodology onto the theological methodology. Viewed as a metaphor, one can readily see that the blurring of the epistemological boundaries between Christianity and science does not mean that one sphere is subsumed into the other: the definitional integrity of each is maintained. Yet, again, as the metaphor suggests, the epistemic relation means one cannot live without the other. This is a good thing: humanity is much better positioned to successfully navigate the threats that it faces if it draws constructively on the wisdom of both Christianity and science. It is clear what occurs when the quality of this integration suffers: the viability of the ethical vision suffers. To the four Christian thinkers I have examined, the liberation of many subjects of creation is at stake. Neither a scientific fundamentalism, nor claims that something is believable because the tradition has believed it will do. It would seem that the epistemological framework with which one approaches the integration of the issues, concerns, and dynamics of religion, science, environment, and liberation matters.

While I submit that the process of integrating these four spheres of concerns, currently being undertaken by Christian thinkers, will become less of a struggle if Christian theorists adopt convergent knowing as a model for engaging with the natural sciences, I put forth no guarantee. Perhaps when more Christian theorists, and indeed scientists, see the fruits of taking Christianity, science, environment, and liberation seriously they will appreciate its value. Certainly, once a Christian thinker and a scientist see that the epistemological bound-aries between their religion and science are less distinct than assumed, they should find it less difficult to allow each of the spheres to not only affirm and clarify but to inform and qualify the other. Convergent knowing is perhaps not a model that we can expect all Christian think-ers (or all scientists for that matter) to follow. It not only demands an openness to the surrendering of sovereignty on the part of the con-tributing disciplines, or traditions, but a tolerance of uncertainty, a welcoming of paradox, and the employment of imagination. Such feats cannot be expected of everyone. Moreover, convergent knowing, as revealed by the four theorists in this book, engages liberation as the primary drive behind much of the integration of their faith and sci-ence. Arguably, a certain kind of person is best suited for the task.

Perhaps this is what Ruether (chapter 1) has in mind when she speaks of the "scientist-poet." When she maintains that nature's voice comes into the conversation through our empirical sciences and through our senses and our poetry, she is not necessarily suggesting that three distinct humans, at least one being a poet and another a sci-entist, are exchanging their ways of knowing the world. She is referring to one person, the "scientist-poet," who does not mark a stark delinea-tion between ways of knowing our world. By way of another example, Berry (chapter 4) calls for a new spiritual guide for our times, one who is ecologically sensitive: an "integral ecologist," as he calls him or her. This is leadership beyond what we can get from the traditional prophet, priest, yogi, philosopher, or scientist. This is a person who "would understand the numinous aspect of a universe emergent from the beginning."[43] An integral ecologist would see song and dance as manifestations of that primordial capacity for language within us that helps us to listen and to hear revelation. Whether a scientist-poet or integral ecologist, those engaging with the natural sciences to unite a liberationist ethic with an environmental agenda will likely have to remain comfortable with relations of mutuality and be audacious in confronting pressures of conformity. They will need to work in this manner to undertake the critical, and at times, bold integration pro-cess that faces the Christian tradition at this juncture in its existence.

Conversation, as Tracy reminds us, is our hope. Convergent know-ing, with its liberationally pragmatic approach is redolent of what and how that conversation might unfold. The journey ahead is great and requires much in the way of boldness, humility, and a love for all creation from participants. It is perhaps only such people, the integral ecologists or scientist-poets, who will be able to take the lead as humans conceive the liberation of the human and the other-than-human. The four interlocutors presented here are themselves integral ecologists; they have presented hope. It is a demanding task, but one that is assuredly not an option.

A Post-Normal Christianity?

By way of culminating my exploration, I return to the three questions I identified arising from the writings of Ruether, Boff, O'Murchu, and Berry, all of which are posed to their Christian faith. To the first question – How might we conceive the liberation of the human and the other-than-human when the future of life on the planet is at risk due to anthropogenic causes? – I suggest as a response an eco-tethered liberation. To the second question – How and in what form might science and Christianity enter into a serious and sustained conversation to help effect the liberation of all creation? – the answer I put forth is convergent knowing. To the last question – What challenges and opportunities does the above conversation present for the Christian tradition? – I think it has become obvious that these four theorists, while recognizing many of the hurdles Christianity faces, have no doubt that their faith tradition must change if it is to remain relevant.

THE IMPENDING CHALLENGE FROM THE MODERN SCIENCE OF ETHOLOGY

To this last point, by way of an example, I would like to identify a more specific challenge to Christianity – one that has not been well developed by my chosen four Christian thinkers, with the possible exception of O'Murchu – which will most likely present itself should Christianity and science continue their serious and sustained theological reflection. I suggest – and I am not the first to do so[1] – that the most significant challenges in the decades ahead will arise from the biological sciences. However, I refer specifically to research on animals and animal behaviour. New research in ethology by scientists like Marc Bekoff, Frans de Waal, and Jane Goodall suggests that current Christian doctrinal and ethical understandings of the role and significance of the human being might have to be reconsidered, and in a radically new way. In his investigation of the behaviours of animals, for instance, Bekoff finds strong evidence that many animals, and perhaps not just mammals, have the capacity for moral behaviour.[2] Moreover, he finds that animals not only have a sense of empathy but also a sense of justice, forgiveness, trust, and reciprocity. He states, "New information that's accumulating daily is blasting away perceived boundaries between human and animals and is forcing a revision of outdated and narrowminded stereotypes about what animals can and cannot think, do, and feel."[3] This new information has come only recently to scientists as new research methods are devised, and as scientists like Jane Goodall – as I have shown – increasingly break with convention by naming their subjects instead of identifying them by numbers. They realize that to understand them, one has to allow some emotional contact and intuition, and long-term observation. One might argue that biologists have employed inference to make judgments on animals for some time, which is true. But its employment has been used principally for animal-to-animal research. Bekoff and others now employ this approach for animal-to-human research.

Indeed, it is hard not to be astonished by the evidence Bekoff has gathered. There is the story of eleven elephants, for instance, who rescue a group of captive antelopes in KwaZulu-Natal: the matriarch undoes all of the latches on the gates of the enclosure with her trunk and lets the gate swing open so that the antelopes can escape. In another example, a teenage female elephant nursing an injured leg is knocked over by a rambunctious, hormone-laden teenage male. An older female sees this happen, chases him away, and goes to the younger female and touches the sore leg with her trunk. A rat in a cage refuses to push a lever for food when it sees that another rat receives an electric shock as a result. A male Diana monkey who has learned to insert a token into a slot to obtain food helps a female who cannot master the skill; the more skilled monkey inserts the token for her and allows her to eat the food reward. And there is a cat named Libby who leads the elderly, deaf, and blind dog friend Cashew away from obstacles and to food.[4]

Succinctly, Bekoff, together with philosopher Pierce, argues, "*Ought* and *should* regarding what's right and what's wrong play an important role in [animals'] social interactions, just as they do in ours."[5] Bekoff and Pierce see morality as being much less conscious and deliberate than has been assumed when morality has been thought about from a human-centric point of view. The authors argue that there exists an evolutionary continuity between human animals and nonhuman animals, and that differences between species – not unlike what Charles Darwin had argued – are differences in degree rather than differences in kind.[6] Bekoff and Pierce stress a species-relative view of morality: "Each species in which moral behavior evolved has its unique behavioral repertoire."[7] In this manner, while there is empathy, altruism, cooperation, and perhaps a sense of fairness within different species, each will also manifest these in different ways.

To be sure, much evidence given above is anecdotal and the field of ethology is relatively new, as Bekoff and Pierce themselves point out. Any conclusions arrived at by the scientists studying animal behaviour are at best tentative. It nevertheless prompts me to wonder what the effect of these findings – should they prove more conclusive – might be on the nature of human ethics, especially as it pertains to the Christian tradition. Can Christian thinkers assume, for instance, that humans alone are moral beings? As Bekoff and Pierce put it, can we assign human morality as the "gold standard" by which to judge the morality of nonhuman species?[8] If it is indeed becoming increasingly difficult to demarcate sharp lines both morally and cognitively between human animals and other-than-human animals, should this not raise questions about the Christian foundation for ascribing an inherent dignity to the human alone? More poignantly, can Christians, in light of the above findings, credibly speak of being uniquely "made in God's image"? The infamous *imago Dei* seems disingenuous in light of the science. I mention this potential challenge not to present answers to the difficult questions above, especially since the science behind them is so new. Yet this example in ethology does point to larger questions that Ruether, Boff, O'Murchu, and Berry have brought to light: to what degree might the findings above challenge the roots of the Christian ethical system?

In their critical survey of Christian literature, comprising over 500 articles, essays, and books by over 300 authors from 1961 to 1993, authors Peter W. Bakken, Joan Gibb Engel, and J. Ronald Engel suggest that Christianity in its continued integration of ecology, social justice – and we can add here science – is experiencing "another reformation."[9] Instead of reformation, I think the better term might be revolution. What appears truer is that we are witnessing not an era of change but a change of era. Berry explains it well when he says, "What is happening now to Christian theology, or any theology or any religious life or moral code, is the most profound change that has taken place during the past 5,000 years. All human affairs are forced to change more than they have changed, certainly since larger civilizations came into being."[10] What indeed is happening to Christianity?

A PARADIGM SHIFT FOR CHRISTIANITY

Throughout this book it is evident that my chosen interlocutors have not necessarily been working from current or popular paradigms for conceiving ethics, approaching science, or for doing theology. They changed the game, so to speak (or certainly the rules), seemingly engaging with the world in an entirely new way: relationally. Such a change appeared necessary. Current dominant ethical models, as well as the moral imagination of the western tradition, seemed woefully inadequate to address the realities of the Anthropocene or to change the social, economic, and political structures that repress the liberation of countless subjects.

In this light, it became apparent that the new ethical vision put forth by my interlocutors had to be assessed on its own merits. Similarly, when assessing the quality with which these four thinkers had appropriated science, it became clear that the science they were appropriating is not the normal science many engage with today. It is a post-normal science, marked by its rejection of reductionist and mechanistic assumptions, and the inclusion of normative social values informed by inputs from the larger population. In short, it too is relational at its core. And finally, when assessing the quality with which they had theologized, here too, it became clear that theological thinking and understanding of truth has drastically changed. The quality of their approach could only be ascertained by assessing the quality of dialogue they had pursued through a relational model of doing theology. What we seem to be witnessing, I propose, is a paradigm shift within Christianity itself.

If it is possible to speak of a post-normal science, can it not also be suitable to speak of a post-normal Christianity? Could this shift be part of a larger civilizational shift? Shifts similar to those in how science is approached certainly appear evident in Christian ethics, ecclesiology, and soteriology. In both science and Christianity a similar theme is arising: relationality as a way of knowing and communicating. It might help to remember that such shifts are not new to Christianity. Theologian Hans Küng, who believes that a paradigm shift is indeed occurring from normal theology to revolutionary theology – much the same way in which scientific paradigm shifts occur, as understood within the Kuhnian framework[11] – notes how a theologian working within a Thomistic paradigm was doing so within a revolutionary mode compared with the "normal" theological Augustinian mode.

As with science, Küng suggests that new models of theological interpretation emerge not simply because individual theologians like controversy or enjoy constructing new models in their studies, but because the traditional model of interpretation breaks down: "'Old thinkers', the 'puzzle solvers' of normal theology, in the face of the new historical horizon and its new challenge, can find no satisfactory answer to great new questions, and thus, 'model testers', 'new thinkers', set in motion an extra-normal, 'extra-ordinary' theology alongside normal theology."[12] I suggest that Rosemary Radford Ruether, Leonardo Boff, Diarmuid O'Murchu, and Thomas Berry are four such "new thinkers." They have engaged in extra- or post-normal theology alongside normal theology. In doing so, they have made a strong case for a new paradigm for knowing and communicating.

Notes

PREFACE

1 Mitchell, *Sea Sick*; Rockström et al., "Planetary Boundaries."
2 The term "uncreating" comes from Cynthia Moe-Lobeda, *Resisting Structural Evil.*

INTRODUCTION

1 Bakken, Engel, and Engel, *Ecology, Justice, and Christian Faith*, 14. The authors map this struggle well in their critical survey of Christian literature, which comprises over 500 articles, essays, and books from 1961 to 1993 by over 300 authors.
2 While not as comprehensive in their survey as Bakken, Engel, and Engel (see *Ecology, Justice, and Christian Faith*), Anne Marie Dalton and Henry C. Simmons in their book (*Ecotheology and the Practice of Hope*) arrive at a similar conclusion about this struggle to integrate environmental and justice issues, and science with precepts of their faith. Dalton and Simmons give anecdotal evidence, for instance, of the resistance "ecotheology" has received within the academy. A volume more focused on the convergence of science and religion within the context of a deteriorating environment is *Ecology and Religion: Scientists Speak*, eds. John E. Carroll and Keith Warner, OFM. Also indicative of the struggle Christians are experiencing to integrate the discoveries from science, ethical frameworks, and traditional affirmations of their faith, consult

Christianity and Ecology, Seeking the Well-Being of Earth and Humans, eds. Dieter T. Hessel and Rosemary Radford Ruether.

3 Hefner, "Religion and Science," 3.

4 Rockström et al., "Planetary Boundaries," 1–32.

5 United Nations Department for Economic and Social Affairs (DESA), "Renewing Commitments to End Poverty," accessed July 2015, http://www.un.org/en/development/desa/news/social/idep2014.html. See also DESA's *Rethinking Poverty,* 15.

6 Quoted in Moe-Lobeda, *Resisting Structural Evil,* 23. The bishop is referring to the serious matter of debts that are crippling real development rather than fostering it (24).

7 Polkinghorne, *Quantum Physics and Theology,* xii–xiii. An early book Polkinghorne wrote has as its title *Serious Talk: Science and Religion in Dialogue* (Valley Forge, PA: Trinity Press International, 1995). Its chapter 3 is entitled, much like the impetus behind my chapter 6, "Taking Science Seriously." By way of another example, Celia Deane-Drummond, also a theologian as well as a scientist, avers that "if biological science is to be taken as a serious issue for debate in theology as such, rather than just by an elite who happen to have combined both careers, then there is a need for more theologians to take biological issues seriously." Deane-Drummond, "Theology and the Biological Sciences," 366.

8 Polkinghorne, *Quantum Physics and Theology,* xii–xiii.

9 Tracy, *The Analogical Imagination,* 13.

10 I do not wish to place too much attention here, as meanings of "transdisciplinarity" vary too much. I am more concerned with what is occurring than naming it. However, the term does seem to fit here insofar as the issue of surrendering sovereignty on the part of the contributing disciplines or traditions is highlighted, a feature of transdisciplinarity, according to Margaret Somerville ("Transdisciplinarity," 94–107). Roderick MacDonald ("Transdisciplinarity and Trust," in Somerville and Rapport, *Transdisciplinarity*) also speaks of a mutual trust and vulnerability – not unlike the project undertaken by Ruether, Boff, O'Murchu, and Berry. These two sentiments become the cornerstone of transdisciplinary projects. MacDonald explains how the lack of these aspects lies at the root of why transdisciplinary projects fail:

> The greatest obstacle to transdisciplinarity is a failure to trust those with whom we work; and the single most important

determinant of this failure is our failure to trust ourselves. A
failure to make ourselves vulnerable in the presence of the
disciplinary other induces us to distrust the sincerity even of
the disciplinary other who renders herself or himself vulnerable
to us. (71)

Echoing this notion, Somerville adds that the trust MacDonald speaks
of needs to be earned: a sort of "trust me because I will show that you can
trust me" scenario ("Transdisciplinarity," 106).

11 Frodeman, *Geo-Logic*; see also Carroll, "Limitations of 'Western Science.'"

12 Tracy, *Blessed Rage for Order*, 6.

13 Ibid., 5.

14 Ibid., 7; Tracy cites the Lonergan formulation of imperatives in method:
"Be attentive, be intelligent, be rational, be responsible, develop and, if
necessary, change" (12).

15 Ibid., 6.

16 Such a pragmatic approach is similar to that of John Dewey ("The
Problem of Truth"). Of course, when aligning my understanding of
pragmatic with Dewey's pragmatism, there is much of his thinking that I
do not include here as it stands in contrast to what my chosen Christian
thinkers espouse: Dewey, influenced by the positivist tendencies of his
day, for instance, negates metaphysical ways of knowing.

17 Jenkins, *The Future of Ethics*.

18 See Chapter VII, *Lumen Gentium*, accessed 8 July 2013, http://www.
vatican.va/archive/hist_councils/ii_vatican_council/documents/
vat-ii_const_19641121_lumen-gentium_en.html.

19 Funtowicz and Ravetz, "Post-Normal Science."

CHAPTER ONE

1 Ruether, "Beginnings," 36; in her teenage years, her ambition was to be
an artist (37).

2 Ibid., 39.

3 Ibid., 47.

4 Ibid.

5 Ibid., 49. She was, in fact, a third-order lay member of the community; it was there that she wrote her thesis on Gregory Nazianzen, the
fourth-century Greek Church father.

6   Miller, "Rosemary Radford Ruether."

7   Hinton, "A Legacy of Inclusion." Ruether implies that it is not parenting per se that grounds a person but the act of concern and acting for the other. She states in an interview: "I'm not saying that people have to necessarily have their own children. But, I do think we have to move to stages of life that we are concerned with helping the next generation of people."

8   Miller, "Rosemary Radford Ruether."

9   Ruether, "Ecofeminism and the Challenges of Globalization," vii.

10   Ruether, *New Woman/New Earth*, 204.

11   Ruether, "Ecofeminist Philosophy, Theology, and Ethics," 77.

12   Ruether, *Sexism and God-Talk*, 79.

13   Ruether, *Gaia and God*, 4.

14   Ibid., 41.

15   Ibid. That we are stardust is a common phrase used by scientists themselves, but it says more than that we are made of the same elements comprising stars. These elements were synthesized within the stars and released into the galaxy when the stars exploded at the end of their lives, releasing elements that eventually make up other stars, planets, and life-forms.

16   Ibid., 45.

17   Ibid.

18   Ibid.

19   Ibid., 4.

20   Lovelock, *The Revenge of Gaia*, 208.

21   Ruether, *Gaia and God*, 254.

22   Ibid., 43.

23   Teilhard de Chardin, *The Phenomenon of Man*, 200.

24   Ibid., 202.

25   Ruether, *Gaia and God*, 243; cf. Teilhard de Chardin, *Phenomenon of Man*, 283–99, 318.

26   Ruether, "Toward an Ecological-Feminist Theology," 89.

27   Ruether, "Ecofeminism: Symbolic and Social Connections," 54.

28   Ruether, "Toward an Ecological-Feminist Theology," 90.

29   Ibid., 90.

30   Ruether, *Gaia and God*, 48.

31   Ruether, "Toward an Ecological-Feminist Theology," 90.

32   Ibid., 90.

33   Ruether, *Gaia and God*, 47.

34   Ibid., 53. Ruether, the reader might note, is alluding here to natural law. I will revisit this notion in more detail in chapter 7.

35   Ibid., 54.

36   I will deal with Margulis's theory in more depth in chapter 8. Though Ruether's portrayal of Margulis's work is fairly accurate, Ruether is not very detailed in her account of it. And while Ruether appears to consult an earlier book by Margulis (Margulis and Sagan, *Microcosmos*), Ruether is not as detailed with her referencing either; cf. Margulis, *Symbiotic Planet*, 37. In this way, a chloroplast is a result of oxygen-breathing bacteria eating green photosynthetic bacteria without being able to digest them. Eventually, a chloroplast is formed into part of the oxygen-breathing bacteria's body, referred to here as organelles. An organelle is to the entire cell what an organ is to the body.

37   Ruether, *Gaia and God*, 56.

38   Ibid.

39   Ibid., 57.

40   This reference to Indigenous comes from a "penultimate draft, 14 November 1997" of what appears to have been a web-lecture that Ruether presented earlier on 7 November 1997 at the University of Wyoming web-based Religious Studies Program (http://uwacadweb.uwyo.edu/religionet/), entitled "Ecofeminism, Spirituality and Justice: First and Third World Women," accessed February 2012, http://uwacadweb.uwyo.edu/religionet/rsp/trnscrpt.htm.

41   Ruether "Toward an Ecological-Feminist Theology," 93.

42   This contrast is found in a number of her writings: Ruether, "Ecofeminism Symbolic and Social Connections," 53, and "Ecofeminism: The Challenge to Theology,"109.

43   Tatman, *Knowledge That Matters*, 174.

44   Ruether, "Ecofeminism Symbolic and Social Connections," 56.

45   Tatman, *Knowledge That Matters*, 179; cf. Ruether, *Women and Redemption*, 254.

46   Ruether, *Integrating Ecofeminism, Globalization and World Religions*, 114.

47   Tatman, *Knowledge That Matters*, 177; cf. Ruether, *Sexism and God-Talk*, 256–7; also, Hintin, "A Legacy of Inclusion."

48   Tatman, *Knowledge That Matters*, 177.

49   Ibid., 178.

50 Ruether, "Ecological Theology," 228.

51 Ibid., 228; cf. Ruether, *Integrating Ecofeminism, Globalization,*150.

52 Bouma-Prediger, *The Greening of Theology,* 141.

53 Ruether, "The Challenge to Theology," 109.

54 Ibid.

55 Ibid.

56 Ruether, *Gaia and God,* 223.

57 Ibid., 226.

58 Ruether, *To Change the World,* 67.

59 Ruether, "Deep Ecology, Ecofeminism, and the Bible," 230.

60 Ruether, *Gaia and God,* 225; cf. McDaniel, "Four Questions in Response to Rosemary Radford Ruether." McDaniel presents a response to Ruether's position on animals and ethics.

61 Ruether, "Toward an Ecological-Feminist Theology," 93.

62 Scharper, *Redeeming the Time,* 163.

63 Ruether, *Women and Redemption,* 253.

64 Ibid., 6–7.

65 Ibid., 7.

66 Ibid.

67 Ruether, *Liberation Theology,* 2.

68 Ibid., 12.

69 Ibid., 178–9.

70 Mary Grey, foreword to *Introducing Redemption in Christian Feminism,* 7–8.

71 Ruether, *Introducing Redemption in Christian Feminism,* 120.

72 Ruether, "Beginnings," 55.

73 Ruether, *Gaia and God,* 39.

74 Tatman, *Knowledge That Matters,* 258.

75 Ruether, *Liberation Theology,* 2.

76 Ruether, "Ecofeminism: Symbolic and Social Connections," 46.

77 Ruether, "Ecofeminist Philosophy, Theology, and Ethics," 89–93; cf. Carol Merchant, "From the Control of Nature to Partnership," accessed 1 January 2012, http://nature.berkeley.edu/departments/espm/env-hist/ Moses.pdf.

78 Tatman, *Knowledge That Matters,* 166–7.

79 Ibid.

80 Ruether, *Gaia and God,* 37.

81 Personal interview.

82 Ruether, *Liberation Theology*, 2.

83 Ibid., 2.

84 Ruether, "Ecofeminism: Symbolic and Social Connections," 389.

85 Ruether, *Gaia and God*, 58. Of interest, Ruether considers Brian Swimme a prime example of the scientist-poet figure (personal interview).

86 Ruether, "Toward an Ecological-Feminist Theology of Nature," 92–3.

87 Ruether, *Gaia and God*, 270.

88 Ibid., 270.

89 Merchant, "From Control of Nature to Partnership."

90 Ruether, "Toward an Ecological-Feminist Theology of Nature," 90.

CHAPTER TWO

1 Boff, *Cry of the Earth*, 208.

2 Ibid., 208.

3 Boff and Boff, *Introducing Liberation Theology*.

4 Boff, *Cry of the Earth*, 101.

5 Boff's biography on his website, https://leonardoboff.wordpress.com/sobre-o-autor/.

6 Boff, "Liberation Theology," 11.

7 Teresa Malcolm, "Ratzinger: Boff's Vision of Church Still Circulates," *National Catholic Reporter*, 17 March 2000, 11; cf. Brown, "Leonardo Boff," 615–17. I will return to this issue in chapter 7.

8 Brussat and Brussat, "Living Spiritual Teachers Project."

9 Dawson, "Mystical Experience as Universal Connectedness," 155.

10 Boff, "Social Ecology," 236.

11 Boff and Boff, *Introducing Liberation Theology*; see also Boff, "La Originalidad de la Teología de la Liberación," 236; cf. 127–44.

12 As Boff's work is never written first in English and always needs translating, the date of original publication is usually a couple of years earlier. *Cry of the Earth*, for instance, was first written in Portuguese and published in 1995: Leonardo Boff, *Ecologia: Grito da Terra, Grito dos Pobres* (São Paulo, SP: Editora Atica, 1995).

13 Boff, "Liberation Theology and Ecology Alternative, Confrontation or Complementarity?," in *Ecology and Poverty*, 67.

14 Boff, *Cry of the Earth*, xi.

15 Vázquez Carballo, *Trinidad y Sociedad*, 220. This is my translation from the Spanish in which Vázquez Carballo quotes Boff as saying, "Ya no estamos tanto en una época de cambios cuánto en un cambio de época." It appears Boff might have been quoting Xabier Grosotiaga, SJ, who stated this in a presentation of a paper at the Second International Symposium on Catholic Social Thought and Management Education, Antwerp, Belgium, July 1997, entitled "The Universities of Christian Inspiration and the Catholic Social Thought Confronting the New Millenium," accessed 16 February 2014, http://www.shc.edu/theolibrary/cst.htm.

16 The works of Nick Herbert, David Bohm, F. David Peat, Menas Kafatos, John von Neumann, Robert Nadeau, and Paul Davies are particular to Boff's collaborative work with Mark Hathaway in *The Tao of Liberation*. To be sure, Hathaway's contribution certainly expands the array of scientists whose work is consulted by Boff and, in many cases, it deepens our understanding of the science (Hathaway, with a scientific background, explains the science lucidly). I do not see a problem in including these scientists as part of Boff's list for two reasons: Boff must have agreed to their incorporation as a senior collaborator, and the inclusion of their work mainly builds upon what Boff says elsewhere and does not alter the main messages of his other works. With this in mind, except where clarification is needed, I do not distinguish between Boff's work and that of both Hathaway and Boff in my writing for simplicity's sake.

17 Boff, *Ecology and Liberation*, 11.

18 Boff, *Cry of the Earth*, 41.

19 Boff, "Ecology and Poverty," ix.

20 Boff, *Ecology and Liberation*, 45.

21 Ibid., 26.

22 Boff, "Calling in Multiple Ecological Debts," 138.

23 Ibid., 138; see also Boff, *Cry of the Earth*, 17.

24 Hathaway and Boff, *The Tao of Liberation*, 263.

25 Ibid., 263ff.

26 Boff, *Cry of the Earth*, 49.

27 Boff, "Calling in Multiple Ecological Debts," 138.

28 Boff, *Cry of the Earth*, 112.

29 Ibid., 19. Cf. Boff, *Global Civilization*, 32.

30 Boff, *Ecology and Liberation*, 124.

31 Boff, *Global Civilization*, 34. This particular understanding of increased complexification comes from Pierre Teilhard de Chardin, *The Future of Man*, 105: "The more complex a being is, so our Scale of Complexity tells us, the more is it centered upon itself and therefore the more conscious does it become. In other words, the higher the degree of complexity in a living creature, the higher its consciousness; and vice versa."

32 Boff, *Global Civilization*, 25.

33 Jantch, *The Self Organizing Universe*, 31.

34 Hathaway and Boff, *The Tao of Liberation*, 207.

35 Boff, *Global Civilization*, 34.

36 Ibid., 34.

37 Hathaway and Boff, *The Tao of Liberation*, 207; this is a play on the butterfly effect, which I will discuss with O'Murchu.

38 Ibid., 214.

39 Boff, *Cry of the Earth*, 14, 20; cf. Boff, *Essential Care*, 134.

40 Boff, *Ecology and Liberation*, 39.

41 Indeed, scientists refer to them under the rubric of attributes, such as vibrating "wave packets" or "events," and Hathaway and Boff prefer to use the term "thinglessness," 172–3; cf. Capra, *The Turning Point*, 78–9.

42 Boff, *Cry of the Earth*, 57.

43 Hathaway and Boff, *The Tao of Liberation*, 174.

44 Ibid., 175.

45 Boff, *Cry of the Earth*, 57.

46 Hathaway and Boff, *The Tao of Liberation*, 183; cf. Boff, *Cry of the Earth*, 57.

47 Boff, *Cry of the Earth*, 58.

48 Einstein, Podolsky, and Rosen, "Can Quantum-Mechanical Description of Physical Reality Be Considered Complete?"

49 Hathaway and Boff, *The Tao of Liberation*, 179.

50 Boff, *Cry of the Earth*, 45.

51 Hathaway and Boff, *The Tao of Liberation*, 180. Original found in Capra, *The Turning Point*, 86.

52 Ibid., 180.

53 Hathaway and Boff, *The Tao of Liberation*, 181; for a further explanation of this phenomenon, see Swimme, *The Hidden Heart of the Cosmos*, 90ff, and Capra, *The Tao of Physics*, 77, 181ff.

54 Hathaway and Boff, *The Tao of Liberation*, 181.

55 Ibid., 182.

56 Boff, *Cry of the Earth*, 45.

57 Hathaway and Boff, *The Tao of Liberation*, 251.

58 Boff, *Cry of the Earth*, 17.

59 Hathaway and Boff, *The Tao of Liberation*, 321.

60 Boff, *Cry of the Earth*, 9.

61 Ibid., 59.

62 Hathaway and Boff, *The Tao of Liberation*, foreword.

63 Boff, *Cry of the Earth*, 219.

64 Boff, "Earth as Gaia," 30.

65 Boff, *Cry of the Earth*, 20.

66 Boff, "The Ethic of Care," 129–45.

67 Boff, *Essential Care*, 6.

68 Dawson, "Mystical Experience as Universal Connectedness," 164.

69 Scharper, *Redeeming the Time*, 172.

70 Ibid., 174.

71 Boff, *Cry of the Earth*, 29.

72 Ibid., 11.

73 Ibid., 11–12.

74 Ibid., 26.

75 Quoted from Andrew Dawson's translation of some of Boff's work found solely in Portuguese (159).

76 Boff, *Cry of the Earth*, 11. Boff employs the term "democratic" in *Global Civilization*, 18.

77 Boff, *Cry of the Earth*, 11.

78 Ibid., 24.

79 Ibid., 12.

80 Boff, *Global Civilization*, 17.

81 Boff, "Ecology and Poverty," x.

82 Boff, *Cry of the Earth*, 24.

83 Ibid., 4.

84 Ibid.

85 Hathaway and Boff, *The Tao of Liberation*, 355–6.

86 Ibid., 356.

87 Dawson, "Mystical Experience as Universal Connectedness," 161; cf. Hathaway and Boff, *The Tao of Liberation*, chapter 11, and Boff, *Cry of the Earth*, chapter 10.

88 Dawson, "Mystical Experience as Universal Connectedness," 160, quoting Boff from the Portuguese in a book Boff co-wrote with F. Betto: *Mistica e Espiritualidade* (Rio de Janeiro: Rocco, 1994), 78–9.

89 Boff, "Calling in Multiple Ecological Debts," 138.

CHAPTER THREE

1 A "Doctrinal Note" on O'Murchu's book *Reframing Religious Life* was issued by *L'Osservatore Romano* in March 2006: http://www.zenit.org/article-15804?l=english; accessed July 2011. There was a subsequent case of the Archbishop of Melbourne, Australia, Denis Hart, withdrawing his permission for O'Murchu to present a series of workshops in his diocese because of such investigations by the Vatican: http://cathnews.acu.edu.au/606/165.php; accessed July 2011 (The series took place in the end at a different venue, due to popular outcry; see http://www.catholica.com.au/tomstake/033_tt_print.php; accessed August 2012).

2 O'Murchu, *Adult Faith*, 1.

3 Ibid., 2.

4 O'Murchu, *Evolutionary Faith*, 2.

5 O'Murchu, *Religion in Exile*, 5.

6 Ibid., 5.

7 O'Murchu speaks of this connection between spirituality and his work as a psychologist in *Religion in Exile*, 7, as well as in personal interview with him.

8 O'Murchu, *Ancestral Grace*, 226.

9 O'Murchu, *Evolutionary Faith*, vii.

10 Ibid., 176.

11 O'Murchu, *The Transformation of Desire*, viii.

12 O'Murchu, *Evolutionary Faith*, 23.

13 Ibid., 81.

14 O'Murchu, *Quantum Theology*, 30.

15 Ibid., 30.

16 Ibid., 51.

17 Ibid., 47.

18 O'Murchu, *Evolutionary Faith*, 49.

19 See Teilhard de Chardin, *The Phenomenon of Man*.

20 O'Murchu, *Quantum Theology*, 36.

21 Ibid., 113.

22 Ibid., 114.

23 O'Murchu, *Quantum Theology*, 197.

24 O'Murchu, *Evolutionary Faith*, 102.

25 O'Murchu, *Quantum Theology*, 39.

26 Ibid., 61.

27 Ibid., 63.

28 O'Murchu, *Religion in Exile*, 136.

29 This phrase is not unproblematic and demonstrates an ambiguity in O'Murchu's thinking as he obviously does care about individuals. I return to discuss this in chapter 5.

30 O'Murchu, *Quantum Theology*, 151. While not a formal theologian or calling himself one, O'Murchu democratizes theology by defining it as "faith seeking understanding," which "belongs to the primal and primordial aspiration that underpin the search for meaning, predating religion by thousands of years" (14–15).

31 Ibid., 37.

32 Ibid., 151.

33 Personal interview with O'Murchu.

34 While I did not discuss this notion in the previous chapter, Boff also explores Sheldrake's hypothesis in Hathaway and Boff, *The Tao of Liberation*.

35 See Sheldrake, *The Presence of the Past*, 250ff.

36 Ibid., 111, 136, and 233.

37 O'Murchu, *The God Who Becomes Redundant*, 132; cf. *Quantum Theology*, 75–6.

38 O'Murchu, *Ancestral Grace*, 50.

39 Ibid., 23.

40 Ibid.

41 Ibid.

42 O'Murchu, *Religion in Exile*, 73; cf. O'Murchu, *Evolutionary Faith*, 96.

43 O'Murchu, *Religion in Exile*, 73.

44 O'Murchu, *Ancestral Grace*, 56. It is not clear how he can arrive at such a claim, as the scientific evidence on it is sparse at best. A more thorough discussion of O'Murchu's speculations and his employment of science will occur in chapter 7.

45 O'Murchu, *Ancestral Grace*, 57.

46 Ibid., 186.

47 Ibid., 188.

48 O'Murchu also bases his assertion, in large measure, on the principles underscoring the cosmogenesis of differentiation, communion, and subjectivity as outlined by Berry, which I will discuss more in chapter 4.

49 O'Murchu, *Evolutionary Faith*, 82.

50 As will become more evident as the book progresses, the *campesina* serves as a symbolic benchmark to discern how our interlocutors deal with liberation. The scenario of a woman walking long and far for water is not fanciful but based on a reality faced by many such women in the global South and on a daily basis. Rigoberta Menchú is a good living model for the campesina I have in mind. She is a woman of Maya Quiché Indigenous origin and leader among Indigenous peoples in Guatemala in the struggle for justice. She also won the Nobel Prize for her struggles for human rights in that country. A good read on her life – though not uncontroversial because of its methodology – is Rigoberta Menchú, *I, Rigoberta Menchú: An Indian Woman in Guatemala*. For a good discussion on this issue of language regarding the term "peasant," see Marc Edelman, *Peasants against Globalization: Rural Social Movements in Costa Rica* (Stanford: Stanford University Press, 1999).

51 O'Murchu, "Discerning the Meaning of Earthquakes," accessed 12 December 2011, http://www.diarmuid13.com/cosmology. Cf. O'Murchu, *Evolutionary Faith*, 102–3, where he cites several similar examples, such as the earthquake in El Salvador in 2000.

52 O'Murchu, *Evolutionary Faith*, 103.

53 O'Murchu, *Adult Faith*, 129.

54 O'Murchu, *Evolutionary Faith*, 108.

55 Ibid.

56 Discussed in my personal interview with O'Murchu.

57 Ibid.

58 Ibid.

59 Ibid.

60 O'Murchu, *Evolutionary Faith*, 106.

61 My interview with O'Murchu.

62 Ibid.

63 O'Murchu, *Quantum Theology*, 113.

64 O'Murchu, *Ancestral Grace*, 179.

65 Personal correspondence with O'Murchu, 6 December 2011.

66 O'Murchu, *Quantum Theology*, 146.

67 Ibid., 92–3.

68 Ibid., 64.

69 O'Murchu, *Evolutionary Faith*, 18.

70 Ibid., 8.

71 Ibid., 176. Much of this information O'Murchu gains from Peter Russell, *The White Hole in Time* (London: Aquarian Press, 1992).

72 Lovelock, *Gaia*, xii.

73 O'Murchu, *Quantum Theology*, 47.

74 O'Murchu, *Evolutionary Faith*, 120.

75 O'Murchu, *Ancestral Grace*, 17.

76 From interview with the author; indeed, O'Murchu makes a point of distinguishing himself from academics.

77 O'Murchu, *Evolutionary Faith*, 203; and he speaks similarly in *Religion in Exile*, 83.

78 O'Murchu, *Adult Faith*, 90.

79 Ibid., 90.

80 O'Murchu, *Ancestral Grace*, xvii.

81 O'Murchu, *Adult Faith*, 82.

82 O'Murchu, *Quantum Theology*, 12.

83 O'Murchu, *Catching Up with Jesus*, ix.

84 O'Murchu, *Evolutionary Faith*, 13.

85 O'Murchu, *Quantum Theology*, 168.

86 Ibid., 168.

87 O'Murchu, "Discerning the Meaning of Earthquakes," accessed 1 January 2012, http://www.diarmuid13.com/cosmology.

88 Ibid.

CHAPTER FOUR

1 Berry, *The Great Work*, 12; Berry devotes an entire chapter, "The Meadow across the Creek," to this experience in this book.

2 Ibid., 13.

3 Tucker, "Biography of Thomas Berry," found on his website, accessed September 2011, https://ecozoictimes.com/thomas-berry-1914-2009-rip/

articles-about-thomas-berry/biography-of-thomas-berry-by-mary-evelyn-tucker-phd/.

4 Taylor, *Green Sisters*, 47–9. Taylor recounts a negative article by a reporter who questions Berry's credentials as a Christian thinker. The reporter "suggests that many of these pantheistic, naturalistic dynamics may have crept into the environmental movement precisely because the Church's absence has left the door open to ideas and philosophies not guided by appropriate Christian beliefs"(47).

5 5 June 1989.

6 Tucker, "Thomas Berry," in *The Encyclopedia of Religion and Nature*, 165.

7 Ruether, "Ecological Theology," 229.

8 *New York Times*, Opinion pages, 2 June 2009, http://dotearth.blogs.nytimes.com/2009/06/04/the-great-worker/; accessed November 2011.

9 Berry, *Dream*, 125.

10 Berry, "Ethics and Ecology."

11 Berry, *Great Work*, 15.

12 Berry, *Dream*, 209.

13 Ibid., 200.

14 Berry, "Ethics and Ecology."

15 Berry, "Religion in the Twenty-First Century," in *The Sacred Universe*, 82.

16 Berry, *Great Work*, 82.

17 Swimme and Berry, *The Universe Story*, 74.

18 Ibid., 73.

19 Berry, *Dream*, 46.

20 Swimme and Berry, *The Universe Story*, 22–9.

21 Berry, *Great Work*, 162.

22 Jantsch, *The Self Organizing Universe*, 10.

23 Berry, *Dream*, 107.

24 Berry, "An Ecologically Sensitive Spirituality," in *The Sacred Universe*, 138.

25 Swimme and Berry, *The Universe Story*, 89.

26 Tucker, "Thomas Berry and the New Story," 11.

27 Berry, "The Universe Story," 215.

28 Swimme and Berry, *The Universe Story*, 138. A similar story is given on page 133 where a population of woodpeckers wandering into a mountain community is confronted everywhere by "demands shouted at them, 'your wings are too stubby … your beaks are too fat,'" and so on. The

birds are told that if they are interested in entering the new community, they must pay attention to the whole community and live in an awareness of the needs of each member of the community.

29 Berry, *Great Work*, 52.

30 Ibid., 51.

31 Swimme and Berry, *The Universe Story*, 52.

32 Berry, *Great Work*, 52; see also *Dream*, 217.

33 Swimme and Berry, *The Universe Story*, 54.

34 Ibid., 54–5.

35 Ibid., 60.

36 Ibid., 59.

37 Berry, "The Cosmology of Religions," in *The Sacred Universe*, 120.

38 Dalton, *A Theology for the Earth*, 111.

39 Berry, *Befriending the Earth*, 22–3.

40 Scharper, *Redeeming, the Time*, 186–8.

41 Scharper, "Democracy, Cosmology, and the Great Work of Thomas Berry."

42 Eaton, "Cosmological Ethics?"

43 Berry, *Great Work*, 100.

44 Ibid., 105; cf. Eaton, 162.

45 Eaton, "Cosmological Ethics?," 164. While Berry argues that he is advocating a more comprehensive perspective, both Scharper and Eaton's cautions are well heeded by Berry himself (in responses to the essays within the same volume), as they "deepen and expand what *The Great Work* seeks to communicate" (198).

46 Dalton, *A Theology for the Earth*, 135; cf. Swimme and Berry, *The Universe Story*, 217–18.

47 Tucker and Grim, introduction to *The Christian Future and the Fate of the Earth*, ix.

48 Berry, *Dream*, 70–1.

49 Ibid., 165.

50 Berry, *Befriending*, 7.

51 Ibid., 11.

52 Berry, "The Gaia Hypothesis," 104.

53 Berry, *Dream*, 2.

54 Berry, *Befriending*, 7

55 See Appolloni, "The Roman Catholic Tradition."

56 Berry, *Dream,* 37–8.

57 Ibid., 38.

58 Berry, *Befriending,* 26.

59 Berry, *Dream,* 21.

60 Berry, *Befriending,* 26.

61 Berry, *Dream,* 46.

62 Berry, *Great Work,* 20.

63 Berry, "An Ecologically Sensitive Spirituality," 136.

64 Berry, *Great Work,* 180.

CHAPTER FIVE

1 Stefanovic, *Safeguarding Our Common Future,* 61.

2 That Christian ethics specifically is currently also inadequate to the task is not discussed here. That is the topic in chapter 7.

3 Schönfeld, introduction to "Plan B: Global Ethics on Climate Change," 129–36; Schönfeld writes this in the introduction to a special edition of *Journal of Global Ethics,* whose underlying assumption is that "conventional modes of thought are bankrupt" (134).

4 Cheney and Weston, "Environmental Ethics as Environmental Etiquette."

5 Ibid., 124.

6 Warner, "The Greening of American Catholicism," 113.

7 Cheney and Weston, "Environmental Ethics as Environmental Etiquette," 115.

8 Ibid., 117.

9 Ibid., 119.

10 Dussel, *Ethics of Liberation,* 39.

11 Gomez, "Ethics Is the Original Philosophy."

12 Dussel, *Ethics of Liberation,* 45; cf. Gomez, where Dussel shares his experience studying in Europe in his youth. He said that he could not truly fully understand being made to feel like a barbarian from the global South until he actually *lived* and studied in Europe.

13 Dussel, *The Invention of the Americas,* 35.

14 Dussel, *Ethics of Liberation,* 39.

15 Willis Jenkins, *The Future of Ethics,* 35–42.

16 Ibid., 22.

17 Cuomo, "Getting Closer."

18 My interview with O'Murchu.

19 Schweitzer, *My Life and Thought*, 270.

20 Schweitzer, *Essential Writings*, 123. Brabazon offers this translation.

21 Ibid., 123.

22 Schweitzer, *A Place for Revelation*, 10–11.

23 Ibid., 15.

24 Schweitzer, *Essential Writings*, 130.

25 O'Murchu, *Quantum Theology*, 206.

26 Cooper, "The Idea of Environment," 174.

27 Ibid., 179.

28 Jenkins, 117.

29 Leopold, *A Sand County Almanac*, xviii.

30 Ibid., 246.

31 Scharper, *For Earth's Sake*, 185.

32 Cheney and Weston, "Environmental Ethics as Environmental Etiquette," 118.

33 Ibid., 118.

34 Ibid., 119.

35 Ibid., 127–8.

36 Ibid., 118.

37 Ibid., 120.

38 Cuomo, "Getting Closer."

39 Berry, "Ethics and Ecology."

40 Dussel, *Ethics of Liberation*, 55.

41 Ibid., 58. Dussel outlines the scientific underpinnings of his ethics in the first part of chapter 1.

42 Ibid., 106.

43 Ibid., 101.

44 Ibid., 103.

45 Gomez, "Ethics Is the Original Philosophy," 34.

46 Barber, *Ethical Hermeneutics*, 107.

47 Ibid., 107. Dussel's response, found in Barber, is taken from "Sobre el 'Documento de Consulta' para Puebla," in *Puebla '78: Temores y Esperanzas*, ed. Clodovin Boff (Mexico City: Centro Reflexión Teológica, 1978), 82–4.

48 Dussel, *Ethics of Liberation*, 375.

49 Rigoberta Menchú is featured throughout *Ethics of Liberation*.

50 See the section on epistemology and methodology in chapter 2.

51 Dussel, *Ethics of Liberation*, 293.

52 Ibid., 294.

53 Dussel with Ibarra-Colado, "Globalization, Organization and the Ethics of Liberation," 504.

54 Scharper, *For Earth's Sake*, 193.

55 Ibid., 193.

56 Hathaway and Boff, *The Tao of Liberation*, 356.

57 Tracy, *The Analogical Imagination*, 363.

58 Ibid., 407ff.

59 Ibid., 421.

60 Boff, *Essential Care*, 6.

61 Stefanovic, *Safeguarding Our Common Future*, 122.

62 Curry, "Who's Afraid of the Naturalistic Fallacy," 238.

63 Were the issue as straightforward as this, I would leave the discussion on this fallacy here. However, the is-ought fallacy is fraught with ambiguities and complexities, and requires some explanation. William H. Bruening ("Moore and 'Is-Ought,'") is certain that Moore's naturalistic fallacy is not the same thing as the *is-ought* problem. Conversely, many philosophers employ the terms almost interchangeably: Holmes Rolston III ("Environmental Ethics and Religion/Science") and Stefanovic (*Safeguarding Our Common Future*, 122–3) both employ the term "naturalistic fallacy" to convey the problems that occur when an *ought* is derived from an *is*. Dussel (*Ethics of Liberation*, 68, 99–100) also appears to employ the two fallacies interchangeably. Bruening posits that Moore is partly to blame, as he uses terms like "naturalistic" misleadingly (144). Oliver Curry ("Who's Afraid of the Naturalistic Fallacy") posits that there are not only these two but many arguments that mistakenly go under the name "naturalistic fallacy," Hume's and Moore's being just two (claiming that good is a natural property or assuming that what currently exists ought to exist, are but two other examples). More important for my purposes here is how Curry finds resonance between both Moore's fallacy and Hume's: both argued that values are not qualities in objects but perceptions in the mind (238). In this manner, where naturalistic fallacy refers to the empirically observed and the ethical

being, as Stefanovic suggests, "defined by distinct categories of thinking" (123), I think it safe to treat the two fallacies interchangeably as long as we keep in mind Moore's greater concern over the indefinability of *good.*

64 De Waal, *The Age of Empathy,* 29–30.

65 DiCarlo and Teehan, "On the Naturalistic Fallacy," 311.

66 Ibid., 313.

67 Rolston, "Science and Religion in the Face of the Environmental Crisis," 394.

68 Berry, *The Great Work,* 194.

69 This point will be discussed in more detail in chapter 6.

70 Midgley and Clark, "The Absence of a Gap between Facts and Values," 207.

71 Ibid., 212.

72 Ibid., 219.

73 Rolston, "Is There an Ecological Ethic?," 100–1. Rolston returns to this notion again in "Environmental Ethics and Religion/Science," 911.

74 Rolston, "Science and Religion in the Face of the Environmental Crisis," 394.

75 Rolston, "Environmental Ethics and Religion/Science," 923.

76 Rolston, "Is There an Ecological Ethic?" 101.

77 Scharper, *Redeeming the Time,* 131.

78 Stefanovic, *Safeguarding Our Common Future,* 61.

79 Ibid., 60.

80 Ibid.

81 Ibid.

82 Ibid., 59.

83 Ibid., 61.

84 Ibid.

85 O'Murchu, *Quantum Theology,* 150.

86 Stefanovic, *Safeguarding the Future,* 64. She also employs the work of physicist and philosopher Henri Bortoft and offers a more nuanced understanding which suggests that "the whole is something *other* [my emphasis] than the sum of its parts, but that the whole can, in some sense, be seen to be present in the parts"; see Stefanovic, "Evolving Sustainability," 199.

87 Stefanovic, *Safeguarding Our Future,* 64.

88 Gutiérrez, *A Theology of Liberation*.

89 Quoted in Bakken, Engel, and Engel, *Ecology, Justice, and Christian Faith*, 10.

90 Eaton, "Forces of Nature," 116.

91 O'Hara and Abelsohn, "Ethical Response to Climate Change."

92 See Guha, "The Environmentalism of the Poor."

93 Ibid., 476–7.

94 See Dewey, "The Problem of Truth."

CHAPTER SIX

1 See, for instance, the work of Brian Swimme, "Science a Partner in Creating the Vision," Celia Deane-Drummond, "Theology and the Biological Sciences," and Philip Clayton, "Theology and the Physical Sciences." Clayton argues that the beliefs a theologian affirms "should be consistent with the results of disciplined study of the natural world" (354). Deane-Drummond argues that there is a need for more theologians to take biological issues seriously, but admits this cannot come about unless theology "becomes a shared task, where mutual encounter and engagement can take place" (366). Along with this must come a "readiness to accept the challenge of the biological sciences in all areas of theology, without necessarily simply accepting biological empiricism as the final arbiter of such theology" (367).

2 Sideris, *Environmental Ethics*, 27.

3 Ibid., 6.

4 Ibid., 27.

5 Ibid., 1; see also Sideris, "Evolving Environmentalism."

6 Sideris, *Environmental Ethics*, 31.

7 Ibid., 76; this adaptation of a biblical quote (Isaiah 65) actually stems from Sallie McFague's writing, which Sideris uses to show how her ethic cannot be supported by science. Ruether, we will see, uses the same quote.

8 Sideris, *Environmental Ethics*, 60. Sideris raises this second point in looking at Ruether's appropriation of Old Testament passages in *Gaia and God* (Ruether's chapters 8 and 9).

9 This quote comes from Ruether *Gaia and God*, 213: passages from Isaiah 65:17–22, 24–5.

10 Sideris, *Environmental Ethics,* 47, quoting Ruether in *Gaia and God,* 58.

11 Ibid., 51, quoting Ruether in *Gaia and God,* 56. See my chapter 1 where I discuss the same quote.

12 Ibid., 48.

13 Ibid., 50, quoting in part Ruether in *Gaia and God,* 55.

14 Ibid., 51.

15 Sale, *Our Dying Planet*; his argument stems from chapter 6 of his book.

16 Ibid., 183.

17 Ibid.

18 Ibid., 168.

19 Ibid., 191.

20 Sideris, "Modern Science and the Varieties of Evolutionary Enchantment."

21 Originally discussed online, Sideris takes up this theme in a more nuanced article: Lisa Sideris, "On Letting a Thousand Flowers Bloom: Religious Scholarship in a Time of Crisis," *Journal of the American Academy of Religion* 83, no. 2 (June 2015): 356–72, doi: 10.1093/jaarel/lfv026.

22 Sideris, *Environmental Ethics,* 294n2.

23 Sideris, "Religion, Environmentalism, and the Meaning of Ecology"; see also Sideris, "Evolving Environmentalism," 63. To be sure, Sideris is mainly targeting the works of Whiteheadian process thinkers such as Charles Birch, John Cobb and David Ray Griffin in her discussion of "the so-called 'new physics,'" but she is decidedly also targeting a larger group (in which arguably not just Ruether but Boff, O'Murchu, and Berry belong).

24 For a balanced report on the incident that addresses this aspect, read Editors of *Lingua Franca, The Sokal Hoax.* See also an editorial from *The Economist,* "You Can't Follow the Science Wars without a Battle Map," 13 December 1997, 77–9. In brief, the "Sokal hoax" was executed by professor of physics at New York University Alan Sokal in 1996, in a leading North American journal of cultural studies, *Social Text.* Concerned about "the spread of subjectivist thinking" within the academy by leftist academics who apply "nonsense and sloppy thinking," which "denies the objective realities" (see also Sokal, "Revelation: A Physicist Experiments with Cultural Studies," in this same book, 49–53), Sokal set out to demonstrate the errors of such an approach to science by crafting a putative scientific article that he felt perpetuated the implausible claims

of postmodernist thinkers, replete with errors regarding physics and obfuscating jargon. The article was published. Sokal thereafter revealed his hoax hoping that a lesson was learned.

25 Sideris, "Religions, Environmentalism," 453.

26 Ibid., 453.

27 Sideris, *Environmental Ethics*, 75.

28 Sideris, "Religions, Environmentalism," 453.

29 Sokal, 51.

30 Editors of *Lingua Franca*, introduction to *The Sokal Hoax*, 1.

31 Kuhn, *Structure of Scientific Revolutions*.

32 Ibid., 24–5.

33 Ibid., 158.

34 Ibid., 155.

35 Jaki, "The Role of Faith in Physics," 197.

36 Kuhn, *Structure of Scientific Revolutions*, 158.

37 Monsanto paid much more attention to the actual degree of carcinogenic risk within the herbicide, arguing, "The mere possibility of risk was not to be considered in isolation from the benefits and relative risks" (Stefanovic, *Safeguarding Our Common Future*, 13).

38 See Bohm and Peat, *Science, Order, and Creativity*, 1–2.

39 Kuhn, *Structure of Scientific Revolutions*, 164.

40 Alvin Toffler, in the foreword to Prigogine and Stenger, *Order Out of Chaos*, xi–xxvi.

41 Midgley, *The Myths We Live By*, 1.

42 Midgley, *Evolution as Religion* 1, 2.

43 Midgley, *Gaia*, 4, 36.

44 Larson, *Metaphors for Environmental Sustainability*, 91.

45 Greene, *The Elegant Universe*, xv.

46 Loften and Northcutt, *Journey of the Universe*.

47 Larson, *Metaphors for Environmental Sustainability*, 4–10.

48 Nancy Abram, from the educational video series *Journey of the Universe*.

49 Larson, *Metaphors for Environmental Sustainability*, 71.

50 Ibid., 214.

51 Bronowski, *Science and Human Values*, 20.

52 Jacob Bronowski, from his television series *The Ascent of Man* (executive producer Adrian Malone; directors Dick Gilling, Mick Jackson, David Kennard, and David Paterson, 1969).

53 Midgley, "Concluding Reflections," 970.

54 Ibid., 968–9.

55 Ibid., 969.

56 Bohm and Peat, *Science, Order, and Creativity*, 5.

57 Sahtouris, "The Conscious Universe," 69.

58 Ibid., 70.

59 O'Murchu, *Evolutionary Faith*, 67–8. Berry himself spoke about this when, as we saw in his employment of Gaia theory, he suggests that even Gaia without the larger cosmological context is insufficient.

60 Midgley, *Gaia*, 38.

61 Ziman, "The Challenging, Inspiring, Irreducible Pluralism of Gaia," in Midgley, *Earthy Realism*.

62 Ibid., 11.

63 Midgley, "Concluding Reflections," 966.

64 Sale, *Our Dying Planet*, 196; Sale himself underlines his preference for individual selection and not group (173, 177), adding, "the work of geneticists, who showed convincingly that self-interest wins over altruism every time when natural selection is involved" (171).

65 Sale, *Our Dying Planet*, 196.

66 Wilkinson, "Homeostatic Gaia: An Ecologist's Perspective on the Possibility of Regulation," in Schnieder et al., *Scientists Debate Gaia*, 72.

67 Numerous international conferences have been held, the first in the United States in 1985 at the University of Massachusetts. Others followed: *Gaia: The Thesis, the Mechanisms and the Implications: Proceedings of the First Annual Camelford Conference on the Implications of the Gaia Hypothesis*, eds. Peter Bunyard and Edward Goldsmith (Camelford, [England]: Wadebridge Ecological Centre, 1988); *Gaia 2: Emergence: The New Science of Becoming*, ed. William Irwin Thompson (Hudson, NY: Lindisfarne Press, 1991); in Perugia Italy; *Gaia and Evolution: Proceedings of the Second Annual Camelford Conference on the Implications of the Gaia Thesis*, ed. Peter Bunyard and Edward Goldsmith (Camelford, Cornwall [England]: Wadebridge Ecological Centre, 1989); *Scientists Debate Gaia: The Next Century*.

68 Ziman, "The Challenging, Inspiring, Irreducible Pluralism of Gaia," 10.

69 Margulis, *Symbiotic Planet*, 125.

70 Ibid., 24.

71 Ibid.

72 Ibid.

73 Schneider et al., preface to *Scientists Debate Gaia*, xiii.

74 Ibid., xiv.

75 Wilkinson, "Homeostatic Gaia," 74.

76 Ibid., 75. Cf. Timothy M. Lenton, "Clarifying Gaia: Regulation with or without Natural Selection," in Schneider et al., *Scientists Debate Gaia*, 15–26, who argues along similar lines.

77 J. Scott Turner, "Gaia, Extended Organisms, Emergent Homeostasis," in Schneider et al., *Scientists Debate Gaia*, 68.

78 Ibid., 68.

79 Francesco Santini and Lodovico Galleni, "Stability and Instability in Ecological Systems: Gaia Theory and Evolutionary Biology," in Schneider et al., *Scientists Debate Gaia*, 353–62.

80 Margulis and Sagan, "God, Gaia and Biophilia," 354.

81 Apart from referencing some papers that attest to this, Wilkinson offers the weak anthropic principle as another reason to conclude that not all is due to chance (72–5).

82 Midgley, "Concluding Reflections," 966.

83 Midgley, *Gaia: The Next Big Idea*, 11.

84 Midgley, *Solitary Self*, 11–12.

85 Fred Pearce, quoted in Midgley, *Gaia: The Next Big Idea*, 22. Originally found in "Gaia, Gaia, Don't Go Away," *New Scientist* (28 May 1994): 43.

86 Lovelock, *Gaia*, xiii.

87 In a personal interview with Ruether, she reiterates the darker side to nature underlining that, "the habit of nature tends to kill off the weak." See also Ruether, "Ecofeminism: The Challenge to Theology," 109.

88 Ruether, *Gaia and God*, 205, the beginning of Chapter 8, "Healing the World: The Covenantal Tradition."

89 Ibid., 205.

90 Ibid., 206.

91 Ibid., 223–4. Ironically, Ruether, in keeping with the writings of biologists Paul and Anne Ehrlich, is arguing that Regan does not take into account the consumer-consumed relation that is an "inevitable part of the biotic condition" (225). But is this not what Sideris claims Ruether herself fails to take into account?

92   Margulis and Sagan, "God, Gaia and Biophilia," 345–64.

93   Sideris, *Environmental Ethics*, 57; cf. Margulis and Sagan, "God, Gaia and Biophilia," 352.

94   Margulis and Sagan, "God, Gaia and Biophilia," 352 and 353. Margulis reiterates this point in her later work, *Symbiotic Planet*, 2.

95   Margulis and Sagan, *Microcosmos*, 16.

96   Ibid.

97   Midgley, *The Solitary Self*, 46.

98   Ibid., 49.

99   Ibid., 11.

100   Ehrlich and Ehrlich, *Earth*, 49.

101   Sideris, "Religion, Environmentalism, and the Meaning of Ecology."

102   The information from Capra I gained in a personal communication I had with him over email in January 2012. Capra mentions some points – but does not go into detail – in the foreword he wrote for Boff and Hathaway's book, *The Tao of Liberation*.

103   Capra prefers to see an attractor as a kind of mathematical description of a morphic field. For a good description of attractors, see W. Teed Rockwell, *Neither Brain nor Ghost: A Nondualist Alternative to the Mind-brain Identity Theory* (Cambridge, MA: MIT Press, 2005), chapter 10.

104   Personal communication with Capra.

105   Capra in his foreword to Boff and Hathaway, *The Tao of Liberation*, xviii.

106   Personal communication with Capra.

107   This is evident in his writings as well as personal conversations I had with him. He was consistently recommending to me new books dealing with new research into various matters, which were not found in his writings.

108   O'Murchu, *Religion in Exile*, 136.

109   Ibid., 37.

110   O'Murchu, in talking about the "dreamer," states that she/he must at times continue down scientific inquiry even "despite the paucity of facts" (*Ancestral Grace*, 17).

111   O'Murchu, *Transformation of Desire*, 79.

112   Swimme, "Science a Partner in Creating the Vision," 82.

113   Ibid., 83.

114   Beller, "The Sokal Hoax." Beller has us consider, for instance, the following extrapolation of Heisenberg's uncertainty and Bohr's complementarity into the political realm.

115 See reports that arose after news of its discovery surfaced: Jon Hembrey, "Why the Higgs Boson 'God Particle' Matters," CBC News, 15 March 2013, accessed June 2013, http://www.cbc.ca/news/technology/story/2013/03/14/f-god-particle-higgs-boson-why-matters.html.

116 Berry, *Great Work*, 20.

CHAPTER SEVEN

1 Harvey, "The Pathos of Liberal Theology"; Northcott, *The Environment and Christian Ethics*.

2 See Chopp and Regan, "Latin American Liberation Theology," 469–84.

3 Boff, *Church, Charism and Power*.

4 Boff, "Encouragement for Those Disappointed with the Church," 13 August 2011, accessed 2 June 2012, http://leonardoboff.wordpress.com/2011/08/13/encouragment-for-those-disappointed-with-the-church/.

5 Berry, *Befriending the Earth*, 77.

6 Ibid., 78.

7 Taylor, *Green Sisters*, 47–9. Taylor recounts a negative article by a reporter who questions Berry's credentials as a Christian thinker. The reporter "suggests that many of these pantheistic, naturalistic dynamics may have crept into the environmental movement precisely because the Church's absence has left the door open to ideas and philosophies not guided by appropriate Christian beliefs" (47).

8 Ibid., 47–8; cf. the Blessed Kateri Tekakwitha Conservation Center website. This site criticizes Berry. Accessed June 2013, http://conservation.catholic.org/creation_spirituality.htm.

9 Berry, *Befriending the Earth*, 21. Cf. Vatican Pontifical Council's "Jesus Christ the Bearer of the Water of Life: A Christian Reflection on the 'New Age,'" accessed March 2013, http://www.vatican.va/roman_curia/pontifical_councils/interelg/documents/rc_pc_interelg_doc_20030203_new-age_en.html. The document, which subsumes Indigenous tradition and all pagan thinking under New Age, is very critical of such notions.

10 O'Murchu, *Quantum Theology*, 217.

11 O'Murchu, *Religion in Exile*, 16.

12 O'Murchu, *Quantum Theology*, 66.

13 Ruether, *The Church against Itself*, 1; cf. Miller, "Rosemary Radford Ruether," 2–4.

14 See Berry, *Befriending the Earth*, 144.

15 Hodgson, *Liberal Theology*, ix.

16 Tracy, *The Analogical Imagination*, 372.

17 Ford, "Introduction to Modern Christian Theology," 1–15.

18 Ibid.

19 Tracy, *Blessed Rage*, chapter 2.

20 See Hodgson, *Liberal Theology*, and Ruether and Grau, introduction to *Interpreting the Postmodern*. There is also the rise of contextual theologies to consider; see Albert Nolan, *Contextual Theologies: One Faith, Many Theologies* (Toronto: Regis College, 1991).

21 Readers can compare the works of Peter Hodgson, *Liberal Theology*; Gary Dorrien, *The Making of American Liberal Theology*; and David Tracy, *Blessed Rage*, for instance. On this issue of inconsistencies closer to my own study of ecotheology, I will convey an anecdotal example as evidence. At a workshop encounter in San Francisco in 2011, comprising approximately thirty Christian religious-theological-environmental scholars from Canada, United States, England, and South Africa, of which I was a participant, the common denominator among the participants was a concern for environmental issues in their research, teachings, and writings from a Christian vantage point. The starting point from which each began his/her research, however, differed among the group – a few individuals took Earth and evolution as their starting point, the majority of scholars took a faith in Jesus Christ and scriptures as their starting point, and some took ecumenism as a starting point. One could say the split was mainly between those ascribing to a natural theology (minority) and those ascribing to a theology of nature (majority). At one point in the three-day discussions, the conversation seemed to have reached an impasse (at least for many hours). It appeared evident to me that one of the reasons for this impasse was this difference in starting points when, at break, I spoke confidentially to one participant, a biblical scholar, who confided in me – in contrast to the view of another scholar who was arguing steadfastly against making her starting point the Bible or faith in Jesus Christ – that (theoretically, he emphasized) were he ever to discern from within the Bible a directive for humans to destroy the Earth, his faith in the primacy of scriptures would impel him to follow that dictate. While I do find this stance personally remarkable,

I offer this anecdote not to denigrate the thinking of any of the scholars, but to point out that even among prominent Christian *eco*theologians, the degree to which they differ can be large, even when they fall under the same grouping.

22 Tracy, *Analogical Imagination*, 373.

23 Ruether and Grau, *Interpreting the Postmodern*, vii.

24 Ibid., vii.

25 This Latin term is considered a "deep well" of wisdom for the Church reaffirmed in Vatican II documents, *Lumen Gentium*. See Dogmatic Constitution on the Church, *Lumen Gentium*, accessed June 2013, http://www.vatican.va/archive/hist_councils/ii_vatican_council/documents/vat-ii_const_19641121_lumen-gentium_en.html.

26 See, for instance, the paper by Catherine E. Clifford and Richard R. Gaillardetz co-authored and co-presented at the Catholic Theological Society of America's annual gathering in 2010 entitled "Beyond Presumption: Reimagining the Ecclesial-Prophetic Vocation of the Theologian."

27 Murray, "Catholic Theology after Vatican II," 276. This 1968 Vatican document on the Church's teaching on married love, parenthood, and sexual reproduction prohibited the use of contraceptives. It was a landmark document that left many Catholics – including not a few bishops – confused, as the *sensus fidei*, which was overwhelmingly in favour of artificial contraception, was unilaterally overturned by Pope Paul VI. Despite this, few Catholics obeyed this edict (see a recent Gallup poll, which found that 82 per cent of US Catholics say birth control is morally acceptable, available at http://www.gallup.com/poll/154799/americans-including-catholics-say-birth-control-morally.aspx), and many thinkers today consider this a pivotal moment in Catholic history, as the authority of the Magisterium since then has been eroded in the minds of many Catholics. A good précis on this is offered by PBS, which did an in-depth film on the story: available at http://www.pbs.org/wgbh/amex/pill/peopleevents/e_humvit.html, accessed 17 June 2013.

28 Gregersen and van Huyssteen, *Rethinking Theology and Science*, 4.

29 Allsopp, *Reviewing Christian Ethics*, 3.

30 Baum, "Personal Experience and Styles of Thought," 7.

31 Ibid., 8.

32 Ibid., 11.

33 Swidler, *Toward a Universal Theology of Religion*, 3.

34 Ibid., 3.

35 Quoted in Swidler, *Toward a Universal Theology of Religion*, 8.

36 Baum, "David Tracy: Pluralism and Liberation Theology," in *Essays in Critical Theology*, 36–7.

37 Tracy, *Blessed Rage for Order*, 6.

38 Ibid., 5.

39 Ibid.

40 Ibid., 7.

41 Ibid., 6.

42 Tracy, *The Analogical Imagination*, 363.

43 See its Baar Statement: Theological Perspectives on Plurality, available at http://www.oikoumene.org/en/resources/documents/wcc-programmes/interreligious-dialogue-and-cooperation/christian-identity-in-pluralistic-societies/baar-statement-theological-perspectives-on-plurality, accessed June 2013.

44 Boff, *Ecclesiogenesis*, 24.

45 Berry, *Befriending the Earth*, 7.

46 Ibid., 75.

47 The notion of the cosmic Christ has biblical roots and is a theme popularized by Matthew Fox (also Catholic). It is a belief that an aspect of God pervades all of creation, the Christ whose church "is his body, the fullness of him who fills all in all" (Ephesians 1:23); cf. Boff, *Cry of the Earth*, Chapter 9.

48 O'Murchu, *Jesus in the Power of Poetry*.

49 Ruether, *Gaia and God*, 206; recall that Ruether is also critical of science that has created the destructive power of various technologies.

50 Hessel and Ruether, "Introduction: Current Thought on Christianity and Ecology," xxxviii.

51 Berry, *Befriending*, 9.

52 Nash, "Seeking Moral Norms in Nature," 230.

53 Ibid., 229. See also Curran, *The Development of Moral Theology*, chapter 3, and Bakken, Engel, and Engel, *Ecology, Justice, and Christian Faith*, 21.

54 O'Murchu, *Evolutionary Faith*, 2.

55 Teilhard de Chardin, *Divine Milieu*, 66.

56 Grim and Tucker, "An Overview of Teilhard's Commitment."

57 Ibid., 158.

58 Teilhard de Chardin, *The Phenomenon of Man*, 312.

59 Ibid., 311 and 313.

60 Ibid., 32.

61 Greeley, *The Catholic Imagination*, 1.

62 Ibid., 1.

63 Ibid.

64 Ibid., 2.

65 Ibid., 7.

66 Ibid., 4.

67 Ibid., 6.

68 Ibid., 8.

69 Ibid., 5.

70 Berry, "Women Religious: Voices of Earth," in *The Christian Future and the Fate of the Earth*, 74.

71 Boff, *Cry of the Earth*, 151.

72 Ibid., 159.

73 Personal interview. In the end, Holy Names University decided Sophia Center could stay and the issue was closed. I should note that the question I asked Ruether, which elicited this response, did not mention the Catholic imagination. Instead, I only asked her, "How much do you suppose your Catholicity comes into play in regards to [the formation of your ethical vision]?"

74 Warner, "The Greening of American Catholicism."

75 Greeley, *The Catholic Imagination*, 10.

76 Bakken, Engel, and Engel, *Ecology, Justice, and Christian Faith*, 3.

77 Sideris, *Environmental Ethics*. We note that her later work on the scientific method was directed primarily at the Evangelical Christian tradition.

78 Sideris, *Environmental Ethics*, 4–5.

79 Greeley, *The Catholic Imagination*, 10.

80 Merchant, *The Death of Nature*, 3.

81 Ibid., 4.

82 Ibid., 33, 41.

CHAPTER EIGHT

1 Whitehead, *Science and the Modern World*, 260.

2 Kenney, "On Convergence," 369.

3 Ibid., 368.

4 Ibid.

5 Tambiah, *Magic, Science, Religion and the Scope of Rationality*, particularly chapter 5. I am not comfortable using the term "primitive" and am conscious of the baggage it carries. I use it here as it is the wording Lévy-Bruhl and Tambiah use themselves.

6 Ibid., 107–8.

7 The "dialogue" typology Ian Barbour (*When Science Meets Religion*, 24–7) employs, for instance, names a number of authors that find methodological and conceptual parallels between these two domains, but a greater integration of how each knows the world is denied. An epistemic demarcation between religion and science is clearly demarcated. See also Bauman, "Religion, Science, and Nature." Bauman argues well how religion and science in dialogue complement the process of arriving at meaning in our world; science may even suggest new ways of relating to the rest of the natural world, but science does "not indicate what or 'how' we ought to become" (788).

8 Swimme, "Science," 84.

9 Flanagan, "Varieties of Naturalism," 430–52.

10 Barbour, *When Science Meets Religion*, 23–7.

11 Ibid., 28; he places Aquinas under this category.

12 Barbour, *When Science Meets Religion*, 34.

13 Scharper, *Redeeming the Time*, Chapter 3.

14 Drees, *Science, Religion and Naturalism*, chapter 1.

15 Peters, "Theology and Natural Science," 649–68.

16 Ibid., 653.

17 Polkinghorne, *Quantum Physics and Theology*.

18 Hefner, "Science-and-Religion and the Search for Meaning," 307–21.

19 Ibid., 311.

20 Ibid.

21 Berry, *Dream*, 124; Berry understands that many today have turned to New Age orientations because of the dysfunctional aspects of traditional "stories." He believes such a spirituality, however, lacks the deep meaning

and social discipline "needed for a life leading to emotional, aesthetic and spiritual fulfillment."

22 Haught, *Christianity and Science*, 116–32. Haught originally developed a typology of four in a previous work (*Science and Religion: From Conflict to Conversation* [Mahwah, NJ, and New York: Paulist Press, 1995]), adding here "conflation" to his new list. Of his first three, the conflict position is akin to scientism, and contrast is similar to Barbour's independence, in that it is believed theology and science address radically disparate sets of questions; thus, there can be no conflict between them. Conflation, as the title suggests, overlooks distinctions and blurs methods and roles (for example using the Book of Genesis as a scientific guide). As I argue in this chapter, I do not see a conflation, but convergence occurring. Further, the convergence is of an epistemological nature, while his deals with methodologies, worldviews, and roles.

23 Haught, *Christianity and Science*, 120.

24 It is not all clear to me why he sees the need to distinguish typologies dealing with science in general and evolution; nevertheless, the one dealing with evolution seems more embracing: Haught, *God after Darwin*.

25 Ibid., chapter 9; cf. Haught (*Christianity and Science*), where he forcibly espouses a theology of nature that takes much of biblical and early church teachings as "givens" for his faith.

26 Scharper, *Redeeming the Time*, Chapter 1. Christian authors in the first category contest Lynn White Jr's famous charges of anthropocentrism against Christianity, while the authors in the second category – which comprises the bulk of Christian writers on the subject – accept aspects of White's claim as being valid, while maintaining that within the Christian tradition there are "deep wells" for producing an environmental theology ("Deep wells" is used by Scharper in "Ecological Theology," 144).

27 Scharper, *Redeeming the Time*, 24.

28 Scharper does not expressly deal with O'Murchu; and Boff, while not exactly identified, as a liberation theologian, would naturally make theology a second act, while listening to the poor and the Earth are primary acts. Ibid., 181–2.

29 Ibid., 37.

30 Ibid.

31 Ibid., 25.

32 Proctor, "Introduction: Rethinking Science and Religion," 3–23.

33 Ibid., 20.

34 Hefner, "Science-and-Religion and the Search for Meaning," 318.

35 While there are plenty of papers explaining her research in scientific terms, for the layperson, she presents her theory in her book, *Symbiotic Planet*. See also Sagan, "On the Origin of Mitosing Cells," 225–74.

36 Margulis, *Symbiotic Planet*, 10.

37 Margulis, "Origins of Species," 121.

38 Dalton, *A Theology for the Earth*, 95.

39 Ruether, *Gaia and God*, 37.

40 Dalton, *A Theology for the Earth*, 111; see also 108, 125.

41 Scharper, *For Earth's Sake*, 184. By way of another example of this absorption, we can look at the argument Timothy Leduc makes in his book *Climate, Culture, Change: Inuit and Western Dialogue with a Warming North* (Ottawa: University of Ottawa Press, 2011). Leduc insists that any interdisciplinary dialogue among the Inuit and the scientists must be understood as occurring with a warming North, not in the North. The distinction is crucial: for "with" implies that the world is involved in co-creating our thought. Such an argument can only be conceived within a multidimensional epistemological framework.

42 Teilhard de Chardin, *The Phenomenon of Man*, 311.

43 Berry, "An Ecologically Sensitive Spirituality," 135.

CONCLUSION

1 See Clayton, "Theology and the Physical Sciences," 352ff. Clayton suggests neuroscience will play a decisive role.

2 Bekoff and Pierce, *Wild Justice*, and Pierce and Bekoff, "Wild Justice Redux."

3 Bekoff and Pierce, *Wild Justice*, x. This approach speaks to the anecdotal methodology or "narrative ethology" for animal research that scientists like Bekoff have developed over the years (chapter 2); also see Jane Goodall, foreword to Bekoff, *Minding Animals*.

4 Bekoff and Pierce, *Wild Justice*, ix.

5 Ibid., x.

6 Bekoff and Pierce, *Wild Justice*, xi. See also Bekoff, *Minding Animals*, 48; Midgley, *The Solitary Self*, 85; and Midgley, *Animals and Why They Matter*, 14.

7   Bekoff and Pierce, *Wild Justice*, 19.

8   Ibid.

9   Bakken, Engel, and Engel, *Ecology, Justice, and Christian Faith*, xvi.

10   Berry, *Befriending*, 6.

11   Hans Küng, "Paradigm Change in Theology: A Proposal for Discussion," in Küng and Tracy, *Paradigm Change in Theology*.

12   Ibid., 20; italics original.

Bibliography

Albanese, Catherine L. *A Republic of Mind & Spirit: A Cultural History of American Metaphysical Religion.* New Haven: Yale University Press, 2007.

Allsopp, Michael E. *Reviewing Christian Ethics: The Catholic Tradition.* Chicago, IL: University of Scranton Press, 2005.

Appolloni, Simon. "The Roman Catholic Tradition in Conversation with Thomas Berry's Fourfold Wisdom." *Religions* 6, no. 3 (2015): 794–818, doi.10.3390/rel6030794.

Bakken, Peter W., Joan Gibb Engel, and J. Ronald Engel. *Ecology, Justice, and Christian Faith: A Critical Guide to the Literature.* Westport, CT: Greenwood Press, 1995.

Barber, Michael. *Ethical Hermeneutics: Rationality in Enrique Dussel's Philosophy of Liberation.* New York: Fordham University Press, 1998.

Barbour, Ian. *Religion in an Age of Science.* San Francisco: HarperSanFrancisco, 1990.

– *When Science Meets Religion: Enemies, Strangers or Partners?* New York: Harper Collins, 2000.

Batstone, David, Eduardo Mendieta, Lois Ann Lorentzen, and Dwight N. Hopkins, eds. *Liberation Theologies, Postmodernity, and the Americas.* New York: Routledge, 1997.

Baum, Gregory. *Essays in Critical Theology.* Kansas City, MO: Sheed & Ward, 1994.

– "Personal Experience and Styles of Thought." In *Journeys: The Impact of Personal Experience on Religious Thought*, edited by Gregory Baum, 5–33. New York: Paulist Press, 1975.

Bauman, Whitney. "Religion, Science, and Nature: Shifts in Meaning on a Changing Planet." *Zygon* 46, no. 4 (December 2011): 777–92. ATLA *Religion Database with* ATLA*serials,* EBSCO*host* (accessed 3 February 2014).

Bekoff, Mark. "Animal Emotions: Exploring Passionate Natures." *Bioscience* 50, no. 10 (October 2000): 861–70. doi:10.1641/0006-3568(2000)050 [0861:AEEPN]2.0.CO;2.

– *Minding Animals: Awareness, Emotions and Heart.* New York: Oxford University Press, 2002.

Bekoff, Marc, and Jessica Pierce. *Wild Justice: The Moral Lives of Animals.* Chicago: University of Chicago Press, 2009.

Beller, Mara. "The Sokal Hoax: At Whom Are We Laughing?" *Physics Today* 51, no. 9 (September 1998): 29–34.

Berry, Thomas. *Befriending the Earth: A Theology of Reconciliation between Humans and the Earth.* Edited by Stephen Dunn, C.P., and Anne Lonergan. Mystic, CT: Twenty-Third Publications, 1995.

– *The Christian Future and the Fate of Earth.* Edited by Mary Evelyn Tucker and John Grim. Maryknoll, NY: Orbis Books, 2009.

– *The Dream of the Earth.* San Francisco: Sierra Club Books, 1988.

– "Ethics and Ecology." Paper delivered to the Harvard Seminar on Environmental Values, Harvard University, 9 April 1996. Accessed June 2013. https://intuerifarm.wordpress.com/philosophy/ethics-and-ecology-by-thomas-berry/.

– *The Great Work: Our Way into the Future.* New York: Bell Tower Publishing Group, 1999.

– "Response to the Essays." *Worldviews: Environment Culture, Religion* 5, no. 2 (2001): 198–222.

– *The Sacred Universe: Earth Spirituality, and Religion in the Twenty-First Century.* Edited by Mary Evelyn Tucker. New York: Columbia University Press, 2009.

– "The Universe Story: Its Religious Significance." In *The Greening of Faith: God, the Environment, and the Good Life,* edited by John Carroll, Paul Brockelman, and Mary Westfall, 208–18. Hanover, NH: University of New Hampshire Press, 1997.

Boff, Leonardo. "Calling in Multiple Ecological Debts." In *Sacred Earth, Sacred Community: Jubilee, Ecology and Aboriginal Peoples,* edited by John Mihevc, 135–41. Toronto: Canadian Ecumenical Jubilee Initiative, 2000.

– *Church, Charism and Power: Liberation Theology and the Institutional Church.* Translated by John W. Dierchsmeier. London: SCM Press, 1985.

– *Cry of the Earth, Cry of the Poor*. Translated by Phillip Berryman. Maryknoll, NY: Orbis Books, 1997.

– "Earth as Gaia: An Ethical and Spiritual Challenge." In *Eco-Theology*, edited by Elaine Wainwright, Luiz-Carlos Susin, and Felix Wilfred, 24–32. London: SCM Press, 2009.

– *Ecclesiogenesis: The Base Communities Reinvent the Church*. Maryknoll, NY: Orbis Books, 1986.

– *Ecology and Liberation: A New Paradigm*. Translated by John Cumming (from the Italian). Maryknoll, NY: Orbis Books, 1995.

– "Ecology and Poverty: Cry of the Earth, Cry of the Poor" (editorial). In *Ecology and Poverty: Cry of the Earth, Cry of the Poor*, edited by Leonardo Boff and Virgil Elizondo, ix–xii. Maryknoll, NY: Orbis Books, 1995.

– *Essential Care: An Ethics of Human Nature*. Translated by Alexandre Guilherme. Waco, TX: Baylor University Press, 2008.

– "The Ethic of Care." In *A Voice for Earth: American Writers Respond to Earth Charter*, translated by Philip Berryman, edited by Peter Blaze Corcoran and A. James Wohlpar, 129–45. Athens: University of Georgia Press, 2008.

– *Global Civilization: Challenges to Society and Christianity*. Translated by Alexandre Guilherme. London: Equinox, 2005.

– "La Originalidad de la Teología de la Liberación." In *Teología y Liberacíon: Ensayos en Torno a la Obra de Gustavo Gutiérrez*, 127–44. Lima, Peru: Instituto Bartolomé de Las Casas, 1989.

– "Liberation Theology: Option for the Poor and Socialism Today." A reproduction of an interview by Jose Maria Vigil. *Liberation Theology*, August 1994, 11.

– "Liberation Theology and Ecology: Alternative, Confrontation or Complementarity?" In *Ecology and Poverty: Cry of the Earth, Cry of the Poor*, edited by Leonardo Boff and Virgil Elizondo, 67–77. Maryknoll, NY: Orbis Books, 1995.

– "Social Ecology: Poverty and Misery." In *Ecotheology: Voices from the South and North*, edited by David G. Hallman, 235–47. Maryknoll, NY: Orbis Books, 1994.

Boff, Leonardo, and Clodovis Boff. *Introducing Liberation Theology* (excerpt reprinted online by permission, Orbis Books). Accessed August 2012. http://www.landreform.org/boff2.htm.

Bohm, David, and F. David Peat. *Science, Order, and Creativity*. New York: Routledge, 1987.

Bortoft, Henri. "Counterfeit and Authentic Wholes: Finding a Means for Dwelling in Nature." In *Goethe's Way of Science: A Phenomenology of Nature,* edited by David Seamon and Arthur Zajonc, 277–98. Albany, NY: State University of New York Press, 1998.

– *Taking Appearance Seriously: The Dynamic Way of Seeing in Goethe and European Thought.* Edinburgh: Floris Books, 2012.

Bouma-Prediger, Steven. *The Greening of Theology: The Ecological Models of Rosemary Radford Ruether, Joseph Sittler and Jürgen Moltmann.* Atlanta, GA: Scholars Press, 1995.

Bronowski, Jacob. *The Ascent of Man.* Executive producer Adrian Malone; directors Dick Gilling, Mick Jackson, David Kennard, and David Paterson, 1969. Accessed August 2012. http://www.youtube.com/watch?feature=endscreen&v=j7br6ibK8ic&NR=1.

– *Science and Human Values.* New York: Harper and Row, 1965.

Brown, Robert McAfee. "Leonardo Boff: Theologian for All Christians." *The Christian Century* 103, no. 21 (2–9 July 1986): 615–17.

Bruening, William H. "Moore and 'Is-Ought.'" *Ethics* 81, no. 2 (January 1971): 143–9.

Brussat, Frederic, and Mary Ann Brussat. "Living Spiritual Teachers Project: Leonardo Boff." Accessed July 2011. http://www.spiritualityandpractice.com/teachers/teachers.php?id=270.

Butkus, Russell A., and Steven A. Kolmes. *Environmental Science and Theology in Dialogue.* Maryknoll, NY: Orbis Books, 2011.

Capra, Fritjof. *The Tao of Physics: An Exploration of the Parallels between Modern Physics and Eastern Mysticism.* 4th updated ed. Boston: Shambala Press, 2000.

– *The Turning Point: Science, Society, and the Rising Culture.* New York: Bantam Books, 1982.

Cheney, Jim, and Anthony Weston. "Environmental Ethics as Environmental Etiquette: Toward an Ethics-Based Epistemology." *Environmental Ethics* 21 (Summer 1999):115–34.

Chociolko, Christina. "The Experts Disagree: A Simple Matter of Facts Versus Values?" *Alternatives* 20, no. 3 (1995): 19–25.

Chopp, Rebecca S. "Seeing and Naming the World Anew: The Works of Rosemary Radford Ruether." *Religious Studies Review* 15, no. 1 [January 1989]: 8–11. doi:10.1111/j.1748-0922.

Chopp, Rebecca S., and Ethna Regan. "Latin American Liberation Theology." In *The Modern Theologians: An Introduction to Christian Theology since 1918*, 3rd ed., edited by David F. Ford with Rachel Muers, 469–84. Malden, MA; Oxford: Blackwell Publishing Ltd., 2005.

Clayton, Philip. Introduction. In *The Oxford Handbook of Religion and Science*, edited by Philip Clayton and Zachary Simpson, 1–4. Oxford: Oxford University Press, 2006.

Clifford, Catherine E., and Richard R. Gaillardetz. "Beyond Presumption: Reimagining the Ecclesial-Prophetic Vocation of the Theologian." Paper at the Catholic Theological Society of America's Annual Gathering in 2010. CTSA *Proceedings* 65 (2010): 43–62.

Conn, Marie A. "Plurality in Unity: The Ecclesiology of Leonardo Boff in Honor of His 70th Birthday (December 14, 2008)." *Theology Today* 66 (2009): 7–8.

Cooper, David E. "The Idea of Environment." In *The Environment in Question: Ethics and Global Issues*, edited by David E. Cooper and Joy A. Palmer, 165–79. London; New York: Routledge, 1992.

Corbett, Jim. *Goatwalking*. New York: Viking, 1991.

Cuomo, Chris J. "Getting Closer: Thoughts on the Ethics of Knowledge Production." Accessed August 2013. http://fore.research.yale.edu/disciplines/ethics/essays/.

Curry, Oliver. "Who's Afraid of the Naturalistic Fallacy." *Evolutionary Psychology* 4 (2006): 234–47. http://www.epjournal.net/archive/2006/.

Dallmayr, Fred. "The Underside of Modernity: Adorno, Heidegger, and Dussel." *Constellations* 11, no. 1 (March 2004): 102–20.

Dalton, Anne Marie. *A Theology for the Earth: The Contributions of Thomas Berry and Bernard Lonergan*. Ottawa: University of Ottawa Press, 1999.

Dalton, Anne Marie, and Henry C. Simmons. *Ecotheology and the Practice of Hope*. Albany, NY: SUNY Press, 2010.

Dawson, Andrew. "Mystical Experience as Universal Connectedness: Leonardo Boff's 'Trans-cultural Phenomenology.'" *Journal of Contemporary Religion* 19 no. 2 (2004): 155–69. doi:10.1080/1353790042000207683.

De Waal, Frans. *The Age of Empathy: Nature's Lessons for a Kinder Society*. Toronto: McClelland and Stewart Ltd. 2009.

De Waal, Frans, and Peter L. Tyack, eds., *Animal Social Complexity: Intelligence, Culture, and Individualized Societies*. Cambridge, MA: Harvard University Press, 2003.

Deane-Drummond, Celia. "Theology and the Biological Sciences." In *The Modern Theologians: An Introduction to Christian Theology in the Twentieth Century*, 2nd ed., edited by David F. Ford, 357–69. Oxford; Cambridge, MA: Blackwell Publishers, 1997.

Deane-Drummond, Celia, and David Clough, eds., *Creaturely Theology: On God, Humans and Other Animals*. London: SCM Press, 2009.

Dewey, John. "The Problem of Truth." In *John Dewey: The Collected Works, 1882–1953*, edited by Anne S. Sharpe, Harriet Furst Simon, and Barbara Levine. Carbondale: Southern Illinois University Press, 1991.

DiCarlo, Christopher, and John Teehan. "On the Naturalistic Fallacy: A Conceptual Basis for Evolutionary Ethics." In *Science and Ethics: Can Science Help Us Make Wise Moral Judgments?* edited by Paul Kurtz with the assistance of David Koepsell, 306–22. Amherst, NY: Prometheus Books, 2007.

Dooley, J.E., and P. Byer. "Decision-Making for Risk Management." In *Living with Risk: Environmental Risk Management in Canada*, edited by I. Burton, C.D. Fowle, and R.S. McCullough, 71–84. Toronto: IES Monograph, no. 3, University of Toronto, 1982.

Dorrien, Gary. *The Making of American Liberal Theology: Crisis, Irony, and Postmodernity, 1950–2005*. Louisville: Westminster John Knox Press, 2006.

Dowd, Michael. Interview with Diarmuid O'Murchu. "Meeting God in Our Evolutionary Story." Accessed 29 December 2010. http://evolutionary christianity.com.

– *Thank God for Evolution: How the Marriage of Science and Religion Will Transform Your Life and Our World*. New York: Penguin Books Ltd., 2007.

Drees, William B. *Science, Religion and Naturalism*. Cambridge: Cambridge University Press, 1996.

Dussel, Enrique "The Architectonics of the Ethics of Liberation." In *Liberation Theologies, Postmodernity, and the Americas*, edited by David Batstone, Eduardo Mendieta, Lois Ann Lorentzen and Dwight N. Hopkins, 273–304. New York; London: Routledge, 1997.

– "Ethics of Culture and Ecology." In *Ethics and Community*. Translated by Robert R. Barr. Maryknoll, NY: Orbis Books, 1988.

– *Ethics of Liberation: In an Age of Globalization and Exclusion*. Translated by Eduardo Mendieta, Camilo Pérez Bustillo, Yolanda Angulo and Nelson Madonado-Torres. Durham and London: Duke University Press, 2013.

– *The Invention of the Americas: Eclipse of "the Other" and the Myth of Modernity*. Translated by Michael D. Barber. New York: Continuum, 1995.
– *The Underside of Modernity: Apel, Ricoeur, Rorty, Taylor, and the Philosophy of Liberation*. Translated and edited by Eduardo Mendieta. New Jersey: Humanities Press, 1996.
Dussel, Enrique, in collaboration with Eduardo Ibarra-Colado. "Globalization, Organization and the Ethics of Liberation." In *Organization* 13, no. 4 (2006): 489–508. doi: 10.1177/1350508406065852.
Eaton, Heather. "Cosmological Ethics? *The Great Work*." *Worldviews: Environment, Culture, Religion* 5, no. 2/3 (2001): 157 –69. doi.org/10.1163/15685350152908228.
– "An Ecological Imaginary: Evolution and Religion in an Ecological Era." In *Ecological Awareness: Exploring Religion, Ethics and Aesthetics*, edited by Sigurd Bergmann and Heather Eaton, Studies in Religion and the Environment, 7–23. Berlin: LIT Press, 2011.
– "Forces of Nature: Aesthetics and Nature." In *Aesth/Ethics in Environmental Change: Hiking through the Arts, Ecology, Religion and Ethics of the Environment*, edited by Sigurd Bergmann, Irmgard Blindow, and Konrad Ott, 109–26. Berlin: Lit Verlag, 2013.
– "Reflections on the Contribution of Rosemary Radford Ruether." *Feminist Theology* 17, no. 2 (2009): 152–7.
Editors of *Lingua Franca*. *The Sokal Hoax: The Sham That Shook the Academy*. Lincoln, Nebr.: University of Nebraska Press, 2000.
Ehrlich, Anne, and Paul Ehrlich. *Earth*. New York: Franklin Watts, 1987.
– *Extinction: The Causes and Consequences of the Disappearance of Species*. New York: Random House, 1981.
Einstein, A., B. Podolsky, and N. Rosen, "Can Quantum-Mechanical Description of Physical Reality Be Considered Complete?" *Physical Review* 47, no. 10 (1935): 777–80. doi:10.1103/PhysRev.47.777.
Eisenberg, Even. *The Ecology of Eden*. New York: Alfred A. Knopf, 1998.
Flanagan, Owen. "Varieties of Naturalism." In *The Oxford Handbook of Religion and Science*, edited by Philip Clayton and Zachary Simpson, 430–52. Oxford: Oxford University Press, 2006.
Fleischer, Barbara J. "A Theological Method for Adult Education Rooted in the Works of Tracy and Lonergan." *Religious Education* 95, no. 1 (January 2000): 23–37. doi:10.1080/0034408000950104.

Ford, David F. "Introduction to Modern Christian Theology." In *The Modern Theologians: An Introduction to Christian Theology since 1918*. 3rd ed., edited by David F. Ford with Rachel Muers, 1–15. Malden, MA; Oxford: Blackwell Publishing Ltd., 2005.

Frodeman, Robert. *Geo-Logic: Breaking Ground between Philosophy and the Earth Sciences*. New York: State University of New York Press, 2003.

Funtowicz, S.O., and J.R. Ravetz. "Science for the Post-Normal Age." *Futures* 25, no. 7 (1993):739–55. doi: 10.1016/0016-3287(93)90022-L.

Gaillardetz, Richard R. *Teaching with Authority: A Theology of the Magisterium in the Church*. Collegeville, MN: Liturgical Press, 1997.

Garvey, James. "Climate Change and Causal Inefficacy: Why Go Green When It Makes No Difference?" *Royal Institute of Philosophy Supplement* 69 (September 2011): 163. doi:10.1017/S1358246111000269.

Gerhart, Mary, and Allan Russell. *Metaphoric Process: The Creation of Scientific and Religious Understanding*. Fort Worth, TX: Texas Christian University Press, 1984.

Gomez, Fernando. "Ethics Is the Original Philosophy; or, The Barbarian Words Coming from the Third World: An Interview with Enrique Dussel." *Boundary2* 28, no. 1 (Spring 2001): 21. Accessed June 2012. http://bibliotecavirtual.clacso.org.ar/ar/libros/dussel/artics/gomez.pdf.

Goodall, Jane. Foreword to *Minding Animals: Awareness, Emotions, and Heart* by Marc Bekoff, ix–xiv. Oxford: Oxford University Press, 2002.

Goodenough, Ursula. *The Sacred Depths of Nature*. New York: Oxford University Press, 1998.

Goodwin, Brian. *How the Leopard Changed Its Spots*. New York: Simon and Shuster, 1996.

Gould, Rebecca Kneale. "Christianity – Natural Theology." In *Encyclopedia of Religion and Nature*, edited by Bron Taylor, 368–9. London and New York: Continuum, 2005.

Greeley, Andrew. *The Catholic Imagination*. Berkeley, CA: University of California Press, 2000.

Greene, Brian. *The Elegant Universe: Superstrings, Hidden Dimensions, and the Quest for the Ultimate Theory*. New York: Vintage Books, 1999.

Gregersen, Niels Henrik, and J. Wentzel van Huyssteen, eds., *Rethinking Theology and Science: Six Models for the Current Dialogue*. Grand Rapids, MI: William B. Erdmans Publishing Company, 1998.

Grey, Mary. Foreword. *Introducing Redemption in Christian Feminism*. Sheffield, England: Sheffield Academic Press, 1998.

– "'My Yearning for Justice': Moving beyond Praxis in Feminist Theology." In *Interpreting the Postmodern: Responses to "Radical Orthodoxy,"* edited by Rosemary Radford Ruether and Marion Grau, 175–94. New York: T and T Clark, 2006.

Grim, John. "Time History, Historians in Thomas Berry's Vision." Accessed 12 December 2011. http://www.thomasberry.org/Biography/grim-bio.html.

Grim, John A., and Mary Evelyn Tucker. "An Overview of Teilhard's Commitment to 'Seeing' as Expressed in his Phenomenology, Metaphysics, and Mysticism." *Ecotheology* 10, no. 2 (2005): 147–64. ATLA *Religion Database with* ATLASerials, EBSCOhost (accessed 3 February 2014).

Gross, Rita M., and Rosemary Radford Ruether. "Christian Resources for Ecological Sustainability." In *Religious Feminism and the Future of the Planet: A Christian-Buddhist Conversation*. London: Continuum, 2001.

Guha, Ramachandra. "The Environmentalism of the Poor." In *Varieties of Environmentalism: Essays North and South*, edited by Ramachandra Guha and J. Martinez-Alier, 3–21. London: Earthscan Publications, 1997.

Gustavo Gutiérrez. "Pobres y Opción Fundamental." In *Mysterium Liberationis: Conceptos Fundamentals de la Teología de la Liberación*. Tomo 1, edited by Jon Sobrino y Ignacio Ellacuría, 303–22. Madrid: UCA Editores, 1990.

– *A Theology of Liberation: History, Politics and Salvation*. Rev. ed. Translated and edited by Sister Caridad Inda and John Eagleson. Maryknoll, NY: Orbis Books, 1988.

Harvey, Van A. "The Pathos of Liberal Theology: *Blessed Rage for Order: The New Pluralism in Theology* by David Tracy." *The Journal of Religion* 56, no. 4 (October 1976): 382–91. http://www.jstor.org.myaccess.library.utoronto.ca/stable/1201996.

Hathaway, Mark, and Leonardo Boff. *The Tao of Liberation: Exploring the Ecology of Transformation*. Maryknoll, NY: Orbis Books, 2009.

Haught, John F. *Christianity and Science: Toward and Theology of Nature*. Maryknoll, NY: Orbis Books, 2007.

– *God after Darwin: A Theology of Evolution*. Philadelphia: Westview Press, 2008.

Hawken, Paul. *Blessed Unrest: How the Largest Movement in the World Came into Being, and Why No One Saw It Coming*. New York: Viking, 2007.

Hawking, Stephen. *A Brief History of Time: From the Big Bang to Black Holes.* New York: Bantam Books, 1998.

Hefner, Philip. "Religion and Science – Two-way Traffic?" (editorial). *Zygon* 4, no. 1 (March 2006): 3–5.

– "Science-and-Religion and the Search for Meaning." *Zygon* 31, no. 2 (June 1996): 307–21; doi:10.1111/j.1467-9744.1996.tb00026.x.

Hessel, Dieter T., and Rosemary Radford Ruether, eds. *Christianity and Ecology, Seeking the Well-Being of Earth and Humans.* Cambridge, MA: Harvard University Press for the Harvard University Center for the Study of World Religions, 2000.

Hinton, Rosalind. "Contextualizing Rosemary." *Cross Currents* 53, no. 1 (Spring 2003). Accessed July 2011. http://www.crosscurrents.org/Hinton spring2003.htm.

– "A Legacy of Inclusion: An Interview with Rosemary Radford Ruether." *Cross Currents* 52, no. 1 (Spring 2002). Accessed July 2011. http://www. crosscurrents.org/Ruetherspring2002.htm.

Hodgson, Peter C. *Liberal Theology: A Radical Vision.* Minneapolis: Fortress Press, 2007.

Hope, Marjorie, and James Young. "A Prophetic Voice: Thomas Berry." *Trumpeter* 11, no. 1 (1994): 1–19. Accessed June 2012. http://trumpeter. athabascau.ca/index.php/trumpet/article/view/349/545.

Hoyningen-Huene, Paul. "On Thomas Kuhn's Philosophical Significance." *Configurations* 6, no. 1 (November, 1998): 1–14. http://muse.jhu.edu. myaccess.library.utoronto.ca/journals/configurations/v006/6.1hoynin gen-huene.html.

Hrynkow, Christopher, and Dennis Patrick O'Hara. "The Vatican and Ecospirituality: Tensions, Promises and Possibilities for Fostering an Emerging Green Catholic Spirituality." *Ecozon@: European Journal of Literature, Culture and Environment* 2, no. 2 (2011): 177–97. http://ecozona. eu/article/view/425/439.

IPCC Fourth Assessment Report. "Climate Change 2007: Synthesis Report." Accessed July 2012. http://www.ipcc.ch/publications_and_data/ publications_ipcc_fourth_assessment_report_synthesis_report.htm.

Jaki, Stanley L. "The Role of Faith in Physics." *Zygon* 2, no. 2 (May, 1967): 187–202. ATLA *Religion Database with* ATLAserials, EBSCO*host* (accessed 2 February 2014).

Jantch, Erich. *The Self Organizing Universe: Scientific and Human Implications of the Emerging Paradigm of Evolution.* Toronto: Pergamon Press, 1980.

Jenkins, Willis. *The Future of Ethics: Sustainability, Social Justice, and Religious Creativity.* Washington, DC: Georgetown University Press, 2013.

Kellert, Stephen, and E.O. Wilson, eds. "God, Gaia and Biophilia." In *The Biophilia Hypothesis,* 345–64. Washington, DC: Island Press, 1993.

Kenney, Jim. "On Convergence." In *When Worlds Converge: What Science and Religion Tell Us about the Story of the Universe and Our Place in It,* edited by Clifford N. Matthews, Mary Evelyn Tucker and Philip Hefner, 367–73. Peru, IL: Open Court Publishing Company, 2002.

Klein, Julie Thompson, Walter Grossenbacher-Mansuy, Rudolf Häberli, Alain Bill, Roland W. Scholz, and Myrtha, eds. *Transdisciplinarity: Joint Problem Solving among Science, Technology, and Society: An Effective Way for Managing Complexity.* Basel; Boston; Berlin: Birkhäuser Verlag, 2000.

Kuhn, Thomas S. *The Essential Tension: Selected Studies in Scientific Tradition and Change.* Chicago: University of Chicago Press, 1977.

– *The Structure of Scientific Revolutions.* Chicago, IL: University of Chicago Press, 1996.

Kumar, Manjit. *Quantum: Einstein, Bohr, and the Great Debate about the Nature of Reality.* New York: W.W. Norton, 2009.

Küng, Hans, and David Tracy, eds. *Paradigm Change in Theology: A Symposium for the Future.* Translated by Margaret Köhl. New York: Crossroads Publishing, 1989.

Lamb, Kara L. "The Problem of Defining Nature First: A Philosophical Critique of Environmental Ethics." *The Social Science Journal* 33, no. 4 (1996): 475–86.

Larson, Brendon. *Metaphors for Environmental Sustainability: Redefining Our Relationship with Nature.* New Haven, CT: Yale University Press, 2011.

Leddy, Mary Jo, Bishop Remi De Roo, and Douglas Roche, eds. *In the Eye of the Catholic Storm: The Church since Vatican II.* Toronto: HarperCollins, 1982.

Leopold, Aldo. *A Sand County Almanac: With Essays on Conservation from Round River.* New York: Ballantine Books, 1966.

Loften, Adam, and Patsy Northcutt, eds. *Journey of the Universe: An Epic Story of Cosmic, Earth, and Human Transformation: Educational Series.* DVD. Northcutt Productions, 2011.

Lovelock, James. *Gaia: A New Look at Life on Earth*. New York: Oxford University Press, 1982.

– *The Revenge of Gaia: Why the Earth Is Fighting Back and How We Can Still Save Humanity*. London: Allen Lane, 2006.

Lumen Gentium. Accessed 8 July 2013. http://www.vatican.va/archive/hist_councils/ii_vatican_council/documents/vat-ii_const_19641121_lumen-gentium_en.html.

Maclean, Iain S., and Lois Ann Lorentzen. "Boff, Leonardo (1938–)." In *The Encyclopedia of Religion and Nature*, edited by Bron Taylor et al., 207–8. London: Thoemmes Continuum, 2005.

Margulis, Lynn, and Dorion Sagan. "The Microbes Contribution to Evolution." *BioSystems* 7, no. 2 (October 1975):266–92.

– *Microcosmos: Four Billion Years of Evolution from Our Microbial Ancestors*. New York: Summit Books, 1986.

– "Origins of Species: Acquired Genomes and Individuality." *BioSystems* 31 (January 1993): 121–5. doi: 10.1016/0303-2647(93)90039-F.

– *Symbiotic Planet: A New Look at Evolution*. Amherst, MA: Basic Books, 1998.

Martín Alcoff, Linda, and Eduardo Mendieta. Introduction to *Thinking from the Underside of History: Enrique Dussel's Philosophy of Liberation*, edited by Linda Martín Alcoff and Eduardo Mendieta, 1–26. Lanham, MD: Rowman & Littlefield Publishers, 2000.

McDaniel, Jay B. "Four Questions in Response to Rosemary Radford Ruether." In *An Ecology of the Spirit: Religious Reflection and Environmental Consciousness*, edited by Michael Barnes, 59–60. Lanham, NY: University Press of America; College Theology Society, 1994.

McErlean, Jennifer. *Philosophies of Science: From Foundations to Contemporary Issues*. Belmont, CA: Wadsworth Publishing Company, 2000.

McFague, Sallie. *The Body of God: An Ecological Theology*. Minneapolis: Fortress Press, 1993.

Mellor, Mary. "New Woman, New Earth – Setting the Agenda." *Organization & Environment* 10, no. 3 (September 1997): 296–7. doi:10.1177/0921810697103004.

Menchú, Rogoberta. *I, Rigoberta Menchú: An Indian Woman in Guatemala*. Edited and introduced by Elisabeth Burgos-Debray. Translated by Anne Wright. New York: Verso 1984.

Merchant, Carolyn. *The Death of Nature: Women, Ecology and the Scientific Revolution*. New York: HarperCollins, 1976.

Meyer, Marvin. "Affirming Reverence for Life." In *Reverence for Life: The Ethics of Albert Schweitzer for the Twenty-First Century,* edited by Marvin Meyer and Kurt Bergel, 22–36. Syracuse, NY: Syracuse University Press, 2002.

Midgley, Mary. *Animals and Why They Matter.* Athens: University of Georgia Press, 1998.

– "Concluding Reflections: Dover Beach Revisited." In *The Oxford Handbook to Religion and Science,* edited by Philip Clayton and Zachary Simpson, 962–77. New York: Oxford University Press, 2006.

– ed. *Earthy Realism: The Meaning of Gaia.* Charlottesville, VA: Imprint Academic, 2007.

– *Evolution as Religion: Strange Hopes and Stranger Fears.* New York: Routledge, 2002.

– *Gaia: The Next Big Idea.* London: Demos, 2001.

– *The Myths We Live By.* London: Routledge, 2003.

– *The Solitary Self: Darwin and the Selfish Gene.* Durhman, England: Acumen, 2010.

Midgley, Mary, and Stephen R.L. Clark. "The Absence of a Gap between Facts and Values." *Proceedings of the Aristotelian Society, Supplementary Volumes* 54 (1980): 208–40.

Miller, Patti. "Rosemary Radford Ruether: Fearless Leader and Change-maker for a Progressive Catholic Feminism." *Conscience Magazine* 31, no. 3 (2010): 38–40. Accessed July 2011. http://digital.graphcompubs.com/publication/?i=54869&p=40.

Miller-Francisco, Grant D. "Rosemary Radford Ruether (1936–)." *Boston Collaborative Encyclopedia of Western Theology.* Accessed July 2011. http://people.bu.edu/wwildman/bce/mwt_themes_908_ruether.htm.

Mitchell, Alanna. *Sea Sick: The Global Ocean in Crisis.* Toronto: McClelland and Stewart, 2009.

Moe-Lobeda, Cynthia. *Resisting Structural Evil: Love as Ecological-Economic Vocation.* Minneapolis: Fortress Press, 2013.

Murray, Paul D. "Catholic Theology after Vatican II." In *The Modern Theologians: An Introduction to Christian Theology since 1918,* 3rd ed., edited by David F. Ford with Rachel Muers, 265–86. Malden, MA; Oxford: Blackwell Publishing Ltd., 2005.

Nash, James A. "Seeking Moral Norms in Nature: Natural Law and Ecological Responsibility." In *Christianity and Ecology: Ecology: Seeking the Well-Being of Earth and Humans,* edited by Dieter T. Hessel and Rosemary

Radford Ruether, 227–50. Cambridge, MA: Harvard University Press for the Harvard University Center for the Study of World Religions, 2000.

Nickles, Thomas, ed. *Thomas Kuhn* (Online). Reno: Cambridge University Press, 2002. doi: http://dx.doi.org.myaccess.library.utoronto.ca/10.1017/CBO9780511613975.

Northcott, Michael S. "Ecology and Christian Ethics." In *Cambridge Companion to Christian Ethics,* edited by Robin Gill, 209–27. Cambridge: Cambridge University Press, 2000.

– *The Environment and Christian Ethics*. Cambridge: Cambridge University Press, 1996.

Numbers, Ronald L. "Simplifying Complexity: Patterns in the History of Science and Religion." In *Science and Religion: New Historical Perspectives,* edited by Thomas Dixon, Geoffrey Cantor, and Stephen Pumfrey, 263–82. New York: Cambridge University Press, 2010.

O'Hara, Dennis Patrick. "The Implications of Thomas Berry's Cosmology for an Understanding of the Spiritual Dimension of Human Health." PhD diss., University of St Michael's College, 1998. https://tspace.library.utoronto.ca/bitstream/1807/10506/1/NQ36598.pdf.

O'Hara, Dennis Patrick, and Alan Abelsohn. "Ethical Response to Climate Change." *Ethics & the Environment* 16, no. 1 (2011): 25–50. Accessed 11 November 2013. http://muse.jhu.edu/.

O'Murchu, Diarmuid. *Adult Faith: Growing in Wisdom and Understanding*. Maryknoll, NY: Orbis Books, 2010.

– *Ancestral Grace: Meeting God in Our Human Story*. Maryknoll, NY: Orbis Books, 2008.

– *Catching up with Jesus: Reflections of a Social Scientist*. New York: Crossroad, 2005.

– "Discerning the Meaning of Earthquakes." Accessed 12 December 2011. http://www.diarmuid13.com/cosmology.

– *Evolutionary Faith: Rediscovering God in Our Great Story*. Maryknoll, NY: Orbis Books, 2002.

– *The God Who Becomes Redundant*. Cork: Mercier, 1986.

– *Jesus in the Power of Poetry: A New Voice for Gospel Truth*. New York: Crossroad Publishing Company: 2009.

– *Our World in Transition: Making Sense of a Changing World*. New York: The Book Guild Ltd, 1992.

– *Quantum Theology: Spiritual Implications of the New Physics*. New York: Crossroad Publishing Company, 2004.

– *Religion in Exile: A Spiritual Vision for the Homeward Bound*. Dublin: Gateway, 2000.

– *The Transformation of Desire: How Desire Became Corrupted and How We Can Reclaim It*. London: Darton, Longman and Todd, 2007.

– "A Tribute to Thomas Berry (1914–2009)." Accessed November 2011. http://thomasberry.org/life-and-thought/berry-award-and-memorial-service/tributes-photos-and-obituaries-1/a-tribute-to-thomas-berry-1914-2009.

Orr, David W. *Earth in Mind: On Education, Environment, and the Human Prospect*. Washington, DC: Island Press, 2004.

Peters, Ted. "Theology and Natural Science." In *The Modern Theologians: An Introduction to Christian Theology in the Twentieth Century*, 2nd ed., edited by David F. Ford, 649–68. Cambridge, MA: Blackwell Publishers, 1997.

Pierce, Jessica, and Marc Bekoff. "Wild Justice Redux: What We Know about Social Justice in Animals and Why It Matters." *Social Justice Research* 25, no. 2 (June 2012): 122–39. doi:10.1007/s11211-012-0154-y.

Polkinghorne, John. "Christianity and Science." In *The Oxford Handbook of Religion and Science*, edited by Philip Clayton, ass. ed. by Zachary Simpson, 57–70. Oxford: Oxford University Press, 2006.

– *Quantum Physics and Theology: An Unexpected Kinship*. New Haven: Yale University Press, 2007.

Prigogine, Ilya, and Isabelle Stengers. *Order Out of Chaos: Man's New Dialogue with Nature*. New York: Bantam Books, 1984.

Primavesi, Anne. *Sacred Gaia: Holistic Theology and Earth System Science*. London: New York: Routledge, 2000.

Proctor, James D. "Introduction: Rethinking Science and Religion." In *Science, Religion, and the Human Experience*, edited by James D. Proctor, 3–23. Oxford: Oxford University Press, 2005.

Putnam, Hilary. *The Collapse of the Fact/Value Dichotomy and Other Essays*. Cambridge, MA: Harvard University Press, 2002.

Rafferty, Agnes. "Sophia and the Cosmic Dance." *Feminist Theology* 9, no. 27 (May 2001): 102–15, doi:10.1177/096673500100002709.

Rediger, Lloyd. "Can Jubilee Lead to Quantum Thinking?" *The Clergy Journal* 76, no. 10 (September 2000): 10–15.

Rockström, Johan, Will Steffen, Kevin Noone, Åsa Persson, F. Stuart Chapin III, Eric Lambin, Timothy M. Lenton, Marten Scheffer, Carl Folke, Hans Joachim Schellnhuber, Björn Nykvist, Cynthia A. de Wit, Terry Hughes, Sander van der Leeuw, Henning Rodhe, Sverker Sörlin, Peter K. Snyder, Robert Costanza, Uno Svedin, Malin Falkenmark, Louise Karlberg, Robert W. Corell, Victoria J. Fabry, James Hansen, Brian Walker, Diana Liverman, Katherine Richardson, Paul Crutzen, and Jonathan Foley. "Planetary Boundaries: Exploring the Safe Operating Space for Humanity." *Ecology and Society* 14, no. 2 (2009): 1–32. Accessed 1 September 2012. http://www.ecologyandsociety.org/vol14/iss2/art32/.

Rodrigues, Luís F. *Open Questions: Diverse Thinkers Discuss God, Religion, and Faith*. Santa Barbara, CA: Praeger, 2010.

Rolston, Holmes, III. "Environmental Ethics and Religion/Science." In *The Oxford Handbook of Religion and Science*, edited by Philip Clayton and Zachary Simpson as assistant editor, 908–27. New York: Oxford University Press, 2006.

– "Is There an Ecological Ethic?" *Ethics: An International Journal of Social, Political, and Legal Philosophy* 18, no. 2 (1975): 93–109. http://www.jstor.org.myaccess.library.utoronto.ca/stable/2379925.

– "Science and Religion in the Face of the Environmental Crisis." In *The Oxford Handbook of Religion and Ecology* (Online), edited by Roger S. Gottlieb. New York: Oxford University Press, 2006. doi:10.1093/oxfordhb/9780195178722.003.0018.

Ruether, Rosemary Radford. "Beginnings: An Intellectual Autobiography." In *Journeys: The Impact of Personal Experience on Religious Thought*, edited by Gregory Baum, 34–56. New York: Paulist Press, 1975.

– *Christianity and Social Systems: Historical Constructions and Ethical Challenges*. Landham, MD: Rowman & Littlefield Publisher, 2009.

– *The Church against Itself: An Inquiry into the Conditions of Historical Existence for the Eschatological Community*. New York: Herder and Herder, 1967.

– "Deep Ecology, Ecofeminism, and the Bible." In *Deep Ecology and World Religions: New Essays on Sacred Ground*, edited by David Landis Barnhill and Roger S. Gottlieb, 229–41. Albany, NY: State University of New York Press, 2001.

– "Ecofeminism: The Challenge to Theology." In *Christianity and Ecology: Seeking the Well-Being of Earth and Humans*, edited by Dieter T. Hessel and Rosemary Radford Ruether, 97–112. Cambridge, MA: Harvard

University Press for the Harvard University Center for the Study of World Religions, 2000.

– "Ecofeminism: Symbolic and Social Connections of the Oppression of Women and the Domination of Nature." In *An Ecology of Spirit: Religious Reflections and Environmental Consciousness*, edited by Michael Barnes, 45–56. Lanham, NY: University Press of America: College Theology Society, 1990.

– "Ecofeminism and the Challenges of Globalization." In *Ecofeminism and Globalization: Exploring Culture, Context, and Religion*, edited by Heather Eaton and Lois Ann Lorentzen, vii–xi. Landham, MD; Toronto: Rowman & Littlefield, 2003.

– "Ecofeminist Philosophy, Theology, and Ethics: A Comparative View." In *Ecospirit: Religions and Philosophies for the Earth*, edited by Laurel Kearns and Catherine Keller, 77–93. New York: Fordham University Press, 2007.

– "Ecological Theology: Roots in Tradition, Liturgical and Ethical Practice for Today." *Dialog: A Journal of Theology*, 42, no. 3 (September 2003): 226–34. doi: 10.1111/1540-6385.00162.

– *Gaia and God: An Ecofeminist Theology of Earth Healing*. San Francisco: HarperSanFrancisco, 1994.

– *Integrating Ecofeminism, Globalization and World Religions*. Lanham, MD: Rowman & Littlefield Publishers, 2005.

– *Introducing Redemption in Christian Feminism*. Sheffield, England: Sheffield Academic Press, 1998.

– *Liberation Theology: Human Hope Confronts Christian History and American Power*. New York: Paulist Press, 1972.

– *New Woman/New Earth: Sexist Ideologies and Human Liberation*. New York: Seabury Press, 1975.

– "Reflections on Being a Catholic." *Conscience: A Commemorative Issue* 23, no. 2 (Summer 2002): 38.

– *Sexism and God-talk: Toward a Feminist Theology*. Boston: Beacon Press, 1983.

– *To Change the World: Christology and Cultural Criticism*. London: SCM Press, 1981.

– "Toward an Ecological-Feminist Theology of Nature." In *Readings in Ecology and Feminist Theology*, edited by Mary Heather Mackinnon and Moni McIntyre, 89–93. Kansas City, MO: Sheed and Ward, 1995.

– *Women and Redemption: A Theological History*. Minneapolis, MN: Fortress Press, 1998.

Ruether, Rosemary Radford, and Marion Grau. Introduction. In *Interpreting the Postmodern: Responses to "Radical Orthodoxy,"* edited by Rosemary Radford Ruether and Marion Grau, vii–xv. New York: T and T Clark, 2006.

Sagan, Carl. "Can We Know the Universe? Reflections on a Grain of Salt." In *Science and Its Ways of Knowing,* edited by John Hatton and Paul B. Plouffe, 3–7. Upper Saddle River, NJ: Prentice Hall, 1997.

Sagan, Carl, Hans A. Bethe, M.I. Budyko, Paul J. Crutzen, Freeman J. Dyson, Gyorgi S. Golitsyn, James E. Hansen, Henry W. Kendall, Lynn Margulis, Roger Revelle, Abdus Salam, Nans Suess, Richard P. Turco, Victor F. Weisskopf, Edward O. Wilson, Jerome B. Wiesner, Robert R. Wilson, Alexey V. Yablokov, Elise Boulding, S. Chandrasekhar, Margaret B. Davis, Richard L. Garwin, Stephen Jay Gould, Mohammed Kassas, Motoo Kimura, Thomas Malone, Peter Raven, Walter Orr Roberts, Stephen H. Schneider, O.B. Toon, Yevgeniy P. Velikhov, Sir Frederick Warmer, and Carl Friedrich von Weizsacker. "An Open Letter to the Religious Community." In *Ecology and Religion: Scientists Speak,* edited by John E. Carroll and Keith Warner, OFM, ii–vi. Quincy, IL: Franciscan Press, 1998.

Sagan, Lynn. "On the Origin of Mitosing Cells." *Journal of Theoretical Biology* 14, no. 3 (March 1967): 225–74. doi: 10.1016/0022-5193(67)90079-3.

Sahtouris, Elisabet. "The Conscious Universe." In *When Worlds Converge: What Science and Religion Tell Us about the Story of the Universe and Our Place in It,* edited by Clifford N. Matthews, Mary Evelyn Tucker, and Philip Hefner, 59–72. Peru, IL: Open Court Publishing Company, 2002.

Sale, Peter F. *Our Dying Planet: An Ecologist's View of the Crisis We Face.* Berkeley: University of California Press, 2011.

Scharper, Stephen Bede. "Democracy, Cosmology, and the Great Work of Thomas Berry." *Worldviews: Environment, Culture and Religion* 5, no. 2/3 (2001):188–97. doi.org/10.1163/15685350152908228.

– "Ecological Theology." In *New and Enlarged Handbook of Christian Theology,* edited by Donald W. Muser and Joseph L. Price, 143–5. Nashville: Abingdon Press, 2003.

– *For Earth's Sake: Toward a Compassionate Ecology.* Edited by Simon Appolloni. Toronto: Novalis Publishing Inc., 2013.

– "The Gaia Hypothesis: Implications for a Christian Political Theology of the Environment." *Cross Currents* 44 (Summer 1994): 207–21.

– *Redeeming the Time: A Political Theology of the Environment.* New York: Continuum Publishing Company, 1998.

Schneider, Stephen H., James R. Miller, Eileen Crist, and Penelope J. Boston, eds. *Scientists Debate Gaia: The Next Century*. Cambridge, MA: MIT Press, 2004.

Schönfeld, Martin. Introduction, "Plan B: Global Ethics on Climate Change." *Journal of Global Ethics* 7, no. 2 (August 2011): 129–36.

Schweitzer, Albert. *Albert Schweitzer: Essential Writings*. Selected with an introduction by James Brabazon. Maryknoll, New York: Orbis Books, 2005.

– *My Life and Thought: An Autobiography*. Translated by C.T. Campion. London: Allen & Unwin, 1933

– *A Place for Revelation: Sermons on Reverence for Life*. Translated by David Larrimore Holland. New York: Macmillan Publishing Company, 1988.

Sharrock, Wes, and Ruppert Read. "Does Thomas Kuhn Have a 'Model of Science'?" *Social Epistemology* 17, no. 2 and 3 (2003): 293–6. doi:10.1080/02 69172032000144324.

Sheldrake, Rupert. *The Presence of the Past: Morphic Resonance and the Habits of Nature*. New York: Times Books, 1988.

Shrader-Frechette, Kristen. "Liberation Science and the Option for the Poor: Protecting Victims of Environmental Justice." In *The Preferential Option for the Poor beyond Theology*, edited by Daniel G. Groody and Gustavo Gutiérrez, 120–48. Notre Dame, IN: University of Notre Dame Press, 2014.

– "Reading the Riddle of Nuclear Waste: Idealized Geological Models and Positivist Epistemology." In *Earth Matters: The Earth Sciences, Philosophy, and the Claims of Community*, edited by Robert Frodeman, 11–24. Upper Saddle River, NJ: Prentice-Hall Inc., 2000.

Sideris, Lisa H. "The Ecological Body: Rachel Carson, *Silent Spring*, and Breast Cancer." In *Rachel Carson: Legacy* and *Challenge*, edited by Lisa H. Sideris and Kathleen Dean Moore, 136–48. Albany, NY: State University Press, 2008.

– *Environmental Ethics: Ecological Theology, and Natural Selection*. New York: Columbia University Press, 2003.

– "Evolving Environmentalism." *Worldviews* 11 (2007): 58–82. doi: 10.1163/156853507X173504.

– "Modern Science and the Varieties of Evolutionary Enchantment." Accessed July 2012. http://www.carsoncenter.unimuenchen.de/download/staff_ and_fellows/projects/project_sideris.pdf.

– "Religion, Environmentalism, and the Meaning of Ecology." In *The Oxford Handbook of Religion and Ecology* (Online), edited by Roger

Gottlieb. New York: Oxford University Press, 2006. doi: 10.1093/oxfor dhb/9780195178722.003.0021.

Slingerland, Edward. *What Science Offers the Humanities: Integrating Body and Culture*. New York: Cambridge University Press, 2008.

Somerville, Margaret A., and David J. Rapport, eds. *Transdisciplinarity: ReCreating Integrated Knowledge*. Oxford, UK: EOLSS Publishers Co. Ltd., 2000.

Stalsett, Sturla J. "Ethical Dimensions of Vulnerability and Struggles for Social Inclusion in Latin America. Paper prepared for the Inter-American Initiative on Social Capital, Ethics and Development." Presented in Washington, 24 February 2006, at the IDB Ethics and Development Day: "How Can Ethical Values and Social Capital Contribute to Development Projects?" Accessed 30 November 2010. http://www.urbeetius.org/news letters/23/news_23_stalsett.pdf.

Stefanovic, Ingrid Leman. "Evolving Sustainability: A Re-Thinking of Ontological Foundations." *Trumpeter* 8, no. 4 (Fall, 1991): 194–200. http:// trumpeter.athabascau.ca/index.php/trumpet/article/view/798/1159.

– *Safeguarding Our Common Future, Rethinking Sustainable Development*. Albany, NY: State University Press, 2000.

Stehn, Alexander V. "Toward an Inter-American Philosophy: Pragmatism and the Philosophy of Liberation." *Inter-American Journal of Philosophy* 2, no. 2 (December 2011): 14–36. http://pages.uoregon.edu/koopman/ events_readings/coast_group/stehn_inter-american.pdf.

Stuart, Kevin. "My Friend the Soil: A Conversation with Hans Jenny." *Journal of Soil and Water Conservation*, May/June 1984: 158–61. Accessed April 2012. http://www.people.ku.edu/~azung/my_friend_soil_Jenny.pdf.

Suzuki, David, with Amanda McConnell. *The Sacred Balance: Rediscovering Our Place in Nature*. Vancouver: Greystone Books, 2002.

Swidler, Leonard. *Toward a Universal Theology of Religion*. Maryknoll, NY: Orbis Books, 1998.

Swimme, Brian Thomas. *The Hidden Heart of the Cosmos: Humanity and the New Story*. Maryknoll, NY: Orbis Press, 1996.

– "Science a Partner in Creating the Vision." In *Thomas Berry and the New Cosmology*, edited by Anne Lonergan and Caroline Richards, 81–90. Mystic, CT: Twenty-Third Publications, 1987.

Swimme, Brian Thomas, and Thomas Berry. *The Universe Story: From the Primordial Flaring Forth to the Ecozoic Era: A Celebration of the Unfolding of the Cosmos*. New York: HarperSanFrancisco, 1992.

Swimme, Brian Thomas, and Mary Evelyn Tucker. *Journey of the Universe.* New Haven: Yale University Press, 2011.

Tambiah, Stanley Jeyaraja. *Magic, Science, Religion and the Scope of Rationality.* New York: Cambridge University Press, 1990.

Tatman, Lucy. *Knowledge That Matters: A Feminist Theological Paradigm and Epistemology.* London: Sheffield Academic Press, 2001.

Taylor, Sarah McFarland. *Green Sisters: A Spiritual Ecology.* Cambridge, MA: Harvard University Press, 2007.

Teilhard de Chardin, Pierre. *Divine Milieu.* New York: Harper & Row, 1965.

– *The Future of Man.* Translated by Norman Denny. New York: Image Books, Doubleday, 1964.

– *The Phenomenon of Man.* Translated by Bernard Wall. London: Collins, 1960.

Toolan, David. *At Home in the Cosmos.* Maryknoll, NY: Orbis Books, 2001.

Tracy, David. *The Analogical Imagination: Christian Theology and the Culture of Pluralism.* New York: The Crossroad Publishing Company, 1981.

– *Blessed Rage for Order: The New Pluralism in Theology.* New York: Seabury Press, 1975.

Tracy, David, and John B. Cobb Jr. *Talking about God: Doing Theology in the Context of Modern Pluralism.* New York: Seabury Press, 1983.

Tucker, Mary Evelyn. "Thomas Berry." In *The Encyclopedia of Religion and Nature*, edited by Bron Taylor, 164–6. London: Thoemmes Continuum, 2005.

– "Thomas Berry and the New Story: An Introduction to the Work of Thomas Berry." In *The Intellectual Journey of Thomas Berry: Imagining the Earth Community*, edited by Heather Eaton. Lanham, MD: Lexington Books, 2014.

Tucker, Mary Evelyn, and John Grim. Series Foreword. In *Christianity and Ecology: Seeking the Well-being of Earth and Humans*, edited by Dieter T. Hessel and Rosemary Radford Ruether, xv–xxxii. Cambridge, MA: Harvard University Press for the Harvard University Center for the Study of World Religions, 2000.

United Nations Department of Economic and Social Affairs (DESA). *Rethinking Poverty: Report on the World Social Situation 2010.* New York: United Nations Publication, 2009. Accessed June 2013. http://www.un.org/esa/socdev/rwss/docs/2010/fullreport.pdf.

Vázquez Carballo, José Mario. *Trinidad y Sociedad: Implicaciones Éticas y Sociales en el Pensamiento Trinitario de Leonardo Boff.* Salamanca, Spain: Secretariado Trinitario, 2008.

Von Bayer, Hans Christian. "The Aesthetic Equation." In *Science and Its Ways of Knowing*, edited by John Hatton and Paul B. Plouffe, 67–75. Upper Saddle River, NJ: Prentice Hall, 1997.

Warner, Keith Douglass, OFM. Epilogue. In *Ecology and Religion: Scientists Speak*, edited by John E. Carroll and Keith Warner, OFM, 353–6. Quincy, IL: Franciscan Press, 1998.

– "The Greening of American Catholicism: Identity, Conversion, and Continuity." *Religion and American Culture: A Journal of Interpretation* 18, no. 1 (2008): 113–42. doi:10.1525/rac.2008.18.1.113.

White, Lynn, Jr. "The Historical Roots of Our Ecologic Crisis." In *Worldviews, Religion, and the Environment: A Global Anthology*, edited by Richard C. Foltz, 30–7. Belmont, CA: Thomson Wadsworth, 2003.

Whitehead, Alfred North. *Science and the Modern World*. New York: Macmillan, 1925.

Whitfield, John. "Biological Theory: Postmodern Evolution?" *Nature* 455, no. 8 (September 2008): 281–4. doi:10.1038/455281a.

Wray, K. Brad. *Kuhn's Evolutionary Social Epistemology* (Online). Cambridge: Cambridge University Press, 2011. doi: http://dx.doi.org.myaccess.library.utoronto.ca/10.1017/CBO9780511997990.

Zalasiewicz, Jan, Mark Williams, Will Steffen, and Paul Crutzen. "The New World of the Anthropocene." *Environmental Science & Technology* 44, no. 7 (April 2010): 2228–31. doi: 10.1021/es903118j.

Index